TELLING IT LIKE IT WASN'T

TELLING IT LIKE IT WASN'T

The Counterfactual Imagination
in History and Fiction

CATHERINE GALLAGHER

THE UNIVERSITY OF CHICAGO PRESS
CHICAGO AND LONDON

The University of Chicago Press, Chicago 60637
The University of Chicago Press, Ltd., London
© 2018 by The University of Chicago
All rights reserved. No part of this book may be used or reproduced in any manner whatsoever without written permission, except in the case of brief quotations in critical articles and reviews. For more information, contact the University of Chicago Press, 1427 E. 60th St., Chicago, IL 60637.
Published 2018

27 26 25 24 23 22 21 20 19 18   1 2 3 4 5

ISBN-13: 978-0-226-51238-9 (cloth)
ISBN-13: 978-0-226-51241-9 (paper)
ISBN-13: 978-0-226-51255-6 (e-book)
DOI: 10.7208/chicago/[9780226512556].001.0001

Library of Congress Cataloging-in-Publication Data
Names: Gallagher, Catherine, author.
Title: Telling it like it wasn't : the counterfactual imagination in history and fiction / Catherine Gallagher.
Description: Chicago : The University of Chicago Press, 2018. | Includes bibliographical references and index.
Identifiers: LCCN 2017021803| ISBN 9780226512389 (cloth : alk. paper) | ISBN 9780226512419 (pbk. : alk. paper) | ISBN 9780226512556 (e-book)
Subjects: LCSH: Imaginary histories—History. | Alternative histories (Fiction)—History and criticism. | Counterfactuals (Logic)
Classification: LCC D16.118 .G35 2018 | DDC 809/.93358—dc23 LC record available at https://lccn.loc.gov/2017021803

TO THE LIGHTS OF MY LIFE: FRANKIE, SAMMY,
RYE, AND BABY SID.
AND TO MAGGIE, IN GRATITUDE
FOR THE LIFE WE SHARED.

CONTENTS

	Introduction	1
1.	The History of Counterfactual History from Leibniz to Clausewitz	16
2.	Nineteenth-Century Alternate-History Narratives	48
3.	How the USA Lost the Civil War	97
4.	Historical Activism and the Alternate-America Novels	147
5.	Nazi Britain: The Invasion and Occupation That Weren't	190
6.	The Fictions of Nazi Britain	237
	Acknowledgments	313
	Notes	315
	Index	351

Introduction

Late in the last century, a certain kind of historical speculation took root in a surprisingly diverse set of venues. Across disciplines, in legal and policy debates, as well as in popular forms of entertainment, Americans seized on past moments of historical indeterminacy and imagined possible but unrealized alternative consequences that might have resulted. We give the general name "counterfactual history" to such thought experiments. It's well known that this mode of conjecture has been around for centuries, but the profusion of guises it has taken over the last several decades is unprecedented. The 1970s were a starting point for several simultaneous developments: historians began serious debates about new counterfactual methodologies and courts employed counterfactuals to assess remedies for historical wrongs suffered by large groups of people. Soon after, high-school teachers began using classroom computer software that allowed students to vary the outcomes of WWII battles so that they could better understand the options of the historical combatants, and multiplayer gamers also began repeatedly fighting and revising past wars.

In popular culture, too, the presence of counterfactual history steadily increased. Writers in the civil rights era imagined that under revised circumstances there might have been independent nations of African Americans and Native Americans; science fiction (informed by popular science primers on the physics of time) explored the backward time-travel paradoxes involved in attempting to make such changes in history by intervening at crucial junctures. In the 1980s and 1990s, television shows and movies featured these themes, acquainting viewers with various alternate-history scenarios. On the literary side, the counterfactual-history mode spread from science-fiction genres (where it had existed since the 1950s) to the mainstream novel in the first decade of this century. As a result, the counterfactual imagination has become a familiar feature of our culture, and the forms of its propagation continue to proliferate.

This study explores why and how we conduct these counterfactual thought experiments. When, it asks, did this mode of speculation start and what forms has it taken in previous centuries and in our own? What uses does it have, and what contexts stimulate its growth? These are the questions I will address in the coming chapters, but a few preliminary issues need to be clarified here. First, what, exactly, does the term "counterfactual-historical mode" mean? When I first started talking about the phenomenon, I found that the phrase implied many kinds of works I had not expected: histories that are simply fictional or even mendacious; "secret" histories that purport to explain the hidden private stories behind the official explanations of historical events; "counterhistories" stressing the forgotten struggles or viewpoints of those outside of the mainstream; or imaginary histories that are "counterfactual" in the sense that they envision states of the world, usually utopias and dystopias, that might be, but have not yet been, realized.

Several of these forms might come close to the mode under consideration here, but they lack what I take to be the definitive characteristic: that the discourse, whether analytical or narrative, be premised on a counterfactual-historical hypothesis, which I define as an explicit or implicit past-tense, hypothetical, conditional conjecture pursued when the antecedent condition is known to be contrary to fact. For example, this sentence—"If John F. Kennedy had not been assassinated in 1963 and had lived to be a two-term president, the war in Vietnam would have been over by 1968"—is a historical counterfactual. The antecedent condition (the *if* clause) is overtly contrary to the normally uncontroversial fact of John F. Kennedy's 1963 assassination; nevertheless, the hypothesis ventures a probable consequence of the assassination's nonexistence. The sentence is not attempting to call the assassination into question or to imply that we should look into it more deeply; it is simply asserting that *but for* the assassination, history would likely have taken a different path. Insisting on this definition of "historical counterfactual" at the outset should not only clarify the topic but also emphasize that the works under discussion are hinged onto the actual historical record, usually at a juncture that is widely recognized to have been both crucial and underdetermined.

This definition clarifies the mode of historical speculation that will be examined here, but it leaves open the question of which expressions of the mode should be included. It ranges across so many media and genres that I could not possibly include them all. I have devoted most of this study to works in the long-lived medium of print and given preference to those appearing in the format of the book, since these seem to reveal the most about the history of the mode. The texts examined here fall into three broad categories. The first, which I've placed under the simple heading of "counterfactual histories," contains a heterogeneous assortment of analytical works prominently featuring counterfactual speculations. These are often histories of wars, economic crises, or assassinations in which sudden, unexpected changes in the status quo occur, but under this category I have also included shorter pieces: essays, newspaper articles, and historical conjectures in theological or philosophical texts, as well as in legal arguments and opinions. The common denominators in this lot, besides their counterfactual-historical hypotheses, are their generally analytical rather than narrative quality and their tendency to indicate multiple possibilities that went unrealized rather than to trace out single historical alternative trajectories in detail.

The next two categories are narrative forms, which have often been lumped together under the category of alternate histories. This book, though, will treat them as separate kinds, reserving the term "alternate history" for works that describe one continuous sequence of departures from the historical record, thereby inventing a long counterfactual narrative with a correspondingly divergent fictional world, while drawing the dramatis personae exclusively from the actual historical record. The third form, which I call the alternate-history novel, invents not only alternative-historical trajectories but also fictional characters. Combining with various novelistic generic forms, these fictions allow for the illusion of a more complete alternative reality, presenting in detail the social, cultural, technological, psychological, and emotional totalities that result from the alterations.

The book is organized around these three categories and their dynamic interactions. Each of the first three chapters traces the origins of one of the kinds, following its development up until it begins to resemble current instances and exploring its links with and means of differentiating itself from the other two. There is both a historical sequence and a geographical movement to this form-creation and differentiation process. The mode established itself among historians first in military history, mainly in France and Prussia, during the late eighteenth and early nineteenth centuries. It then appeared in the form of alternate histories several decades later in France, and spread to Great Britain and America by the end of the nineteenth century. Alternate-history narrative fictions featuring invented protagonists are a twentieth-century innovation and began appearing in both France and the United States between the World Wars. They did not become an established subgenre until the postwar period, primarily in the United States and Britain.

This sequential progression from the earliest through the most recent of the mode's expressions thus gives us a sense of both their genealogical links and their larger national contexts. Each kind of text inherits some features from the earlier ones but also owes its existence to separate conjunctures of circumstances. Each is bound by distinctive constraints, has unique resources, and serves a different set of cultural functions. The last four chapters explore the interactions as well as the disconnections among the three types by investigating the writings that cluster around two long-established counterfactual-historical loci: (1) the American Civil War and (2) the period of World War II when Great Britain was Nazi Germany's sole undefeated opponent (from May of 1940 to the end of 1941). The two case studies, which form the majority of the book, let us see how the different forms shape similar hypothetical questions in ways that let both countries reflect on their national identities by imagining how—or if—they would have changed under altered circumstances.

This sketch of the book's organization brings us to the third question that needs to be addressed explicitly in this introduction. Why, despite its odd-looking logic, does the counterfactual-historical mode deserve our serious attention? To start with, it has a centuries-long connection to a constellation of basic and perennial issues: the role of human agency and responsibility in history, the possibilities of historical justice and repair, and the coherence of identity—of individuals, nations, and peoples—through time. Indeed, even before it was harnessed to military history, the mode began in the context of theological and metaphysical debates during the seventeenth and eighteenth centuries; reconciling God's nature (his omniscience, omnipotence, and omnibenevolence) with human free will and the existence of evil entailed the question of whether human history might have been different. And that question continued to remain open long after it was fashionable to think of history as the work of God's providence; historians and philosophers of history argued about determinism, causality, and contingency, all of which touched on the possibility of alternatives and their ontological status, throughout the nineteenth and twentieth centuries. Moreover, in the last half of the twentieth century, analytical philosophers borrowed from the old metaphysical debates by arguing that we need the concept of other possible historical worlds in order to explain how conjectural propositions about the past become meaningful, while others insisted that all causal statements make counterfactual claims. Philosophical interest in the nature and uses of counterfactual-historical thought experiments shows no sign of abating.

Another reason for paying serious attention to historical counterfactuals is that they tend to be used in contexts where historical understanding aspires to be consequential in the world. Instead of being satisfied with merely scholarly exercises, counterfactualists often want to apply history to other purposes. This book, as I've already indicated, will look closely at the mode's central importance to the professionalization of war, where counterfactual speculation about the past was used to define the nature and improve the practice of the enterprise. When the Prussian military theorist Carl von Clausewitz insisted that perfecting the art of warfare entailed knowing not only what had occurred in previous wars but also everything that *could have* occurred, he articulated the link between counterfactual speculation and the ability to gain knowledge from the past for the sake of future planning. And that premise, we'll see, carried over in the twentieth century into other fields, so that today counterfactual analyses tend to cluster in areas where historical data might inform current policy debates, such as economic history, diplomatic history, developmental studies, and international studies. And, of course, we frequently hear politicians drawing lessons from history that rely on counterfactual assumptions. If the free-trade agreements had not been made, American workers' wages would have increased over the last fifteen years; if we had not invaded Iraq, the Middle East might still be relatively stable; if we burned fewer fossil fuels, the sea levels would not be rising so fast. The debates that take place around such assumptions allow ordinary people to assess the policies of the recent past and decide whether to continue, revise, or abandon them. They obviously do not settle the disputes, but they may help strengthen collective historical awareness by stitching together decisions about what the nation should do next with judgments about what it has done. They encourage people not only to think about the causes of present conditions but also to imagine what the probable alternatives might have been, which is a necessary step in judging them and making use of those judgments in deciding about the future. In other words, counterfactual speculation is one way in which debates about history take on consequences in democratic politics.

Of all the ways in which historical counterfactualism has become consequential for us, perhaps the most important involve its affiliation with legal and political historical justice projects. The explicit use of past counterfactual hypotheses in the field of law began shortly after their appearance in military history, and they have become an indispensable tool of legal reasoning. To be sure, most legal counterfactuals do not concern events we consider historical, and perhaps that is why the resemblances between Clausewitz's ideas and those of the nineteenth-century German jurists who recommended the use of counterfactuals in discovering liability and guilt have gone unrecognized.[1] The legal and historical practices of counterfactualizing might be said to have developed along parallel paths for most of the nineteenth and twentieth centuries, but in the last seventy years, they have frequently converged in criminal prosecutions for war crimes and crimes against humanity as well as in historical restitution efforts and demands for reparations for collective wrongs. Even when not pursued through judicial processes, counterfactual legal-historical reasoning has become a way of exploring the identities and responsibilities of political and genealogical communities emerging from imperialism, tyrannous regimes, civil wars, calamitous change, or deep subjugation. Through its uses in these various endeavors, the counterfactual mode has not only intertwined itself with our ideas of progress and justice but also become an instrument for shaping history.

The ease with which historical justice movements have adopted historical counterfactualism underlines several other features of the mode that make it useful outside of the discipline of history. From its earliest modern appearances, its overriding impulse has been to judge historical outcomes, rather than simply to know, understand, and analyze events, episodes, and agents. In many of its manifestations, the imperative is to assess the actions of responsible and identifiable human actors. Clausewitz, for example, explained that one counterfactualizes in order to judge the skill (as opposed to the luck) of the combatants and, thus, place praise and blame. And, going beyond the evaluation of individuals, counterfactualism encourages the judgment of anonymous and impersonal occurrences as well, as if we could weigh them against possible options on a scale that would reveal their greater or lesser effect on the common good of a community, a people, a cause, a nation, the environment, or humanity as a whole. Indeed, making such an evaluation is precisely what the seventeenth-century philosopher Gottfried Leibniz, who first suggested the use of counterfactual possible worlds, claimed God does. Leibniz argued that no historical occurrence should be regretted because God sees and judges all the simultaneous alternatives and choses the best among them. Throughout the eighteenth century, most historical counterfactuals were formulated either in support of this possible-worlds "theodicy," which always found actuality superior to any imaginable replacement, or in opposition to it, imagining examples of how history might have been improved.

Entailed in the activity of judging, of course, is the necessity for comparative options, but it is a truism that history studies unique and thus largely *in*comparable situations, a point that is often illustrated by contrasting the discipline of history to the laboratory sciences, where controlled and replicable experiments can be used to manipulate variables and discover what factors determine which outcomes.[2] History, we are frequently reminded, must make do with thought experiments because it is, by its very nature, a record of unusual and unique occurrences, each not only situated in a singular, nonreplicable spatiotemporal configuration but also ipso facto standing out from the ordinary, unrecorded progression of human affairs and the actions of unremarkable or at least forgotten people. Leibniz's followers explained that this is the reason we have trouble reconciling history—mainly an account of wars and disasters as they saw it—with the idea that God is taking providential care of mankind. Since we cannot share God's vision of the other possible worlds, we have to imagine the worse alternatives, thereby demonstrating that it is reasonable to declare our own the "best" even though our past may seem a chronicle of horrors. Conversely, when Clausewitz proposed counterfactual analysis for improving the military sciences, he often visualized alternatives superior to actuality, attempting to demonstrate that even the best commanders leave opportunities unexploited. Although Leibniz and Clausewitz were making very different kinds of judgments, they shared two assumptions: that history does not allow for exact comparisons between its always highly unusual events, episodes, and personnel and that counterfactual speculation compensates for the deficiency.

The uses to which the mode has been put are thus various, but the motivation to make comparative judgments about history remains steady, and it illuminates many other features of the texts that will be examined in this study. It clarifies their predilection for catastrophic histories, which focus either on infamously horrific actual episodes or on even worse imaginary ones.[3] But the mode also, somewhat paradoxically, tends to derive alternatives to the catastrophic events from probabilistic models of what is ordinary, thus placing a heavy emphasis on normality. A good modern example is historian Jay Winter's calculation (using statistically adjusted data from life insurance policies) of what the normal life expectancy for young British males would have been in 1914–18 if there had been no war. Winter demonstrated through this method that the British government consistently underestimated its war losses.[4] Such appeals to what normally happens in order to learn what would have been the alternative if the historical event had not interfered are typical of counterfactual modes of assessment in most periods, and especially in alternate-history novels, they tend to privilege private life over public history. In this example, the reliance on a commonsense preference for peaceful private life in describing the alternative possibility also suggests a general antiwar stance. In other cases, though, counterfactual-historical analyses might design their comparative alternatives with the intention of changing, rather than expressing, current norms. For example, in prosecutions for war crimes and crimes against humanity, defendants often claim that they were just following orders or that their vows of allegiance to the state had limited their ability to follow the dictates of their consciences, and prosecutors often respond by instancing people in similar situations who refused to cooperate with the criminal actions. They thus construct norms for alternatives in which the victims might have gone unmolested if the perpetrators had held themselves to higher levels of accountability. And they often further claim that convicting the perpetrators will set a precedent for the adoption of new norms by the agents of the state, who will no longer consider themselves immune to prosecution.[5] We thus return once again to the counterfactual mode's ambition to shape history rather than merely record, analyze, or understand it.

Many of my readers will be aware that the reasons I've just given for taking an interest in the counterfactual-historical mode have also been adduced by academic historians as reasons for avoiding it. The perennial theological and philosophical debates with which it is associated, they note, have no actual bearing on the practice of the modern discipline, even if they may bear fruit in other ways. And they contend that the various uses I've just enumerated—justifying "the ways of God to men" (to use John Milton's phrase); improving warfare and economic policy; meting out historical justice; and shaping democratic political cultures—have contributed little to historical knowledge *per se* and may even hinder it. For example, recent uses of counterfactuals in fields like military and economic history—now reliant on modeling, sophisticated statistical techniques, innovations in applied mathematics, and modern computing—are often criticized for narrowing our view of the past to fit the confines of ahistorical abstractions about human behavior (such as rational choice theory). Counterfactual history's ambition to be consequential is often decried by academic historians for its distortion and instrumental subordination of scholarship to other aims. They similarly complain about its general focus on judgment and on making value-laden comparisons between what happened and what might have happened. Even the recent uses of counterfactuals in finding and prosecuting wrong-doing or compensating its victims have been accused of narrowing and simplifying the complex historical issues, especially of combing the historical record to dislodge identifiable suspects and actionable wrongs. And, of course, the constant appropriations of history for political purposes, with their attendant counterfactual speculations, are often viewed as even less respectable.

These criticisms seem reasonable to me, and refuting them is no part of my purpose in writing this book. Instead of arguing for or against the use of such methods by historians, this book takes the counterfactual-historical mode in all of its guises to be itself a historical object, whose long-term development and motivations might give us some significant insights into our ways of making history meaningful. That said, I am not free simply to set aside or ignore the historians' critique as irrelevant, for it is both a part of the history of counterfactual history and sometimes even reflects on itself as such. It has, indeed, played important roles in the composition of this book as both a continual goad and an immense archival resource. Most participants in the debate, to be sure, fold the question of the mode's history into their arguments for or against the method: supporters tend to universalize it by insisting that historians implicitly use counterfactuals whenever they make causal statements, even in a casual explanatory mode, and opponents often disparage it as a recent development, little more than a postmodern fad, a right-wing plot, or a symptom of the general decline of confidence in the possibility of achieving complete objectivity or unbiased "truth."[6]

But despite their polemical frameworks, the debaters have called attention to numerous works, especially from the early twentieth century, that have come to form something like a canon for counterfactual history. Moreover, the parts of the debate that have been conducted in particular fields over the specific merits of certain recent forms of historical counterfactualism provide an invaluable record for the case studies that form the majority of this book.[7] Those few academic historians whose intellectual curiosity has taken them outside the confines of the methodological debate to a more nonpartisan consideration of the mode's history have paved the way for this study.[8]

While academic historians often disparage the use of counterfactual methods, other social scientists—especially in political science, government, demography, and economics departments, schools of international studies, and military academies—have not. As a result, this book's general account of the current state of historical counterfactualism draws heavily on interdisciplinary works, especially on a cluster of probing and impartial overviews of the methodological issues.[9] And yet these works, too, have little time to spare for the mode's longer history or its cultural and intellectual contexts because they focus on defining and developing the methods. Another source of inspiration for this book, the philosophical literature on counterfactualism, focuses on a few episodes in the longer-range history by pointing to the early contributions of Leibniz and David Hume but are also not interested in the historical contexts of those contributions. In short, there is a large and informative academic discourse on the topic of historical counterfactualism, a discourse that makes the current study possible, but much of it tends to be ahistorical.

The exception to this generalization is the scholarship specifically on the two counterfactual *narrative* forms. Works by literary and cultural historians on alternate histories and alternate-history novels have given us a fairly full picture of their chronological development, dissemination, and general cultural contexts.[10] They have traced the forms across nations and explored their roles in national myth-making. The narratives have been placed in various disciplinary contexts, analyzed as expressions of popular understandings of scientific discoveries (especially of twentieth-century developments in the idea of space-time), and read as symptoms of collective self-justification, regret, and guilt. Their literary genres—which include utopias and dystopias, historical novels, science-fiction genres, avant-garde experiments, and adventure pulp fiction—have also been examined historically. However, the one context for the alternate-history forms that has not been explored is the body of works, more analytical than narrative, that I've categorized under counterfactual history.

In this book, I try to remedy that lack by looking across the barrier between the "constrained" analytical kind of counterfactual and the more "exuberant," imaginative, and extended narrative varieties of alternate history.[11] But rather than effacing that distinction I instead take it to be central to the phenomenon's dynamism, its ability to generate formal variety in order to meet developing needs. I extend my exploration across the formal divisions first by retrieving the earliest uses of counterfactual history in my opening chapters. And second, in my case studies on the American Civil War and the threatened Nazi invasion of Britain, I uncover the initial framing of the counterfactual questions and the stages of their subsequent development. Once the changing shapes of the hypothetical questions, which began as future conjectures in the debates leading up to the historical episodes, are visible, we can then see what functions the later narratives have played in rearranging our perspectives on the actual history. The current book differs from previous studies of historical counterfactualism by emphasizing the interactions among the various forms within the more general ecology of the mode.

I've already mentioned many features of the entire counterfactual-historical mode that become prominent when we take this longer and wider perspective, and I will close this short introduction with a glance at one further role it plays: it helps satisfy our desire to quicken and vivify historical entities, to make them seem not only solid and substantial but also suspenseful and unsettled.

To explain how the mode performs this function, I'll need to outline one of its most common and controversial practices: counterfactualists tend to vary *events* while holding historical *entities* constant between Our Timeline and the Alternate Timeline. Thus they seem to assume that the entities (e.g., persons, governments, institutions, armies, political parties, nations, families, dynasties, empires, races, etc.) remain identical to those in our actual history even though their destinies—the totality of what they think, do, and suffer—are changed. The assumption maintains what philosophers sometimes call transworld identity, although the framers of most counterfactual thought experiments cannot be said to subscribe to any such elaborated theory.[12] They merely follow a long-standing convention that takes the entities to be the usual constants of the thought experiments and the surrounding events and circumstances (their histories) to be the variables.[13] The convention, we should note, allows for the subtraction of historical persons and other individuals as the result of some altered event—how many times have Hitler and the Nazis been extirpated?—but even then the subtracted entity (the Hitler whose birth never occurs) is considered identical to the one in actual history. Moreover, the assumption does not prevent the thought experiment from including entirely fictional persons, as alternate-history novels do. The transworld-identity assumption applies only to the referents of the names of *historical* individuals or collectivities, so a fictional backward time traveler might prevent JFK's assassination or his birth, but it is still our JFK who has been saved or lost.

The notion that the same person could have contradictory destinies has always seemed, on reflection, to be both necessary and problematic: considering JFK's possible second term, for example, we note that we must assume we are talking about the *same* John Fitzgerald Kennedy who was murdered, for otherwise the thought experiment would not be an experiment about our history. But once the story is changed, how can we maintain that the *person* is the same? What do we mean when we say that *our* JFK might have had a second term if he had not been assassinated? This is the sort of question that Leibniz tried to answer with the conceptual expedient of possible worlds: God sees worlds populated by the *same* people doing and suffering different things. And modern philosophers draw on that idea when describing the meaning of past counterfactual conditionals. Saul Kripke tells us, for example, that the modal semantics of the JFK counterfactual require us to think of a possible world that is identical to our own, right down to the identity of the person called John Fitzgerald Kennedy, except for the assassination and its consequences.[14]

This is, to be sure, a strangely minimal idea of "identity," limited to the bio-physiological and genealogical continuity that allows for maximal expansion across modal registers.[15] Indeed, philosopher Bernard Williams calls this the zygotic principle of identity and explains that it keeps "the different life story of the same individual" from being read as "the life story of a different individual" (225). Moreover, as the stress on that word "individual" in Williams's formulation indicates, this idea of identity might not be easy to transfer to the collective entities that are so often the objects of historical thought experiments. In such cases, something other than a zygote must serve as an identifying substance, and our case studies will show how complex the idea of collective identity becomes in counterfactual histories. For the time being, though, I want to stress that, because it minimizes its criteria for identity, the counterfactual-historical mode proportionately enlarges ideas of its "characters." Indeed, the nature of a "counterfactual character" is one of the mode's most distinctive features. When a person or a group is detached from what it actually thought, did, and suffered, a space opens up for the attribution of different characteristics to the same entity: different thoughts, actions, and experiences that might plausibly have belonged to it had it faced different conditions. This might at first glance seem like the eradication of what was formerly thought to be the person's character, but instead it tends to produce an expansion of that category.

Ascribing a "character" to someone is always a highly probabilistic and speculative activity. We try to fathom what they are capable of or what they "have it in them to do." We use the word "character" to sum up traits that are consistently enough manifested to lead us to expect a certain range of behavior without being perfectly predictive. Unlike identity, character is expected to vary through time, changing, developing, and both gaining and revealing different facets in response to experiences. It thus seems to retain a certain plasticity, even as some qualities that were once merely nascent congeal into a reliable core while others that once protruded become invisible again, suggesting the existence of further imperceptible possibilities. The concept of character is thus not limited to the entity's actualized traits at any particular moment but also includes further qualities, capabilities, projects, and potentials. Some of these, moreover, might happen to remain latent or submerged under all the actual circumstances of the entity's existence and yet might nevertheless have surfaced into prominence if events had permitted.[16]

The counterfactual mode makes this connection between imagining diverse possibilities and establishing character unusually clear by explicitly inventing lots that are incompatible with the individual's known destiny and allowing an accretion of contradictory stories. Even the simplest counterfactual hypothesis has at least two versions: the one we knew before (JFK was assassinated) and the one being proposed (if he had survived). As in our usual activity of character making, when we create this plausible multistoried character out of counterfactuals, we also both base it on the most frequently displayed characteristics in the actual historical record and then purposely try to enlarge the character beyond the most apparent qualities. We might think of the process as melting down the materials that history solidified into particular shapes in order to see what else might have been made of them. Thus we imagine the circumstances under which seemingly persistent traits and habits would have broken down, measuring how far into the range of improbability such an exercise would take us. Or, conversely, if the entity was prone to unreliable behavior, we imagine circumstances that would have allowed for its ideally consistent behavior. In all cases, though, the thought experiments create counterfactual characters charged with a peculiar kind of indeterminacy, visibly wavering between actual and alternative destinies and saturated with unspent potential. No longer flattened against the outlines of their actual destinies, these counterfactual characters have the vitality of the permanently unfinished.

The following chapters will develop the many permutations and ramifications that appear in the construction of such beings, but there is one additional aspect of counterfactual characters that should be mentioned here: they almost automatically scale up into larger collectivities, stretching our normal view of what can count as a character. Debates about the counterfactual careers of JFK or Napoleon may begin with arguments about the parameters of the individual's character, but their ultimate aim is usually to speculate on how the nations they led would have been different under the changed circumstances. Would Kennedy have been able to withstand the pressure to escalate the war in Vietnam more successfully than Lyndon Johnson did? Could Napoleon have become just another European monarch if left unmolested in France after escaping from the Island of Elba in 1815, or would the world have been plunged once again into imperial wars? Questions of this sort impinge on the issue of the nations' characters in at least two senses: the qualities of their people (their stomach for war, their desire for world dominance) and the natures of their states (democratic, republican, monarchical, imperial).

The scaling-up activity is most evident in the counterfactual narrative forms, for the alternate histories and alternate-history novels might begin by looking at individuals, but they almost always become more permanently focused on changes in collectivities. What we seek in these speculations are might-have-been peoples and nations, other versions of our common lives against which we might measure our actuality and through which we might define the norms and limits of our communal characters. Because the plots that we follow in these narratives usually subordinate stories of both historical-counterfactual and fully fictional individuals to the unknown stories of the peoples and the nations, it is those collectivities that tend to emerge as the protagonists. This feature is particularly apparent in the alternate-history novel form, which seems to turn the genre inside out. Whereas in most novels national histories and characteristics are mere background against which the stories of individuals are played out, in counterfactual novels the destinies of these larger entities are the central dramas. And because aspects of what are normally the "setting" thus stride into the foreground and take on character functions, the dynamic interactions between the communal and the individual are far more fundamental than they are in normal novels.

Moreover, because the continuity of collective characters is often at stake, the mode seems designed to explore a paradox in our conception of character as it is used in both history and fiction. We must, as I've been arguing here, imagine alternatives in order to conceive of character, and thus the difference between identity and destiny is constitutive. Nevertheless, to assert a continuity of character, we must also probe the degree of allowable divergence, the breaking point beyond which the identity of the character, bending to the arc of a different destination, might be altogether disconnected from the original being. For example, speculations about alternative national destinies—what the United States of America would have become if it had lost the Civil War, or what Great Britain would have done if it had been invaded by Germany—are attempts at realizing collective characters, and yet such stories continually veer toward and often reach transformations that would produce unrecognizably different collectivities. At that point, the thought experiment may be said to end with the expiration of the given national identity.

This scaling-up effect accounts for yet another distinctive feature of the alternate-history fictions: collective-character testing is paired with an emphasis on thickly described world making that often goes beyond the circumstantial realism of normal fictions. Their world making resembles that of other kinds of speculative narrative; indeed, the fictions are often entwined with utopian, dystopian, and science-fiction elements, but the extent to which the invented place resembles our own is a more pressing issue here than it is in the related forms. And the urgency of the transworld relations may explain why some alternate-history novels engage with the question of larger systems of variations, touching on multiverse theories and possible-worlds ontology.[17] This book will not often cross over into those parallel universes of dispute, although it will occasionally point out commonalities between specific theories and the literature under discussion. Instead it will focus on how the different forms construct possible *historical* worlds, for that activity epitomizes the raison d'être of the mode in general. No matter how distant the resulting creations seem from ours, they are meaningful primarily as plausible offshoots of some phase of our world, some version of what it nearly became. The mode's vigorous "worlding" thus deepens our perceptions of actuality by shadowing and estranging them. And perhaps most typically, the alternate worlds strip our own of its neutral, inert givenness and open it to our judgment.

CHAPTER ONE

The History of Counterfactual History from Leibniz to Clausewitz

THEODICY AND THE INVENTION OF COMPARABLE POSSIBLE PASTS

Writers have used counterfactual thought experiments in narrating history since ancient times, but the practice underwent a significant change during the Enlightenment. Whereas the ancient instances were usually rhetorical exercises, designed to emphasize or call into question the importance of a person or event, the later ones are apt to imagine the reality that might have resulted from an alteration. When the Roman historian Livy asked what would have happened if Alexander the Great had invaded the Roman Empire, to take a prominent example, he tested a full-blown counterfactual hypothesis, which he attributed to the Greeks: if Alexander had invaded Italy, he would have interrupted the growth of the Roman Empire. This certainly qualifies as a past-tense hypothetical conditional conjecture ("if it had been the case that *a*, then it would have followed that *b*"), which is pursued when the antecedent condition (the if clause) is known to be contrary to fact. Alexander never invaded Italy, and yet Livy went into considerable detail about the possible battle that might have ensued if he had, which results in Alexander's defeat. The exercise, though, was mainly designed to praise the superiority of Roman armies and display their combined force in Alexander's time.[1] Thus he used his historical counterfactual as a rhetorical showcase.

Livy did not speculate about possible alternative outcomes of the battle or long-term historical changes; that sort of conjecturing, some historians of history have argued, seems to require a more modern idea of history as the product of aggregated human actions over time, composed of sequences of causes and effects that might be explained without recourse to divine or supernatural intervention. The secularization of historical writing during the Enlightenment has thus been seen as a necessary condition for the appearance of the counterfactual mode, because divine determination apparently ruled out the very possibility of alternatives. Counterfactual speculation is thus supposed to have arisen as an offshoot of the new interest in causal explanation once teleological explanations were discredited.[2] Some current advocates of the counterfactual mode have placed its appearance at an even more recent date, arguing that all forms of determinism—not only divine intervention and predestination but also modern "scientific" nineteenth-century determinism—needed to be discarded before the counterfactual mode could arise. These accounts, though, ignore the nature and contexts of the counterfactualism that was actually practiced during the Enlightenment. By examining those initial thought experiments, this chapter will present a very different, indeed almost an opposite, understanding of the mode's genealogy: instead of emerging inside a secularizing historical discipline, it arose out of the theorization of a new version of God's Providence. And instead of rejecting teleology, it embraced the practice of explaining events by identifying their overarching rational purpose. The first development in this actual history of counterfactual history was Gottfried Leibniz's apparently paradoxical theorization of contingent immanent historical causes as *the basis of* divine supervision.

Leibniz is usually seen as a preventer, rather than a progenitor, of modern counterfactualism because he is understood simply as a champion of providential determinism.[3] He is, of course, the philosopher satirized as Pangloss in Voltaire's *Candide*, and he invented the mode of justifying actuality commonly known (and frequently reviled) as theodicy. But Leibniz's importance to the philosophy of history goes beyond these simplifications, for he also insisted that historical events were caused by natural and human activity rather than directly by God. History's events, he insisted, were contingent, and Leibniz's interest in contingency was a constant feature of his thinking. He was, after all, a pioneer of probability theory, often credited with the invention of the calculus underlying its modern mathematical transformation, who envisioned the actual as a subset (rather than the obverse) of the possible. And yet he insisted on combining his insight into historical contingency with the idea that God nevertheless exercises providential care. Scholars have offered various accounts of the connections between his theodicy and his understanding of probability, but central to most is the role played by contingent possibilities. When dealing with the topic of history, his book *Theodicy* (1710) argues that all actually occurring events ultimately serve the greatest good *even though* their efficient causes were produced by the play of random variations. To reconcile these apparently contradictory notions, he presented a God who chooses among naturally or humanly created contingencies, which do not lose their accidental nature simply by being chosen.[4] History may therefore be "determined," in the sense that its causes and effects have been selected by God throughout eternity, without being "necessary" in the old Aristotelean sense of the word (*Theodicy*, 146–48). Admittedly, the difference between God *causing* events and his *choosing* among randomly occurring variations may seem small to us, but its impact on the development of counterfactual history was enormous.

Leibniz's peculiar providentialism gave alternative contingencies a prominent place in God's mind and thereby inspired the activity of counterfactual imagining; moreover, he posited a new mode of being for all of those unrealized possibilities by locating them in "possible worlds." The invention of these realms was a way of reconciling the fact of evil in this world with God's omnipotence, omniscience, and unfailing beneficence, as well as with the freedom of both divine and human will. So it addressed multiple theological problems, but its importance for the concept of history was that it helped change the status of historical accidents: mere contingencies could now find existence inside God's consciousness as part of the very process of divine planning.[5] The idea that God's view of history included countless unrealized contingencies also encouraged speculation about His reasons (insofar as they could be fathomed by humans) for choosing our actuality from among those infinite options. It went without saying that only God can truly know the other possible worlds, existing as they do in his thought; but the rest of us can—indeed should—speculate about their natures. We know only that they must be inferior to our, best, world, but actively imagining their deficits can give us a clearer view of the hand of providence operating in the field of randomness: "Let us . . . by our reflexion supply what is lacking in our perception, in order to make the good . . . more discernible" (133). Hence, unlike many theologians (Calvin, Luther, or Wellesley), who stressed God's role in shaping history by asserting that there are no accidents, Leibniz recommended reaching the providential insight precisely by dwelling on the importance of contingency and envisioning the inferior alternatives.

Leibniz exercised his own historical counterfactual imagination only once in the *Theodicy*, but the single example he gives is highly elaborated and prominently placed at the end of his formal argument. The historical incident is the rape of the Roman matron Lucretia by Sextus Tarquinius, son of Rome's last king, Lucius Tarquinius Superbus. Because the crime and Lucretia's subsequent suicide led to the king's overthrow and the eventual institution of the Roman Republic, it had long been considered an important turning point in world history. Leibniz treats this story as the kernel of a parable in which the young Sextus Tarquinius behaves as he did in our history, and then, in response to the question of how else he might have behaved, we are given a vision, supposedly provided by Pallas Athena, in which Sextus is shown in myriad possible worlds where he acted differently. In one such world, for example, he reins in his lust, "And lo! he goes to a city lying between two seas, resembling Corinth. He buys there a small garden; cultivating it, he finds a treasure; he becomes a rich man, enjoying affection and esteem; he dies at a great age, beloved of the whole city." In another world, he goes to Thrace, "marries the daughter of the king, who had no other children; he succeeds him, and he is adored by his subjects" (377). All of these vignettes play out simultaneously in parallel worlds, and in many of them Sextus is virtuous. Nevertheless, the worlds as a whole are consequently worse than ours, representing what theorists now call "downward" counterfactuals. Indeed, Leibniz seems to have inaugurated the vertical ranking scheme of incompatible possibilities at the end of his parable, when we get a view of the totality of possible worlds arranged "in a pyramid, becoming ever more beautiful as one mounted towards the apex." At the top of the pyramid, of course, is our own world "the most beautiful of all," a world that would not have been actualized without the rape of Lucretia: "The crime of Sextus serves for great things: it renders Rome free; thence will arise a great empire, which will show noble examples to mankind." Conversely, if God "had placed here a Sextus happy at Corinth or King in Thrace, it would be no longer this world . . . which forms the apex of the pyramid" (377).

Leibniz's vision of the pyramid of possible worlds emphasizes several things: first, belief in a God who determines history is consistent with imagining other histories; and second, justifying God's choices might even entail such imaginative activity. Third, the vision stresses that the alternatives are only imagined in order to be qualitatively judged against actuality. The *Theodicy* thus inspired later writers to combine counterfactual history with religious apologetics, explicating historical events, especially the most apparently incomprehensible and horrific, as preferable to other possibilities; and it also gave the enterprise its *comparative* emphasis, its stress on judging the relative merits of alternative outcomes. For centuries after the publication of *Theodicy*, writers incorporated these characteristic Leibnizian traits into their historical speculations, and counterfactualism grew as a form of pious reflection, which was capacious enough to accommodate different sectarian and political tendencies.

Looking at a couple of examples from eighteenth-century Britain can give us a more detailed view of how the Leibnizian legacy developed and help us identify features that persist in counterfactual-historical speculations right up to the present, becoming especially important in the extended narrative varieties. My first example comes from an anonymous British eighteenth-century historian, who imagines a counterfactual victory of Charles II at the Battle of Worcester (the last battle of the English Civil War, actually won by Cromwell's forces). Even though the writer clearly sympathizes with the Royalist cause, he hypothesizes that a royal victory in 1651 would ultimately have been bad for the crown and thus for Britain as a whole. A victory at Worcester, he assures the reader, would have been followed by factionalism among royalists, struggles over the succession, and finally "a civil war would have contained within itself another civil war."[6] The loss at Worcester thus eventually turned into a "blessing" (in Royalist hindsight) because Charles II's defeat "left the commonwealth's men masters of the three kingdoms and afforded them full leisure to complete and perfect their own structure of government. The experiment was fairly tried; there was nothing from without to disturb the process." The loss for Charles II thus allowed the United Kingdom to "experiment" with a Commonwealth form of government long enough to prove its weakness.

Leibniz's possible-worlds model is deeply embedded in this writer's scheme, where it is also partially secularized. Instead of residing merely in the mind of God, the competing possibilities of royal and republican government reside as well in the divided mind of Britain, and a premature royalist victory would only have enlarged the supposed attractions of the republican possibility in the imaginations of the people. In our actual history, the possible world of republican Britain was temporarily actualized during the Interregnum, manifesting its inferiority and creating a national consensus for the Restoration; its actualization thus destroyed it as viable possibility. In the counterfactual scenario, though, the Commonwealth would not have been allowed to display its intrinsic defects and would thus have persisted as a tantalizing and dangerous idea. Indeed it would have spawned its own counterfactuals, as the historian explains: the Commonwealth men would later have claimed that "had their republic not been overthrown their free and liberal government might have diffused its universal happiness through the three kingdoms." In short, if they had lost the battle, the alternate counterfactual vision would have persisted as a challenge to royal legitimacy. In this convoluted turn of the argument, counterfactuals are shown to be not only tools for reflecting on history but also weapons in the political-ideological battles that could determine its outcome. Thus, although the Leibnizian conclusion returns all to God's judgment, demonstrating "how much better events are disposed of by Providence, than they would be if the direction were left to the choice even of the best and the wisest man," the analysis also implies that possible-world visions might additionally be used to shape history. This notion—that counterfactualizing about history can activate dormant or suppressed possibilities—later becomes characteristic of the mode.

One late eighteenth-century thinker, Joseph Priestley, makes the connection between theodicies and Enlightenment thought especially clear. Priestley was a prolific political writer, Unitarian minister, and scientist (who is often credited with the discovery of oxygen). His *Lectures on History* (1788) uniquely blend Leibnizian providentialism with materialistic determinism, arguing that scientific and technological progress, which proceed with God's oversight, will eventually produce a Christian millennium of equality and peace.[7] *Lectures on History* is a full-throated theodicy, which proclaims on its first pages that imagining what might have happened but did not is the key to recognizing the beneficence of God's decisions. Counterfactual speculations, he assures us, "will throw an agreeable light upon the most gloomy and disgusting parts of [history]" by revealing how "all evils lead to, and terminate in, a greater good."[8] But Priestley was not content to heap up particular instances of ironic reversal, although he mentions several—if Henry VIII had not been a lustful adulterer, England would still be in thrall to Rome; if Philip II of Spain had not been such a relentless oppressor of Holland, the states of that region would not have revolted and gained their liberty—in order to illustrate the principle that great progressive events are "brought about contrary to the intention of the persons who were the chief instruments of them, and by the very means which were intended to produce a contrary effect" (79).

Priestley's greater ambition was to find in history's very confusion and disorder the principle of its order. Contrasting the study of natural history with that of human history, he remarks that nature's regularity is both an obvious fact of our daily existence and one that can be further understood through controlled experimentation, whereas history records irreproducible and abnormal human behavior: "Times of peace and tranquility are passed over in silence by all historians," who concentrate instead on events of chaotic upheaval (560). So Priestley hypothesized that those very disruptions of peaceful order were the motive force of long-range progress and that warfare especially, normally cited as evidence that history is a record of meaningless suffering, was the most effective general mechanism for worldwide historical transformation. Typically, he casts his argument as a counterfactual hypothesis: if we imagine the world without war, we can see that it has been the main engine driving scientific knowledge: "In early ages, before mankind had acquired a taste for intellectual pleasures, when they studied nothing but the gratification of their lower appetites, they would have sunk into a state of such gross bestiality . . . as would have been almost inconsistent with the continuance of the species, had it not been for the salutary alarms of war, which roused the activity, and excited the ingenuity, of men" (462). And warfare's "salutary" effect carries on long after the dawn of civilization: at every stage the urgencies of war spur scientific discovery and material progress, which are then put to peaceful uses. Eventually, Priestley believed, the resulting scientific enlightenment, technological prowess, and universal "taste for intellectual pleasures" would reach such high levels that warfare would no longer be needed for advancement. However, the progress leading up to that utopia was the periodic disruption of civilization and not its uninterrupted, harmonious development. Priestley, in short, took the common Leibnizian trope of ironic reversal, in which historical evils are transformed into greater goods, and fashioned it into a proto-dialectical principle of world-historical development.

Priestley's *Lectures on History* might therefore be seen as a step toward the secular dialectical philosophy of history articulated by Georg Hegel. As Reinhart Koselleck has demonstrated, that philosophy takes from Leibniz the idea that historical events arise contingently, in the realm of human freedom, even though God guarantees that only those accidents that lead to an optimal world will be actualized. Priestly kept that stress on divinely controlled contingency and also built into history itself a large-scale mechanism of incremental betterment, which makes use of the very ills it ultimately overcomes. In this way, God's goodness needn't be illustrated by the piecemeal recounting of numerous particulars, for it can be clearly seen in the general rule of human development. Priestley, like many other thinkers of the last quarter of the eighteenth century, illustrates that the notion of history as a process with an immanent *direction*, as well as immanent causes, was taking hold even among those who professed theodicy. And once it had become widely accepted, the philosophy of history could stand on its own as a secular discipline.[9] Moreover, the secularization that made teleological necessity internal to history suppressed the very interest in chance and in the counterfactual method that

Leibnizians had stressed. For if there was no divine mind doing the choosing, then there was no need for alternate possible worlds and no warrant to imagine them. From the point of view of the many varieties of historical determinism that dominated the nineteenth century, counterfactual speculation, we're often told, seemed useless.

ANTI-TELEOLOGICAL COUNTERFACTUALISM

We'll shortly see that the suppression of counterfactualism by historical determinism was by no means complete; the mode actually survived and matured during its apparent nineteenth-century eclipse. But before examining the secular context in which it managed to thrive in the next century, we will look at an earlier Enlightenment tradition that attempted to remove the Leibnizian constraints on counterfactual speculation. The practitioners of theodicy did not entirely have the mode to themselves in the eighteenth-century; their control over it was hotly contested by secular writers, whose attack on the *Theodicy* is best known through the medium of Voltaire's perennially popular satire in *Candide* (1759). There Leibniz is portrayed as an ingenious producer of justifications for the docile acceptance of every imaginable evil, whose philosophy results in complacency and callous insensitivity to actual suffering. The satire can be placed in political terms: Voltaire, the progressive Enlightenment thinker, attacks the *Theodicy* for defending the social-political status quo of the ancien régime. But Voltaire's satire also partook of a longer-running dispute about God's inscrutability and human fallibility, which is important to the history of counterfactual history because it contributed an anti-teleological strand to its genealogy. Even though Leibniz was the presiding genius behind most eighteenth-century counterfactualizing, those who opposed teleological historical explanations also used the counterfactual mode in their own arguments.

Indeed, the anti-teleological counterfactual impulse might be said to have chronological priority, for it can be traced back to Blaise Pascal's cryptic remarks in 1662 about how the world might have been different if Cleopatra's nose had been shorter.[10] Pascal was both a theologian and an early theorist of probability, who, like Leibniz, thought that historical causes arose from human actions or natural forces and were thus both immanent and contingent. Unlike Leibniz, however, Pascal chastised the desire to see God in history and used its contingency to debunk the idea that it should be read as a manifestation of divinity. He was musing not on God's goodness but on our weakness when he wrote the famous aphorism that has served for centuries as a byword for the whole phenomenon of counterfactual-historical speculation:

> He who will know fully the vanity of man has only to consider the causes and effects of love. The cause is a *je ne sais quoi* (Corneille), and the effects are dreadful. This *je ne sais quoi*, so small an object that we cannot recognise it, agitates a whole country, princes, armies, the entire world.
>
> Cleopatra's nose: had it been shorter, the whole aspect of the world would have been altered.[11]

These thoughts on vanity come under the general heading of "The Misery of Man without God," so it would seem that Caesar's infatuation with the Egyptian queen and all that it brought in its train were by no means the work of Providence. Indeed, the overarching theological difference between Pascal and Leibniz was that the former promoted the "irrationalization of religion," arguing that reason can yield some kinds of truths but should not try to comprehend God.[12] His famous counterfactual was designed to challenge, not exalt, our ability to find divine reasons in history, and thus the cause he identifies is irrationality itself.

By denying historical causes any transcendent status, even that of having been chosen by God, Pascal can be seen as a forerunner of history's complete secularization, and his Cleopatra aphorism exemplifies an early stage in that process by singling out a cause that is itself inexplicable, a private motivation that cannot be known or further analyzed (a "je ne sais quoi"). Moreover, the aphorism stresses that the cause is a "small thing," a hypothetical snippet of Cleopatra's nose, which nevertheless altered the "face de la terre" (as the original French puts it). The tiny counterfactual economically contains everything needed to open an aperture on a possible world without suggesting divine intervention, and it exemplifies the "petites causes" that came to fascinate Enlightenment writers who treated causality as immanent activation rather than transcendent teleological reason. They thought of genuine causes as phenomena that could not be traced back beyond themselves: as end points in a backward-moving explanatory sequence, *termini ad quo* that are not amenable to further explanation. They were accidental in the sense that they apparently came from nowhere. Reinhart Koselleck notes that "precisely the inconsequentiality and superficiality of the chance element suited it as a *causa*."[13] Their very meaninglessness proved their immanence, their status as brute facts, and the possibility that they easily might have been different.

The practice of deriving counterfactual possibilities from historical *petites causes* continued through the late seventeenth and eighteenth centuries, especially in France, where Pierre Bayle's *Dictionnaire historique et critique* (1697–1702), Adrian Richer's *Essai sur les grands évènements par les petites causes* (1755–59), and Voltaire's own "Observations" in his edition of Frederick of Prussia's *Anti-Machiavel* all contained influential examples.[14] Quickly translated into English, such works increased skepticism about theodicies while demonstrating that the counterfactual imagination could be easily separated from teleological piety. In English, this trend culminated in the first essay devoted entirely to analyzing the pitfalls and potential benefits of counterfactual history, Isaac D'Israeli's "The History of Events That Have Not Happened." D'Israeli, father of the future Victorian prime minister Benjamin Disraeli, wrote the essay in the early 1790s as a derisive attack on Priestley's recently published *Lectures on History*, beginning it with an assault on the "theodiceans" for arrogantly presuming to act as God's accountants, as if they had some special insight into the divine mind.[15] Their plots of ironic reversal, showing how "events which at first were adverse to [the party favored by the historian] finally terminate in their favour," come in for special disapprobation as expressions of "human error and intolerant prejudice" (251). In discussing the anonymous story of Charles II's possible victory at the Battle of Worcester, for example, he upends the providential historian's conclusion by extending the chronology to create a second ironic turn: "The story . . . would have a brighter close, if the sovereign and royalists had proved themselves better men than the knaves and fanatics of the commonwealth. It is not for us to scrutinise into 'the ways' of Providence; but if Providence conducted Charles the Second to the throne, it appears to have deserted him when there" (255). This is a repeated refrain in D'Israeli's essay: there is no ultimate point when the books are closed and the debits and credits computed so that the "on balance" analyses can take place. History, he claims, is "so ductile . . . in the hands of man" that it almost always tends to bend with special ease "to the force of success" and to "wrap with the warmth of prosperity" (268).

D'Israeli thus seems to be the first writer to identify what has now come to be called "hindsight bias" and to use counterfactual hypotheses to overcome it. The object of his essay is not to find a pattern in history that is different from Priestley's progressive enlightenment—a pattern of decline, for example—but merely to sow doubts about our ability to judge the relative merits of actual historical occurrences when compared with unrealized possibilities.[16] "The History of Events That Have Not

Happened" examines each of the Leibnizians' ironic plot forms—reversal of intended consequences, the use of sordid instruments to affect righteous ends, and the disproportion of cause and effect—making its argument into a counter-discourse, a tissue of previously used counterfactuals with their theology curtailed or attacked. It repeats many of the skeptical dicta already visible in the works of Bayle, Richer, and Voltaire, but it also clearly expresses a newer idea: that we can develop a more accurate knowledge of historical events simply by placing them in the context of their reconstructed alternatives.[17] Counterfactuals teach D'Israeli not about the nature of God but about the nature of history itself, which follows no pattern of reason and arises out of a complex variety of causes: "Important events have been nearly occurring which, however, did not take place; and others have happened which may be traced to accident, and to the character of an individual" (268). Thus, when we pause in our reading of history to reflect "on certain events which have not happened," the purpose should not be to fathom God's plans or engage in pious contemplation of his goodness but rather to "enlarge our conception of human events" by including a multiplicity of motives and accidents (268). D'Israeli was thus one of the first writers to defend counterfactual hypothesizing solely on the grounds that it can contribute to historical knowledge.

COUNTERFACTUALISM AND CRITICAL MILITARY HISTORY

Historians of counterfactualism have claimed that nineteenth-century history was deterministic in both theory and practice. Reinhart Koselleck, for example, remarks that both the philosophy of Hegel and the aesthetics of Novalis were hostile to the previous century's emphasis on chance and helped to launch plots of necessary development (Whig, nationalist, Marxist, Darwinian) that dominated the professionalization of the discipline.[18] Niall Ferguson also traces various forms of "scientific determinism," all of which supposedly precluded imagining alternatives, from the nineteenth century into the twentieth.[19] Indeed, as we'll see in the next chapter, one of the nineteenth-century practitioners of alternate history, Charles Renouvier, thought of his own work as a protest against the prevailing historical determinism. We are thus used to hearing that the counterfactual imagination was stifled in the late eighteenth and the nineteenth centuries by new secular necessitarian philosophies. Once again, however, the generalizations ignore the counterfactual history that was actually written at the time, which includes one of the most flourishing historical practices of the last two centuries, albeit one to which cultural and intellectual historians seldom look: military history. When we take military history into account, we can see that the counterfactual mode not only survived in the nineteenth century but also underwent a prolonged period of growth and disciplinary development.

Military historians have made copious use of counterfactualism, and, in the late eighteenth and early nineteenth centuries, they even developed a specialized form of history—critical military history—that regularized its use. It was called critical because it went beyond reporting the facts of wars to judging their conduct, thus taking up the Leibnizian practice of arranging alternative possibilities along with actualities on a spectrum from worst to best. But it also stressed the importance of knowing which among the numerous factors in a battle were actually decisive in its outcome. In making its judgments about how best to fight wars, it used large amounts of empirical historical data about causes and effects on the battlefield, calculated probabilities, and tried to formulate principles of modern warfare. Thus, although professionalizing most forms of history in academic environments may have inhibited counterfactual speculation, professionalizing warfare gave it a new impetus and new institutional homes.

Military historians are at ease with counterfactualism, it has often been said, because wars are notoriously full of unpredictable turning points, meeting the counterfactualists' need for contingency and multiple possibilities, and yet they have unusually long-range and widespread ramifications.[20] They lend themselves as well to the spacialization and mapping of actions in time, thus encouraging a tendency toward the synoptic overview. The hierarchical chains of command in organized battle also make it relatively easy to trace decisions to individual commanders and decipher their purposes, as well as to distinguish between tactical mistakes and unforeseeable accidents, so the gaps between intention and result are ever present to the military historian. Moreover, military historians who have access to the archives of the absolutist states of the late eighteenth century or the later nation-states can often see unused plans, developed to cover contingencies that did not arise, as well as the correspondence and memoirs describing the options as they appeared at the time. In military history, events that did not happen are obviously a vast part of the historical record and cannot be ignored. Military historians are thus regularly drawn into "virtual" battles and campaigns that were thoroughly conceived and, in some cases, meticulously prepared for but never actualized, and there is a general consensus that these potential battles are important pieces of evidence in filling out the reasons for the conduct of the actual battles.

These affinities between military history and counterfactualism are largely products of late eighteenth-century developments in military institutions and sciences. Only in the Enlightenment did military histories, as a kind set apart from general histories, begin to appear, and they took two forms: memoirs of wars and campaigns principally written by combatants, and the more rigorous critical military history that tried to distill lessons, in the form of general rules, laws, and principles of war, which could then be applied to planning and carrying out future wars.[21] Several developments in late eighteenth-century warfare and statecraft encouraged the critical project and helped reshape the counterfactual comparative operation into a modern historical tool. The vast growth in state information gathering and bureaucratic organization, which began on the Continent in the seventeenth century and spurred improvements in geographical, demographic, and commercial knowledge, as well as more precise record keeping, certainly extended to early modern states' militaries.[22] In France, by the middle of the eighteenth century, a need for mathematical and other technical proficiency in warfare had also begun to break the nobility's traditional monopoly on officer commissions, and technical military academies began to emerge. There was, thus, not only a new premium placed on collecting and consolidating information but also new state-run institutions for fostering its systematic use in the military sciences. The earliest military academies were founded in France in the middle of the century and were soon imitated elsewhere.[23] The new information and technological discoveries were thus funneled into the competition to train professional officers. The efforts also encouraged military thinkers to systematize and shape the new knowledge into more general principles about warfare, and critical military history arose out of that attempt. Drawing on historical data about past wars, this historical practice often used counterfactuals both to pass judgment on the conduct of the commanders and to sort out the determining causes of failure or success from among a swarm of conditioning factors.

Its pioneering practitioner, a Welsh soldier of fortune named Henry Lloyd was, for unknown reasons, teaching military sciences in France during the very decades when the new academies were taking shape. He was born in Wales in 1718 and educated at Oxford but was in France by the early 1740s, where he privately tutored officers in geography and field engineering before joining the French army himself. The French employed him as a highly skilled draftsman and ground surveyor, gave him a junior commission, and sent him along on the Young Pretender's invasion of Scotland in 1745. From there he went on to Wales in disguise and began a career in international espionage: he secretly surveyed and made maps of Britain's southern sea shores in preparation for a possible French invasion in 1746, was arrested and jailed, and then returned to France in 1747. During the Seven Years' War, he changed sides repeatedly, doing reconnaissance for the French, Prussians, and Austrians; he even went back to Britain in 1756 to make more extensive surveys of the coast for Louis XV's ultimately abandoned invasion. After the Seven Years' War, his peripatetic career continued: he spied for the British in Italy and in the early seventies took command of a division in the service of Russia against the Turks.

It may seem odd that it was a Briton who took advantage of the intensive officer training on the Continent to write a book of critical military history, for Britain was notoriously late in instituting formal army officer training and in using the system of thought that Lloyd invented.[24] However, the Welshman's apparent lack of national loyalty to any of the combatants was precisely what made him such a flexible mercenary and unbiased observer. He fought creditably for numerous European powers and seems to have spied on all, so he had a multiperspectival knowledge of the era's armies, an understanding of their operational organizations and their battlefield tactics, a geologist's and surveyor's familiarity with the terrains, and an engineer's mastery of arms. He was, in short, ideally situated to write a history of the Seven Years' War, which he set about doing in the mid-1760s. Moreover, his unusual combination of knowledge, experience, and skill came together in that work as a new *kind* of military history. In its introduction, he explains that it is intended to combine teaching texts on the principles of warfare, which he found too abstract, with historical study of their application. Lloyd's initial ambition was to historicize the science of warfare, making it more concrete and improving its practice. The work was titled *The History of the Late War in Germany: Between the King of Prussia, and the Empress of Germany and Her Allies* and appeared in numerous volumes between 1766 and 1781. It gives exhaustive descriptions of the strategic, operational, logistic, and geographical aspects of various Continental campaigns, pointing out alternative possibilities and general lessons as it proceeds. Written from no single political or national perspective, Lloyd's volumes aspire to synoptic objectivity, and in that regard as well as in their assessments of the relative values of possible alternatives, they bear formal resemblances to the theodicies.

The similarities, moreover, do not end there. If we compare Lloyd to his contemporary Priestley, we can see a similar inventiveness in the spatial and visual rendering of historical change. Priestley was the creator of the horizontally oriented timeline, which he thought could mimic God's view of the omnitemporal totality of history, and Lloyd invented sequential and highly accurate maps of battles that gave compact, fluid views of the action over time.[25] Priestley claimed that his charts let the viewer see at a glance the "movement" of history, and Lloyd's were designed as well to superimpose repeated movements over a single battlefield so that the patterns of the total battle were revealed free of any particular vantage point or single moment. Providing such a synchronous and synoptic vision, moreover, seems to have been related in both cases to the activity of imagining the alternative lines of untaken actions. Both also used relatively recent computational and comparative techniques, like ledgers, grids, and distribution analysis for aggregating historical information. These similarities (as well as the contemporaneity of Lloyd's and Priestley's works) should prevent us from seeing the theodicies as merely benighted precursors, which the military practice left behind: both were saturated in the new sciences and the mathematics of probability, and both inspired technical breakthroughs that are still in use.

And yet, of course, they had divergent aims, and the differences do seem to outweigh the similarities. Lloyd hardly ever thought the actual history was the best among the possibilities. He sought the mistakes and disappointing outcomes as assiduously as Priestley sought the benign results, for it was only by being critical of the decisions of actual commanders that one could learn how to fight wars more effectively. To make his judgments, moreover, Lloyd looked only at military criteria; he was completely uninterested in speculations like Priestley's about any distant repercussions that might have made the world a better place. His concrete mastery of the events of the battles and the operational maneuvers is an end in itself, requiring no transcendent justification. Thus, whereas Priestley was given to moral summaries, Lloyd tends to prefer numbers. He tries to be as precise as possible about the degree of a victory or loss, enumerating the prizes—numbers of troops, size of towns taken, numbers of dead—and he gives tables of the exact number of battalions, garrisons, and squadrons involved in the battles he describes. Explaining one Prussian victory, for example, he goes into great numerical detail listing the fire power taken along with a captured fort: "twenty twelve pounders, three twenty-four pounders, three of ten, eight mortars, ten pounders, one of thirty, ten of sixty, all brass, and six iron of sixty, in all fifty-one pieces, cannon and mortars."[26] This list is immediately followed by the cost to the Prussians and Austrians in casualties; as in an account book, it sets credits off against debits: "two officers, three under officers, one bombardier, ninety-one soldiers, and five common men killed; fourteen officers, ten under officers, two bombardiers, two hundred and thirty-one soldiers, and four men belonging to the army wounded" (3).

Lloyd uses these accounting procedures, calculating the degrees of success and failure of the campaigns, so that he can compare similar campaigns, as he did, for example, in describing the almost annual battles in which the Prussians and Austrians took, lost, and retook Schweidnitz. He begins the second volume of his history with an overview of these conflicts, looking both at sieges prior to 1758, which is the starting time of the second volume, and at instances to come: "This place is by no means strong; it was taken the preceding year by the Austrians in nearly the same space of time. In one thousand seven hundred and sixty-one [three years after the battle he is describing] Laudohn [sic] took it in a few hours sword in hand, without opening the trenches; and it was finally retaken in one thousand seven hundred and sixty-two, after a defence of ten weeks. Whence proceeded this very great difference?" (3). Such passages underline the importance of the detailed comparison of historically similar battles in order to learn what factors were decisive. The numbers served as the basis for such evaluations; minutely and precisely described in standardized and quantifiable terms, each successive siege of Schweidnitz adds to an abstract model of its own possible versions.

Synoptic and synchronous views of multiple actions thus helped him to create models, and models allowed Lloyd to formulate principles of warfare that he thought would pertain generally. Indeed, he was interested in Schweidnitz primarily because the variations in outcome there supported his most important theoretical premise: that the key to success in modern warfare was keeping one's own operational line intact and disrupting that of one's enemy.[27] Once he had that general principle, he began to speculate counterfactually about alternate consequences. For example, he uses the retaking of Schweidnitz to bolster his general claim that the Austrians had no chance of achieving their war aim of wresting Silesia from Prussian control because they had not succeeded in holding Leuthen and therefore could not take Glogau, which would have changed everything because it was an important center of operations for the Prussians. In an almost unreadable passage that mixes actual and counterfactual occurrences, he tries to sum up the state of play in 1758 and its relation to the war's final outcome:

> The retaking of Schweidnitz [by the Prussians] reduced the state of the war to what it was at the breaking out of it; the fatal battle of Leuthen was the cause. Had the Austrians avoided it, being in possession of Glatz and Schweidnitz, and their army powerful, this campaign might and ought to have begun with the siege of Glogau, which the approach of the Russians would have facilitated. Neisse must have fallen of course. The war was finished; Silesia conquered: the Prussians could not pretend to defend Brandebourg and Pomerania after the taking Glogau, when attacked and surrounded by the Austrians, Russians, and Swedes. (3)

Even if one were intimately acquainted with the Seven Years' War, this would be a difficult passage to understand because Lloyd's hypotheticals quickly take on certainty for him and lose the grammatical conditional altogether. Austrian war aims are thwarted at the outset of 1758 by the loss of Leuthen, but if they had held Leuthen, they "might and ought" to have moved on Glogau, and the rest follows automatically: Neisse *must* have fallen, and the Prussians "could not pretend to defend" other targets after losing Glogau. As we proceed further into this alternate version of history, indeed, it takes on greater conviction and inevitability. Leuthen is the condition for the imaginary decisive victory of the war: the Austrian seizure of Glogau, which would have severed the operational line of the Prussians. Thus the puzzling declaration in the middle of the paragraph—"The war was finished; Silesia conquered."—is in the simple past tense because it is written from *inside* a possible world where these events were actualities.[28]

Lloyd's confidence in his representation of this other possible combat in 1758 is thus based on a causal logic quite different from that of earlier counterfactuals: he has a generalization about successful tactics which he uses to identify the weightiest causal factors, and he also supports his judgment of their importance, not by selective anecdotes but by the cumulative evidence from sequences of similar operations. To be sure, many conditions need to come into alignment even in this short counterfactual history: both Russian and Swedish allies are important. But the key—the sine qua non—remains the ability to disrupt the enemy's operational line, to which the seizure of Glogau (which was disabled by Leuthen) would have been necessary. So by the late eighteenth century the comparative operation of counterfactual history had taken on a new object: finding alternatives to actuality in order to perfect an art, in this case the art of war. And it became more closely tied to identifying truly decisive causes, to sorting out the salient from the incidental in a sea of antecedent conditions and also discerning patterns in the sea itself. The desire to frame the general principles of successful warfare merged the comparative and causal functions of counterfactual history, and in military history that merger has lasted from the time of Henry Lloyd in the 1760s to the present. We might conclude, then, that the specialization of military history and the belief that it could be systematized into a set of widely applicable although historically variable generalizations yielded a durable, albeit highly instrumental, role for counterfactual history.

While Henry Lloyd was inventing this new form of history, the institutionalized pursuit of military science was developing another technique for imagining alternative historical wars—three-dimensional gaming to model and simulate operations—and we will take a quick detour here from the history of critical military writing to describe its contribution to counterfactualism. War games evolved quickly during the late eighteenth and early nineteenth centuries in the German and Austrian courts and military academies, and they fostered the practice of revising battles and perfecting past campaigns over time, so that military history and an open-ended future merged. In 1780, the mathematician Johann Christian Hellwig, who was also the tutor of the page boys training to be officers at the court of the Duke of Brunswick, published his rules for an elaborate game board on which to teach both strategic and tactical maneuvers, consisting of 1,666 squares. Their colors symbolized different types of terrain, and the assembled board accommodated hundreds of game pieces representing different sorts of forces and armaments. The game was so complex that it required a director to keep track of the action, a kind of super critic, who would decide when a battle was won or lost. The rules were supposed to mimic the principles of warfare, and the inventor claimed to have it examined by "numbers of military men, profound in the theoretical and practical science of their profession."[29] At the same court in the beginning of the Napoleonic era, the table-top war game became even more intricate and realistic, drawing more explicitly on recent military history. The military theoretician Johann Georg Julius Venturini published the rules for his *Neues Kriegsspiel* in 1798, which used a thirty-six hundred–square grid over an actual map of the much disputed Franco-Belgian border. Each square represented one square mile, and each player had at his command twenty-five hundred units, as well as special pieces for logistical factors, like convoys and supply magazines. With a rule book over sixty densely written pages long, this game also purported to set forth the essence of the "laws of warfare."[30] Even though this particular game proved unwieldy, it stimulated a taste for playing "with possible outcomes of specific events, detailed down to the single soldier." As one modern historian of war games remarks, "Would-be Napoleons could toy with the course of history."[31] Napoleon's sound defeat of the Prussian forces only intensified the desire in Prussia to train an elite class in the principles of warfare, and as the emphasis shifted from tactical to strategic agility, the games were modified appropriately. Among the most significant innovations, both included in a game published in 1806 by a certain Giacomo Opiz, were explicit rules about how terrain should factor into the game and the use of dice to add the element of chance.[32] The most important Prussian war-game inventor, Georg Leopold von Reisswitz, a civilian adviser to Friedrich Wilhelm III, incorporated Opiz's ideas in his widely used *Kriegsspiel* (invented in 1812), which was later modified into a smaller, more portable version. The rules were disseminated in an 1824 publication, and the game was played intensively by the officer corps for decades, especially, but not exclusively, in Prussia. One person stood outside of the action and judged the outcome of each engagement, using statistical tables with data accumulated from historical battles.

The *Kriegsspiel* was a practical embodiment of the idea that military history might be summed up in tables of statistics, which could in turn be mathematically manipulated to model probable futures. The use of the dice to build randomness into the game was also an important feature for learning that practitioners of military science could calculate probabilities, but they also needed to be prepared to confront unforeseeable and uncontrollable accidents as they arose. The mathematical rules became more refined through the early decades of the century, and the player designated referee was "armed with tables of logarithms" and functioned as "a calculator"; thus officers learned even in their leisure hours to apply the mathematics of probability to the activity of warfare.[33] And, of course, the games strengthened the connection between numerical analysis and military history. Historical enumeration had served as the basis for Lloyd's evaluations, and such numerical records continued to serve as the raw data underlying the *Kriegspiel*'s tables of logarithms, which were even higher-level abstractions of history's lessons and allowed the players to perform further virtual military experiments out of which revised historical scenarios emerged. The games themselves later became caught up in debates about military theory, and, especially after Carl von Clausewitz placed a strong emphasis on individual inventive genius, some versions of the

Kriegsspiel began reducing their reliance on mathematics in determining the ultimate results. To accommodate players who wanted greater leeway for strategic creativity, the game split into two versions: the "rigid" mathematically dominated rule-bound sort (mainly used for tactical exercises); and a "free" form, used in strategic exercises, which made some use of the mathematical tables but also called for more individual judgment. However, the mathematics continued to undergird both versions, and the many cadets and officers who spent hours playing the war games continued to tighten the connection between probabilistic mathematical thinking and counterfactual-historical reasoning, as they unconsciously pioneered a technology that became universal in military education and planning.

The changes in the *Kriegsspiel* correspond to developments in military history in the early nineteenth century. Antoine Henri de Jomini's *Art of War* (1836), which was the most important piece of military writing to result from Napoleon's wars, attempted to further the historicization of military theory by deriving rules, principles, and other supposedly scientific laws from actual combat. Jomini's work was the basis of military training in both France and the United States for most of the nineteenth century. He was the son of a Swiss banker, who had not received a professional military training but had read widely in French theory and served under Michel Ney in the Napoleonic Wars. He wanted to prove that those wars had changed the very nature of the enterprise, so all of warfare's fundamentals needed to be adjusted to the new reality. He began writing military history after reading Lloyd's history of the Seven Years' War, which, of course, had also articulated general principles. Jomini, however, claimed to be addressing larger "strategic" issues—such as whether to wage a defensive or offensive war—and to be revising Lloyd's theory of the operational line for modern campaigns. Although he acknowledged the former critical military historian's influence on his own thought, Jomini saw Lloyd's concentrating on tactical operational questions as appropriate to ancien régime "wars of position" as opposed to "the modern system of marches," in which mobility, maneuvering while protecting one's operational line, taking the initiative, and surprising the enemy were keys. However, he imitated the earlier writing by starting his career with his own history of the Seven Years' War, which he commenced immediately after reading Lloyd's. Jomini's *Traité de grand tactique, ou relation de la guerre de sept ans* (1804–5) has Frederick the Great at times prefiguring Napoleon and at other times falling short.[34] And in making these judgments and imagining a more successful Frederick, Jomini expands and improves Lloyd's counterfactual method.

Jomini's work is far easier to read than Lloyd's *History* in part because he has a strong focus: Frederick II is its central figure, a protagonist whose audacity, like Napoleon's, is admirable in itself, but whose strategy must nevertheless be tested by both the actual events and other possible results. His counterfactually framed judgment of the monarch is a cornerstone of his historical writings and is summed up early in the *Art of War*: "Frederick II, while Austria and France were at war, brought forward an old claim, entered Silesia in force and seized this province, thus doubling the power of Prussia. This was a stroke of genius; and, even if he had failed, he could not have been much censured; for the grandeur and importance of the enterprise justified him in his attempt, as far as such attempts can be justified."[35] Whether judged from the standpoint of actual or alternative history ("even if he had failed, he could not have been much censured"), the military critic's verdict would remain the same: Frederick was strategically brilliant, although (as the last phrase of the above quotation indicates) morally dubious. Jomini makes the point explicitly that a commander's skill is not to be judged by his success or failure, for these may be the result of mere accident, what he often calls "conditions." Putting too great an emphasis on those would derail the entire project of systematizing a "science of war": "An order misunderstood, a fortuitous event, may throw into the hands of the enemy all the chances of success which a skillful general had prepared for himself by his maneuvers. But these are risks which cannot be foreseen nor avoided. Would it be fair on that account to deny the influence of science and principles in ordinary affairs? ... For a general's science consists in providing for his side all the chances possible to be foreseen" (*Art of War*, 33). "Chances" are always in the mix, and they may fall to the lot of the "inferior" general, which is why commanders must be judged not by the outcome but their plans, which must include foresight, but cannot provide for every contingency.

Jomini's critical military history thus tries to reconstruct from the evidence of the army's movements what the possibilities envisioned by the planner probably were, and then he assesses the commander's thoroughness and ability to calculate probabilities. His narrative of the campaign of 1758, for example, follows Frederick's movements and interprets them as a coherent strategy to maintain the offensive and, if faced with defeat, to be able to fall back onto his own operating line. The succession of campaigns is presented in a far more continuous and logical fashion than it was in Lloyd's account, and the possibilities are more imbedded in accounts of the warring parties' long-term aims and calculations. After recounting the taking of Schweidniz (same place, different spelling), Jomini begins his account of Frederick's eventually unsuccessful invasion of Moravia. Jomini's purpose is not so much to explain the failure as to assess the wisdom of the attempt by stepping back and re-creating the choices then available: Frederick could "either . . . content himself with defending his own territories, or . . . invade those of Austria." If he had merely tried to defend his possession of Silesia, he would have given the enemy "the time to recruit, to establish magazines upon their line of operation, to conduct their movements with the Russians and the troops of the Empire, in a word, to invade the Prussian states." Jomini gives a thorough inventory of all the negative probabilities that would follow from adopting a defensive posture: *If* he had merely tried to defend Silesia, he would have "had to make war at her expense," and *if* defeat were the outcome, it would have been a "disaster" to lose on his own territory (*Treatise*, 319). Frederick could not have risked these possibilities, and so Jomini finds his attempt to invade Moravia blameless even though unsuccessful.

Of course, Jomini has no access to Frederick's actual reasoning, so the hero's choice is not really narrated as an event; we are not told, for example, that the king considered a series of options and, at some specific time, came to a determination. Instead, the choices are laid out as the objective conditions obtaining during a span of time between April 15, 1758, when Schweidniz was taken, and April 27, when the Prussian forces begin to move toward Moravia. The descriptions of the various forces' placements and capabilities during this time, including many counterfactuals about what they might have done, are also couched as incentives or disincentives for Frederick's eventual action. It is only when Frederick actually sets his forces in motion that Jomini infers a decision must have been taken: "The invasion of Moravia having been decided upon by the king, he started on the 27th of April from Neisse for Neustadt" (324). Jomini's work thus displays the sideways and often impersonal nature of counterfactual history; a great deal of time is spent canvassing unrealized possibilities on the assumption that they formed the basis of decision making, and yet these are often inferred from the resulting action and not explicitly located in the minds of particular actors who make choices at definite moments.

In Jomini's histories we can clearly see not only the dependence of military counterfactual history on the reconstruction of prior future conditionals but also the dependence of the reconstruction on an assumption of strategic coherence. The future conditionals in the minds of the combatants turn into the historian's past counterfactuals only if they can be grasped according to some larger principle. To be workable, this sort of counterfactualism needed both a systematic endeavor, in which the choices seem rational to an observer, and one subject to plenty of contingencies that would stimulate the planning. To make sense of Frederick's ill-fated march on Moravia, Jomini asks which of the hero's possible choices best conformed to his strategic design of maintaining the offense; ultimately the campaign on Moravia is repulsed at Olmutz because the Austrians capture a supply convoy bound for the Prussians, but that does not diminish the fact that "had the king succeeded in gaining a great battle, it is probable nothing would have prevented him from pushing forward even to Vienna" (320). Other possibilities having been eliminated as even riskier in the historian's analysis of conditions, the failed campaign appears to have contained the best chance of piercing deeply into Austrian territory.

Jomini realizes, though, that choosing the course most likely to achieve one's aims has the disadvantage of predictability. If your decision is objectively dictated by the prevailing circumstances, then it might easily be anticipated by the enemy, so the art of war requires weighing all chances while attempting to make one's movements as surprising as possible. Sometimes, indeed, a general must play against the odds. In the campaign under discussion, for example, Jomini shows that Frederick chose Moravia rather than Bohemia as an object because the latter was too predictable a choice. Taking up the viewpoint of Austrian General Daun, who reckoned that Frederick would march instead on Bohemia, Jomini comes to the conclusion that Daun "was not far wrong; for it could hardly be presumed that the king, after having neglected the invasion of Moravia in the course of two campaigns when it offered great advantages, would have then undertaken it" (323). The phrase "not far wrong" reminds us that Jomini imagines Daun's mind reviewing a spectrum of probabilities and calculating the relative advantages and disadvantages of the Moravian campaign with considerable accuracy. As it happened, of course, Daun's prediction of what Frederick would do was dead wrong, but the critic Jomini shows that Daun was better at seeing the disadvantages of the Moravian campaign than Frederick was. Intent on a high-stakes gamble, the Prussian concentrated on its "greater and more favourable chances," and he was also "not wrong" to do so because opting for the choice that was *not* favored by the circumstances gave him the advantage of surprise (324). Thus, although both generals were, if we apply a simple binary test of right and wrong, wrong about what the future held, the critic nevertheless approves their strategic calculations. Both played the game well given their assumptions; Frederick knowingly took the bigger risk in order to win a bigger prize, and he lost while following the correct principals of staying on the offensive but behaving unpredictably. The passages of criticism in both Jomini's *Art of War* and his *Treatise* emphasize that risk and randomness are built into the enterprise, so that all courses of action are side-shadowed with unrealized results.

Jomini's writings thus assume the constant pressure of possible accidents on all military planning: the zero point of randomness is, after all, necessary to the calculation of probabilities, and generalship is a contest of such calculations. This episode in the *Treatise*, though, highlights another complication in the relation between the calculation of probabilities and the changing nature of warfare in historical time: a strategy that is close to the improbable side of the scale in one era may move to the probable side at a later date. Indeed, Jomini had written his history of the Seven Years' War in order to make the point that Frederick was altering the enterprise by waging a war of offensive momentum rather than clinging to defensive positioning. It seems that General Daun and Frederick occupy different temporal frames, different eras in the history of war, with incommensurate probability spectra. Moreover, Daun's more defensive assumptions are visible to Frederick—he knows he can surprise the Austrian by invading Moravia—whereas Daun does not imagine Frederick's unprecedented risk taking. Of course, this is partly just another version of the epistemological asymmetry of historical time: the past is always visible and the future is always unknowable.[36] Jomini, however, was developing the argument not just that Frederick anticipates Napoleon as a practitioner of a future stage of warfare but also that he is already in its ultimate stage: the essence of war is strategic offensiveness combined with operational integrity, mobility, and surprise. But that argument also implies that it would always be premature to make generalizations about what sorts of actions would satisfy these criteria, for the innovations that would be necessary to any side's surprising momentum must be unpredictable. To use a common example, from within the Napoleonic framework, nothing could have been more surprising than the Russian General Kutuzov's "wise passivity," as Tolstoy's narrator put it, in abandoning Moscow.

Perhaps Jomini had an inkling of this inconsistency in his method, for he did not explicitly lay out the connections between his probabilistic reasoning and his formulation of universally applicable principles. Moreover, he soon came under criticism for being rule-bound and insufficiently historical in his analyses. The censure was forcefully delivered by the most famous of all Western military theorists, Carl von Clausewitz in an 1808 work on strategy. He accused Jomini of leaving out of his analyses the importance of moral forces, the larger political-historical context, and the uniqueness of each individual case.[37] The historian Azar Gat maintains that the argument Clausewitz developed against ahistorical and putatively scientific principles of warfare—the argument finally published posthumously as On War in 1832—owes a great deal to Immanuel Kant's *Critique of Judgment*, which gave him a flexible model of the relation between the concrete, manifold, and constantly evolving particularity of warfare and its comprehension through general propositions.[38] In book 2 of *On War*, Clausewitz seems to allude to Kant's distinction between two ways of aligning the particular and the general: through the "determinant" judgments often used in the sciences, where the universals and particulars are both given and the latter are subsumed under the former; and through the "reflective" judgments used in the arts, where only the particulars are given and the governing principles must be actively sought by the theoretical critic. Warfare, according to Clausewitz, tends to resemble an art more than a science, for it seeks understanding in "creation and production" rather than merely "inquiry and knowledge."[39] Moreover, because war is a creative activity directed at objects that react, it is also both social and political and, hence, deeply embedded in other historical processes that change over time.[40] To be sure, Clausewitz by no means abandoned the search for a general understanding of the nature of war, but the precepts he sought needed to factor in ever-proliferating complexity and uncertainty, and they needed to account for changes in the precepts themselves. His new practice of critical military history would thus require a constant striving to derive principles from living instances, in all their intricacy, rather than a mechanical application of precepts to circumstances: "What genius does is the best rule, and theory can do no better than show how and why this should be the case" (84).

But how does this way of articulating the general and the particular affect Clausewitz's use of counterfactuals? We should note at the outset that he built on the traditions of earlier counterfactualists. There is even a faint echo of Leibniz's description of God in his characterization of the mind of a military genius, which possesses "a sense of unity and a power of judgement raised to a marvellous pitch of vision, which easily grasps and dismisses a thousand remote possibilities which an ordinary mind would labour to identify and wear itself out in so doing" (60). But since military geniuses are not Gods and thus cannot choose among the possible accidents of a campaign, they must instead consider them in their planning beforehand or react to them on the spot with maximal opportunism. Clausewitz, like Jomini, judges strategies and planning, but he is far more inclined than the earlier military critics to censure commanders for failing to contain or exploit unforeseen chances. The fact that a campaign ends in a decisive victory does not prove that its conduct was praiseworthy nor does it clear the air of what Clausewitz famously called the "fog of war"—the confusion, chaos, and indeterminacy of actual conflict. He vastly expanded the criteria for judging commanders by factoring in how well they accomplished the long-term political aims of the states they served; having defined war as politics by other means, he could not limit his analyses to the quantifiable results on which Henry Lloyd, for example, concentrated. Thus he expanded the scope of what the historian must consider in order to assess the worth of a commander while also insisting that even a complete mastering of actual history was insufficient: one must know "the full extent of everything that has happened, or *might have happened*" (110; emphasis added). This unrealistically tall order is a constant spur to historical counterfactualizing.

His method can be illustrated by looking at a passage from *On War*. I've chosen one in which Clausewitz analyzes Napoleon's options after defeating the Archduke Charles on the Tagliamento in 1797. He introduces his critique by noting that Napoleon's surprise march across the Alps had been hailed as an act of astonishingly brilliant and successful generalship, and to demonstrate that it was not, he assumes a series of overlapping points of view.

> How could Bonaparte make use of this success? Should he press on into the heart of the Austrian Empire, ease the advance of the two armies of the Rhine under Moreau and Hoche, and work in close conjunction with them? That was how Bonaparte saw it, and from his point of view he was right. But the critic may take a wider view—that of the French Directory; whose members could see, and must have realized, that the campaign on the Rhine would not begin for another six weeks. From that standpoint, then, Bonaparte's advance through the Norican Alps could only be considered an unjustified risk. (111)

In other words, although the consensus is that Bonaparte was successful because of his boldness, the introduction of the counterfactual test reveals that his daring was actually foolhardiness and might just as easily have ended in catastrophe; moreover, it reveals that his partial success was due to luck and a strategic armistice. Napoleon actually took an unnecessary risk and when he became aware of his exposed position, according to Clausewitz, he signed the armistice of Leoben.

But Clausewitz is not yet finished with this example. He then asks,

Was signing the armistice the right thing to do? Assuming an even wider point of view brings up other possible aims, calling the wisdom of the armistice into question: "If the critic takes a still wider view, he can see that the Austrians had no reserves between the Archduke's army and Vienna, and that the advance of the army of Italy [Napoleon's army] was a threat to the capital itself" (111). If Napoleon knew this and still judged the armistice to be the most important aim, considering the threat to Vienna a sufficient means to achieve the armistice, "the critic would have no more to say." But did Napoleon consider yet another possibility, that the Austrians would not be swayed by that threat? "The critic," continues Clausewitz, "must take a more comprehensive point of view, and ask what would have happened if the Austrians had abandoned Vienna [as the Russians later abandoned Moscow], and withdrawn into the vast expanse of territory they still controlled." Once faced with this possibility, the critic must calculate the outcome of "the probable encounter between the two armies on the Rhine" (which would have come about absent the armistice) and, assuming a French victory there, would at once be faced with the question of what the Directory would have done with that victory: "Would the French have pursued their advantage to the far frontiers of the Austrian monarchy, breaking Austrian power and shattering the Empire, or would they have been satisfied with the conquest of a sizable part of it as a surety for peace?" (112). Answering this question, of course, puts us back into the collective mind of the Directory and forces us to "ascertain the probable consequences of both possibilities before determining the probable choice of the Directory." But we are only temporarily confined to this point of view before shifting to another, more omniscient, perspective (which can now only be that of the historian) in which the critic assesses "the question of whether the Austrian government would even pursue its reflections and thoroughly evaluate the potential limits of French success" (112).

This counterfactual bears a certain family resemblance to the passages from Henry Lloyd and Jomini analyzed earlier. Here we are also taken quite far out in a hypothetical chain. Indeed, Clausewitz takes us to sixth-order hypotheticals: if Napoleon had not signed the armistice but continued to threaten the capital, the Austrians might have abandoned Vienna, in which case there would have been an encounter on the Rhine, in which case the French would have won, in which case they might have pursued their advantage and tried to destroy the Austrian empire, in which case they might have overextended themselves, but only if the Austrians had continued to resist, and so on. In other ways, though, Clausewitz departed radically from earlier military historians. His complex analyses of the totality of interests at play are unprecedented, and they follow from his willingness to imagine both individual and collective mentalities, thinking across myriad historical actors. These he judges not by how well they illustrate general principles but by how well they played the political and military cards dealt them in the course of their campaigns: the uses they made of changing circumstances and intelligence, the adaptability of their strategies, even their creativity and finesse in resolving conflicts with their own confreres (the conflict, for example, between Napoleon's glory seeking and the Directory's limited war aims). Throughout this analysis, Clausewitz is careful to point out that, in understanding the causes of events, we can neither limit ourselves to the perspectives of the historical actors nor altogether dispense with them; just as history continues to divide into new possibilities, the critical perspectives must continually shift in order to follow them.

There is, moreover, one final way in which Clausewitz's *On War* departs from previous historical counterfactualism: in its methodological self-reflectiveness and candor about the historian's creative role. Clausewitz believed that the truth of history—the overall shape containing its facts—was only perceivable with the help of "critical analysis," and it was *therefore* partly the invention of the historian: "Critical analysis is not just an evaluation of the means actually employed, but *all possible means*—which first have to be formulated, that is, invented" (113). He answers the questions that earlier critical military historians evaded: What consciousness sees the combination of those future conditionals? When does that comprehensive understanding of all the possibilities occur? He acknowledges that it comes into being only in the retroactive analysis of the historian. Even in cases where the "range of possible combinations" may be small, analyzing them is "not a mere analysis of existing things but an achievement" of the "creativity of the intellect" (113). To be sure, Clausewitz also believed in the objective existence of the possibilities on which the historian's inventions rest, but he is nevertheless the creator of the counterfactual histories he records. The historian is the closest thing to Leibniz's God in Clausewitz's system, for he visualizes the alternative military histories simultaneously and judges which best suited the antagonists' policy aims. And yet his creativity is limited by the requirement to demonstrate that the options were immanent in the historical action and exerted differential pressures according to their degrees of probability. The critical historian must weave his tapestry, to use one of Clausewitz's metaphors, out of contingencies, which are the historical fabric's "countless threads" (60), the very identity of pattern and medium indicating that the total interplay already structured the possibilities of the historical action. In this regard, Clausewitz anticipates many later writers who have tried to take history beyond the binary opposition between constructivism and objectivism.

⸺

We've been tracking the spread of counterfactual-historical speculation, starting in theological debates in the late seventeenth and early eighteenth centuries, into critical military history, where it became a sophisticated and self-reflective mode of exploring the nature of warfare in Clausewitz's *On War*. It is now time to sum up by taking stock of the ways in which these early works established narrative patterns that will evolve quite differently in the two counterfactual forms whose early stages we'll trace in the next two chapters: alternate histories and alternate-history novels. The later genres are narratively structured whereas the works we've examined in this chapter tend to be organized as arguments that both generate stories and present challenges to the stability of their foundational elements: plot, character, and narrative temporality. Looking at the anomalous nature of each of these categories in the early counterfactual histories will identify what the later writers try to exploit and overcome.

First, even though we've traced here a movement in the use of counterfactual speculation from theological controversy to military history, in both contexts the writers stress that the actuality of the past (what we think of as history proper) is merely a small subset of what "might have happened." Moreover, in the ambition to explore the larger category of the possible, the smaller one—the actual history—tends to get short shrift, which makes for highly unusual plotting. Most historians concern themselves with unrealized possibilities occasionally, but here the might-have-beens tend to dominate the discourse, especially when it surrounds decisive moments. To be sure, the military historians do not question the ontological status of the outward events and their sequences—Napoleon indubitably surprised and defeated the army of the archduke on the Tagliamento and then signed the armistice of Leoben; only the linking relations (including the motivations and other mental states of the actors) and their relative values are at issue. Moreover, the historians stress that they hypothesize alternatives mainly in order to better judge and explain the reasons for the actual eventualities, and thus they acknowledge that a deep and firm substratum of consensus about some facts must already be established before the counterfactual inquiry begins. Nevertheless, the swarm of possible stories arising from the speculations has an oddly de-realizing effect on the givenness of the actuality, which is often only cursorily described since it is assumed that readers already know it. Counterfactual speculation is a plot-generating machine, but instead of coexisting peacefully as in other multistrand narrative forms, these plots compete, cutting each other short and shoving each other to the side. Thus, the putatively main plot—the actual history—dwindles and comes to seem marginal to the real interest and energy of the narrative segments.

A second narrative anomaly arises on the level of character delineation, and it is visible as early as the parable in Leibniz's *Theodicy*, when something of a muddle arises over the nature of the historical persona:

> I will show you [possible worlds], wherein shall be found, not absolutely the same Sextus as you have seen (that is not possible, he carries with him always that which he shall be) but several Sextuses resembling him, possessing all that you know already of the true Sextus, but not all that is already in him imperceptibly, nor in consequence all that shall yet happen to him. You will find in one world a very happy and noble Sextus, in another a Sextus content with a mediocre state, a Sextus, indeed, of every kind and endless diversity of forms. (377)

The question that arises here about the identity of Sextus across worlds—are these "forms" avatars or counterparts of a singularity or mere simulacra of an original that exists only in our world?—is not convincingly resolved here. If they are simulacra, then the whole point of exploring what Sextus might do in another world is lost, for the name refers to a different entity. But if they are avatars, then the unity between the person and the destiny God has chosen for him ("he carries with him always that which he shall be") is broken.

Because they have no commitment to providential history, the critical military historians can ignore this sort of problem, but it nevertheless tends to come back in their work. On the one hand, critical military history emphasizes individuality, sometimes even imputing its hypothetical conditionals to some historical consciousnesses. The "invention" (to use Clausewitz's word) of alternative courses of action is often limited to options that might have been known by actual decision makers or historical actors. This desire to locate the possibilities in the minds of individuals also encourages the military historians' tendency to limit the number of decisive agents, and so counterfactual history, as is often remarked, is best suited to endeavors like war, in which single actors or small groups make the decisions and others follow their commands. But these historians also create dramatic forms of character indeterminacy. To follow Clausewitz's multipronged hypotheses, for example, we must hold in our minds one Napoleon who signs the Treaty of Leoben and returns to France while we are told of another who fights a battle on the Rhine; then the fighting Napoleon splits again into one who secures some Austrian territory before heading back to France and another who marches on to Vienna, and so forth. And yet, to make sense of the hypothetical exercise we must see all these actions as the behavior of the same person, the unique individual referred to as Napoleon. The form thus fractures the singular destiny of each actor into numerous hypothetical versions, creating increasingly wider rifts between identity and destiny, whereas in normal narratives the two things tend to converge.

Finally, the temporal trajectories of these works are far more multidirectional than those of most narratives. Historians, to be sure, must always cope with the difficulty of negotiating the relation between their own retrospective view and the time-bound, future-blind vision of their subjects, but the critical military historians emphasize additional temporalities. Because they are designed to perfect the practice of warfare, counterfactual questions are framed in answer to questions about the future: if we were in a position like Napoleon's, armed with our analysis of his past experience, how should we plan our campaign? They are not only addressed to the future in the same way that any text is, since the reader is always on its forward temporal horizon, but also striving to form that future. The critical historian aspires to an overview above not only the temporal plain of the war under discussion but of all wars, a perspective from which higher-order abstractions would take in both past and future. In this regard, it seems omnitemporal like the theodicies. An ambition to foretell the future might even seem built into the critical-history enterprise. Indeed, at the turn of the eighteenth century, Adam Heinrich Dietrich von Bülow tried to reduce the theory of the operational line to geometrical formulas, arguing that by taking up certain positions and maintaining specific proportions and angles between the army's base and its operational line, a general could so predetermine the outcome of an impending battle that there would be little need to engage in extended combat. Such "wars of maneuver" would therefore become mainly hypothetical. To Clausewitz, von Bülow represented everything that was wrong with previous military theory: it was ahistorical, abstract, mathematical, and combat averse. Von Bülow, he claimed, made war into a mere game on paper, whereas the very essence of war was combat and consequently it could never truly be predictable.⁴² But even Clausewitz sought a temporal vantage from which he could look backwards to establish synthetic generalizations—for example, combat is the essence of warfare—and improve the future practice.

The most unusual features of critical military history's temporality, though, are its repeated sideways maneuvers. Napoleon might have done many things instead of what he did, and each of the options appears at a tangent to the actuality. As we've seen, these historians sometimes did carry a hypothetical line of action forward for several steps, but their dominant inclination is just to multiply the simultaneous possibilities. This tendency of counterfactualism to stop the forward movement of time and take a 360-degree survey of a particular moment, radiating possible lines of development in all directions, is one of its most useful features, for it helps recover and explore history's cul-de-sacs and unfinished projects, aspects of "the way it was" that are often overlooked in unilinear histories. Nevertheless, the lateral, as opposed to forward, temporal movement of counterfactualism overwrites its omnitemporality with constant reminders of discreet sequences of time starting and stopping again, appearing and disappearing.

These three aspects of counterfactual history—the proliferating competition of plots; the fissuring of singular actors into a variety of hypothetical versions; and the multidirectional movement of narrative chronology —contrast not only with normal narrative history but also with the two narrative forms the counterfactualists so clearly inspired. The next chapter will explore the ways in which the inventors of alternate history and alternate-history novels managed to harness the story-generating energy of historical counterfactuals while steadying their narrative instabilities.

CHAPTER TWO

Nineteenth-Century Alternate-History Narratives

Turning from critical military counterfactualism to nineteenth-century alternate-history narratives, one is mainly struck by their differences: the alternate-history forms are both far more coherent as narratives and much less serious as history. They usually trace a single plotline from counterfactual premises, elaborating a hypothetical historical trajectory that results in an altered world. To be sure, they often start by changing the outcome of some decisive battle or other well-known historical crisis, so these stories definitely descend from the earlier histories, but instead of probing the moments of indeterminacy for their multiple possible consequences in the manner of Leibniz or Clausewitz, the alternate-history writers extend and embellish particular imaginary aftermaths, sometimes spreading them over generations or even centuries. These forms have all of the features we associate with narrative fiction: character development, suspenseful plots, and invented settings are far more prominent in these works than they were in the eighteenth-century counterfactual mode. They appeared in two book-length forms in the nineteenth century: alternate histories, which draw their dramatis personae exclusively from the actual historical record, and alternate-history novels, which invent not only fictional historical events but also fictional characters. Thus they extended the reach of the counterfactual mode into the realm of imaginative literature.

In addition to developing the narrative potential of the mode, the alternate-history forms also provided substantial amounts of reflective analytical commentary about the nature and purposes of their own counterfactualism. Their authors lifted the hypothetical mode from contexts where its aims had become relatively easy to discern—understanding

God's goodness or fighting better wars—and began asking readers to explore unrealized alternatives in far greater detail and for longer periods of time. They needed to explain what the point of such prolonged hypothetical exercises might be, and they came up with a variety of answers. The first half of this chapter explores the rationales given by a trio of French writers, analyzing their narratives in their national-political contexts and tracing the aesthetic, philosophical, legal, and cosmological currents of thought that ran through their work. The second half turns to the specifically literary contexts of alternate-history narratives as they developed alongside other kinds of prose fiction in the nineteenth century. It describes the earliest instances of alternate-history *novels* in the last years of the century, explaining why fully fictional characters—as opposed to counterfactual versions of historical figures—became important to the alternate-history imagination as it sought to formulate the potential actions and destinies of collective characters, like nations and peoples.

PART I: FRENCH ALTERNATE HISTORIES AND THE SEARCH FOR HISTORICAL JUSTICE

The first alternate histories were French, and they candidly expressed their authors' disappointment about the nation's early nineteenth-century reversals of military and political fortunes. Formally, the first two combined counterfactual speculation with utopian visions, depicting imaginary ideal societies that were located not in a "no*where*" (which is what the Greek-derived word "utopia" means) but instead in a *time* that never was. The narratives begin in familiar geographical spaces under actual historical conditions but then quickly alter events to produce vastly superior alternatives to the dreary realities of our history. The form's first full-length example—Louis Geoffroy-Château's *Napoléon Apochryphe* (published initially as *Napoléon et la conquête du monde* [*Napoléon and the Conquest of the World*] in 1836)—is steeped in regret about the nation's loss of a glorious empire, and its utopia is presented as literary compensation. Twenty-one years later, the French philosopher Charles Renouvier was similarly wistful about the defeat of the 1848 revolutions when he wrote a lengthy tome, *Uchronie (L'Utopie dans l'histoire)*—*Uchronia (Utopia in History)*—(1857), which gave the form its French name and an enduring testament to the principles of French secular republicanism.[1] Fifteen years on and another disappointed French revolutionary, Auguste Blanqui, was lamenting the suppression of the 1870 Paris Commune when he wrote *Éternité par les astres* (*Eternity through the Stars* [1872]), which carried the French longing for alternate histories deep into cosmological and metaphysical territory.

And yet melancholic regret is not the dominant emotion of these works, nor are they merely exercises in wish fulfillment.[2] Wishing that the course of history had gone differently is as old as history writing itself, but not until the nineteenth century did anyone elaborate such wishes into full-blown alternative narratives. These writers pioneered a form that could only have been written in a modern era when the idea of progress was widely taken for granted and history was thought to have an optimal direction. Of course, among these writers, visions of the best of all possible paths toward prosperity and peace differed widely, as did their ideas of justice. Nevertheless they shared the assumption that history would eventually vindicate their hopes and produce a superior civilization. Moreover, their efforts to revive the alternative histories, those that would have led more directly to what they considered humankind's greater good, are designed to keep the destination in view rather than to mourn its loss. Present actuality appears to be a temporary delay in the forward progress. Consequently, instead of getting mired in nostalgia for a time that never was, these narratives aspire to resurrect and redeem sidelined possibilities as guides for the future. They are acts of retrieval and attempts to reanimate unrealized possibilities.

We can also see in these works anticipations of the late twentieth century's determination to bring the concept of justice into history. Although the current idea of historical justice, which stresses redressing historical wrongs, is usually thought to be a post-WWII innovation, we can discern earlier ways of making history just—the opposite of justifying history—in these nineteenth-century counterfactual narratives. Geoffroy-Château's and Renouvier's books especially reveal that alternate histories germinated the desire to subject history to norms of justice, a desire that continues to enliven the form. They connected the critical procedures of the earlier military historians—reviewing past options to identify mistakes and missed opportunities—with grand stories of how the entire world might have been remade according to better standards on the basis of some particular adjustment. Thus combining Clausewitz's project of "placing praise and blame" with a new effort to envision an overall direction for the ramifications of particular actions, the narratives became deep explorations of the interplay between individual historical characters' potentials and the making of a just world.

Geoffroy-Château's *Napoléon and the Conquest of the World* revises the years 1812–32 and depicts a Napoleon Bonaparte who realizes his "vision of a united Europe, and even of a whole world joined in peace."[3] Instead of suffering chaotic decline and ultimate defeat between 1812 and 1815, the Napoleonic Empire grows steadily until it encircles the entire globe, spreading civilization and enlightenment to all. The book was produced and published in the early years of King Louis Philippe's July Monarchy (the liberal constitutional monarchy established after the 1830 revolution deposed the Bourbons), and in many ways it fit perfectly into its national political and cultural contexts. Louis Philippe's government had purposely adopted a cultural strategy of reconciliation to unite republican, Bonapartist, and royalist factions, hoping to end the destabilizing dynamic of revolution/counterrevolution. The July Monarchy therefore laid claim to the totality of French history in a carefully sanitized version from which internal strife and conflict were banished, and it actively encouraged idealization of Napoleon Bonaparte and his era.[4] The author of *Napoléon and the Conquest of the World* seems to have been eager to join the effort, perhaps because his personal history gave him a deep emotional attachment to the Napoleonic era combined with the generational distance that spawns nostalgic longing: the child of a French officer killed in battle in 1806, he was adopted by the emperor and "Napoleon" was added to his first name: hence renamed Louis-*Napoleon* Geoffroy-Château.

In its idealization of Napoleon and its hunger to envision the glories of his empire, this first alternate history is comparable to other contemporary art works. It goes even further than the newly completed Arc de Triomphe, the decorations of which were put up during its composition, in imagining scenes of martial victory and triumphal celebrations, adding dozens of imaginary new campaigns in distant lands. And its uniform depiction of *gloire* resembles the succession of battle paintings, in which Napoleon himself always calmly presides at the center of the action, which were then being produced by Horace Vernet for the new national museum at Versailles.[5] The book's political vision further spread the liberal Bonapartism that was promulgated by works like the *Memorial of Saint Helena* (1823), a volume of Napoleon's recollections redacted by Emmanuel de Las Cases, in which the emperor presents himself as the defender of the freedom of religion, equality before the law, and popular sovereignty won by the French Revolution as well as the protector of the nation's independence from foreign powers. It even intermittently indulges the sentimentality that was on display in the 1830s Napoleonic bric-a-brac produced by French ceramics manufacturers: in the alternate history Queen Marie Louise tells Napoleon on her deathbed to reunite with Josephine, the love of his life.

So like many other French writers and artists of the time, Geoffroy-Château was determined to do justice to the deposed emperor, whose reputation had suffered under the Bourbon restoration, but he did it in an altogether novel way. Instead of reviving and rehabilitating the actual history, he completely changed it. We might wonder how the author expected this unprecedented form of historical narrative to be interpreted. After all, in a milieu full of praise for Napoleon's actions, a work praising him for what he did *not* do might have seemed ironic or implicitly critical. Already surrounded by numerous more familiar ways of revitalizing the Napoleonic legacy, what unusual aspirations prompted Geoffroy-Château to invent this odd and risky new vehicle? What kind of historical justice did he think this new form could uniquely achieve?

To answer these questions, we need to see just what, at the time, was so unusual about the form. The counterfactualism itself was not new; indeed, Geoffroy-Château obviously followed the example of the critical military historians by identifying a moment of indeterminacy when the emperor might have acted differently. However, unlike his predecessors, he did not dwell on or even explicitly mention an actual error but instead simply replaced Napoleon's notorious delay in Moscow in the fall of 1812 with an imaginary action that starts a different causal sequence. The structure that Geoffroy-Château created through this innovation is now so well established that it has spawned its own specialized terms. The definitive instant of divergence from the actual historical record has come to be known in alternate-history lingo as the "nexus," and the ensuing invented history is called the ATL or the Alternate Timeline, in contradistinction to OTL, or Our Timeline. The diachronic line of Geoffroy-Château's ATL keeps moving forward even as it departs increasingly from Our Timeline, creating an implicit Y-shaped pattern, which is often likened to a tree: a unified narrative trunk (e.g., Napoleon's history until September 1812) terminates in a bifurcation (nexus) point, from which two separate branches (ATL and OTL) diverge.[6]

Since Geoffroy-Château invented this structure, almost every alternate history has used it. In 1836, though, a narrative beginning with the burning of Moscow in September of 1812 would hardly have been expected to depart from the historical record twenty pages later by announcing the emperor's decision to march on Saint Petersburg and spend the winter there, thus avoiding his mistake of lingering in the ashes of Moscow for a month and then undertaking the fatal march back to Western Europe. The improved strategy allows the hero to proceed, through several hundred pages of imaginary campaigns and enlightened reformation, to the subjugation of all the world's peoples in a universal, but nonetheless perfectly French, empire. Following the logic of this new form required both recognizing the fictionality of the story that begins with the nexus and registering the implicit modal transformation: this, the reader must realize, is the story of what *would have* happened if Napoleon had not erred.

Unlike the scenarios in most critical military histories, though, *Napoléon and the Conquest of the World* is not narrated in the conditional mode. The author separated its hypothetical proposition from its narrative, placing the former in a preface explaining the past-conditional status of the history and then putting the narrator inside the alternative utopian timeline, where he recounts the events as actual history. So this work is not just an analytical conditional speculation but a full-fledged *fiction* with a counterfactual premise. Nevertheless—and this is another key feature of the new form—the alternate reality keeps us mindful of its conditional mode by balancing the fictional events with unnarrated but implicit events from our actual history, which are brought to the reader's mind by frequent allusions to well-known anecdotes. For example, Geoffroy-Château makes the Peninsular War the decisive European conflict between the Duke of Wellington and Napoleon, and yet when surrendering in the alternate 1813, Wellington remarks that the combat "was still a close run thing" (88), reminding us of the widely quoted remark he supposedly made after Waterloo.[7] The phrasing ("*still* a close run thing") indicates the prior version of the story repeated in the current adaptation, acknowledging the actual history as epistemologically prior to the revision we are reading. So despite the fact that the narrative maintains linear time, it makes sideways glances, keeping the reader aware of the parallel timeline of history and creating a continuous margin of side shadows. Napoleon's invasion and destruction of England are set in the spring and summer of 1814, in reality the disastrous months when the Coalition powers forced Napoleon's first abdication and the Bourbon monarchy was restored. When Napoleon conquers England, he sets off on a triumphant journey through Britain and stops at Hartwell Castle (where the Bourbons held court in exile) long enough to scold the unrepentant French royal family before confining them on the tiny Isle of Man, in a reversal of his actual incarcerations on the islands of Elba and Saint Helena. The book even briefly recounts the actual post-1812 history of the French Empire as a "pretended history," both false and absurd, that has somehow got into circulation. We could multiply the examples endlessly, but the point should be clear: even when the narrator is supposedly located in the parallel world, alternate histories create significance by continually contrasting their narratives with actual historical events. In this first example of the form, the contrasts serve to remind us of the reason for the counterfactualism: to rectify the injustices done to Napoleon by actual history.

What could it mean, though, to claim that *history* was unjust to Napoleon? And why should such an abstraction be blamed if the tale implies that Napoleon himself was the author of his own doom? The structure of this alternate history seems to accommodate a pair of opposed ideas of historical justice. One descends from Clausewitz's desire to criticize commanders, and it bears a striking resemblance to patterns of thought used in legal reasoning. In courtrooms, things that might and should have happened are commonly contrasted with actuality when determining responsibility for a harmful event. Looking for the causes of injuries, for example, lawyers mentally eliminate various factors until they find a sine qua non, a prior action without which the injury would not have occurred: for instance, "if the defendant had not been speeding, there would have been no collision." The legal technique thus relies heavily on past counterfactual hypotheses, and its model of faultfinding, as we will see in later chapters, generated numerous counterfactual scenarios over the centuries. Although explicit justifications of legal counterfactual logic only began appearing in the mid-nineteenth century, they seem to have been based on older practices. Geoffroy-Château was himself a jurist and hence probably familiar with the use of counterfactuals to explain what went wrong in the past. In *Napoléon and the Conquest of the World*, he seems to have applied his professional mode of reasoning to locate the cause of the empire's demise: "If Napoleon had not lingered in the ashes of Moscow, his empire would have increased to cover the world." Lawyerlike, Geoffroy-Château has mentally *subtracted* the erroneous act (Napoleon's delay), replacing it with a more characteristically Napoleonic maneuver, and hypothesized that the ensuing harm would thus have been prevented.[8] His work built a certain legal model of justice, already used by military critics, into the very structure of the form.

But there is another model of justice at work here as well, which opposes and overwhelms the legal variety. The overall structural pattern may point to Napoleon as the person at fault for the fall of the French Empire, and yet the book is one long paean to the emperor's greatness. The preface articulates the competing principle that vindicates Napoleon: the comprehensive unfolding of the hero's *real* character remained merely potential because of a flaw in the very nature of actual history, which "permits neither a person, nor a dream, nor an existence to flow long enough to fill the cup completely" (10). Works of imagination are therefore needed "to supplement history, to avoid this unfulfilled past, to reach the longed for goal" (10). History, according to this scheme, is interruption and incompletion, a domain in which portions fall short; fiction, in contradistinction, allows the cup of possibility to fill, so that ethos and epos, character and destiny, coincide. History's events, the author claims, were more than simply inappropriate to Napoleon's character; they also obviated a proper conclusion. His story merely stops but has no apt ending. Hence it is up to Geoffroy-Château not only to give Napoleon the history he should have had, one worthy of the lofty and visionary hero, but also to make an aesthetic improvement by finishing the story. Actuality, in his view, lacked a suitable cadence through which the historic march might be brought to a dignified close. His altered history is the *histoire juste*, the history not only *proper* to Napoleon but also the one with the right aesthetic proportions. It is in this sense that Geoffroy-Château's book seeks historical justice for Napoleon's character by separating it from his actual biography.

That division between a person and his actual destiny is a feature of the form that Geoffroy-Château took from earlier counterfactualists and embellished: it assumes that historical figures might have lived different lives and yet remained themselves. The pattern of the side shadowing produces two destinies for each character—the narrated counterfactual and the implied actual—but both are believed to belong to singular identities. Geoffroy-Château's account makes this assumption not only about Napoleon but also about the hundreds of other Napoleonic-era personages who appear in his narrative, reinforcing their cross-world identities by repeating elements of their historic roles. As in his actual life, for example, Joachim Murat betrays his brother-in-law, indicating that he was incapable of avoiding fraternal betrayal; but in the revised history, the emperor pardons him because the logic of Napoleon's character in this narrative demands magnanimous actions that reconcile all of his contemporaries to his absolute ascendency. The episode is typical of Geoffroy-Château's method of making a plausible alternative character for Napoleon without creating an entirely fictional person. He takes the most heroic aspects of Napoleon's behavior to constitute his highest potential and then writes a destiny that would have allowed for their ample display. The ideal character of Napoleon, we are led to believe, would have marched on Saint Petersburg under the conditions he faced in Moscow, and his potential action persists even though the actual man suffered an unfortunate lapse on this one occasion, destroying its achievement. The difference between the person's biography and his *character* is thus central to the form, for without it the idea of potential alternative action becomes incoherent. And with it, the author has considerable latitude in construing a Napoleonic norm against which certain historical actions can be judged uncharacteristic or highly implausible and, thus, mere side shadows to the man's proper character. Geoffroy-Château chose his nexus wisely, for Napoleon's inaction in Moscow was already considered to be a bizarre, unaccountable deviation from his normal behavior; it seemed a self-betrayal, a failure to be sufficiently Napoleonic. Put most simply, he was not himself. From this vantage point, the separation between Napoleon's identity and his actual biography is a space where the alternative truth of his character can be visualized.[9]

The narrative, in short, tried to display Napoleon's unfulfilled potential, and it is thus an example not of legal but of "poetic" justice, an attempt to establish the correct proportions between Napoleon's potential and its fulfillment in world-historical events.[10] Geoffroy-Château's railing against actual history in the work's preface brings to mind Aristotle's distinction between the forms of history and poetry: history merely deals in accidents whereas poetry is properly philosophical because it imposes considerations of appropriateness on events.[11] *Napoléon and the Conquest of the World* seems to map that distinction onto the bifurcated timelines: OTL is a tissue of contingencies, whereas ATL follows the logic of poetic proportionality, in which protagonists adhere to heroic ideals that are exhaustively manifested in action. In the altered timeline, Napoleon unfurls himself through the labor of conquering and reforming the world, and thus he completes the arc of his own entelechy (to use another Aristotelian word meaning inner purpose or vital principle).[12] In our history, though, "all remains incomplete and unfinished: men, works, glory, fortune and life" (10). Perfection, always aborted by the accidents of particularity, cannot rise above latency in the actual world, but in a counterfactual one we can find an appropriate ending for "these incomplete stories" (10). Our timeline, on this account, seems unjust by nature, and yet we should also notice that its injustice only becomes clearly visible when juxtaposed against the alternative, which also imaginatively rectifies it.

By transferring Aristotle's distinction between history and poetry to a different pair—actual and counterfactual history—Geoffroy-Château created a new dimension for an imaginary, utopian world. Aristotle's opposites became two *historical* options, one actual and the other utopian, one broken and the other complete. Even though the utopian ATL is introduced as a daydream, its attachment to history as the result of a revision of the actual record sets it inside the domain of mundane possibility. Thus historicized, utopian expectations could be thought of not just as a paradigm against which history might be judged but as a missed opportunity inside history, which might therefore be somehow retrieved. The actual series of events in a national space and time was for the first time compared in detail with a perfected alternative sequence pertaining to the same nation and the same rulers. So even though the preface claims that actuality will always be disappointing, the tale concentrates on the cross-world similarities: all three hundred characters are drawn from the historical record; new foreign campaigns depict the actual terrain, political leadership, and military capabilities of the enemy; and in all cases emphasis is placed on the probability of the imagined world. Practicality, we are repeatedly told, is its watchword: Napoleon, for example, encourages the spread and implementation of Saint-Simon's socialism but finds the man himself useless as a state administrator and is forced to fire him (215–19). Geoffroy-Château, in short, labors to make his utopia seem normal (as well as normative) so that readers might question which is the natural course of history and which the anomaly. Building on the comparative counterfactual impulses that came earlier, from both Leibniz and the critical military historians, Geoffroy-Château added the Aristotelian notion of an intrinsic animating dynamic, an entelechy, and *if* we accept the idea that Napoleon's character had such an inherent arc, the emperor's actual history seems like a deviation from the right path, a diversion into a cul-de-sac.

This sense of uncanny similarity-in-difference between our reality and some historical alternative has been sought by almost all alternate historians who followed. To be sure, the first work's utopian exuberance and near deification of a world leader's potential are now atypical of the form, but alternate histories continue to use Geoffroy-Château's structures and they often follow his ambition to complete some historical trajectory perceived as interrupted, diverted, or cut short in actuality. If it had not been for the interference of this or that abnormality, they imply, the story would have stayed on track to its more justifiable end. Indeed, dystopian alternate histories, in which movements thought to be anomalous are extended into the future (e.g., American slavery or Nazism), are only variations on this structure, which plays with the reversibility of norms. For all of his book's exaggerations, implausibilities, and idealizations, therefore, Geoffroy-Château invented something that answered a cultural need of its time and has endured into ours, a form for realizing the desire to imagine a more meaningful and perhaps morally consequential history.

❧

The next lengthy alternate history to appear—Charles Renouvier's *Uchronia*, subtitled *An Apocryphal Historical Sketch of the Development of European Civilization as It Wasn't but as It Might Have Been*—came from a very different French political perspective, and yet it shared that ambition to make history morally meaningful. First published in 1857, it was an obvious protest against the policies of the Second French Empire, ruled by Napoleon III. Charles Bernard Renouvier was a highly influential neo-Kantian philosopher, and his alternate history is much more complex and demanding than Geoffroy-Château's. To do it justice, I will consider first the counterfactual parable in its contemporary context, and then I will try to explicate the philosophy of history it was designed it to illustrate. Finally, in the second half of this chapter, I will come back to this sprawling text yet again as an example of alternate history's penchant for elaborate fictional framing devices.

Politically, the utopia of Renouvier's dreams is the opposite of Geoffroy-Château's: the founders of Renouvier's utopia are not conquerors imposing their wills but guardians of the liberty of action and belief. It is set in the late Roman Empire, and it comes about by Rome's reversion to a republican form of government and commitment to religious neutrality. Indeed, the success of the revived Roman Republic is proved not in the growth of the empire but in its final dissolution and replacement by independent states resting on just and equal laws. Whereas Geoffroy-Château's Napoleon compelled adherence to a Catholicism that was in turn submissive to his will, the alliance of cross and sword is precisely what Renouvier's historical revision is designed to avoid. And whereas *Napoléon and the Conquest of the World* imagines a swift, massive change, *Uchronia* never tires of explaining that all real transformations must occur slowly, over multiple generations, for only when freedom is deep in the customs and mores of a people can they truly make use of the emancipatory legislation of enlightened rulers.

Nevertheless, *Uchronia*, like its predecessor, launches its alternate history by revising the action of a pair of powerful historical individuals. The utopian narrative begins in the second-century Roman Empire, the period of the Antonines, and places its nexus in the decisions of Marcus Aurelius and Avidius Cassius. As the lengthy analytical passages in *Uchronia* tirelessly explain, the civilized republican virtues of ancient Greece and Rome had been undermined by the Roman Empire's prolonged occupation of eastern territories, where Occidentals came into contact with forms of tyranny and despotism nurtured by religious fanaticism, a tendency that permeated the sect of early Christianity. Renouvier does not offer an explanation for the profound cultural division between the religion-crazed east and the civic-minded west; it is simply stated as a historical given in the book's first sentences: "Since early antiquity, the nations of the Orient have obeyed their priests or their absolute rulers," whereas those of the Occident subordinated their priests to civil interests. Instead of grand monarchies, Greeks and Italians had free cities, where "law, that abstraction destined to become one of the great realities of human civilization," was invented.[13]

But in the process of trying to spread the rule of law throughout the ancient world, the Romans were corrupted by the mores of the conquered peoples: the emperors began to destroy the rights of the citizens, the army became a mass of mercenaries, and the actual endpoint of the whole process was the triumph of Christianity—presented in *Uchronia* as one of the most fanatical and intolerant of the Oriental sects. To avoid the approaching calamity of Christian Rome, the author invents a partnership between the emperor Marcus Aurelius (161–180 CE) and the general Avidius Cassius. In actual history, Cassius was the governor of Syria in 175, when he marched on Rome to become emperor on hearing rumors that Marcus Aurelius was dead, and he was subsequently killed in his own camp when he pressed on after realizing that Marcus Aurelius was alive. In the nexus that launches the alternate history, Cassius writes a letter to the emperor and convinces him that they should rule together, restoring and extending the rights of citizens and reforming the state administration in preparation for returning Rome to republican government.

At the end of their joint reign, the two philosophical emperors devise a plan to get rid of the Christians without really engaging in religious persecution: they require all citizens (including the women, who have been given full civil rights) to take an oath of allegiance to the state, swearing that they will recognize the equal rights of their fellow citizens to practice the religion of their choice. Any citizen who does not sign must migrate to the eastern territories; the Christians, who refuse to say that all religions should be equal in the eyes of the state, are thereby removed. In the two hundred pages that follow, there are many struggles and setbacks for the secularist republican vision of Marcus Aurelius and Cassius, and there are pitched battles between the Occident and the Orient, where Christian and (later) Muslim sects, which are in perpetual tumult, frequently mount crusades against the West. But finally in the eighth century (the thirteenth century in Roman years), religious tolerance and civil rights are universal, most empires have devolved into smaller polities, trade flourishes, arts and sciences thrive, and the world is usually at peace.

Nothing, it might seem, could be further from Geoffroy-Château's Napoleonic fantasy, but in the year of *Uchronia*'s publication, it was the earlier work that chimed more harmoniously with the sentiments of the majority of French people. They had gone through decades of political instability and were weary of the warring republican, monarchical, and imperial factions. The July Monarchy had come to an end in the revolutionary year of 1848, and the Second Republic had been declared. Within months, though, the venomous divisions between the moderate liberal and radical socialist republicans, combined with some disastrous economic policies, had so alienated the newly enfranchised voters that they elected Louis-Napoleon Bonaparte (the very pretender who had made a fool of himself in the previous decade) president of the Republic. In 1851, after numerous struggles with the elected National Assembly, Louis-Napoleon effected a coup d'état, later ratified by a plebiscite, dissolved the Second Republic, established the Second Empire, and had himself declared Napoleon III, emperor of the French. Renouvier wrote his alternate history as a protest against this Napoleonic takeover. He had been politically active in the short-lived Second Republic, when the government asked him to write a handbook of rights and duties for the use of the lately enfranchised national electorate, but the manual proved far too radical for the Constituent Assembly, which promptly banned it. The year 1848 was thus Renouvier's political debut and his finale.

By the time he wrote *Uchronia* in the mid-1850s, his political views were more moderate; he was living on his independent income in southern France, far from the centers of political power, but he was still an ardent republican and he set his alternate history in ancient Rome to emphasize that France's recent illiberal path had international as well national repercussions. Among the numerous revolutions of 1848 was a successful revolt in Rome against the pope's temporal rule, which sent Pope Pius IX into exile in Sicily. An election was held in Rome, and a Constitutional Assembly convened in early 1849 declared the founding of the Roman Republic and religious freedom in the Papal States, guaranteeing as well a safe return for the pope if he would give up his claim to temporal power and be content to be the spiritual leader of the Catholic Church. The papal standard was replaced by a new tricolored flag, which was put in the hands of the huge bronze equestrian statue of Marcus Aurelius in the Campidoglio. From Sicily, the pope appealed to Catholic countries for help in regaining his states, but the army that actually besieged the short-lived Roman Republic and brought it to an end was, ironically, that of the French Second Republic, sent by then-president Louis-Napoleon under pressure from French Catholics. French soldiers restored the temporal power of the pope and stayed to maintain it until 1870. Louis-Napoleon's destruction of the Roman Republic of 1848 and his unholy alliance with a reactionary and intolerant religious leader were obviously the immediate contexts for *Uchronia*. To Renouvier's contemporaries, it would have been clear that the book's insistence on the destructive alliance of Catholicism and oppressive imperialism, its vision of a centuries-long battle between virtuous republicans and fanatical autocrats, and even its choice of Marcus Aurelius as the last of the Romans who might have been able to restore the ancient republic were references to contemporary European history.

In the mid-1850s, moreover, Renouvier was becoming convinced that political freedom needed firmer philosophical foundations, and *Uchronia* gave him the appropriate form for simultaneously articulating his philosophical ideas about history and reflecting on the previous eight years in French politics. He thus made his book a hybrid affair, combining narratives with explicit arguments against all kinds of historical determinism. As we saw in the last chapter, counterfactualism was already entangled in religious controversies that reflected on historical necessity and contingency, but Renouvier is the first writer to attack all systems of thought, religious and secular, that he considered deterministic. In the course of his long career, he attacked not only predestination, theodicy, the eighteenth-century French Enlightenment, and German historicism but also Marxist materialism and Darwinism. Even some nonmaterialist Hegelians came under his censure. And he did not restrict his targets to philosophers but refuted numerous contemporary social theorists and historians who concentrated too exclusively on inexorable anonymous processes in their analyses, ignoring the role of free human choices. *Uchronia* was thus not only an alternate history but also a self-conscious updating of the debate about historical necessity and the logic of counterfactualism, and since that blend of issues continues into the present, it behooves us to understand Renouvier's manner of combining them.

The debate over the philosophy of history, moreover, is not relegated to the background of *Uchronia*; the book begins with it, claiming that modern philosophers were unable to appreciate the benefits of alternate history because, like the theologians of old, they were busy affirming that some "universal necessity" shapes history.¹⁴ He blames the French philosophes especially for letting their materialist determinism undermine their ethical pronouncements against tyrannical oppression. If all of the stages of history, even those that entailed systematic injustices, were somehow necessary, then how might any of them be held abhorrent?¹⁵ And he asks the same question of German historicists, detecting in them as well merely another perpetuation of the error. They may have professed to reject Enlightenment materialism, but by regarding each epoch as equally "close to God" (in Leopold von Ranke's memorable phrase) and judging past acts only by the moral standards of the time under consideration, the German philosophers also practiced a form of exoneration.¹⁶ What was missing in both the mechanical progressive determinism of the eighteenth century and the all-accepting historicism of the nineteenth was any true spirit of *critique*, any ambition to discriminate between good and bad in history. And that lack led, in turn, to a failure to appreciate the uses of historical counterfactualism.

The opening pages of *Uchronia* present alternate history as an antidote to these modern philosophies, for it stimulates the critical comparative function, which they had disabled. Renouvier thus stands out as the writer who surrounded his alternate-history narrative with the most ambitious claims for the counterfactual comparative method: it deepens our awareness of our own moral freedom by imaginatively exploring that of others; it reinforces the concept of historical moral responsibility; and it thus shores up the only solid foundation for a just social order. Whereas Leibnizians had seen counterfactualizing as a pious exercise, Renouvier made it an exercise in civic responsibility: when we judge the decisions of historical figures, we assert that our own actions should be subject to similar judgments. If such a practice leads us to believe firmly in our moral liberty, he claimed, then we would grasp "the essence of progress itself" (ix), and the face of the world would change.

We do not have space in this chapter for a detailed account of Renouvier's neo-Kantian philosophy, so suffice it to say that he attempted to reconcile a belief in free will with nineteenth-century ideas about psychological conditioning.¹⁷ The result was an account of human action that lent itself well to the elaboration of alternate-history narratives. Occasions for the exercise of free will are, he claimed, rare because the majority of our thoughts and actions are habitual or automatic, prompted by individual life experiences, self-interest, training, culture, outright coercion, or other historical and social situations. But the capacity for making moral judgments and freely deciding among alternatives is nevertheless a definitive human trait and rises to the fore in extraordinary circumstances. Free will, he claimed, becomes possible only when we are at a crossroads where we can envision alternative paths and judge which is morally superior. His objection to determinism was that it made people unable to recognize such crossroads and imagine the options. Free will, he went on to say, requires faith in the efficacy of one's actions; it is never capricious but, instead, always linked to a rationally informed judgment, although it does not follow mechanically from reason alone. In his philosophy, every instance of free will constitutes a nexus, when the normally conditioned chain of cause and effect in our lives, of which we are seldom highly conscious, arrives at a point of indeterminacy. Then, if we are willing to accept the responsibility of freedom instead of simply taking the path of least resistance, we may seize the opportunity to make a moral judgment.

The formal similarity between Renouvier's description of free will and the narrative structure of alternate history should be obvious: both have that Y-shaped configuration in which a unified stem reaches a point of bifurcating branches. Moreover, additional branching and further crossroads must continually emerge, for every act of free will, Renouvier asserted, creates a new series of events, which would not otherwise have existed. Free choices are more than just special events in a series, therefore, but are instead initiators of new sequences, like the decision that diverts the alternate-history course of events in *Uchronia*'s Roman Empire from the line of actual history. Renouvier brought Marcus Aurelius to the crisis where he sees "ambiguous futures," a conjuncture at which more than one consequence can be envisioned.[18] The universe, therefore, must have the measure of indeterminacy that allows for free will but cannot be entirely indeterminate; for that would preclude the predictable continuity of the new sequences.[19] These two features of Renouvier's universe—allowing just enough indeterminacy to start a new chain of causes and effects but not so much as to precipitate a chaotic cascade of further nexuses—are also frequently remarked traits of alternate histories generally and *Uchronia* in particular.

The alternate-history form also conforms to Renouvier's philosophy simply by being an instance of rhetorical persuasion, as opposed to rational argumentation, for Renouvier claimed that rationality alone could not convince people that they were free. Indeed, he thought the doctrine of free will was unprovable and suggested (in a manner reminiscent of Pascal's wager) that we should choose to believe in our moral liberty, for that choice would enable further choices until choice became a habit. For Renouvier, as for the American pragmatist William James (on whom he had a strong influence), reason could never supply completely adequate grounds for any belief, which will always require the extra operation of the faculties of judgment and will. Thus, although we cannot be completely certain of the historical efficacy of our actions, we must act *as if* our choices would be consequential in order to have any effect at all. By allowing us to imaginatively experience such as-if choices, alternate histories could provide vicarious training in the habits of liberty.

The first episode of the alternate history illustrates this point by describing how Marcus Aurelius might have been converted from a passive Stoic to a moral philosopher who chooses to act *as if* he were an agent of history and thereby brings about radical change. The emperor was the one man in the world who had the necessary knowledge, inclination, and power to put Rome (and therefore the entire ancient world) on the track to republican liberty, but he is at first paralyzed by the fatalistic doctrines of his Stoical training. Only the intervention of Avidius Cassius rouses him from his indifference by presenting him with a clear choice: either decide to pull Rome back toward republican virtue or let it drift onward the gathering current of decadence. Like Geoffroy-Château's Napoleon, Renouvier's Marcus Aurelius casts a side shadow of wrongdoing onto the historical emperor's actual behavior: if he could have taken action to prevent the decline of the Roman Empire, then he most certainly should have. The attempt, however precariously accomplished, would at least have begun a process of reform that could serve as a precedent in the future, and the actual Marcus Aurelius would have been free from posterity's censure. The stories of the emperor heroes in both alternate histories must be read as implicit indictments of the inaction of their actual doubles. Napoleon could have kept the French Empire alive, and Marcus Aurelius could have arrested the decline of Rome, but both failed to act. An important difference between the two plots, though, is that Marcus Aurelius's fault is essentially philosophical. The actual Napoleon failed to be himself, but Renouvier emphasizes that Marcus Aurelius's inaction was all too consistent with his philosophical fatalism. The tale thereby reinforces the book's larger polemic against historical determinism by casting the classical form of that philosophy, Stoicism, as the root cause of Rome's decline. *Uchronia* is not only an alternate history larded with philosophical reflections but also a tale in which the first nexus event is a philosophical conversion.

If Renouvier implicitly singled out Stoicism as the cause of Rome's decline, he explicitly identified Marcus Aurelius's stepson and heir, Commodus, as the embodiment of its moral effects. A symbol of the degeneration of the Roman aristocracy into a pack of mere sensualists, Commodus was widely regarded by his contemporaries as unfit to rule the empire. Avidius Cassius convinces Marcus Aurelius to disinherit Commodus and thereby avoid the disastrous rule that nearly everyone foresees. This single act of revision does not suffice to amend the entire course of Roman history, though, and according to Renouvier's philosophy it could hardly be expected to. There can be no turning point after which history glides automatically down a better path, frictionless and without any great moral effort. Renouvier emphasized this lesson by the return of Commodus, who succeeds in assassinating Avidius Cassius after the suicide of Marcus Aurelius and reigns in the alternate timeline much as he did in ours. In this alternative version, though, Commodus's abuses of his will are countered by other citizens, who, inspired by the example of Marcus Aurelius and Avidius Cassius, assert their right to freedom by overthrowing the tyrant. The telos of this utopia is thus not the installation of a perfect order but the gradual evolution of the conditions for morally meaningful public action.

By placing philosophical belief and moral responsibility at the heart of historical processes, however, Renouvier also made it difficult to describe how such factors would become determinate at the level of collective agents, like nations and peoples. He tried to solve the problem of collective agency by insisting on the creation of just social arrangements, laws, and republican institutions that would allow for group decision-making, but he nevertheless remained distrustful of actual collectivities and their tendency to assert their priorities over individual consciences. Indeed, the irrational power of the crowd and the need for individual resistance to it is a theme raised repeatedly in *Uchronia*. By overlaying the possibility of starting alternate paths of development with the possibility of making free moral choices, he limits the positive and purposeful agents of his alternate history to powerful individuals. To be sure, this limitation was part of his argument: the fact that it would have taken a Marcus Aurelius to revive the republic demonstrates how far the Roman people had declined from their previous condition of moral coherence. Thus the conditions for their concerted moral action needed to be re-created.

And yet, we must admit that *Uchronia* never does illustrate deliberate historical action taken by a collective agent, and hence it seems to merit the criticism often leveled at the counterfactual-historical mode for privileging "great man" history. Renouvier's reflections on contemporary historians also underline that bias toward the individuation of moral action. For example, in his critique of Jules Michelet's celebrated narration of the fall of the Bastille in the *History of the French Revolution* (1847), where the people are characterized as a pure collectivity, undifferentiated into leaders and followers, but acting infallibly, magnanimously, and irresistibly, Renouvier complains that Michelet has no right to call the people's action moral: "Nothing less moral than such a justification of popular passion and its outbursts, nothing less liberal than the abasement of the individual before the instinct of the crowd."[20] The accomplishments of the French Revolution, Renouvier admits, were unquestionably progressive, but he nevertheless insists on distinguishing between their value and the morally compromised means by which they were attained. Indeed, he identifies Michelet's focus on the collective as his primary mistake; he envisions history as "a sort of ontogenesis of collective organisms, or . . . of the souls of nations." The effective forces inside Michelet's national organism, he complains, "are not individuals; . . . they are functions, or abstract principles" (138). And the result is that "the individuality of men in history disappears" (139). Michelet, he claims, portrays a collectivity, which is actually merely a context in which choices might be made, as a unified being already morally active in its own right.

Uchronia, in contrast, keeps promising to show us the transformation of a group, through centuries of purposeful striving and shaping on the part of individuals, into an entity that could have a moral life of its own, but it never reaches that culmination. Renouvier, it seems, used alternate history to chasten the tendency to tell the nation's story as if it were already ethically meaningful, a tendency that he thought might actually retard the effort to bring a collective moral agent into existence by directing attention away from responsible individual action, which was currently the repository and potential source of a moral nation. Thus, although *Uchronia* definitely conforms to the pattern of privileging individual historical actors in alternate histories, it also gives us insights into that preference, displaying its connections to the form's ambitions toward historical justice, moral judgment, and utopian imagination.

In 1871 another politically disappointed French writer, Auguste Blanqui, also took consolation in the idea of alternate histories. Blanqui had already spent a significant portion of his sixty-six years in prison for sedition of one kind or another, and it was in prison that he wrote his book about alternate worlds, *Éternité par les astres* (*Eternity through the Stars*). A radical socialist republican, he had been at odds with every French government of his lifetime, even the Second Republic and the nascent Third Republic (which was just then emerging in the wake of the Franco-Prussian war), but he had particular reasons for bitterness when, in 1871 he was imprisoned on the eve of the formation of the Paris Commune. When the French were forced to surrender to the Prussians, the Assembly appointed a provisional government to serve until new republican institutions could be established, and it began peace negotiations with the victorious enemy. However, the Paris National Guard refused to disarm, held out against the peace, and denied the authority of the provisional government. Parisians elected a city government composed of radical republicans and socialists, declaring themselves to be the Paris Commune.

As this crisis began to develop, the provisional government arrested Blanqui for inciting civil unrest, and by the time the Commune was declared, he found himself far from the scene of action, imprisoned in the damp cell of a fortress on the northwestern coast, in the middle of the Bay of Morlaix, cut off completely from the outside world. As the French went through the last of their major nineteenth-century paroxysms, this notorious rebel looked out on a solitary landscape of sea and sky, with plenty of leisure to contemplate what might be taking place in Paris and what he might have accomplished if he had been there. Blanqui was not the only person to imagine he could have made a difference; the leaders of the Paris Commune offered to exchange their prisoners—including an archbishop and numerous priests—for Blanqui, but the provisional government rejected the offer. As Karl Marx explained in his pamphlet *The Civil War in France*, they knew that Blanqui "would give the Commune a head; while the archbishop would serve his purpose best in the shape of a corpse."[21] Lacking a "head," the communards killed Archbishop Darboy and were in turn brutally wiped out.

The book Blanqui published the following year was not, however, an alternate history of the Paris Commune with himself at its head; it was not an alternate-history narrative at all but, instead, a treatise explaining how modern astronomical and statistical sciences prove the necessity of the existence of multiple worlds that are copies of our own but allow for different histories. We could think of *Éternité par les astres* as an atheist's updating of Leibniz's *Theodicy*, in which the logical necessity of alternate worlds is defended once again but placed on a materialist foundation and deprived of its providentialism. The work can also be seen as a descendant of such French baroque fantasies as Bernard le Bovier de Fontenelle's *Plurality of Worlds* and Cyrano de Bergerac's *The Other World*, and its influence on the development of Friedrich Nietzsche's idea of eternal recurrence has been noted.[22] But the most original contribution of *Éternité par les astres* was its argument that science and mathematics prove the universe must contain many planets identical or nearly identical to ours in all particulars, including the individual human inhabitants, who might nevertheless follow disparate destinies. Whereas Leibniz placed all of the possibilities of our world in the mind of God, Blanqui placed them in the immensity of space, which he thought logically infinite in that we cannot imagine a boundary to it. The part of space filled by matter, he reasoned, may be only a fraction, but the force he calls nature is constantly expanding to fill as much of it as possible. Creation presses toward infinity, but the number of elements at nature's disposal for the fabrication of matter is small. Blanqui hypothesized that the table of primary substances might not yet be complete, but when it is, it will not exceed one hundred elements. Thus, he concluded that an infinity of truly unique beings (in his terms, "types originaux," or original types) would be impossible.[23] It is simply a statistical necessity that each separate combination be replicated in numerous copies as the universe of material things, arranged in the various organizations of astral bodies, expands in infinite space and time, through the stellar life cycle of birth, solar-system development, star death, collapse, and rebirth in new nebulae.

It is one of those fine ironies of intellectual history that Leibniz himself had laid the mathematical groundwork for the theories of infinity and statistics on which Blanqui (through the mediation of Pierre-Simon Laplace) conceived of the necessary realization of all possibilities. A possibility (as Blanqui understood it) is simply something that will happen in the course of infinite combinations of the same variables. The God of Leibniz's theodicy was thus no longer necessary; the possible worlds, which Leibniz thought only the deity could conceive, were, in Blanqui's view, physically realizing themselves in the incalculable numbers of our planet's "copies, répétitions, épreuves" (copies, repetitions, tests [360]) scattered over the universe and constantly multiplying into the expanses of infinite space.

On a first reading, the politics of the book may seem elusive or even reactionary. Indeed, Walter Benjamin, coming across it in 1938, wrote to Max Horkheimer that its speculations were "infernal" and that it "represents an unconditional surrender" to the "social order that Blanqui must have recognized in the evening of his life to be the victor."[24] Benjamin seems to have been focusing on the passages that stress repetition, which are, indeed, some of the most arresting and which do, as he notes, anticipate Nietzsche's writings on eternal return. Strewn across the infinities of time and space, Blanqui writes, numerous complete copies of the earth must exist on which there is "not a pebble, not a tree, not a rivulet, not an animal, not a man, not an incident that has not found its place and its minute" (364). And on some of these other planets, living in the midst of different cycles of solar development, Our Timeline is repeated on different schedules.[25] Political hope in this treatise, though, is frequently expressed in its many passages about repetition with variation, and this theme is certainly the most original in the work. Indeed, it sometimes appears that his motive for elevating probability to the position of primary explanation for the universe's organization is to assert that everything possible must eventually be actualized somewhere in an infinite time and space. As in the work of Renouvier, moreover, variation that occurs on our planet doubles as a result of the human will: "Nature has only inflexible, immutable laws. As long as these govern alone, everything follows in a fixed and fatal succession. But variations start when there are animal beings who have wills" (370). Thus planets that have developed identically to ours, even down to the same flora and fauna may nevertheless have diverged so radically from ours in their human populations that their "pasts are not at all ours" (364). Blanqui asks us to acknowledge this possibility but then to set it aside as distracting. More interesting are those that fall into the category of "veritable earth-double," where the human personnel are duplicated. On these, identity of events can only be said to hold until the present moment, for each future second presents crossroads allowing divergence. "The future of our earth, like the past, will change the route millions of times. . . . From here, each second leads to its bifurcation, the road which one will take, that which one could have taken" (364). Thus, although duplication of events from the beginning of the planet to its end is possible and must happen somewhere, it is not as frequent, and certainly not as interesting, as copying with variation. And through this emphasis on repetition with variation, Blanqui arrives at several familiar alternate-history scenarios: "The English have lost perhaps many times the battle of Waterloo on globes where their adversary did not commit the blunder of Grouchy. . . . On the other hand, Napoleon does not always carry off the victory of Marengo everywhere, which was here a lucky fluke" (365). Alternatives to these events are especially highly likely, we are told, because their comparative versions in our past were the result of mere *fatalité*, a word Blanqui often uses as a synonym for "chance."

Certain chances play out here, whereas others play out elsewhere; we cannot avoid those to which our particular planet is subject, but we should also understand that our existences are not confined to them. To understand Blanqui's vision, one must notice his belief that the incessant expansion of sameness and diversity on other planets is distributed within a delimited set of human beings: "One cannot escape fatality. But fatality cannot find a foothold in infinity, which knows not [exclusive] alternatives and has a place for all. One world exists where a man follows the road scorned in the other by his copy. His existence is redoubled, a globe for each, then is bifurcated a second, a third time, millions of times. He possesses thus complete copies and innumerable variant copies, who multiply and represent always his person, but taking only fragments of his destiny. All one might have been down here, one is somewhere else" (365). The last sentence certainly resonates with Blanqui's political predicament, and one can easily read it as the primary consoling idea of the book: from "down here" (*ici-bas*) in his dungeon, he looks out at the stars and affirms that somewhere else ("quelque part ailleurs") he is leading a political upheaval. The sentence is, indeed, so important to him that he repeats it word for word at a more pessimistic moment in the treatise, in which he imagines the necessary eternity of his imprisonment: "That which I write at this moment in a dungeon of the fort at Taureau, I have written and I will write during all eternity, at a table, with a pen, in the clothes, in the circumstances completely the same" (380). This is the great defect of eternity actualized in the infinity of space and time, he concludes: "There is no progress" (380). Nevertheless, by the end of the same paragraph, he returns to his consolatory formulation: "Only the chapter on bifurcations remains open to hope. Do not forget that *all one might have been down here, one is somewhere else*" (381, emphasis in the original).

That stable binary pairing of what might have been and what is—so typical of the structure of alternate history—recurs in Blanqui's text frequently enough to receive emphasis, but each time it lasts only a moment, and then the might-have-been fractures and ramifies into innumerable possibilities: "Beyond one's entire life, from birth until death, as one is living it in a crowd of worlds, one lives it on the others in ten thousand different editions" (365). The vision cannot sustain a Y-shaped narrative pattern but, instead, points at once toward unnumbered why-nots? The fan of possible vectors radiating toward different destinies at every moment of a life is far more radically imagined here than in even the critical military histories, and the difficulty of asserting that each resulting copy is only a manifestation, an "avatar" (381), of the *same* person is proportionately greater as well. Perhaps because of this difficulty, Blanqui is particularly adamant about the unified identity of the "one" who lives these myriad lives: "We know that all men can take at the same time many variants, by following changes in the route that his copies follow on their respective planets, without touching the personality" (372). And again, "He is infinite and eternal in the person of his other selves, not only those of his own age but of all ages" (378). The important insight seems to be that, despite the lack of communication between instances, each person is a crowd dispersed throughout time and space, all sharing one identity. For the idea of progress, Blanqui trades this eternal camaraderie of the copies, each of whom can take comfort, despite the local isolation of the moment, in knowing himself to be constantly "on thousands of worlds, in the company of beloved people who are today nothing more than memories" (381). All alone under the stars, he can reflect that "we have tasted and will taste that happiness, under the figure of a copy, of millions of copies" (381).

Eternity through the Stars presents us with no utopias or dystopias like those of Geoffroy-Château and Renouvier. It contains no direction of development or decline, no restoration of order or just compensation for history's crimes. But it is nonetheless an exercise not only in imagining alternatives to an incessantly frustrating political process but also in reflecting on the necessity of imagining alternatives. Blanqui may have been the first writer to find this necessity in a specifically *scientific* theory of possible worlds, but he was by no means the last. His work anticipates that of late twentieth-century scientists, who base their ideas on the multiverse theories deriving from quantum mechanics. These theories have, of course, been a major inspiration for alternate-history writers during the last sixty years. It is important to notice, though, that their introduction makes a definitive break with the methods of the other writers discussed in this chapter and remains in tension with contemporary alternate histories. The scientific explanations offer an equal ontological footing to all options, but their random distribution of possibilities also eradicates the hierarchies—aesthetic, moral, and legal—on which judgments are based. As the first to import such a theory, Blanqui makes it obvious that when one chooses a comparison world from among the myriad options, the choice will be predetermined by the kind of justice one wants to accomplish.

For his part, Blanqui decided to forgo those exercises and instead declared his solidarity with all of his possible existences, accepting each with philosophical resignation and taking particular comfort in the happier ones. He reserved his negative judgment for those people who refused to come to the same conclusion and who might, even after reading *Éternité par les astres*, persist in the delusion that they are unique beings, the only versions of themselves in the universe. In a neat reversal at the end of his treatise, he accuses this mistaken humanity of being "infatuated with its grandeur, believing itself to be the universe, and living in its prison as in an immensity" (382). At least Blanqui, whom contemporaries often referred to simply as *L'Enfermé* (the prisoner), understood that he was in jail even as he imaginatively expanded himself into a multitude of prisoners. Consoled by realizing his potential elsewhere and comforted by the fraternity of numbers in his imprisonment, Blanqui tries to reach a still point from which he need not choose among destinies any more than the universe does.

Blanqui's importance for this study lies not only in the pathos of this vision, which we'll often encounter in later fictions, but also in its preview of two of the most important developments in alternate-history writing of the twentieth century: the crossing with scientific thought to produce a subcategory of science fiction, and the affiliation with the avant-garde narrative experiments pioneered by writers like Jorge Luis Borges.[26] It is further proof that, despite the limited number of nineteenth-century alternate-history speculations, the genre's main lines of development were already apparent in that century. What had not yet appeared was its specifically novelistic manifestation.

PART II: THE SLOW RISE OF THE ALTERNATE-HISTORY NOVEL

The alternate histories we've been examining are not novels because they do not have fictional protagonists. Their characters are well-known historical figures, whose names carried preexisting semantic and referential information for the intended readers. The statements made about them may be described as hypothetical, untrue, fictional, legendary, or apocryphal, but they nevertheless refer to actual historical persons.[27] In contrast, novels, regardless of the timelines in which they are set, are not only invented narratives but also narratives concerning completely invented personae, fictional characters without singular, embodied personal referents. The distinction between fictions that use proper names to refer to characters who are hypothetical versions of historical persons, and those, like novels, that use them to create entirely fictional personae is crucial to understanding why counterfactual history spawned two separate fictional forms, each with its own functions.[28]

By drawing their characters exclusively from the historical record, alternate histories assert that the world created in the hypothetical timeline remains comparable to ours. When writers like Leibniz, Renouvier, and Blanqui make explicit statements about the identity of individuals through a range of different destinies, they are revealing the basis of what narratologists call the "cross-world identity" between the actual and hypothetical histories: it resides in their shared personnel. Simply put, the possible history under discussion is "ours" because the identities of the persons who made it are continuous with those in Our Timeline. Blanqui is quite explicit about this requirement when he notes that, in the infinity of possibilities, there are three kinds of possible earth copies: those where all is exactly the same as it is in our own history, so there is no distinction between OTL and ATL; those where the personnel has deviated so far from ours that it is no longer truly a copy at all; and those containing all of the same people, where some live different lives. The last category is the setting for Blanqui's hypothetical history scenarios: a "Goldilocks" zone for alternate-history planets, it is neither too close nor too far for comparison. This is the kind of setting other alternate-history writers seek as well, binding the altered history to the one we know and thereby maintaining an indirect form of historical reference through the use of proper names.[29] The structure of characterization—a constant set of identities across which variations in behavior occur—allows access to our history from the alternatives, so that we can apply insights gained from the suppositional exercises to our actual ongoing narrative. Because the function of alternate history is to imagine difference-in-sameness based on historical persons, the fully fictional characters we usually read about in novels tend to be excluded as confusing distractions.

There are, though, other kinds of counterfactual-historical speculation and reflection that cannot be easily accomplished without the kind of normal novelistic characters whose proper names have no specific actual-world counterparts and whom we understand to be entirely imaginary entities. Alternate histories give us the general outlines of large-scale progressions, but their focus on historically prominent characters tends to keep them from imagining the changed reality in any great detail. The possible worlds they evoke tend to be thin and anemic, providing scant space for the different psychological, social, cultural, familial, economic, and emotional dimensions of ordinary people's lives under the altered conditions. To examine the possible ramifications of a change on these levels, the alternate-history *novel* was invented. When the first books in this form arrived at the very end of the nineteenth century, they enlarged and diversified the social range of the counterfactual mode, exploring the probable effects of the alteration on average people, the great majority of whom remain anonymous in the historical record. They introduced novelistic norms of formal realism by attending to daily life and giving thick descriptions of its ambience. They have since also come to seem necessary to imagining histories extending so far in time from the nexus that a widely different set of persons, with no actual historical versions, would have come into existence. The accessibility of such fictional consciousnesses gives writers the opportunity to imagine both the subjective experience and the cultural totality that might have resulted from the hypothesized change. Fictional characters, moreover, solicit the reader's more intense emotional involvement; to borrow terms from Marshall McLuhan, the novel had already developed as a "hot" medium, immersing readers in deeply imagined experiential details and generally demanding more attention than the "cool" form of historical narrative, with its more schematic and abstract representations of general conditions. In their imitation of historical writing, alternate histories also tend to stay on the cool end of the media thermometer, whereas the novelistic form attempts, we might say, to lend warmth and vitality as well as fullness and particularity to the counterfactual mode by depicting the interplay between representative individual consciousnesses and their possible worlds.

The alternate-history novel was a long time in the making partly because of the technical difficulties in integrating the two types of fictional beings. Putting versions of historical persons behaving counterfactually together with wholly fictional characters requires readers to switch frames of reference repeatedly.[30] For example, the name "Napoleon" in an alternate-history novel will continue to *refer* like all natural names, denoting (as John Stuart Mill pointed out about proper names generally) a unique individual assumed to be independent of the text, and yet it will also have a purely textual "fictional" meaning, where his deeds and destiny are in a tacitly subjunctive mood. The fully fictional characters in the same narrative, however, are not construed in that double mode. Unlike natural names, novelistic ones are motivated by the author's intention to produce characters rather than refer to them; they are at first mere promises of characters, and their repetition allows us to assemble scattered information into a persona.[31] Novel readers understand that the givenness of the character is a convention and that the text's proper names only signify what they (with the active participation of the knowing reader) are simultaneously creating. As we work to construct characters, we may make and then later discard hypotheses about them, and we may be informed about possible destinies they did not follow, but we do not take the information we get as continuously and systematically hypothetical—hypothetical in its essence—as we do when reading about a counterfactual Napoleon in the same story. The events involving the novelistic characters are taken to be simply the "facts of the fiction," whereas those involving the counterparts of the historical characters are simultaneously "facts of the fiction" and historical counterfactuals.[32] Furthermore, personae formed for the purpose of counterfactual speculation are explicitly designed for comparison with real-world individuals, whereas normal novel characters come with no specific contrasting twins. They are often intended to be read as "typical" of broad social, psychological, or moral categories but not as portraits of actual persons. While reading about Anna Karenina, for example, we are not continually prompted to compare her with some individual in the real world; and, of course, when we read about her actions, we are not prompted to reflect that in actuality she did something else instead.[33] It is that *instead-of* structure, when the incompatible realities are displayed, that activates the counterfactual modality and explains the crucial role played by nexus moments in alternate histories. Fully fictional characters can thus be easily accommodated in Our Timeline, whereas counterfactual ones belong to Alternate Timelines.

This distinction between the two kinds of fictionality is especially apparent in a small number of nineteenth-century works where alternate-history narratives are presented as the discourses of fictional characters in Our Timeline. The resulting hybrid structures might be said to anticipate the alternate-history novels, which began making a tentative appearance at the turn of the century. We'll look at three examples of the hybrid texts: *Uchronia*, which I've already introduced, and two shorter American pieces that seem to be the first alternate-history narratives in English, Nathaniel Hawthorne's "P's Correspondence" and Edward Everett Hale's "Hands Off."[34]

Renouvier did use fictional characters in *Uchronia* but not inside the alternate-history parts of the text. Instead, he invented three fictional framing characters, who supposedly lived in Our Timeline, to personify the reasons for exercising the counterfactual imagination. He introduced two of them as the putative authors of alternate-history narratives and the third as a reader and preserver of the manuscripts. Thus, the alternate histories, which internally feature only counterfactual counterparts of historical personae, are framed by the life stories of their fictional authors. The book contains two alternate histories at its innermost narrative level: the utopia about ancient Rome, which we've already examined, and a contrasting dystopia, which reminds us that if history is truly indeterminate, then it must have had the potential to be worse as well as better. The utopian alternate history is attributed to a seventeenth-century narrator, who is said to have narrowly escaped from the Inquisition at the end of the sixteenth century and to have written the alternate history while in exile in Amsterdam. That story, from which the whole volume of *Uchronia* takes its name, is thus a fictional author's consolatory *wish* for a different history that would have precluded his personal sufferings. The second, dystopian, alternate history is next framed as the work of the first author's son, writing in the seventeenth century and expressing his despairing sense that dynastic and religious European wars had become so brutal that the present seemed to be consistent with an even worse past than that which actually occurred. These are followed by a short narrative said to be written by the seventeenth-century writer's son, which ends the volume by telling of the family's further sufferings after the French invasion of Holland in the reign of Louis XIV.

The frame of *Uchronia* thus tells the stories of three generations whose lives span approximately one-and-a-quarter centuries of religious wars on the Continent, and the embedded alternate histories are meant to resonate against this background of continual, lethal fanaticism. The sufferings of the fictional narrators are described with a subjective vividness that provides a fuller appreciation of the ruination of private lives. Indeed, these novelistic renderings are the places where the horrors of state religious persecution and religious war really come alive, even more so than in the dystopian narrative, which adopts an impersonal world-historical perspective greatly removed from individual sufferers. So whereas Renouvier, in the guise of the putative "editor," prefaced the whole volume with a philosophical introduction, the novelistic character-narrators make the alternate histories seem less intellectual exercises than expressions of both personal suffering and human resilience under extreme duress. In short, the fictional frame reminds the reader of the historical reasons for counterfactualizing about history.

Viewing the entirety of *Uchronia*, though, we also take in the gap between reading about fictional characters in Our Timeline and reading about counterfactual ones in an Alternate Timeline. Readers must continually transition between one kind of fiction and the other, and each time we are aware of moving between "modalities," as the possible-worlds theorists would say.[35] But instead of just stressing the difference between actuality and counterfactuality, this arrangement also emphasizes the contrast between normal fictional characters, on the one hand, and counterfactual characters, with their shadowy twins in the actual world, on the other hand. The latter already contain their explicitly contrasting destinies and all the other complexities of their identifying characteristics. A table of the two kinds might look like this:

Our Timeline/Our World	Alternate Timelines/Alternate Worlds
Fictional Characters	Counterparts of Historical Characters
Fictional Personal Destinies	Fictional Personal Destinies
Actual Historical Events	Counterfactual-Historical Events

Uchronia displays other distinctions between the two modes as well, perhaps the most important of which is that, by staying on the level of public persons, institutions, and events, the alternate histories seldom grasp how the changes described would have affected the subjective experience of ordinary people. They may assert that imperial and national history—religious beliefs and international conflicts—would have had profound personal consequences on the private lives of humbler people and on their individual morality, but the elevated altitude of the narratives does not allow us to see those ramifications. The framing narratives, in contrast, revivify the past, as good historical novels do, by immersing us in the life experiences of the narrators. Since the personae in the Alternate Timeline are limited to world-historical actors, who might have caused or sustained the alterations, and the introduction of common fictional characters is prohibited, the alternate worlds produced by the divergences never seems densely realized despite the effort expended on them. For possible-world-making to become a generic ambition of alternate histories, therefore, Renouvier's attempt suggests that its successful completion would ultimately require the mixing of the character types in the alternate-history novel.

Renouvier's book usefully exposes the differences between normal novelistic fiction and alternate histories, but it also makes them seem unmixable. In contrast, Nathaniel Hawthorne's "P's Correspondence" (1845) builds a more permeable barrier between its counterfactual narratives and its fictional narrator's reality, mainly because the narrator's grasp on reality is quite weak.[36] Although "P's Correspondence" has been called the first English-language work in the alternate-history form, it might be more accurate to call it a proto-alternate-history, for the changes it makes in our historical timeline concern only the individual lives of certain famous people; no world-transforming events are identified. It is a humorous piece that was first published as a magazine sketch, and it has none of the political or philosophical ambitions of the two French works we examined in the last section. It does, however, give us an early attempt at blending fictional and counterfactual characters. As in Renouvier's book, there is an editor and a narrator, P whose supposed letters we read. P is said to be a delusional mental patient, who is locked away in a sanatorium in New England but imagines himself to be in London meeting various historical figures, all of whom, we know, were already dead by 1845. In these satirical alternate biographies, Lord Byron and Percy Shelley live on to embrace reactionary politics and orthodox Anglicanism while suppressing or revising beyond recognition their own earlier work, and Napoleon spends his dotage under guard in London, where he experiences constant anxiety and crippling fear. P's letters conform to the ironic counterfactual plots we examined in the first chapter, implying as they do that the actual early deaths of the poets were good for the survival of the poetry and that Napoleon's reputation for bravery depended on his having been imprisoned while still in his forties. They are witty retorts to those, like Geoffroy-Château, who naively regretted that genius should have been cut off in its prime before having fulfilled its destiny.

Behind P's madness, we can discern Hawthorne's satiric intention quite easily, noticing, for example, that the imagined maturities of Byron and Shelley are retributive poetic justice for the way the young Byron and Shelley publically taunted their elders in the first generation of Romantic poets. When reading P's encounter with Shelley, we are prompted to think of the concluding quatrain of the poet's sonnet "To Wordsworth," published in 1816, thirty-some years before Wordsworth's death:

> In honoured poverty thy voice did weave
> Songs consecrate to truth and liberty,—Deserting
> These, thou leavest me to grieve,
> Thus having been, that thou should cease to be.

The youthful poet Wordsworth was thus praised by Shelley but only as someone who has ceased to be, although the man Wordsworth lived on. So Hawthorne creates an alternate Shelley, who, like Shelley's Wordsworth, no longer produces "Songs consecrate to truth and liberty." And to drive home the point, Hawthorne has P imagine Shelley's later works as a complete about-face, far more reactionary than anything the older Wordsworth produced: in 1845 Shelley is composing a "poetico-philosophical" proof of Christianity "based on the Thirty-nine Articles" of Anglicanism. Extending the satire even further, Hawthorne's P encounters a Shelley who is nevertheless unrepentant; still expressing the bland self-approval that gave him such wide latitude of behavior in his actual life, the Shelley of 1845 indulgently interprets his own earlier poetic and philosophical apostasy as part of "a regular progression" toward a higher knowledge. The contrast between the young poet's attack on Wordsworth and his self-forgiveness in Hawthorne's satire is a swipe at Shelley's egotism, but it also raises a serious question about the accidental nature of posthumous reputation more generally. Shelley's actual poem seems to lament Wordsworth's survival, and Hawthorne suggests that Shelley's continued life would have blotted out his actual significance: "I felt half inclined to ask him what would have been his fate had he perished on the lower steps of his staircase, instead of building his way aloft into the celestial brightness" (295). As in so many alternate histories, actuality is the hypothetical "would have been" of the Alternate Timeline.

All of Hawthorne's ironic and satiric tropes were already in the repertoire of counterfactualism by the late eighteenth century; as we saw in chapter 1, writers like Voltaire and D'Israeli used them, without creating a fictional narrator. What P's epistolary framework adds is a tone of personal regret and wonder at the changes wrought by time, which are captured in strikingly grotesque images. Poor sequestered P hallucinates the exciting circumstances of coming into contact with famous men, but the encounters invariably take bizarre turns, as the letter writer's imagination presents him with monstrous images of the deteriorating bodies and minds of his heroes. Byron's body is a case in point:

> His early tendency to obesity having increased, Lord Byron is now enormously fat,—so fat as to give the impression of a person quite overladen with his own flesh, and without sufficient vigor to diffuse his personal life through the great mass of corporeal substance which weighs upon him so cruelly. You gaze at the mortal heap; and, while it fills your eye with what purports to be Byron, you murmur within yourself, "For Heaven's sake, where is he? . . ." Would that he were leaner, for, though he did me the honor to present his hand, yet it was so puffed out with alien substance that I could not feel as if I had touched the hand that wrote Childe Harold. (290)

P often describes the objects of his fantasy in terms like these, as strange amalgams of living and dead substances.

"P's Correspondence" thus characterizes alternate-history speculation as a fluctuating, unstable indistinction between the veracity of death and loss and our ability to resuscitate vanished possibilities in our imaginations. Of course we readers do not share P's visionary confusion; we are only meant to take advantage of it for the purpose of "realizing" the weirdly detailed, irreverent, and literal-minded episodes. The supposedly sane editor, indeed, presents the letters as a combination of misplaced belief and creative imaginative play: "In my opinion, all this is not so much a delusion as a partly wilful and partly involuntary sport of the imagination, to which his disease has imported such morbid energy that he beholds these spectral scenes and characters with no less distinctness than a play upon the stage, and with somewhat more of illusive credence" (287). The sane/insane duality is a heightened version of the real/imagined binary, and P's movement from one state of consciousness to the other provides the generic transition from our reality to the alternate one.

This fictional characterization (insanity) of the actual counterfactual impulse (satire), though, also allows some mixing of the two kinds of personae because, unlike Renouvier's narrators, P believes *himself* to be in the altered biographies. He meets Byron, Shelley, Napoleon, Burns, and so on, walks the same streets, inhabits the same rooms, observes and sometimes interacts with them. The two kinds of fictionality do not remain rigidly separated by the divide between timelines. In placing the fictional character on both sides of the divide instead of confining him to the actual historical world, "P's Correspondence" resembles the structure we'll see in early versions of the alternate-history novel, where a single character tells the story of his travel between timelines. Rather than engaging in thought experiments, like Renouvier's characters, these narrator-protagonists cross the boundaries between the parallel realities; they tend to start out in Our Timeline and arrive in the altered world; the plots of the novels thus revolve around their transworld trajectories. To be sure, the small scale of Hawthorne's counterfactuals obviates the need to create alternate worlds: the continued existence of Shelley and Byron are not imagined to have been highly consequential. But in other ways these stories tilt more toward the counterfactual than toward the normally fictional poles. They are, for example, far more concerned with the alternate lives of the historical personages than with P's dismal lot, and thus the fictional character's function remains largely narrative; his insanity also reminds us that he (unlike the aging, obese Byron) belongs to Our Timeline, even though his wandering mind allows us to perceive him in both sequences. This story nevertheless has the germ of a different type of fiction, centered on the fictional character's dislocations and experiences, his consciousness of participating in competing realities, and the abundant predicaments of being (either apparently or literally) between parallel worlds. Numerous American alternate-history short stories and novels will spring out of this seedbed.

In addition to the fictional narrators who stay firmly in Our Timeline and those who cross over, a third sort seems to occupy a place altogether outside of time. A later nineteenth-century American example, also first published as a magazine story, Edward Everett Hale's "Hands Off" (1881), even begins by complaining about English as a language that requires the use of verb tenses. Tenses, he claims, are false to his "condition," which is "free from the limits of Time, and in new relations to Space."[37] So we are to understand that the events narrated are sequenced merely to accommodate our time-bound mentalities, reinforced by our language; viewed from his dimension, they are all simultaneous. In a way, of course, this might be said of any historical narrative, since the events related are all in the past and their records might be said to exist simultaneously in the archive. As some linguists would have it, once they have occurred, their status becomes omnitemporal, for it will always be the case that they have occurred. "Omnitemporal" might therefore be a better word than "eternal" for the dimension occupied by this narrator, and in the course of the story, we learn to think of him as the immortal soul of a dead man who once inhabited our earth. Indeed, he seems quite recently dead since he is still under the supervision of a "Mentor" and in life was adept at the modern science of optics, skilled in the operations of telescopes and microscopes, learned in history, a man of "scholarly tastes" (8). The counterfactualist is thus characterized as an omnitemporal scientific historical demigod, who can see history from vast spatial and chronological distances and yet achieve minute observations.

In some ways, this narrator's abode resembles Blanqui's sprawling expanse of a universe; he has "twenty or thirty thousand solar systems" in his observation when the story begins. However, this universe has none of the sublime chaos of Blanqui's astronomical vision, in which stars are forever collapsing into nonbeing or bursting into existence. Instead, the astronomical bodies move about "in perfectly harmonic relations, of planets around their centres, of satellites around planets, of suns, with their planets and satellites, around their centres, and of these, in turn, around theirs" (4). Whereas Blanqui emphasized that the universe has no center, Hale seems to believe that it is nothing but centers. Like Blanqui's universe, Hale's also contains numerous world doubles, but these, we learn, exist in a separate expanse, "which the astronomers call the starless region" (12), and on a different ontological plane. They are "an immense and utterly unaccountable series" with many duplicates of creation, and yet they are "not the same." "I do not know myself what these are for," the Mentor tells the narrator, "unless—I think sometimes they are for you and me to learn from. He [God] is so kind" (13). Thus despite the apparent modernity of this narrator, he inhabits an orderly universe, presided over by a deity who has been "so kind" as to provide a store of practice worlds, on which the newly deceased immortals are allowed to experiment, trying out alternative histories.

We have encountered these attributes of the counterfactual impulse before in the Leibnizian God whom Priestley encouraged us to imitate. In true Victorian fashion, Hale makes a fictional character out of a sliver of that all-seeing mind, inventing a still partly human person with godlike powers, who cannot help wanting to improve history. The practice worlds are brought to his attention only when he is about to make that mistake. The narrator tells us that while viewing the actual abduction to Egypt of the biblical Joseph (remember the omnitemporality idea), he spies a moment when the boy might have escaped and returned to the encampment of his father. As the narrator reaches out from his perch on the other side of time and space, intending to silence a dog that is about to alert the slave traders to Joseph's escape, he is himself abruptly stopped by his Mentor: thus the title "Hands Off." Given a practice world—"here's a fresh one; no one has touched it yet"—and assured that the people in it are not actually God's free and conscious children but mere representations, he begins the alternate history. Many features of nineteenth-century alternate history are compressed in this short scenario: (1) the fictional narrator is motivated by an irresistible personal impulse to make a change; (2) the difference between the two timelines is instantiated in two spatially separate worlds, which are also understood to be ontologically different; (3) although the product of a personal wish, the narrative point of view is nevertheless outside of time and space and capable of tracing long arcs of cause and effect; and (4) although beginning with a small change (the death of a barking dog), the narrative traces a world-historical transformation.

But a problem sometimes encountered in alternate histories also comes to the fore in this text: the convention of using only historical personae can lead to a shortage of characters, especially if the story is dystopian. In "Hands Off," the narrator indulges his impulse to help the biblical Joseph escape from the slave traders, and the boy is reunited with his family. For a while, the Israelites prosper and the narrator feels gratified; but then scarcity begins to set in, and, since Joseph was not in Egypt advising the Pharaoh to store food against famine, the Israelites have nowhere to turn when their crops fail and their animals become diseased. Within a few hundred years, the whole of the ancient world either collapses or fails to come into being, leaving the narrator to look for putatively historical figures who never appear or are unrecognizable: "When it came time for Cadmus, there was no chance for Cadmus. Perhaps he came, perhaps he did not. . . . If Cadmus came, he was rather more low-lived than the Pelasgians among whom he landed" (25). In the decline, the supply of historically available people altogether runs out, and the narrator finds "not a man or a woman, nor a boy or girl, left in that world" (34). The relentlessly catastrophic direction of the altered history is the condition of this extinction, but the limitation of the personae to history's pre-given figures, combined with the constant threats to their chances of coming into being, insures the outcome. The story comes to a predictably pious Leibnizian conclusion—"from what I call evil, He educes good"—but it also reads as a parable of the entropy threatening a fictional genre that confines fictional persona to the narrative frame.

Hale was by no means the last alternate-history writer to face this difficulty of the narrative's chronological scope. Alternate histories may be especially good at rendering detailed accounts of historical turning points and the immediate aftermaths of those events, but when they depict long passages of time, enough time to have extinguished the historical personae alive at the nexus, certain genealogical difficulties arise. Charles Renouvier, who stayed at a very high altitude above the private and reproductive lives of historical characters, was able to avoid this difficulty, but even he relied less on the agency of individual personages and more on that of aggregate entities as the centuries represented in his stories progress. Twentieth-century alternate-history fiction writers, though, became fascinated by the question of how the alteration would affect the genetic sequences of the historical record. In these novels, the world is always repopulated, but differently. As we'll see in the chapters to follow, American alternate-history novelists, who are often drawn to science-fiction plots, frequently stress the genealogical puzzles arising when characters become dislocated in time and make unintentional alterations. Hale's story seems to be the first of many in which some trans-time agent alters the events he planned merely to observe. Hale's character is prevented from changing the "real" world, but once he is given his "experimental" alternate world, he intervenes, and the Leibnizian apparatus goes into motion, proving that what happened in Our Timeline was absolutely necessary. Although Hale's message may seem hopelessly old-fashioned, it not only introduces a modern theme but also anticipates a common twentieth-century technique of resolution: the use of a "time patrol" function, in which a group of characters are charged with the responsibility of maintaining the integrity of Our Timeline.

Thus Hale's story invents novelistic fictional resources for alternate history and creates an impetus for the expansion of fictionality in the alternate-history diegesis itself while still adhering to the assumption of alternate history: in order for "you and me to learn from" these experiments (to use the Mentor's words), they must exclusively contain exact replicas of the actual world's people. That assumption would need to be set aside in order for the alternate-history *novel*, properly speaking, to come into existence; moreover—the corollary assumption that fictional personae indicate a textual world sharing our familiar historical reality— would also need to be suspended. These transitions are made at the very end of the nineteenth century, when fictional protagonists finally take center stage inside alternate-historical settings. To be sure, the earliest examples of the alternate-history novel continue to register the stresses between the two forms of fictionality, but they also suggest that the new form will have its own internal tropism toward our world and Our Timeline. Indeed, they might even be said to dramatize the gravitational pull of actuality.

If we want to catch the earliest instances of fully novelistic counterfactual narratives, we must turn to some truly obscure texts. Renouvier, Hawthorne, and Hale were all well-known writers compared to the amateurs, one British and one American, who wrote the first two alternate-history novels. Indeed, Edmund Lawrence's *It May Happen Yet; a Tale of Bonaparte's Invasion of England*, was written in 1895 but never found a commercial publisher; Lawrence published it at his own expense four years later in London. The American novel, Frank Williams's *Hallie Marshall: A True Daughter of the South*, found a publisher and even a couple of reviewers in 1899, but it was very soon forgotten. For all of their originality, both novels are weak performances, and there is no evidence that they had any effect on the form's later development, but that just makes it all the more telling that they already contain so many features of later alternate-history novels in English.

In the first place, they anticipate the most popular counterfactual-history topics in their respective national literatures: *It May Happen Yet* imagines an invasion of the British Isles, and *Hallie Marshall* envisions a Southern victory in the Civil War. Between them, moreover, they divide the two tendencies we'll see in the subgenre as a whole: *It May Happen Yet* primarily narrates the nexus, setting the novel inside counterfactual-historical events as they occurred, while *Hallie Marshall*, only briefly identifying the nexus, mainly depicts the aftermath, exploring the eventual social consequences of the alteration. The books thus establish separate literary traditions into which we can still divide alternate-history novels: one group takes after the historical novel, which is a new departure for counterfactual fictions, whereas the other conforms to the utopian (or dystopian) mode, which had already been established as a norm for alternate histories (witness Renouvier and Hale) as well. The British book follows the pattern of the historical novel as inaugurated by Walter Scott in his 1814 *Waverley*: the narrative is set at the time of the putative historical events, which interrupt the lives of the novelistic characters. Usually in nineteenth-century historical novels, the lives of the characters eventually return to normal, although changes linger about the edges of their individual destinies. In the alternate-history version of this plot, reestablishing normality sometimes requires merging the two timelines at the conclusion, which will prove a very problematic (although interestingly persistent) move. In contrast, the American book draws on utopian fictions, reminding us not only of the alternate histories we've surveyed but also of Edward Bellamy's best-selling 1888 novel *Looking Backward: 2000–1887* and William Morris's 1890 *News from Nowhere*. In Bellamy's and Morris's novels, the protagonist finds himself mysteriously transported to a different reality, and most of the "action" consists in learning about the superiority of the utopian world. In utopian novels, a courtship plot often develops between the protagonist and a young woman encountered in the alternate reality, serving mainly as a device to integrate the newcomer and provide him with a guide. The late nineteenth-century utopias, moreover, usually separated their worlds by leaping forward into an already accomplished future perfection, so the actual moment of change is only briefly described by a character rather than narrated at the novel's primary diegetic plane. The first two alternate-history novels in English were thus conceived inside distinct, indeed almost opposite, nineteenth-century subgenres: the historical novel, set in the past and dramatizing critical events, and the utopian novel, often set in a future state where social conflict has been quelled.

It May Happen Yet appeared at the peak of the popularity of a genre known as *guerre imaginaire*, or "imaginary wars," which usually described wars that, the authors claimed, were imminent and almost always featured invasions of Britain. The books were avidly read in Britain, Germany, and France as national rivalries increased between the end of the Franco-Prussian War in 1871 and the outbreak of WWI in 1914, and *It May Happen Yet* would have been just another such invasion fantasy if it were not for the fact that it uniquely placed its action in the past rather than the future. Indeed, at the outset, it seems to be quite an ordinary historical novel, introducing its middle-class characters with exacting attention to time and place and emphasizing that the lapse of time between the implied present of the writing and the past of the tale puts it outside of living memory: the year of the action is 1805, "about when the grandfathers and grandmothers of middle-aged people of the present time were undergoing the process of being born."[38] It is February of 1805, the town is Norwich, and the drawing-room conversation of the main characters—the physician protagonist Richard Fenthorpe, his mother, and several members of the minor provincial gentry—provides the exposition for both the private and public plots to follow. The private part of the story is unremarkable in the extreme: a courtship plot is slightly complicated by a lost will, which if found would prove the protagonist to be the rightful inheritor of a local landed estate.

Meanwhile, a much greater threat to the little community is brewing unsuspected on the Continent. In the first pages, the impending surprise attack by Napoleon's forces is only hinted at by the presence of a thick fog in the channel and the overly confident (and therefore probably mistaken) opinion of certain characters who want the reserve volunteer corps of the region dissolved, since there is no longer any danger of invasion. The scene then shifts to the Dover coast, where another character, a lawyer only slightly connected to the Fenthorpe family via the legacy plot, learns from local smugglers that hundreds of French ships had been transported overland in pieces to Holland, from whence they are about to carry the French army across the channel and into the northern English ports of Norwich and Yarmouth. The lawyer rushes to London and tries to warn the prime minister, Pitt the Younger, but is too late: the French army has already crossed, under cover of the dense fog, and begun disembarking at Norwich. The novel's action returns to the northern port, and our hero is launched from there into the ensuing battles, as the French push their way through Norfolk, into a devastating victory over the English at Cambridge, and down into London, where they are finally repulsed and turned back.

Lawrence probably took the outlines of his invasion from *Napoléon et la conquête du monde*, where the French invaders also landed at Norwich, defeated the English at Cambridge, and continued on to London. But this similarity is the only evidence that Lawrence was aware of the alternate-history conventions into which he might have been expected to fit his tale. For example, there is no framing material, not even of the sort provided by

Geoffroy-Château's introduction, to put the narrative in the conditional mood; instead, the narrator, at one particularly awkward moment, facetiously asserts that the events are "true" although now forgotten. Later, invoking the model of counterfactual military history, he implies that the point of his exercise is to argue for erecting certain kinds of fortifications that would protect London in case of an attack coming from the northeast. All of this may be put down to lack of craftsmanship, but it also indicates how unprecedented the idea of merging novelistic fiction with alternate history would have seemed at the time. To someone who had never read an alternate-history novel, why not think of it as just like a historical novel, except that obviously counterfactual events would be substituted for actual ones? After all, the historical novel form, especially when set in wartime, provides the novelist with a ready-made tradition of history writing—critical military history—already closely linked to counterfactuality precisely through the multiple contingent turning points it contains. Thus the historical war story helps the novelist negotiate the seemingly opposite aesthetic criteria of unpredictability and plausibility, and the counterfactual war story gives those criteria even greater weight. Wars also have extensive consequences, presumably affecting all citizens in the nation, so they are self-evidently significant, and their actual scope might seem best gauged by the impact they have on civilians. Focalizing the action through a noncombatant like the physician Richard Fenthorpe, whose profession gives him battlefield access, allows for the individuation of nonmilitary historical consciousness amid the exciting action. Indeed, even today a significant part of the interest in British counterfactual invasion narratives (which continue to be produced) is a desire to imagine how the general population might react to a foreign occupation. This first experiment with the form is no exception.

It's easy, therefore, to see why the historical novel would be one of the most frequently chosen generic templates for the alternate-history novel, but historical novels also have some internal tensions that become especially pronounced when combined with alternate history. Although historical novels purport to demonstrate that all phases of human experience are "historical" and that even the most private dimensions of our selfhood are culturally specific, their "history" nevertheless has two quite distinct temporalities: one is associated with quotidian everyday life—a sort of *longue durée* of relatively static conditions—and the other narrates disruptive changes through upheavals like wars and revolutions. In contrast to the eventful history that initiates the plot in these novels, the quotidian status quo ante preceding it can resemble an almost ahistorical normalcy.

Moreover, since novels in general, as opposed to romances, ordinarily specialize in the representation of the quotidian, the large historical events that disrupt it seem to be entering from a different plane of reality. So even as the historical novel enlarges the repertoire of plausible action (journeys, battles, abductions, imprisonments, etc.), it still depicts eventful public history as something that intrudes into everyday life—for good or for ill—rather than a broad underlying condition subtending private existence.

The two planes of history further map onto the two sorts of personae. Historical and fictional characters exist on the same diegetic level and in the same timeline in alternate-history novels, but just as in normal historical novels, their modes of action are not exactly commensurable. The historical personae cause the events to which the ordinary novelistic characters react, but those fully fictional characters center the plots that are organized around their individual destinies. Again, the temporal distinction comes into play: the long-term cultural conditions that underpin personal lives are assumed to be more persistent, outlasting changes in political arrangements. The private fictions depicting the mores, modes of communal and family formation, social hierarchies, and traditions of inheritance therefore represent not only individual microhistories but also the *longue durée*, where transformations are glacially slow compared to those at the more eventful level of military and political change.[39] *It May Happen Yet* overtly makes this point about the nonintersecting levels of historical experience when the protagonist explains that the French invaders have no intention of setting up a military government in Britain but merely hope to liberate it from what they mistakenly imagine to be an unpopular monarchy. He advises his countrymen to go about their lives in a normal way because the invaders will not try to make deep social changes.

Alternate-history novels of this sort also follow the lead of historical novels in giving us far more access to the consciousnesses of novelistic than historical personae. For example, in *It May Happen Yet*, when we glimpse Napoleon in England, he is (to revise a description attributed to Hegel) "alternate history sitting on a horse" and has an appropriately impenetrable subjectivity.[40] Lawrence invests even less time in trying to compass Napoleon's inner state than did Clausewitz or Geoffroy-Château. Instead the world-historical personage par excellence is an object of perception, a phenomenon creating a certain kind of sublime experience in the fictional perceiver and protagonist:

> It was a face and a figure that could not be seen by the least observant without attention and almost fascination. But as Richard continued

to look, although not a motion of the features of this remarkable face could be perceived, it appeared to him as if the face itself had changed. For a moment he admired, and was entranced by its beauty, power, and intellectuality; then, while the power and the intellectuality remained, the beauty seemed to die out of the face, and be replaced, as by transformation, by something far transcending mere human ugliness, something whose origin could be ascribed to nowhere but the depths of the bottomless pit. (196)

British writers had frequently portrayed Napoleon as the fallen angel, on a par with Milton's Satan, so this vision, alternately lofty and demonically abysmal, was a cliché by 1895.[41] Nevertheless it illustrates—all the more clearly for the exaggeration—the gap that frequently opens in both historical and alternate-history fiction between the superhuman world makers and the characters whose stories we are following.

The tensions in the historical novel are part of its dynamism: we thrill to the historical events and prodigious figures, but we also anticipate the end of their tyrannical "invasion" of the novel's everyday world. Historical novels usually begin in the peace and the obscurity of private life, and the narrative logic is that they should end with its restoration, although often on new and improved foundations. Thus a strong presumption in favor of establishing a status quo post that resembles the status quo ante seems built into the form, giving the sense that, as we approach the end of the novel, we will return to a state that resembles the earlier order. The urge to restore the world, though, creates greater tension in the alternate-history novel, where the change should create not just a temporary interruption but an entirely new and parallel reality. In these novels, the reappearance of the status quo ante requires the deflection of the newly divergent trajectory back toward Our Timeline. *It May Happen Yet* accomplishes this tricky restoration when the protagonist, in a trance state, sees Napoleon sneaking out of England in the middle of the night, having failed to subdue the population of London to his will. Here the conditions of the moonlit vision might indicate that the whole narrative was a kind of dream, but the narrator nevertheless invokes a historical precedent for Napoleon's abrupt withdrawal, reminding the reader that the general abandoned his campaign in Egypt in a similarly precipitous way. The main impact of the invasion on the novel's private plot is that it hastens the marriage of the hero and heroine and indirectly leads to the discovery of a lost will, which gives Richard Fenthorpe an estate. Thus, ironically, the French invasion leaves England even more firmly in the hands of its rightful owners.

Bizarre and amateurish as it may seem, the conclusion of *It May Happen Yet* previews a widespread tendency in later alternate-history novels to follow the historical-novel's restorative instinct by not only taming and normalizing eventful counterfactual history (especially when it takes an unfortunate turn) but also bracketing and even nullifying it at the conclusion. In dystopian novels especially, hopes for the return to our own form of normality often create the narrative energy. A well-known twenty-first-century example would be Philip Roth's 2004 *The Plot against America*, but many lesser instances, some of which carry on the struggle against the alternate option for several volumes, might also be cited. They solidify our allegiance to the status quo by envisioning the means of its extinction: in this earliest example, we see an England absorbed into the French Empire; in later ones we see an America in league with Nazi Germany, a Britain under German occupation, or a victorious and dominant Confederate States of America. In these fictions, the reader's actual situation is estranged, appearing not as the state of affairs given by past events but as an improbable achievement snatched from the jaws of perdition. As the ATL merges back into OTL, though, its lingering traces become the most problematic aspects of the narrative's closure. If the events were so momentous as to be pregnant with an alternate world, how could their remains have folded so seamlessly back into our world? This formal problem has never been resolved entirely, and in succeeding chapters we'll see a number of ingenious attempts. Suffice it to say here that when the narrator of *It May Happen Yet* says the invasion happened but has been lost to memory, the remark makes some overall generic sense: alternate-history novels that borrow the historical-novel form have a built-in tropism toward the reestablishment of Our Timeline.[42]

And finally, *It May Happen Yet* displays the tendency of the alternate-history novel to shift attention from the actions of individual counterfactual characters to those of collectivities, whose typical ways of thinking and acting are represented sometimes by particular fictional characters and sometimes by crowds or other manifestations of the people's will. Napoleon initiates the action in this novel and wins the battles, but he loses the campaign because the British people as a whole simply refuse to cooperate in the dismantling of their political institutions, which would require the abandonment of the great compromise of 1688 and disestablishment of their parliamentary monarchy. This refusal, said to be typical of Britons' stubborn resistance to both outside interference and Continental European ideologies, conforms to the gravitational pull of the status quo ante. No great leader defeats the French army, and there is no heroic uprising; instead, the outcome is produced by the overwhelming inertial pressure of the national character.

F. P. Williams's *Hallie Marshall: A True Daughter of the South* seems to have exactly the opposite valuation of the status quo: it implicitly presents our reality as dystopian and envisions an alternative utopia. The protagonist, an embattled manager of a New England factory facing a strike, falls asleep on a snowy summer evening and wakes up in the morning on a sweet-smelling veranda in the Confederate States of America (CSA). The date is the same as that on which he lost consciousness, but he has awakened to a radically altered present, in which the South won the Civil War over thirty years earlier by convincing the slaves to fight on the side of their masters. The CSA is a paternalistic slave culture, where kindly masters treat their slaves like children and none of the "old abuses" that were common in the antebellum South have survived. The North, in contrast, is a nightmare of unbridled free-market capitalism, where laborers and factory owners incessantly fight and discarded workers and their families are left to sicken and die in the streets.

There was nothing new in the claim that Southern slavery was a more humane arrangement than industrial capitalism; the idea had been around since the late eighteenth century and had been frequently used by both proslavery writers and critics of early industrialism on both sides of the Atlantic.[43] To be sure, it was somewhat rare by the end of the century, when many Southern apologists had given up on the defense of slavery and had begun defending the erection of Jim Crow racial segregation, often on constitutional grounds, instead. The Supreme Court case *Plessy v. Ferguson* had just recently (1896) upheld the constitutionality of racial segregation, even in public accommodations, so racialist apologetics had moved into a different phase. But slavery was not an entirely ignored issue, for there was a concurrent rise in nostalgic depictions of the antebellum South as a part of the overall vilification of Reconstruction that accompanied the consolidation of a segregationist consensus throughout white America, North and South. The unusual ideological feature of *Hallie Marshall* is that it places the idealized South not in the past of the lost cause but in an alternate present. Antebellum slavery, it admits, was often corrupt and abusive; it simultaneously asserts, though, that slavery as a system contained the seeds of paternalism, which would have had time to ripen into a fully harmonious way of life if the South had won the war. One denizen of the alternate world explains:

> The slavery that exists in the South today is a modified form of slavery—there is nothing oppressive about it. The rights of the negroes are protected; their right to life, that great natural right of mankind. Sick or well, young or old, every slave is sure of subsistence. The family rights of the slaves are also guarded—no negro is sold away from his immediate family, nowadays. We cannot buy or sell a married negro alone—we must take wife or husband also, and children, too, if we buy, and we must put them together when we sell. That is the condition of labor in the Confederate States of America today.[44]

The emphasis on the "today" of 1899 is typical of this kind of novel, in which the altered *present* occupies the forefront and is explicitly contrasted with the implied readers' familiar actuality. In addition to noting the differences between the "modified" paternalistic slavery and its antebellum precursor, the passage also calls attention to "the condition of labor in . . . America today," where all were not "sure of subsistence." The class conflict of the 1890s thus serves as one implied negative alternative to this particular utopia: prolonged and bloody strikes—the garment workers' strike of 1890, the Homestead Steel strike of 1892, the Pullman strike of 1894, and a series of violently suppressed miners' strikes from 1896 to 1899—marked the decade in the North and West, while the thirteen Southern states were the scene of widespread child labor in factories and extensive convict labor.

The present-mindedness of the book accounts for many of its formal differences from *It May Happen Yet*. In contrast to the British novel, *Hallie Marshall* relegates its counterfactual history to the interpolated narration of a former Confederate colonel, uncle to the at-first skeptical protagonist. The plot of *It May Happen Yet* included imaginary battles and decisive councils of state, whereas *Hallie Marshall*'s scanty history is delivered indirectly as exegesis, the background necessary for the protagonist to understand the world in which he mysteriously finds himself. We learn that Abraham Lincoln inadvertently provided a "teachable moment" in the Emancipation Proclamation: "When the proclamation was first heard of there was more or less turmoil among the slaves. They thought, as a matter of course, that freedom carried a means of independence with it; they expected forty acres and a mule apiece—every mother's son of them" (96). But Lincoln is one of the very few historical figures to be named in the novel, and the critical changes brought about at the moment of the nexus are accomplished by collective agents—"the masters," "the slaves," "England," "the South," "the North"—rather than by particular persons:

We showed the slaves that the freedom that 'Marsa Linkum' wanted to give them was a condition that would set them free to work or starve, as they could or could not find employment; and would set their masters free from all responsibility as regarded the negroes—children, aged, helpless and all. . . . And when we made them understand what the North was fighting for—to subjugate us and to force the blacks to accept liberty that was not real liberty; freedom without independence—our slaves demanded that they should be enlisted to repel the invaders. (97–98)

These slave volunteers, the kindly colonel continues, then "poured into the field of Gettysburg at a critical moment," and as a result the South won not only the battle but also (with the help of Great Britain) the war.

As we'll see in later chapters, this particular fantasy—that the slaves might have fought to maintain the plantation system if they had been given the chance—can still be found among twenty-first-century Civil War counterfactual hypotheses. And even more common in alternate-history novels is the emphasis on collective agency, although in this novel it takes a blatantly racist form. The utopian logic is familiar: the change not only is accomplished by groups of people but also supposedly gives full expression to the natural propensities of these protagonists, conceived of here as races. The slaveholding Southern gentlemen were essentially magnanimous and protective, we are told; slaves were essentially childlike in their loyalty, dependency, and tractability. By nurturing these inborn tendencies in the two races, the slave utopia perfects their natures. We've already seen this notion of utopia as the completed social manifestation of an inner entelechy in Geoffroy-Château's alternate Napoleonic history; the novel replaces the alternate-history utopia's interest in a great man's potential with an equally energetic creation of collective characters. And this earliest example clearly demonstrates that the shift has a strong tendency to draw on and reinforce national and racial stereotypes.

Hallie Marshall, though, is not a novel of the nexus but of the aftermath, and its task is to gauge the degree of difference that the alternate outcome of the war would have made to the lives of ordinary people in the contemporary moment of the novel's composition. The historical agents are collective entities, and the individual personae are fictional, all the better to explore the effects of the change on the intimate levels of cultural, psychological, and personal experience and to elaborate the imaginary world from the perspective of a typical inhabitant. Thus the first half of the book is devoted to trying to realize the unfamiliar world, to make it seem substantial, and Ralph, the narrator-hero, is our proxy in that exercise. He describes the food, social rituals, work rhythms, and daily routines of the people, and as the narrator's belief in the reality of his experience increases, our willingness to credit the represented world as a realistic possibility is also supposed to increase. Williams's attempted thick description of the slave utopia, however, is little more than a pile of threadbare clichés. Indeed, its primary mode of familiarizing its world is to imagine it as a kind of a minstrel show, where happy darkies go back and forth to the cotton fields singing and the humorous Negro butler dances with the golden-haired daughter of the plantation owner. *Hallie Marshall* thus shows us what alternate-history fiction might aspire to do even as it raises the question of how to separate our sense of plausibility from the mere indulgence of popular prejudices.

The novel's narrative structure, in which a protagonist is abruptly deposited in an alternate reality and forced to orient himself through a series of intensive tutorials and close observations, had been used before by authors like Edward Bellamy in *Looking Backwards* (1888) and Mark Twain in *A Connecticut Yankee in King Arthur's Court* (1889), and in these books, too, the protagonist's acceptance of the alternate world is designed to model our acceptance of the fictional premise. But this is the first use of the technique in an alternate-history narrative, and it produces a shape very different from those we've been examining: in the earlier books the stories start shortly before the nexus and develop as the two timelines gradually diverge; they begin in the trunk of the familiar Y-shaped pattern. Novels of this pattern, though, start at the tip of one of the branches, indirectly and retrospectively validating the origin of the alteration while removing it from strong scrutiny. As the possible world becomes more intricate and compelling, the change that produced it is also supposed to seem more plausible.

Hallie Marshall's failure in this regard is by no means unique, and it cannot be solely attributed to its racism, for the problem with utopian novels in general is that their lack of social friction and dissatisfaction keeps them from generating plots. The early episodes of *Hallie Marshall* are dominated by what is *not* happening; for example, the protagonist mistakenly imagines that a runaway slave is being pursued, whereas it turns out that the runaway is merely a lost dog. On the blandly predictable plantation, the harrowing tales of the old South have been replaced by trivial happenings hardly worth the telling, but they are resurrected when some interesting fugitives from the North arrive, with their stories of inhumane treatment and starvation at the hands of hard-hearted capitalists. Since no other plot has managed to take hold—and Hallie and her father the colonel have run out of things to tell the narrator-hero about their slave utopia and its history—the rest of the book, over half of it, tells the story of the Northern refugees, in the course of which the North of the frame (in Our Timeline) and that of the tale (in the alternate one) become increasingly identified. Whether as starting point or dystopian alternative the North is the place of dynamic disequilibrium, where plots are born, and the South is the place of static tranquility, where they end.

Hallie Marshall thus solves the problem of utopian plotlessness with a device common to such fictions: it creates a contrasting dystopia, which soon becomes the main object of attention. Thus the novel, in addition to starting with the usual contrast between OTL and ATL, also creates an exaggerated version of actuality as a separate space internal to the alternate world. This is a pattern we've seen before, in Renouvier's alternate history, which separated out the conflicting strands of contemporary history into a utopia of liberal secular republicanism developing in the West and a dystopia of bellicose autocratic religious fanaticism confined to the East. In both books, the geographic separation is the very basis of the establishment of the utopia: just as Marcus Aurelius and Avidius Cassius contrived to keep Christianity in the East, the masters and slaves of the South decide together to prevent the capitalist free-labor market from entering the CSA. And yet in both books, the threat of reversion to Our Timeline seems constant. Because *Hallie Marshall* must leave the plantation to find a story, its plot bends toward our actuality, just as Renouvier's republic is constantly under siege. Alternate-history novels based on historical fiction are thus not the only ones in which our world reappears inside the Alternate Timeline. Indeed, the utopian variety can seem even more heavily dominated by the presence of actuality, since it often both frames the alternate-history story and plays a major role inside of it. In *Hallie Marshall*, the utopian Confederate States of America actually seems surrounded and outnumbered by its negative alternatives.

~

We've been exploring the nineteenth-century origins of the counterfactual mode's narrative forms in this chapter, using early versions of each to describe their basic assumptions and formal features, and we've discovered what seem to be their different motivating ambitions. The alternate histories drive toward historical justice, while the alternate-history novels seem intent on demonstrating that ordinary people, often acting collectively, might be the agents of historical change. At first these two ambitions appear to be at odds; recall Renouvier's insistence, for example, that large groups were usually incapable of moral decision-making and thus could not be held responsible for their actions. Since they often did not have organs of rational deliberation and thus acted irrationally and instinctively or in blind obedience to the wills of powerful individuals, the norms of justice simply did not apply to them any more than they applied to children or madmen. But over the course of the twentieth century, the impulses toward historical justice and collective responsibility became intertwined, and in the post-WWII period when the alternate-history novel was reinvented, they were becoming inextricable even if difficult to reconcile. To be sure, the burst of counterfactual storytelling in the last decades of the twentieth century was also inspired by other developments—especially the revolutions in scientific conceptions of time. But, as we'll see in the following chapters, when organized into counterfactual-historical conjectures, even these tend to center on the possibilities of reversing or undoing massive wrongs perpetrated by one collectivity (nation, race, class, empire) against another.

CHAPTER THREE

How the USA Lost the Civil War

The works we'll examine in the remainder of this book seem to violate the rule we identified in chapter 2: that people normally use past counterfactual hypotheses to learn why some regrettable event occurred. That norm seemed to explain why the alternate-history narrative modes began in nineteenth-century France, where writers from different sides of the political spectrum found plenty to regret in their nation's recent past and seemed to take solace in retrieving lost chances for better histories: if only Napoleon or, conversely, the Republic had prevailed. In contrast, American and British counterfactual suppositions have gravitated toward the question of how our nations might have lost the important wars they actually won. Instead of wondering how we might have won the war in Vietnam, for example, alternate-history writers in the late 1970s and 1980s preferred instead to refight the Civil War and World War II. In our fantasies, these are the two wars that we continually lose, and our reasons for dwelling on the possibilities of our own defeat are complex and various. In the next four chapters I'll look in detail at counterfactual versions of these two wars and their aftermaths, tracking them across the three textual forms I described in the previous chapter—counterfactual history, alternate history, and alternate-history novels—and analyzing the changing contexts in which they emerged. This chapter and the following treat the American Civil War and Reconstruction, while chapters 5 and 6 describe Britain's counterfactual Second World Wars.

To be sure, U.S. losses in the Civil War and World War II would not have been equally *American* defeats, for Americans fought on both sides of the

War between the States, as some historians prefer to call it. But insofar as the United States of America is the political entity whose singularity was preserved in that conflict and into which former combatants on both sides were reincorporated, imagining that the CSA prevailed is tantamount to imagining the loss of *our* nation no matter what our region. Consequently, in what follows I will often say "we" when referring to the USA, not only because I'm a Northerner without sympathy for the causes espoused by the Confederacy but also because all citizens of the USA belong to the nation that survived. What degree of actual unity survived, what varieties of opposing regional and political identification persist, what conflicted and ambivalent ideas of the nation appeared and disappeared over time are the topics of this chapter, and yet it is undeniable that the continuing struggles played out in the context of one nation's history.

That Americans have often imagined it otherwise, have envisaged a two-nation outcome to the Civil War, and have thereby depicted themselves as the losers, is a curious fact attesting to our continuing national identity crisis. Even more curious is the fact that most of the writers who inaugurated this thought experiment were not at all like the author of the novel *Hallie Marshall*, which I described in the last chapter; Frank Williams was a white supremacist who wanted to vindicate the rebellion, but the writers we'll examine in this chapter express no regret for the abolition of slavery or the passing of the plantocracy. They are mainly Northerners and political liberals, the earliest of whom published magazine pieces at the turn of the twentieth century arguing that the North's aims might have been better served either by not fighting at all or by losing the war.[1] This chapter will try to account for the origins of this paradoxical tradition as well as to trace its development and impact on the nation's view of its history into the twenty-first century.

DEMOCRATIC POLITICS AND COUNTERFACTUAL REASONING

The prehistory of Civil War counterfactuals begins before the war itself started, in the national debate over whether to fight. Could war between the states be avoided? Would it be the only solution to the complex regional tensions that were converging toward a crisis during the 1850s? If some Southern states were to secede after a Republican victory in the 1860 presidential election, should the United States let them go in peace? If a war were to be fought, what should be its purpose: to save the union or end slavery? What might alternative courses of action for achieving those ends be? Prior to the event, the pros and cons of the American Civil War were broadly and publicly canvassed to an extent unprecedented in the history of modern warfare. Americans had debated war before; the Mexican-American War had also been hotly disputed: Lincoln probably lost his congressional seat for seeming to oppose it, and Henry David Thoreau went to jail for refusing to pay taxes to support it. But that was only an early skirmish in the ongoing sectional conflict preceding the Civil War, and it is to the proliferation of Northern perspectives on that longer conflict, which persisted through the war years and into the aftermath, that we will look first for an understanding of how the institutions of democracy encouraged the growth of historical counterfactualism in public discourse. The possibility of civil war in a country with a large electorate and a free press—in which the two combatants would ultimately need to justify their actions to their own citizens, their future soldiers, and the foreign powers whom they hoped to interest in their causes—encouraged a torrent of future conjectural speculations.

This is not to say that hypothetical speculations about the future are themselves in the counterfactual mode; obviously, they can only refer to events that are as yet still merely in the realm of the possible, and thus there are no "facts" to which they are counter. However, in the course of time, if the sequences of events they describe are not tested in actuality and the crucial moments for testing have gone by, they are often revived as past hypothetical conjectures. For example, because the USA did not let the Southern states secede in peace, the possible consequences of their having done so remain forever unknown, neither corroborated nor invalidated by historical experience. The unused future scenarios convert easily into past-tense hypothetical conjectures, which are pursued even though the antecedent clause of the hypothesis (e.g. "If the USA had let the Southern states secede in peace . . .") contains an idea indisputably contrary to fact; so the earlier debates are crucial to understanding the later counterfactual-historical discourse, with all of its deep ambivalence about Northern victory and its constant casting about for different solutions.

Despite the many well-known incidents of mob violence against abolitionists and the suppression of their free speech, the range of expressed prewar opinions in the North about how to resolve the issues remained broad. There were Northern abolitionists in favor of dissolving the union with slaveholders: "I do not know what anti-slavery men mean by saying they are opposed to slavery, and yet for preserving the Union," William Lloyd Garrison exclaimed in 1855. "Let this slave-holding Union go; and when it goes, slavery will go down with it."[2] As far as the single issue of union was concerned, they were in substantial agreement with Southern "disunionists," followers of John C. Calhoun, who as early as 1850 were certain that North and South should be independent nations. Most people in both sections, though, thought there would be continuing compromise, although they disagreed over which compromises would be necessary. Four mainstream candidates ran for president in 1860, each envisioning a different set of alternatives for the future. And even after Lincoln was elected and the six states of the deep South resolved to "disunite" themselves from the North, war by no means seemed necessary to many north of the Mason-Dixon line. Peace Democrats, especially strong in the midwestern states, were vociferous in their opposition to the use of force; for example, Wilbur Storey predicted in an editorial for a Detroit newspaper in February of 1861 that if Lincoln sent troops "to march against the people in the South, a fire in the rear will be opened upon such which will . . . stop their march altogether."[3] In that month, too, the states of the upper South watched to see how the new administration would react to secession, seceding themselves only after Lincoln's April 15, 1861, proclamation declared the original Confederate states to be insurrectionary. And even then large numbers of Northerners thought the South should be allowed to go its own way.

Nor did the positions staked out in the years leading up to the war change much after it started; the same debate continued in the daily newspapers throughout its course. In the North, Peace Democrats kept up a constant antiwar campaign in their electioneering and through their newspapers ("fire-in-the-rear" Storey still edited the *Chicago Times* in the war years), despite a few attempts on the part of military commanders to suppress them.[4] All of the papers in the major northern cities were heavily invested in the war news, and most of them had professional correspondents in the field. War correspondents had earlier been used by a few New York papers in the Mexican-American War and by British papers in the Crimean War; it was reports from that conflict—famously excoriating the army for its ineptitude and indifference to the condition of the soldiers—that demonstrated how much of an irritant independent press correspondents could be to a state waging war. Union commanders, though, had to contend with a far larger number of newspaper reporters than had ever before descended on an army's camps, many of whom viewed the enterprise skeptically. Antiwar Democrats were only part of the problem. At the other extreme, the abolitionist wing of the Republican press (the *New York Tribune*, the *Chicago Tribune*, and the *Philadelphia Enquirer*) often carried reports and editorials that were highly critical of the way the war was actually being prosecuted, for they suspected most of Lincoln's West

Point-trained generals, some of whom were Democrats, of at least apathy and perhaps outright disloyalty. Even more moderate Republican papers, like the *New York Times* and the *Boston Journal*, which seldom editorialized against the Union generals, were certainly keen to place blame by exploring alternative tactics when the North lost battles.[5]

Thus a form of journalistic counterfactual "military criticism" came to be circulated as the daily reading of civilians. The war spurred a rapid growth in the profession of journalism, but there was as yet no agreed-upon way for the government to control information about troop movements or battle plans, let alone ways of distinguishing between official and unofficial accounts of battles. Nor was there any journalistic norm of objectivity or political neutrality. On the contrary, the expectation was that the competing Northern political factions would spin the news in their various directions and would editorialize incessantly about how battles and campaigns should have been fought. This military criticism was highly partisan, amateurish, and misinformed, but that only made it all the more riveting, for it seemed a pastime in which all citizens could participate. To guard against the worst excesses of partisanship, such as the spreading of false or badly timed information, the administration struggled to control the news from the fronts, and by 1862, it had gained considerable control over the actual reporting from the battlefields by commandeering the telegraph wires and the railroads, forcing all war correspondence through the War Office, where Secretary of War Edwin Stanton oversaw its rewriting and distribution through the Associated Press.[6] But newspapers nevertheless found unofficial sources and sought out facts that would corroborate their views: copperhead Democrats looked for evidence that the war was unwinnable and peace should be negotiated, while abolitionist Republicans tried to demonstrate that West Point generals lacked enthusiasm for the cause or even secretly supported secessionists. And there was plenty of evidence for both of these positions, so the swift conversion of future hypothetical conjectures ("If we pursue tactic X, it will lead to outcome Y") into past counterfactuals ("You see, if only we'd pursued tactic X, it would have led to outcome Y") was incessant.

An important source of information for the abolitionist press of the Republican Party—and the main vehicle for the radical Republicans' campaign against the army hierarchy—was the Congressional Joint Committee on the Conduct of the War. It was established in 1861, after repeated early Union losses shattered the optimism of Republican congressmen regarding the chances for an easy victory and prompted great distrust of the Union's military leaders; although many of its hearings were held in closed sessions, its members leaked large amounts of testimony to papers they considered friendly. A complicated three-way tug-of-war between the Congress, the Lincoln administration, and the military over who would make war policy ran through that committee's hearings. Its dominant Republicans believed that officers trained at West Point, where they had been the classmates of the treasonous Confederate officers, should not be in charge of Union forces. In one of his many counterfactual declarations Senator Benjamin Wade, for example, assured his colleagues that, "if there had been no West Point Military Academy, there would have been no rebellion. . . . That was the hot-bed from which rebellion was hatched and from thence emanated your principal traitors and conspirators."[7] Indeed radical Republicans tended to hold the view that a civilian-run army would be a better fighting force than one led by specially trained military professionals; they agreed with Congressman Owen Lovejoy, who supported the motion to found the committee with the argument that "men who have received a military education are more in the way of the success of our arms than anything else."[8] Thinking that what mattered most was the commander's personal dedication to the cause of eradicating slavery as quickly as possible, they pressed Lincoln to appoint people with the right abolitionist credentials and to remove any who had been Democrats or had no history of supporting the antislavery cause. After the Emancipation Proclamation and substantial Democratic gains in both the 1862 and 1864 elections, it seemed all the more imperative to abolitionists that they should be in charge of the war effort.

Lincoln was himself an object of suspicion to radical Republicans, both because he was a gradualist on the issue of emancipation and because he had appointed a "compound cabinet," some of whose members held opinions very far from those of the abolitionists. He also irritated the committee by not following its suggestions in appointing and removing commanders, and the committee used its hearings to promote the idea that Congress, as the branch of government most directly representative of the people, should set the agenda for the war and insure that the army comply with it. Like all presidents, Lincoln wanted to preserve his rights as commander in chief, but he also shared the committee's worry that Union generals might not fully appreciate the nature of the war, which was not the kind of conflict they'd been trained to fight. Instead of a struggle between sovereign nations, it was a rebellion within a single state, and Lincoln thought his generals had trouble understanding the very concept of a civil war. When, for example, after the crucial Union victory at Gettysburg, commanding general George Gordon Meade sent a message to his troops calling for even "greater efforts to drive from our soil every vestige of the presence of the invaders," Lincoln exclaimed, "Will our generals never get that idea out of their heads? The whole country is our soil!"[9] Lincoln, too, sometimes wondered if the generals' confusion about the status of the enemy and the proper extent of Union jurisdiction kept them from pursuing a more aggressive war. Especially in the immediate aftermath of Gettysburg, he seriously entertained the counterfactual hypothesis that General Meade might have more promptly counterattacked and pursued Lee's army if he had not thought in defensive terms about driving out an invader but had instead thought in offensive terms about rooting the rebellion out of the land.

This was one of the counterfactual suppositions underlying a protracted series of hearings held by the Joint Committee on the Conduct of the War in the winter of 1864, which investigated in great detail the actions of Meade during and after the battle. Meade had been given the command of the Army of the Potomac only a few days before encountering Robert E. Lee's Army of Northern Virginia at Gettysburg, and he was not the sort of general the committee's leaders supported; he was a West Point man, apolitical, and not well-connected in Washington. The abolitionists wanted his predecessor, General Joseph Hooker (a Republican), reinstated, and so they tried to discredit Meade, arguing that he had not really wanted to engage the enemy at Gettysburg and had not followed up with a vigorous counterattack or pursuit once Lee's army was repulsed. The latter charge echoed Lincoln's earlier private feelings, but the president had already decided not to replace Meade and was unresponsive when, after hearing only a few witnesses, the Republican leaders of the committee unofficially recommended the general's removal. The committee therefore pressed on, eventually calling Meade himself as a witness as well as other West Point–trained generals, so that finally all three parties to the dispute over military authority were involved: the committee asserting its control over the military; the administration resisting the committee's intrusion; and the professional soldiers defending the principle that only the commanders in the field were competent to decide what strategies and tactics should be adopted.

The committee's method resembled that of the tradition of military criticism, the origins of which we examined in chapter 1, with its incessant questioning of whether victories should really be credited to the commander's foresight, planning, and bravery and its focus on taking maximum advantage of a situation. Just as Carl von Clausewitz examined Napoleon's 1797 options and determined that he had not gone far enough into Austrian territory, the committee interrogated numerous witnesses and Meade himself about his failure to pursue and destroy Lee's army. Each witness was asked to give a précis of his experience at Gettysburg, but the questioning that followed was almost entirely in the conditional mode, especially when the topic of the counterattack-that-should-have-been arose:

> Question: Under the circumstances, as you understand them, could there have been any great hazard to our army in venturing an engagement [on the banks of the Potomac]? (46)
>
> Question: Our troops were in good condition and eager to renew the fight.... And the enemy were on the bank of the river, so that it is ... a very plain case that they should have been vigorously attacked? (51)
>
> Question: Was not such overcaution well calculated to weaken the confidence of the army in the ability and resolution of their officers? (93)
>
> Question: As a military man, do you think it possible for us ever to conquer the rebellion by defensive operations alone? (144)
>
> Question: If we had made a reconnaissance in force, as was suggested, and had been repulsed, would any serious disaster have followed us? ... Suppose, on the other hand, we had broken their lines, what would have been the consequence to them? (201–2)[10]

The committee members began by calling witnesses already known to be hostile to Meade, whose answers to these questions were emphatic and uncomplicated, if a little short on technical particulars; Major General Daniel Sickles, who was not a West Point–trained professional but had joined the army as a commander of volunteers, assured the committee: "If we could whip them at Gettysburg, as we did, we could much more easily whip a running and demoralized army, seeking a retreat which was cut off by a swollen river; and if they could march after being whipped, we certainly could march after winning a battle" (46). But as the sessions went on, the committee was eventually obliged also to hear members of Meade's staff and other professional officers with a fuller knowledge of his motives and intentions and a greater respect for the ways in which local conditions shape decisions.

QUESTION: Immediately after the final repulse of the enemy . . . were we not in a condition to have attacked the enemy, and why was not that done?

ANSWER [BY BRIGADIER GENERAL HUNT]: I think we might have attacked the enemy there if the troops in hand had been formed so that they could push forward at once. But our troops were very roughly handled where they were attacked. I thought that the troops that were on the right of the point of attack, near the 2d corps, and which moved out beyond their lines, and continued to move down the front of our line after the first assault was repulsed might have joined in an attack upon the right of the enemy, of course taking the chances of his position. On the evening of the 2d of July, when the re-enforcements came up, just at dusk, I thought it would be well to move forward. But on the evening of the 3d I did not feel so positive about it by any means, because I did not see a disposable force sufficiently large, immediately on the ground, to attack the enemy in position in those woods, where I knew, from my experience of that day, that they had more than one hundred guns in position, a much larger force of artillery than we could bring to bear against them. And they had been planted behind that wood long enough to have made such defenses as were found so effective where the 12th corps was. It was one of those cases where it was a question of risk and opportunity, and the general commanding must decide for himself whether he will run the risk or not. (314)

Responses like this one thwarted the committee's purposes not only by concluding that generals needed the authority to weigh risks and opportunities but also by overwhelming the congressmen with complex and detailed knowledge of the dynamics on the battlefield. The professional military testimony was useless for the counterfactualism the majority of the committee was willing to practice. Composed mainly of lawyers, the committee just wanted to hear that another line of action was possible, which would have kept Lee from escaping with his army to Virginia. They were not particularly interested in the exact feasibility of the options and were more than content simply to have them asserted. In their questions, they reason like plaintiffs trying to show that Meade was negligent in allowing the escape; his action was exceptional because he had Lee trapped and did not press his advantage as, they assume, a normally competent and sufficiently energetic general would have. But most of the career military men described instead the shifting alternatives and the precariousness of the positions; they produced the fog of war. The officers' contempt for the committee is often palpable in their terse responses to naive questions: no, an attack could not have been mounted at night; no, a commander could not begin an attack just as a probe and then abruptly reverse it.[11] Military criticism, their manner implies, is not to be attempted by mere civilians. The disdain of the brass, though, did not deter the committee, which finally produced a report censuring Meade in the spring of 1865, when it was no longer of interest to anyone, having been overtaken by such events as the assassination of Lincoln and the surrender of Robert E. Lee.

Nevertheless, the proceedings of the War Committee reveal the way historical counterfactual narratives come to be constructed in democratic political processes. When word of Meade's victory at Gettysburg was first reported, the expectation that Lee could be finished off, bringing the war to a speedy end, was publicly expressed in a wide variety of media, and when Lee then escaped unhindered, there was immediate disappointment. But Meade was not publicly blamed until the committee's struggle with the executive branch intensified.[12] The Lincoln administration's judgment of Meade's delay might have been as negative as that of the War Committee, but they had nothing to gain from replacing him with the equally dilatory Hooker, whom they had removed for his own reluctance to take the offensive against Lee. Constantly changing the command of the Army of the Potomac, the administration thought, gave the impression of unsteadiness and indecision and lowered the morale of the troops. So they stuck by Meade, which prolonged the hearings and led to more hostile hypotheses about his behavior and motives in the press. Both in the hearings and in other venues, the anti-Meade faction tried to craft a consistent narrative in which all of the general's actions leading up to and following the battle could be explained by his reluctance to fight Lee, which was then traced to his putative copperhead leanings.[13] Their total counterfactual narrative was therefore something like the following: if the Republican Congress had been allowed to keep West Point Democrats from commanding federal armies, Lee would have been vigorously pursued and the war would have been over in 1863. A battle had been won, to be sure, but it seemed more important that an opportunity had been lost.

The committee's version of Gettysburg has not survived in critical military history, where the controversy over its denouement was soon made into an illustration of a more all-pervasive strategic point: "It will always remain a striking instance of the controlling influence exercised in this war by defensive positions, that the two decisive points of this great campaign were mainly determined by the simple incident of securing the defensive," wrote William Swinton in the first critical history of the Army of the Potomac (1866).[14] Nevertheless, the War Committee's attempt to organize the controversy against the background of an alternate war—shorter, more energetically prosecuted, and less costly in lives—not only illustrates the link between historical counterfactuals and wartime partisan politics but also lets us see the making of a trope in Northern Civil War remembrance: we were losing even when we were winning. The actual war was routinely diverging from the course it should have been taking, so even in victory some preferable, possible alternative was lost. Gettysburg in particular continues to fascinate counterfactualists. Its imperfections and incompleteness invite constant imaginative revision, and in this regard it stands for the Civil War conflict as a whole, lamented as it was being fought and regretted in recollection. For most of American history, it has been remembered in a pall of melancholy retrospective dissatisfaction, which pervades the accounts of the victors.

To be sure, the melancholy tone of Civil War histories was by no means always paired with counterfactual imaginings; indeed, Southern commentators on the war quite soon constructed an ideology that cast their defeat in a predetermined tragic mold, precluding alternative outcomes. In personal memoirs and regimental histories, theirs became the "lost cause," noble but doomed, overwhelmed by the sheer size of the Union fighting force and its superior industrial base. Victims of the dynamics of modernity, they had never even had a chance to prevail. In time, this lost-cause interpretation spawned its own preferred counterfactual hypotheses—"If we had been allowed to secede . . ."; "If we had been left to ourselves after the war . . ."—emerging as the dominant American belief at the end of the nineteenth century. However, in the immediate aftermath of the war, the lost-cause idea provided the balm of an elevated, tragic narrative mainly for Southerners. Meanwhile, the North also had its own providential accounts, including Lincoln's famous claim in his second inaugural address, delivered as the war drew to a close, that it had been God's punishment of the whole nation for the sin of slavery:

> He gives to both North and South, this terrible war, as the woe due to those by whom the offence came. . . . Fondly do we hope—fervently do we pray—that this mighty scourge of war may speedily pass away. Yet, if God wills that it continue, until all the wealth piled by the bondman's two hundred and fifty years of unrequited toil shall be sunk, and until every drop of blood drawn with the lash, shall be paid by

another drawn with the sword, as was said three thousand years ago, so still it must be said "the judgments of the Lord, are true and righteous altogether."

Lincoln's address—contrite, mournful, eschewing triumphalism, and uniting North and South in guilt as well as in exculpatory suffering—is yet another way in which the winners presented themselves as the losers. If we were winning, it was only because we were atoning for *our* sins and submitting to God's punishment. The North was not the righteous instrument of God's justice, as in the *Battle Hymn of the Republic*, but one of the culprits.

As complex and even magnanimous as Lincoln's address was, many have seen it as a harbinger of less admirable things to come, namely, the defeat of those who wanted a true reconstruction of Southern society and a clear national policy of racial equality. The sorry outcome of the North's reluctance to act like a victor was that, by the turn of the century, it had, in fact, lost the peace. The story is well known: President Andrew Johnson's initial mild reconstruction effort seemed to signal that the South would be allowed to make its own internal postwar social and political arrangements, and the result was that the Southern states replicated their antebellum political institutions and went on to pass a series of "black codes," which restricted the mobility of the freedmen and even reattached them to their former masters.[15] These attempts to reverse the effects of emancipation convinced many in the North that the South was unwilling to accept the consequences of its defeat, and after the midterm election of 1864, the augmented radical Republicans in Congress undertook a more robust Reconstruction effort: a Civil Rights Act was passed over the president's veto, in which a state's ratification of the Fourteenth Amendment was made a requirement for reentry into the Union, the Fifteenth Amendment outlawing the denial of the vote on the grounds of race or religion, was passed and ratified, and the activities of the Freedman's Bureau, which were mainly directed at education and employment, were extended. But by the mid-1870s, white supremacist paramilitary organizations in the South had emerged to intimidate freedmen, in 1877 the last federal troops were withdrawn from the South, and Southern states began systematically subverting the Fifteenth Amendment. Reconstruction was tacitly repudiated in the 1876 national election, and the federal government began its long career of appealing to the doctrine of states' rights, using constitutional arguments to justify its refusal to protect the franchise, life, and property of the freedmen and their descendants.

COUNTERFACTUALISM IN THE JIM CROW PERIOD

In the postwar period, then, the North began as a timid, apologetic victor, passed through a phase of reforming zeal, and ended as an opportunistic supporter of segregationist Southern institutions. No wonder some disappointed Northerners went so far as to say that history had reversed the outcome of the conflict: the South really had won. Perhaps the most explicit and extended exposition of this belief came from the writer Albion Tourgée, a Northerner who had lived through Reconstruction in North Carolina. His best-selling 1878 novel, *A Fool's Errand*, was a thinly fictionalized account of his own struggle to resist the reversal of the war's outcome, and he often describes his experience explicitly as the uncanny sensation of living in a counterfactual reality. For example, one of the novel's Southern characters, who supported the Union during the war and by 1870 finds himself openly persecuted by his Southern neighbors, complains to the narrator, a former Union officer,

> I can't understan' it, Colonel. They say our side whipped; that the Union won, an' the Confederacy lost: an' yit here they be a-puttin' it on tu me like they all possessed day arter day, an' abusin' my wife an' children too bad for white folks to hear about, jes cos I was a Union man. There must be some mistake, Colonel, about the matter. Either 'twas the t'other folks that surrendered at Appomattox, or else you an' I was on t'other side, an' hev jes been a-dreamin' that we was Yank an' Union all this time![16]

Like the protagonist of Frank Williams's *Hallie Marshall: A True Daughter of the South* (1900), Tourgée's abolitionist characters seem to have awakened in an alternate-history reality, where "'twas the t'other folks that surrendered at Appomattox." But in *A Fool's Errand*, it was the actual history of the aftermath that produced the bizarre reversal; no what-if thought experiment was necessary. We might also think of Tourgée's ironic use of the counterfactual mode as descending from the military criticism practiced by the abolitionist Congressional Committee after Gettysburg, for they contain the same message: we have won, but we are losing for want of zeal in the prosecution of our cause.

A Fool's Errand is not an alternate-history novel, for it is undergirded by no hypothetical premise. Instead, it uses the metaphor of counterfactualism—reality is *like* a counterfactual history—to track the dynamic of a historical reversal. The metaphor of suddenly finding oneself in the alternate world underlines the swiftness and thoroughness of the North's capitulation to the will of the putatively conquered. Moreover, for the purposes of our analysis, it marks a historical moment when abolitionists could still register the wide discrepancy between what their victory should have meant—a reconstructed South where freedmen were granted the full rights of citizenship—and what it actually meant—a USA in which racial inequality became the national norm. Finally, it helps us to see a connection between counterfactualizing and protecting the principles of abolitionism from the sordid actual history of their betrayal. This is a dynamic we earlier encountered in Renouvier's *Uchronie*: by imagining simultaneous parallel phases in the evolution of an animating idea, such as Republicanism or racial equality, the concept is rhetorically liberated from its historical decline and preserved as a source of energy for future use. Counterfactuals keep the *cause* of racial justice and equality in a realm of possibility, by which readers can orient themselves amid the seemingly chaotic reversals of current events.

Tourgée's counterfactual imagination, though, does not always move in an upward direction; he also sometimes notes that the war might have had an even worse outcome. For example, while supporting his argument that the North must rule as a conqueror to achieve "the results she fought for," the narrator hypothesizes a dystopian version of the present: "Suppose the South had been triumphant, and had overwhelmed and determined to hold the North? Before now, a thoroughly organized system of provincial government would have been securely established. There would have been no hesitation, no subterfuge, no pretense of restoration, because the people of the South are born rulers,—aggressives, who, having made up their minds to attain a certain end, adopt the means most likely to secure it. In this the North fails. She hesitates, palters, shirks" (153). And this scenario of complete Southern victory must not be counted out as a future possibility. "The South has lost—lost her men, her money, her slaves," we are told, but nevertheless "the most reckless and unworthy of those who led in the war will again come to the front" (154). Their steadfast, fanatical purposefulness, we are warned, will be a marked contrast to the weakness of the Southern Republicans and freedmen, abandoned by the federal power, against whom they will direct their vengeance.

In the timeline of the story, this prediction is supposed to have been made in 1868, ten years before the novel's appearance, and contemporary readers would have recognized it as already fulfilled, like a series of other warnings in the same chapter: "The prestige of the Federal soldier will begin to wane throughout the land. In the course of another decade, one will almost be ashamed to confess that he wore the blue. On the other hand, the glory of the Confederate leader will hourly wax greater and brighter" (153). The novel then goes on to describe the rise of the Ku Klux Klan, the Southern states' toleration of terror, dispossession, and lynching, and even the takeover of the Northern press by Southern propaganda: "The most amazing thing connected with this matter . . . was the fact that the press of the North, almost without exception, echoed the clamor and invective of the Southern journals" (158). Near the end of the story (when another seven years are supposed to have passed), the narrator again calls on the federal government to reverse the historical reversal, "The impotence of the freedman, the ignorance of the poor-white, the arrogance of the late master, are all the result of national power exercised in restraint of free thought, free labor, and free speech. Now, let the Nation undo the evil it has permitted and encouraged" (346). Undoing the federal government's surrender to the South, though, hardly seems likely to the narrator, and his pessimistic prediction is delivered with greater conviction: "The North is disunited: a part will adhere to the South for the sake of power; and, just as before the civil war, the South will again dominate and control the nation" (346).

Through this complicated diachronic pattern, in which future-conjectural warnings go unheeded and turn into past counterfactuals, the novel stresses that the war is not over, which is both the bad news and the good news. On the one hand, since the North cannot perceive that the military combat was a mere skirmish rather than a decisive blow against the enemy, it continues to lose by refusing to press its advantage. But on the other hand, the fact that the war endures implies that there is still time for victory. Thus, although its counterfactual discourse is only intermittent, *A Fool's Errand* displays the connection between the perception that history has already been reversed—both through the inversion of power relations between victor and vanquished and through the reversion of history to an earlier stage—and later alternate-history imaginings of how we lost the war and yet might still win it.

By the time the first analytical counterfactual essay on the Civil War was published in 1903, Tourgée's pessimistic predictions had been realized in full. The essay was a short magazine piece by Ernest Crosby titled "If the South Had Been Allowed to Go," and before analyzing it I want to measure the distance between the discourse surrounding it and the one that had informed *A Fool's Errand* twenty-five years earlier. The abandonment of Northern interference on behalf of the freedmen and the turn toward "reunification" grounded in the nation's acceptance and even imitation of the South's disenfranchisement and terroristic control of black Americans was complete by the turn of the century. Emblematic of the "reunification" period as a whole was the Supreme Court's 1896 decision in *Plessy v. Ferguson*, which upheld the constitutionality of state laws requiring racial segregation in private businesses and established the segregationists' "separate but equal" principle as a doctrine of national law, which would stand until the 1950s. The federal legal reaction against Reconstruction, though, started earlier (the court's 1883 decision in the civil rights cases struck down the Civil Rights Act of 1875) and went on well into the first decade of the new century (*Giles v. Harris* legalized the de facto exclusion of blacks from voting roles in 1903). As Michael T. Gilmore has shown in stunning detail, reunification involved a willingness on the part of Northerners to accept the South's version of the history leading up to and following the Civil War.[17] To be sure, Lincoln was a revered martyr in the North, and the legitimacy of saving the union generally went unquestioned. Indeed, that goal merged with the fin de siècle aim of cultural reunification, while Reconstruction, with its ambition of racial equality, was retroactively substituted for secession as a cause of national disunity. Thus, while still mourning their own war dead, white Northerners came to share the South's nostalgia for an idyllic plantation culture and adopted the lost-cause analysis of its defeat. The nation as a whole came to accept, even share, the increasingly institutionalized policies of racial segregation, including the denial of civil and political rights and tolerance of the violence against black citizens. The revisionist climate at the end of the nineteenth century made the regretful tone of *A Fool's Errand* obsolete; fewer radical Republicans like Tourgée were left to object when the federal government legalized racial disenfranchisement and segregation. Since the South's victory was complete and Reconstruction generally despised, a novel like Frank Williams's *Hallie Marshall*, with its alternate-history fantasy of Southern victory and paternalistic slavery, could appear without causing any stir.

No one would accuse Ernest Crosby—the liberal Northerner, pacifist, anti-imperialist biographer of William Lloyd Garrison—of sharing the prevailing nostalgia about the antebellum South, and yet he claimed in "If the South Had Been Allowed to Go" that the North had lost its Republican soul when it *won* the Civil War. Crosby traced "almost all the pressing evils of the day" to that conflict, including the national debt, an epidemic of crime, class and civic strife of every kind, speculation, plutocracy, physical degeneracy, and—especially in the wake of the Spanish-American War—American imperialism. All of this, he argued, might have been avoided if the South had been allowed to go. And more importantly—and counterintuitively—the freedmen would have been truly emancipated instead of being subjected to civil discrimination and violence. He gives the following brief though enduring outline of "what the upshot of peaceful Secession might have been":

> It is easy to predict . . . that a nation built upon the principle of free secession would not have remained long intact. It is clear, too, that slavery could not have lasted long along the Northern border. . . . If nothing but an ordinary boundary-line had separated the slave States from free soil, a general exodus of slaves would have begun, and ere long the border States would of necessity have ceased to be slave States. With slavery extinct, the reason for their separation from the North would have ceased, and their commercial interests would have demanded reunion with the United States, while the kindly action of the North in permitting them to secede without interference would have left no hostile feelings in their minds to prevent such a reunion. With the border States once annexed, a new boundary would have been created along their southern frontier, and here again history would repeat itself, until the nation was again one.[18]

This, he explains, would have been "the natural evolution of the race difficulty" as well as the cure for disunion.

Crosby's was the first of several early twentieth-century counterfactual analyses by Northerners arguing that the racial situation in the South was so bad that it could not have been worse and *would have been better* if the Confederate states had seceded. He was the first to imagine a victorious South as the fulfillment of the abolitionists' dream. Because it was a *war*, the pacifist Crosby insisted, the Civil War "did not settle the race question, but merely aggravated it." No war could have realized the abolitionist aims of his heroes, "and now, after forty years, we are beginning to learn that the Negro has yet to be emancipated" (871). He then states succinctly a counterfactual hypothesis that has remained in circulation to this day: "If the South had been permitted to secede, slavery would have died a natural death, the Southerners would have felt that they had consented to its demise, and they would have accepted the new order with that attitude of acquiescence which is necessary to the success of any social experiment" (871).[19] Crosby's causal logic is clear: if there had been no war—and therefore no Reconstruction—then there would have been no resentment and no reactionary racism. By locating his nexus at the moment of the North's declaration of war, he could represent everything following from that mistaken decision as destined to failure. We have lost, he concluded, by having fought the war in the first place.

The counterfactualism here follows some familiar patterns. We recognize the ironic plot, dating back to seventeenth- and eighteenth-century examples, in which the agents of history—here the Northern unionists—defeat their own purposes by the very success of their zealous methods.[20] In Crosby's later hagiographic biography of Garrison, moreover, we can see his self-conscious revival of prewar future conjectures as the basis of his counterfactualizing: he insists that the abolitionists had always known war would be counterproductive, and thus his analysis, rather than that of a hardline Reconstructionist like Tourgée, maintains the true spirit of abolitionism. He quotes Garrison's "No union with slave holders" slogan, conveniently ignoring the fact that Garrison eventually expressed support for the Union war effort. Using the well-worn counterfactualist method of pressing his abolitionist heroes into a greater degree of consistency than actual history allowed them, Crosby depicts both Garrison and the abolitionist activist and editor Horace Greeley as men who had all along seen the fruitlessness of the war. He calls Greeley's putative advice about the seceding states—"Let the erring sisters go"—"the words, and the only words, of wisdom" spoken by a Northerner at the outbreak of the war.[21] Garrison, we're told, must privately have disapproved of the war because on principle he opposed forcing men to remain in political unions not of their choosing; he accuses unscrupulous politicians, without any real regard for emancipation, of forcing war on the abolitionists. Indeed, Crosby makes Garrison into a timeless seer, rather than a constrained historical actor, who was not only innocent of fomenting or supporting war but was also prescient about the long-term results: "If Garrison were alive and could visit the South to-day and read 'Up from Slavery' [Booker T. Washington's 1901 autobiography], 'The Leopard's Spots' and 'The Negro a Beast' [Thomas Dixon's works, illustrative of the contemporary South's racism], he would find sufficient reason for congratulating himself upon his course. Slavery was a crying evil . . . but it was abolished the wrong way" (122). The biography comes close to being a frustrated theodicy, in which Garrison is the God who knows eternally that "the race question" could only be settled by peaceful and voluntary means, but the stubborn, short-sighted mortals refused to obey him, and history wandered into the wrong path.

Crosby's hypothesis that it would have been better for American race relations, especially for black Americans, if the South had been allowed to secede was later transformed into the proposition that it would have been preferable if the South had *won* the war. The arguments for the eventual necessity of the South's emancipating its own slaves were repurposed to demonstrate that Southern victory would have been the next best thing to peaceful secession. During and after World War I, the Ku Klux Klan was revivified and even glamorized by its depiction in the 1915 film *Birth of a Nation*, which D. W. Griffith adapted from the Thomas Dixon works Crosby had cited as proof of the region's growing bigotry. Pointing to increases in lynching and other forms of violent suppression of blacks, antiracist and anti-vigilante groups, including African American organizations, began a national campaign against the Klan and even succeeded in introducing a bill in Congress to force states to crack down on the organization and prosecute its crimes. White brutality against blacks therefore became a well-publicized national disgrace at just the time when American ambitions for world leadership were growing. As the nation headed for the seventieth anniversary of the Civil War in 1930, the search for an alternative Southern history, one that would not have produced mob rule, revived, so when a few national periodicals invited contributors to speculate on possible alternative outcomes to the war, several writers responded by continuing Crosby's line of argument. This time, though, the favorite scenario was the victory of the CSA.

One of these, a 1930 essay by H. L. Mencken titled "The Calamity of Appomattox," argued that the defeat and subsequent migration from the region by the Virginian "aristocracy" caused the horrors perpetrated by the Southern rabble: "If the war had gone with the Confederates no such vermin would be in the saddle," he explained; "nor would there be any sign below the Potomac of their chief contributions to American *Kultur*—Ku Kluxry, political ecclesiasticism, [negro]-baiting, and the more homicidal variety of wowserism."[22] Mencken draws on the cliché that the Civil War was a struggle between Puritans and Cavaliers; ever the iconoclastic contrarian, though, he provocatively takes aim at what he considers the negative consequences of Puritan victory: "No doubt the Confederates, victorious, would have abolished slavery by the middle 80s. They were headed that way before the war, and the more sagacious of them were all in favor of it. But they were in favor . . . on sound economic grounds, and not on the brummagem moral grounds which persuaded the North. . . . In human history a moral victory is always a disaster, for it debauches and degrades both the victor and the vanquished. The triumph of sin in 1865 would have stimulated and helped to civilize both sides" (199). Despite the shocking phraseology, the sentiment was not at all unusual; one of the things that had come to mark the Civil War as wrongheaded was the Northern abolitionists' claim that their cause was neither regional nor national but a matter of universal morality, that it was indeed a holy war. Thus the very thing that had once justified the struggle and its aftermath in the minds of abolitionists—that it was selflessly undertaken to free others—became the sign of its delusional faultiness. The putative "fanaticism" of Reconstruction (i.e., black enfranchisement) was especially thought to have been driven by mere self-righteousness and opportunism, to which the adjective "hypocritical" was inevitably joined.

Long before the 1930s, Reconstruction had come to be viewed retrospectively as a program of punitive measures directed against former slaveholders, rather than as an attempt to benefit former slaves, who were usually represented in both the North and South as unready for civil and political rights and therefore the ignorant pawns of unscrupulous "carpetbaggers." Mencken's prose instances the seamless transition from the so-called violence of Reconstruction to white mob rule: "First the carpetbaggers ravaged the land, and then it fell into the hands of the native white trash, already so poor that war and Reconstruction could not make them any poorer" (197). His preference for "economic" over ethical motivations also echoes an analysis that, as we'll see in the next section, had become the basis of a counterfactual consensus among American historians by the 1930s: "no doubt" economic forces would have made Southern slavery inefficient sometime in the 1880s. Indeed, the idea was so frequently repeated and so often coupled with condemnations of Reconstruction that the logical interdependence of the two notions emerged: *because* manumission was inevitable in the "natural" course of things, Reconstruction should be thought of as a counterproductive policy, which only bred impossible expectations and murderous resentments.

Once again the irony of unintended consequences dominates the plot, but for Mencken the defeat of the North would also have constituted poetic justice, for the very moralism of its claims deserved to be chastened. By this logic, of course, all campaigns claiming to have some higher aim than immediate self-interest were futile, and the actual failure of Northern self-righteousness, represented by the collapse of Reconstruction, was merely the reassertion of the natural course of things. The details of Mencken's alternative South place it in opposition to a contemporary North conceived as the inheritor of the Puritan spirit; the victorious, aristocratic South would, he argues, have been a counterweight not to the North of class strife and social dislocation, which we've seen in other alternate-history fantasies, but to the North of Progressive Era moral reform, including Prohibition: "The University of Virginia would be what Jefferson intended it to be, and no shouting Methodist would haunt its campus. Richmond would be, not the dull suburb of nothing that it is now, but a beautiful and consoling second-rate capital, comparable to Budapest, Brussels, Stockholm or The Hague. And all of us . . . would be making frequent leaps over the Potomac to drink the sound red wine there and breathe the free air" (198). The connection between an aristocratic, victorious South without a KKK and one without Prohibition was not a great stretch; a 1926 book called *Klansmen: Guardians of Liberty* by Alma Bridwell White depicted the Klan as "The Defender of the 18th Amendment."[23] In Mencken's piece, the KKK, the shouting Methodists, the temperance movement, and the canting Reconstructionists are lumped together as intolerant crusaders, and his aristocratic South would have precluded them all.

Mencken, therefore, contributes a new twist to the usual ironic plotline: he claims, like Crosby, that the Northern abolitionists have in actuality lost their cause by their methods of achieving it, *and* he then adds that they have reproduced their own moral vindictiveness in the monstrous shape of the Ku Klux Klan. The good cause not only undoes itself ("in human history a moral victory is always a disaster . . .") but also spawns an opposing zealotry, which locks both sides into intransigent moralism. Other contemporary counterfactual reflections on the sorry state of the American South, all published in Northern magazines, make the same point: history had already reversed the outcome of the Civil War by creating an anti-type of progress, a region rife with the very vices the North had hoped to abolish, but which nevertheless presents its mob violence as a holy crusade.[24] One must, therefore, imagine a Northern loss in order to visualize either an enlightened South or a better North.

The early 1930s were, of course, experienced by many as a time of seeming historical reversals: worldwide financial collapse and depression, democratic political arrangements under siege, and signs of revived militarism and international conflict all presented examples of what might have been avoided had the Civil War turned out differently. For Mencken, mob violence and crusading bigotry in the South were American echoes of fascist mobilizations in Germany and Italy.[25] We shouldn't be surprised, therefore, to see at least one non-American writer focusing on the international consequences of the Civil War. Winston Churchill, in his 1930 piece "If Lee Had Not Won the Battle of Gettysburg," explicitly imagined that Southern victory would have created a world in which the contemporary economic and political downward spiral would never have occurred. The best known of the era's victorious-Confederacy essays, it was the first that we can call a full-blown alternate history: an imaginative realization of a single line of development from a particular counterfactual premise to a substantial alternate reality. Originally published in *Scribner's*, it was anthologized the next year in a popular collection of "what-if?" essays and stories, which gave it a longer shelf life than the other counterfactual magazine pieces from those years. It may seem like cheating to introduce Churchill here among Northern American writers, but the story was, after all, solicited by a New York–based magazine, and in the early 1930s Churchill led a remarkably peripatetic transatlantic life, spending months at a time in his mother's home city of New York and trying to pay his debts by writing for American periodicals. Perhaps the most important reason for including it here, though, is the influence Churchill's story had on subsequent American writers: he gave them a new counterfactual Gettysburg, an alternate Great Emancipator, and a Southern victory with global ramifications, all of which are still common features in Civil War alternate histories.

Counterfactualism was a settled habit of Churchill's thought by 1930: he had been educated at the Royal Military Academy at Sandhurst, served in the Boer War, and was first lord of the Admiralty under Asquith; moreover, he had written both military journalism and military history, in which he happily practiced the art of critical speculation.[26] It stands to reason, therefore, that he would write the most formally self-conscious and playful of the period's Civil War counterfactuals, and his story comments most obviously on the trope of ironic reversal. Even the title reverses the usual reversal: instead of asking what would have happened if Lee had won—reversing actuality—he asks what would have happened if Lee *had not* won—imagining that we are already in the reversed world and, therefore, the "counterfactual speculations" are really comments on our actual history while the actual history alluded to is counterfactual. Churchill, moreover, begins his story with reminders that this is an imitation—almost a pastiche—of other counterfactual histories:

> The quaint conceit of imagining what would have happened if some important or unimportant event had settled itself differently, has become so fashionable that I am encouraged to enter upon an absurd speculation. . . . Once a great victory is won it dominates not only the future but the past. . . . The hopes that were shattered, the passions that were quelled, the sacrifices that were ineffectual are all swept out of the land of reality. Still it may amuse an idle hour, and perhaps serve

as a corrective to undue complacency, if . . . we meditate for a spell upon the debts we owe to those Confederate soldiers who by a deathless feat of arms broke the Union front at Gettysburg and laid open a fair future to the world.

It always amuses historians and philosophers to pick out the tiny things, the sharp agate points, on which the ponderous balance of destiny turns.[27]

From motivating the speculation as both a safeguard against deterministic habits of mind and an exercise in judgment to noting the preference for *petites causes* ("sharp agate points"), this opening announces its mastery of the genre with a slightly facetious aplomb. We read everything that follows, therefore, as the product of a dramatis persona who supposedly speaks from a foreign "land of reality" but nevertheless within a thoroughly familiar world of discourse.

The large arc of the plot is as follows: a few small changes in the Southern tactics at Gettysburg were the first steps in a long process leading ultimately, in the twentieth century, to the establishment of a three-nation coalition, the English-Speaking Association (ESA), comprising the British Empire, the USA and the CSA. This ESA so dominates world politics by 1930 that it single-handedly averts the First World War and the onset of the Great Depression, both of which are explored only as disastrous counterfactual possibilities. The method of reversing the reversals, the ironization of the ironies of history, as usual turns history back to its proper orientation: the Confederate victory forces Gladstone and Disraeli, for example, to change their party allegiances, bringing them into alignment with their true political characters. The grandest of Churchill's turnarounds, though, is his undoing of the American Revolution, which is reversed with the founding of the ESA at the moment when Britain intervenes to keep the CSA and the USA from entering into a second war: "Henceforward the peoples of the British Empire and of . . . the 'Re-United States' deemed themselves to be members of one body and inheritors of one estate" (191). In the long-run, therefore, the victory of the CSA leads to a new form of North-South unity and merger with the empire, so Churchill's vision exceeds the provincial American outlook of previous Civil War counterfactual scenarios, and later alternate-history writers, especially novelists, have imitated Churchill by altering the Civil War as a mere preliminary to much grander sagas, replete with continuing wars and dueling empires.

Before Churchill's essay swells into its enthusiasm for a world-saving transatlantic British-American polity, though, it follows the domestic script of the American essay writers: the slaves were freed by the CSA and life was better for them there than in the actual American South. His CSA, indeed, is founded on the ironic undoing of Southern racial oppression by a Southern victory, since it is the abolition declaration delivered by General Lee on his triumphant arrival in Washington, DC—"the victorious Confederacy would pursue no policy towards the African negroes, which was not in harmony with the moral conceptions of Western Europe"—that makes an alliance between the South and Great Britain, breaks the North's naval blockade, and definitively ends the war. Lee-the-emancipator has been a staple of alternate Southern history ever since, and the general's actual antislavery sentiments have been frequently invoked to support the appropriateness of such a destiny. Churchill also follows his American contemporaries in getting rid of Reconstruction; in keeping with his theme of world salvation through "English-speaking" reunification, he depicts a CSA that learns from "the long statecraft of Britain in dealing with alien and more primitive populations": "There was not only the need to declare the new fundamental relationship between master and servant, but the creation for the liberated slaves of institutions suited to their own cultural development and capable of affording them a different, yet honourable status in a commonwealth, destined eventually to become almost world-wide" (179). Churchill contrasts the racial harmony following voluntary CSA slave emancipation, accompanied by no "idiotic assertion of racial equality," with the dreadful state of things had a victorious North imposed liberty: "We might have seen the sorry farce of black legislatures attempting to govern their former masters. Upon the rebound from this there must inevitably have been a strong reassertion of local white supremacy. By one device or another the franchises accorded to the negroes would have been taken from them.... And many a warm-hearted philanthropist would have found his sojourn in the South no better than 'A Fool's Errand'" (179–80). Once again we read the truism that the North defeated its own purposes by precipitously inverting the social order, but the device of making the historical defeat of Reconstruction a matter of speculation adds to the sense of its inescapability; even if it had never actually happened, one could reason from general principles that it was bound to happen, given certain "obvious" facts, like the inequality of the races, the natural resentment of conquered people, and the predictable reassertion of white power. He echoes the Northern American writers by implying his disapproval of the extralegal means by which black Americans have been disenfranchised while seeming to assert that there was no alternative.

The uniquely Churchillian part of the above quotation, though, is the concluding allusion to Tourgée's book, which at once indicates an acknowledgment of the Northern Reconstructionists' laudable, if quixotic, motivations, and reminds us, once again, of the piece's intertextuality. Churchill's story, with its awareness of the state of the discourse, seems to sum up the development of Northern Civil War counterfactual thinking from the 1870s through the 1930s. Tourgée may have been its starting place, but by the 1930s the current of thought and feeling ran in opposition to his. The later writers admit that history did reverse itself, but they blame the attempt on Reconstruction rather than on the failure to complete it; and they admit it would be desirable to undo the reversal, but not by a repetition of the original mistake of strong federal intervention. The alternate histories of Crosby and Mencken may briefly imagine other Souths with prosperous and pacific people, cosmopolitanism, and even good local wine, but the writers conceive no way of making progress toward such visions. Instead, they use alternate history to assert that the opportunity for better race relations has ended, and they thus might be said to convert Tourgée's consciousness of defeat into a settled defeatism. Finally Churchill, assuming an attitude of superiority to all of these provincial Americans, imagines a program for "improving" the situation: British Empire–style legal institutionalization of second-class citizenship, a version of Jim Crow legitimized to remove both the promise of equality and the threat of racial confrontation. Cooperation among English-speaking nations was a favorite theme of Churchill's throughout his career; he even served as the chairman of the English-Speaking Union to promote such cross-Atlantic solidarity in the early 1920s, and his fantasy of reabsorbing North America might seem continuous with such efforts. But the reunion imagined here is an extension of the North-South agreement to sanction official segregation: an authorized inequality of citizenship based on race, Churchill implies, might have become part of an alliance spreading "almost world-wide."[28]

This style of Civil War alternate history had only one last gasp before the civil rights era made it obsolete, after which the form simply disappeared for several decades. In 1960, for the centenary of the war's commencement, *Look* magazine commissioned the popular historical-novel writer MacKinlay Kantor to write a serial narrative with the premise (and title) *If the South Had Won the Civil War*, and the resulting piece illustrates just how unready alternate-history writers were to adjust to the realities of the civil rights era. Commissioned in preparation for the centennial of the conflict, Kantor's was the longest and most elaborate American alternate history to have appeared by 1960, and it came out in book form the following year. It developed both a detailed alternate military history and an account of the continuing political history of the two nations, USA and CSA, tracing their separate western settlements, international relations, and eventual reunification. But on the topic of race relations, it echoes the early twentieth-century scenarios, not only invoking the usual bête noire of Reconstruction to explain white American racism in Our Timeline but also echoing previous estimates of when and why the victorious CSA would have freed the slaves. In short, even after the 1950s' school integration conflict had broken the taboo against federal intervention to enforce African American's civil rights and Southern whites had massively once again resisted that intervention, Kantor simply repeated the previous consensus that "enforced amalgamation" (i.e., Reconstruction) was responsible for "a common hatred directed against the Negro."

And his vision of how much better things would have been had the CSA won independence also stays true to the form. Swept along in the rising tide of worldwide social change, we are told, Southern emancipation would have been accomplished entirely without struggle in the same decade that Cuba and Brazil freed their slaves: "Progressive enlightenment and reform among the nations at large had deleted any excuse for a protraction of human slavery," and therefore "the Liberation Act . . . passed both houses of [the Confederate] Congress early in 1885."[29] The only indication Kantor's book gives that the Southern states in actuality were not currently demonstrating any willingness to accept gradual racial amalgamation is a short passage toward the end, which explains that even in the imaginary alternate world, "the color question" remains unsettled. The passage seems a hasty afterthought, and the narrator, like Churchill's located in the Alternate Timeline, maintains his neutrality by casting blame on "extremists of both factions," who have once again destroyed racial harmony by disrupting the progress toward "a fair adjustment in professional, commercial and industrial enterprise, in rural economics, and in higher education" that had been made by "sagacious moderates." The brief, offhand interruption is jarring not only because it was earlier indicated that racial tensions dissolved after the CSA's voluntary emancipation of the slaves but also because it reminds the reader that in the book's representation of the history of the CSA between 1880 and 1960, which goes on for many chapters, race relations had not been mentioned at all.

It appears, therefore, that not much had changed between the turn of the century and 1960 in the alternate history of the Civil War and its aftermath, except that the fate of African Americans had become much less important to it. Ernest Crosby, after all, had been primarily motivated by his alarmed reaction to Southern racism when he imagined the squandered possibilities for what he thought of as a better, more highly evolved, well-prepared, and voluntary emancipation; MacKinlay Kantor, in contrast, gave only a few perfunctory sentences to the issues of slavery and race relations. Although he was published at the beginning of the decade that was to see the end of legal segregation in the South, Kantor's book evinces little insight into its own historical moment, and that failing was typical of the genre. We will therefore leave the alternate-history form where it stalled during the civil rights era and move on to the forms of counterfactualism that arose during that period: new methods of counterfactualism in academic history and new uses of legal counterfactualism in social policy.

ACADEMIC COUNTERFACTUAL HISTORY AND THE POST-WWII REVISION OF CIVIL WAR HISTORIOGRAPHY

To be fair to these alternate-history writers, we must note that their scenarios merely popularized the beliefs held by most academic historians of the Civil War and Reconstruction for the first half of the twentieth century. One need only read the excoriating introduction to W. E. B. DuBois's 1935 *Black Reconstruction* to realize how fervently the academic establishment—analyzed in withering detail by DuBois—alleged that the Civil War was unnecessary to end slavery and Reconstruction was a colossal injustice. From Woodrow Wilson's *A History of the American People* (1901) to J. G. Randall's *The Civil War and Reconstruction* (first published in 1937 but reissued as late as 1969), many influential historians in all sections of the country presented the Civil War as arising from a series of "misunderstandings" and declared that it might have been avoided if it had not been for the machinations of radical abolitionists and a few Southern fire-eaters. James G. Randall was a professor of history at the University of Illinois, the country's leading expert on the life and career of Abraham Lincoln, and the author of the book that stood for decades (last reprinted in 1969) as the standard authoritative account of the Civil War and Reconstruction. Slavery, Randall taught generations of American educators, was a paternalistic arrangement in which, "On the master's side the sense of proprietorship tended to encourage better treatment while in the slave there developed a sense of family loyalty, indeed an amusing tendency to identify himself with his master's family connection."[30] "In a real sense," Randall wrote, "the whites were more enslaved by the institution than the blacks. The Negroes were in their midst. They had to be looked after" (73).

In promulgating this version of history, Randall was following in the already deeply imprinted footsteps of William Archibald Dunning, professor of history at Columbia University (*Reconstruction, Political and Economic* [1907]), who believed African Americans to be incapable of exercising political rights and therefore condemned Reconstruction as a corrupt imposition on the Southern states, which was bound to fail. In a 1901 essay, "The Undoing of Reconstruction," Dunning frankly celebrated the reversal of the undoing of slavery:

> The ultimate root of the trouble in the South had been, not the institution of slavery, but the coexistence in one society of two races so distinct in characteristics as to render coalescence impossible; slavery had been a *modus vivendi* through which social life was possible; . . . after its disappearance, its place must be taken by some set of conditions which, if more humane and beneficent in accidents, must in essence express the same fact of racial inequality. The progress in the acceptance of this idea in the North has measured the progress in the South of the undoing of reconstruction.

In that early essay, Dunning went on to express his hope that this latest reversal of sentiments, which had converted most of the white population of the country to the cause of its own racial supremacy, would be the final: "In view of the questions which have been raised by our lately established relations with other races, it seems most improbable that the historian will soon, or ever, have to record a reversal of the conditions which this process has established."[31] The "Dunning school" had a virtual monopoly on the academic study of Reconstruction until well into the 1960s. As late as 1969, the last edition of Randall's *The Civil War and Reconstruction* (in which large sections had been rewritten by David Donald of Johns Hopkins) still cites Dunning on the necessity of the "black codes" in the postwar South: "Had the Southern states not passed some legislation on these subjects, chaos would have resulted" (572). In short, the essayists who wrote explicitly counterfactual magazine pieces in the first half of the century mainly explicated and embellished the counterfactual assumptions that had developed and spread as the lost-cause interpretation of the war, with its bias toward the Confederacy and regret that the war had ever been fought, took over Civil War historiography.

This interpretation of the war was resoundingly overturned in the post-WWII years, but not by discarding counterfactualism entirely. The pressure exerted by the civil rights movement in favor of a Second Reconstruction, affirmative action programs, and claims for reparations all had a tendency to spread historical counterfactual modes of thought through the general discourse on racial justice, as we'll shortly see. In this section, though, we'll look specifically at the new kinds of counterfactualism that entered the academic historical field in the 1950s. It was in that decade that some economic historians started using sophisticated quantitative, rather than anecdotal, ways of introducing counterfactual speculation. On the specific topics we've been tracing—was the war necessary? would the CSA have freed the slaves anyway if they had won?—these scholars turned to new kinds of economic evidence for answers, and their efforts significantly expanded the reach and ambition of historical counterfactualism at the same time that they overthrew the previous academic consensus.

To set the scene for this transition, let's look specifically at Civil War *economic* historiography. At the beginning of the twentieth century, the analyses of U. B. Phillips (a student of William Dunning and later professor at Yale) had been instrumental in creating the belief that slavery hadn't been so much brutal or immoral as simply inefficient. It had created irrationalities in the plantation system, which exacerbated regional tensions. Phillips seemed to provide plenty of archival sources and appeared to be rigorously objective, so he was credible when he announced, in a 1910 article called "The Decadence of the Plantation System," that an unmolested CSA would probably have made a transition to free-labor capitalism, combining plantations with other economic activities:

> If no cataclysm of war and false reconstruction had accompanied the displacement of slavery, the plantation system might well have experienced something of a happy further progress with free wage-earning labor. The increase of its service to the community would have required some provision whereby such laborers as the system had schooled into superior efficiency might easily withdraw from the gangs and set themselves up as independent artisans, merchants or farmers. The gangs must graduate at least the ablest of their laborers into the industrial democracy, and the regime must permit small farms, factories and cities to flourish in the same districts as the plantations. In a word, for the best economic results, industrial resources and the industrial mechanism of society must be made varied, complex and elastic, and every distinctly capable member of the community must be permitted to find his own suitable employment.[32]

There is no obvious nostalgia for the antebellum way of life here, just a seemingly objective assessment of what would have been necessary to maintain the Southern plantation economy. The implication, worked out at length in Phillips's *American Negro Slavery* (1918) and *Life and Labor in the South* (1929), was that the war and the "false reconstruction" had prevented this natural progress. Phillips's counterfactual speculation passed as proven historical knowledge. It allowed H. L. Mencken, for example, to make the unsupported claim we've already quoted about the "many Southerners" before 1860 who wanted emancipation "on sound economic grounds, and not on the brummagem moral grounds which persuaded the North." And it helped solidify a consensus among academic historians that slavery had been economically moribund and would have been naturally superseded.

There were, to be sure, a few dissenters in the 1930s and 1940s; Phillips's analyses about slavery's profitability were challenged in periodicals like *Agricultural History* and the *Journal of Southern History*, and W. E. B. DuBois cited the research of many other scholars who disagreed with the orthodoxy, but it wasn't until 1952, when Kenneth Stampp, at that time an assistant professor at the University of California, Berkeley, published a highly visible and extremely negative assessment of Phillips's whole corpus in the *American Historical Review* that the tide began to turn in the direction of what was then called "revisionism."[33] In that early article, which was a preview of his seminal book, *The Peculiar Institution: Slavery in the Ante-Bellum South* (1956), Stampp concluded, first, that the evidence showed slavery to have been as profitable as most enterprises in the antebellum period and, second, that Phillips's analysis (based on inadequate sampling and faulty reasoning) was part of his systematic bias in sympathy with the slaveholding class. By the 1950s, therefore, academic historians were beginning to disprove the interpretation of the Civil War that had been at the center of American explanations of the conflict since the end of Reconstruction. The old counterfactual consensus would no longer pass for "knowledge," and numerous social, political, and cultural historians contributed to the revision of America's understanding of its Civil War.

It was in this revisionist climate that a new breed of economic historian, trained in economics departments and practicing what became variously known as the new economic history, cliometrics, or econometrics, made its appearance. The intervention of the economists marked a turning point in the history of academic counterfactual history, and at its inception, the method was closely tied to the specific debate we've been following. In 1958, Alfred Conrad and John Meyer, two Harvard economists, used a new kind of counterfactual economic methodology to negate Phillips's speculative conclusions; their article was not only the first application of that methodology to a Civil War topic but also the first cliometrics article ever published. Their intervention confronted an old (ad hoc and unself-conscious) counterfactualism with an emerging variety that incorporated neoclassical economic modeling. Phillips had been engaged in counterfactual thinking not only when he drew his conclusion about what would have happened "if no cataclysm of war and false reconstruction had accompanied the displacement of slavery" but also when he simply claimed slavery was economically inefficient. In order to draw that conclusion he must have had in mind some superior alternative use to which cotton planters might have put their capital instead of slave property. Conrad and Meyer pressed on the missing comparative data in Phillips's analysis: slavery was unprofitable compared to what? "In a strict conceptual sense," Conrad and Meyer explained, "the relevant rate of interest is that which plantation owners or their investors in southern agriculture could have earned on their money in other pursuits if slavery had gone out of existence. This is difficult to arrive at on the basis of historical evidence, since it assumes circumstances contrary to the facts. The closest substitute would be earnings on other investments that were *least* dependent upon cotton and southern agriculture."[34] Conrad and Meyer came up with might-have-been interest rates by first taking investment returns in the North during the actual war years—that is, in an American economy owing nothing to slave-grown cotton—and then adjusting them to correct for such things as war inflation and what they called Lincoln's "Keynesian" policies. On the basis of their computations, they concluded that slavery was profitable in both the plantation states and in those where the slaves were bred. They unambiguously stated that the South was not forced into an unnecessary war "to protect a system that must soon have disappeared because it was economically unsound." "This," they added in a clear swipe at lost-cause ideology, "is a romantic hypothesis which will not stand against the facts" (121). Furthermore, they linked their historical analysis to current policy debates about how to treat developing countries with "slave-like" labor forces: "Indeed, economic forces often may work toward the continuation of a slave system, so that the elimination of slavery may depend upon the adoption of harsh political measures." And their concluding sentence identified those necessary "harsh measures" with the Civil War and Reconstruction: "Certainly that was the American experience" (122). Cliometrics was thus an early ally of revisionist Civil War history, although their conjuncture may have been largely fortuitous, based more on the availability of data than on a prior interest on the part of economic historians in the debate over the profitability of slavery.[35] Another seminal cliometric work—Douglas North's 1961 *The Economic Growth of the United States, 1790–1860*—came to similar conclusions about the necessity of the war in ending slavery, although for slightly different reasons, and it further strengthened the revisionist-cliometric association.[36]

But there was also a strong disciplinary distinction between the revisionists and the new economic historians. Stampp and the other revisionists were trained in history departments as social, political, or intellectual historians. Conrad and Meyer were Harvard economists, not historians by training, and North was also an economist at the University of Washington. They shifted the debate over this particular Civil War counterfactual into a new register by claiming to have an innovative methodology especially designed to settle debates over what might have been. They seemed to declare that such debates would no longer be indeterminable matters of mere opinion. Henceforth, if counterfactual arguments about economic history were to be made, they would need to be tested and defended according to methods developed outside the historian's profession, using economic modeling and relying on new developments in statistics, applied mathematics, and computer technology.[37] Although the revisionist historians might use the conclusions of the cliometricians, few actually adopted the methodology, and, indeed, some have claimed that the triumph of cliometrics in the field of economic history has led to its disappearance from history departments and migration into economics departments and business schools.

Cliometrics would have a long-lasting effect on the direction taken by academic historical counterfactualism, since it implied that the enterprise had its own kind of proper analysis and, by extension, its legitimate objects. Some kinds of history (for example, demographic and economic history) would lend themselves to high levels of certainty about counterfactual propositions, whereas less quantifiable and data-driven historical fields probably should avoid them. The disciplining of counterfactualism may have given it new professional credibility, but not inside history departments. By the 1980s, historical counterfactualism had two institutional homes—military academies and economics departments—neither of which had much contact with the mainstream of academic history.

Indeed, one of the most famous cliometric books addressing the debate over the profitability of slavery (and, by extension, the necessity of the war) created an outcry among historians. In 1974, two economists from the University of Rochester, Robert Fogel, who was already well known to historians through a previous book, and Stanley Engerman published *Time on the Cross*, a work that repeated many of Conrad and Meyer's conclusions: "The slave system was not economically moribund on the eve of the Civil War. There is no evidence that economic forces alone would have soon brought slavery to an end without the necessity of a war or some other form of political intervention. Quite the contrary; as the Civil War approached, slavery as an economic system was never stronger and the trend was toward even further entrenchment" (4–5).[38] Fogel and Engerman, though, went further than Conrad and Meyer in computing economic data for the hypothetical late nineteenth-century slave economy. For example, using regression analyses they charted the probable course of slave prices "in the absence of a Civil War, for the decade 1881–1890" (97). Moreover, they also stepped way over the line into social history when they argued that slavery might have withstood the diversification of the Southern economy and opined that it could have been maintained in urban settings. *Time on the Cross* was a notorious book, but not because of its claims about the economic health of the antebellum Southern plantation system; rather, Fogel and Engerman normalized slavery in ways that discounted its moral dimensions. They wrote, for example, that *economically* the slaves had not really been worse off than mid-nineteenth-century free laborers (a point on which they came into collision with other economists), and they claimed that slaves gained skills and made "progress" under the system. Of course, to anyone deeply familiar with the intellectual history of the issues and their broad social and political implications, these arguments sounded shockingly similar to nineteenth-century defenses of slavery. The debate they generated, like the earlier attacks on lost-cause historiography, had the uncanny quality of seeming to require that slavery's immorality be once again asserted and proven. Reading the book today, it seems clear that the authors had only a partial grasp of the larger historical period and a very faulty sense of the complete historiography. Claiming that they were defending African Americans against charges that they were inefficient, the authors (perhaps unwittingly) echoed U. B. Phillips in denouncing the abolitionists' supposed exaggerations of slavery's brutality while they simultaneously debunked Phillips's assessment that slavery made plantations inefficient. Oddly, Fogel and Engerman created new ways to undercut the victory of the North. First, they suggested that, although the Civil War was certainly necessary to end slavery, perhaps the realities of slavery had to be misrepresented by abolitionists in order to stoke the North's martial spirit. Second, they left their readers wondering why, if slavery wasn't such a bad thing after all, we should think that its abolition was an important triumph.

The controversy surrounding *Time on the Cross* therefore seemed to revive one of the earliest doubts about the righteousness of the Northern cause—were the evils of slavery so bad that their eradication justified a war?—but only briefly, for the book's claims regarding the benefits of slavery to the slaves were swiftly and decisively rebutted.[39] A more lasting effect of the controversy was that it increased historians' familiarity with the debates over Civil War counterfactuals, and the publicity surrounding its most extreme generalization also made the reading public acquainted with the issues. Its reception demonstrated once again how sensitive the question of the fate of American slavery remained, especially in the decades of the affirmative action debates. Although the book was most often criticized for underestimating the antebellum exploitation and suffering of the slaves, Fogel and Engerman's insouciant chapters about how the system might easily have persisted, evolved, thrived, and spread without any natural historical limits, perhaps right into the twentieth century, probably gave it additional connotations of contemporary relevance. So even though it widened the gap between mainstream historians and cliometricians, we should also say that *Time on the Cross* hit a deep nerve and illustrated the peculiar ability of counterfactual projections to emphasize the present consequences of historical events. Their Civil War counterfactuals, like those of all the writers we've examined in this chapter, implicitly point to comparisons between the world we now inhabit and those that we could be inhabiting if the national past had been different.

Did the revisionists and cliometricians between them put paid to the counterfactual debates about the Civil War's necessity and slavery's possible fates? Many previous points of contention do seem to have been settled; no historians are now arguing that slavery had been unprofitable and the war therefore unnecessary, although many contend that an independent postbellum CSA, facing a cotton market that had changed greatly during the war, might well have been forced to abandon the system after another generation.[40] In this scenario, though, even "voluntary" emancipation would have required the Northern war effort. Historians now, moreover, are no longer arguing about whether to blame Reconstruction for white racism. The revisionists saw Reconstruction as a potentially revolutionary moment that was completely and utterly defeated by the compromise of 1877, but this bleak view has now been surpassed by a "neo-revisionist" consensus, best represented by Eric Foner, that has less confidence that radical change could have been effected in the period and more appreciation for what was accomplished.[41] Of course, that has not meant the end of Civil War counterfactuals. Indeed, a 2005 special issue of the journal *Civil War History* dedicated to "Reconstruction as It Should Have Been" may indicate that historians are more apt to use them now than they were in the past. Five professors of history teaching in different regions of the country came up with separate alternate-history scenarios for how the United States might have won the postwar peace.[42] It is, moreover, probable that the attention to Reconstruction counterfactuals in 2005 reflected the fact that the first years of the twenty-first century saw a campaign, largely waged through lawsuits, for the federal government to pay reparations to African Americans; those lawsuits often used counterfactual arguments about "possible pasts."[43] In short, the connection between contemporary social movements and academic historical counterfactualizing is still evident.

THE SECOND RECONSTRUCTION: REMEDIAL JUSTICE AND ALTERNATE HISTORY

The connection between the social movements of the period and historical counterfactuals is also apparent when we look at government policies. We tend to forget that an official U.S. government drive for greater racial equality began immediately after the Second World War, with Truman's appointment of the President's Committee on Civil Rights in 1946. *To Secure These Rights*, the report issued by the committee in 1947, stressed that the country had reached a crucial juncture in its history, which paralleled two previous moments—drafting the Constitution and ending slavery—as opportunities to review and remake its record of civil rights. Although careful not to dwell on what it called the "failure" of Reconstruction legislation, the committee thoroughly explained the rationale for passing similar new legislation and concluded with a ringing call for immediate action. "THE TIME IS NOW" announced the heading of the report's final section, where it further emphasized that the "NOW" of 1947 was a repetition of earlier opportunities: "It is our profound conviction that we have come to a time for a third re-examination of the situation, and a sustained drive ahead. . . . [We] have a moral reason, an economic reason, and an international reason for believing that the time for action is now."[44] Deciding to make a civil-rights record fit for the leading nation of the Free World was thus already framed as a repetition (and by implication a reversal) of previous decisions. The committee's sense of urgency, though, was not felt by Congress, and its recommended legislation was put off for ten years, until the civil rights era, the years between 1957 and 1968, which the historian C. Vann Woodward dubbed "Second Reconstruction."

People on both sides of the desegregation struggle presented the civil rights years as a repetition of Reconstruction and noted that the federal government was again pursuing goals it had abandoned almost eighty years earlier. For example, in the summer of 1964, Representative Howard Smith of Virginia opposed Lyndon Johnson's Civil Rights Act by declaring it "unmatched in harshness and brutality . . . since the tragic days of Reconstruction," and he likened freedom riders and other student activists to a "second invasion of the Southland." "Hordes of beatniks, misfits, and agitators from the North," he claimed, "are streaming into the Southland mischief-bent, backed and defended by other hoards of federal marshals, federal agents, and federal power."[45] On the other side, the civil rights movement had a strong consciousness that it was restoring rights fleetingly granted during Reconstruction and then removed by Jim Crow laws; it was therefore proud to see itself as Reconstruction revived. The metaphor of "Second Reconstruction" harks back to DuBois's prediction in 1935 that "the rebuilding, whether it comes now or a century later, will and must go back to the basic principles of Reconstruction in the United States during 1867–1876."[46]

The resemblance between this ambition to retrieve and reverse the outcome of Reconstruction and alternate-history narrative patterns should be obvious: there had been two possible tracks, and the country had previously taken the one that, in hindsight, was obviously wrong; now we had regained the right trajectory. A keen awareness of how the history of race relations might have turned out differently was thus built into the intellectual foundations of the civil rights movement. Moreover, alternate-history racial scenarios appeared in federal government programs and legal cases founded on the concept of remediation. Hypotheses about what might have been *if* the country had allowed the first Reconstruction to succeed, for example, were folded into attempts to undo past wrongs, and the resulting remedial plans put counterfactual speculation into play as an immediate pragmatic concern in those decades. For all of these reasons, remedial legal thought encouraged historical counterfactualism in our political culture and our modes of imagining national identity.

It soon became clear that merely having regained the right road by ending legal segregation was by no means sufficient, for the country had to mitigate the effects of the intervening eighty years of inequality. One of the earliest official indications that we would be called on to remediate the past, rather than merely leave it behind, came in Lyndon Johnson's 1965 address to the graduating class of Howard University, which emphasized that it was already too late to expect formal and legal safeguards alone to bring about actual social and economic equality: "Freedom is not enough. You do not wipe away the scars of centuries by saying: Now you are free to go where you want, and do as you desire, and choose the leaders you please. You do not take a person who, for years, has been hobbled by chains and liberate him, bring him up to the starting line of a race and then say, 'you are free to compete with all the others,' and still justly believe that you have been completely fair."[47]

Johnson uses the metaphor of the starting line here to emphasize that there is no common point of departure from which all Americans might move forward on the road of opportunity. Referring to the fact that the 1964 Civil Rights Act had placed two groups, African Americans and white Americans, at the beginning of a free competition for social and economic advancement, he insists on the need for different starting lines to compensate for the present effects of past discrimination. Programmatically, the different starting lines were to take the form of the "war on poverty" (for the benefit of all children living below the poverty line) and a set of further remedial measures, which collectively became known as affirmative action, promising to bridge the distance between the relative positions of the races.[48] "This is the next and the more profound stage of the battle for civil rights," Johnson explained. "We seek not just freedom but opportunity. We seek not just . . . equality as a right and a theory but equality as a fact and equality as a result."

For the first decade of their existence, the affirmative action programs were thus conceived as remedial and were modeled on civil tort-law cases. When deciding in 1974 that the city of Detroit had to devise a plan to achieve racially integrated schools, for example, the U.S. Supreme Court used the language of equitable remedy: "The decree must indeed be *remedial* in nature, that is, it must be designed as nearly as possible 'to restore the victims of discriminatory conduct to the position they would have occupied in the absence of such conduct.'"[49] Such formulations made it clear that the plan was to "make whole" the lot of African Americans by "restoring" them to the position they would have occupied but for the legal and extralegal disabilities imposed on them by the white majority. They were to be restored, in short, to a condition they had never been allowed to occupy, but might have held in an alternate history, so connection to counterfactual history in this reasoning is obvious. As one legal theorist describes it, remediation "involves using the imagination to create a counterfactual hypothesis. One creates a mental picture of the situation identical to the actual facts of the case in all respects save one: the . . . wrongful conduct is now 'corrected.'"[50] Like lawyers constructing any other kind of counterfactual hypothesis, the framers of affirmative action in the various federal administrations and departments asserted that *but for* the wrongs suffered—denial of equal access to jobs, education, representation, goods, and services—the overall condition of black people in America would have improved over the last eighty years at rates similar to those among white Americans. Hence, black Americans were entitled to a remedy, just as an injured party in a civil case would be. As a result, affirmative action temporality was unlike that of earlier progressive programs—for example, those of the New Deal—which assumed that we were building on the past; it required us to take action against the effects of our past omissions and commissions, to overturn and reverse the direction of our racial history. We could not just go back to an earlier moment of opportunity, such as Reconstruction, to regain a lost trajectory, because those who had been forcibly retarded in their progress toward prosperity now needed to be sped along the road at an accelerated rate; access to the fast lane of affirmative action programs would be the equivalent of a tort-law remedy for African Americans. Thus the first step was to imagine a parallel present, the one that would have occurred on the alternate timeline in which Reconstruction had prevailed—and then we would try to bring that imaginary condition into actuality.

In some ways, the tort-law model was highly appropriate to the process through which antidiscrimination laws came to be enforced. Since Title VII of the Civil Rights Act of 1964 mandated the establishment of the Equal Employment Opportunity Commission, an independent federal agency, the laws have been implemented by filing suits, mainly against employers but sometimes also against trade unions, on behalf of alleged victims of workplace discrimination. When in 1973, the commission, for example, charged AT&T with "pervasive, systemwide, and blatantly unlawful discrimination in employment against women, blacks, Spanish-surnamed Americans, and other minorities," it sought and won back-pay compensation for the lost wages that women and minority employees would have been paid under nondiscriminatory conditions. To take another sort of example, when the Nixon administration's Department of Labor pressured the building-trades unions to integrate in the early 1970s, threatening the denial of government contracts if they did not meet specific goals for minority membership, they estimated what the racial makeup of the trades would have been *but for* the unions' discriminatory practices. The man who led the Labor Department's effort, Arthur Fletcher, declared himself to be uninterested in compensation or in a "fruitless debate about slavery and its debilitating legacy."[51] In his mind, setting "visible, measurable goals [i.e., quotas] to correct obvious imbalances" was a way of avoiding recriminations, a "no-fault" policy designed to pull more African Americans out of poverty and reduce the welfare rolls. Nevertheless, the policies, known as the Philadelphia Plan, were justified as a means of hastening progress toward the economic conditions that would have prevailed had it not been for "years of segregation and discrimination."[52] Consequently, they followed the "but for" tort-law logic even though they did not name, as the AT&T case did, any particular individuals who had been the victims of particular discriminatory acts.

But handy as tort-law logic was for prosecuting actual civil cases and for explaining why some kinds of Americans should receive temporarily advantageous treatment to compensate for previous disadvantages, the model was in other ways ill-fitting. First, as the Philadelphia Plan indicated, there was often great reluctance to identify a wrongdoer, a counterpart for the defendant, who is usually held responsible for making the plaintiff "whole." The pro–affirmative action rhetoric of the 1960s and 1970s, indeed, avoided pitting segments of the population against each other as plaintiff and defendant, stressing instead that the nation in general would benefit from the programs, that they would be supported by all taxpayers, and that no group would be singled out as the responsible party. For example, James Farmer, head of the Congress of Racial Equality, was careful to use inclusive language when testifying before a congressional committee in 1963: "You see none of us are really innocent because we are caught in a society, the social system of which has tolerated segregation."[53] The fact that Farmer, a black man, included himself along with white Americans among the "not really innocent" implied that all races share the same degree of blame; black and white are merged, as well as "caught," in the wrong-producing machinery of an impersonal social system. A tort without a wrongdoer, though, was a paradoxical thing; James Farmer filled its place with a pernicious social system, but often "past discrimination" was laid at the door of an even more vaguely defined "history"; affirmative action might serve, therefore, as an exemplary instance of judging large swathes of history negatively, which we have noted in each chapter as an element of counterfactual thought.

And yet it was also obvious that even if the *beneficiaries* of past discrimination—mainly white male Americans—were not being overtly blamed, they sometimes felt that affirmative action programs turned their race and gender into competitive handicaps. As is well known, rejected applicants brought civil suits against those programs for violating the very Civil Rights Act that the Equal Employment Opportunity Commission was trying to enforce, which required treating all candidates without regard to race or sex. The case of the *Regents of the University of California v. Bakke* (1978) illustrates the clash of counterfactual arguments that had begun to arise by the late 1970s. The complainant, an unsuccessful applicant to the medical school at the University of California, Davis, argued that *but for* the university's preferential program of minority admissions, he, a white applicant, would have been admitted. He argued that the minority admissions program violated federal law by making race a factor in admissions and he asked the courts to reverse the medical school's decision against admitting him.[54] When the case reached the U.S. Supreme Court, Justice Thurgood Marshall wrote a minority opinion (in which he was joined by Justices Brennan and White) that used a different but-for argument against the plaintiff: "*If* it was reasonable to conclude—as we hold that it was—that the failure of minorities to qualify for admission at Davis under regular procedures was due principally to the effects of past discrimination, then there is a reasonable likelihood that, *but for* pervasive racial discrimination, [the plaintiff Bakke] would have failed to qualify for admission even in the absence of Davis' special admissions program."[55] In Justice Marshall's supplementary remarks, he advances further alternate-history claims, some of which accuse the U.S. Supreme Court itself of creating the social conditions that made affirmative action necessary: "This Court in the Civil Rights Cases [of the late nineteenth century] and *Plessy v. Ferguson* [1896] destroyed the movement toward complete equality."[56] Marshall holds the earlier court responsible for its actions by demonstrating that it had other options, quoting the dissenting opinions. He argues as well that the decision in *Plessy* bred the Bakke suit by creating an unequal educational legacy that would require affirmative action as well as spawn such reactions to it as Bakke's. Marshall presents an alternate history of the Supreme Court which, he claims, would have obviated the very existence of the case under consideration: "Had the court been willing in 1896, in *Plessy v. Ferguson*, to hold that the Equal Protection Clause forbids differences in treatment based on race, we would not be faced with this dilemma in 1978."[57] The ironic paradox of this story is that the wrong (failing to forbid "differences in treatment based on race" in railroad facilities) superficially resembles the remedy (allowing such difference in the University of California at Davis's admissions procedures), except for the crucial distinction between differential treatment designed to segregate society and treatment designed to integrate it. Marshall is pointing out that it would be both too late and counterproductive for the court to adhere to the abstract principle at this stage when it failed to do so eighty years prior. Indeed, the court would be doubly guilty, for it would have caused the problem and then outlawed the remedy.

To visualize this counterfactual logic, it helps to recall yet again the forking-branches pattern so familiar to us from alternate-history narratives. Branch A coming out of the fork represents an alternate history of U.S. black-white race relations of ever-increasing equality, where the reaction against Reconstruction was defeated and the civil rights cases of the late nineteenth century and *Plessy* were decided differently. Branch B represents the actual history of inequality, only recently departed from at another fork in 1954, when *Brown v. Board of Education* tilted the court back toward the road to equality. Then, in 1978, a third fork could once again change its direction toward inequality. Those who hoped to uphold affirmative action viewed it as a means of accelerating advancement along the vector that points from *Brown* so that its line would intersect with Branch A more quickly and thereby undo the consequences of the earlier courts' actions. This counterfactualism is not only an imaginative historical exercise but also a means of actualizing the future of an alternate past designed "to restore the victims of discriminatory conduct to the position they would have occupied in the absence of such conduct." Moreover, Marshall's hypothesis was itself a miniature example of the alternate-history form.

Marshall's big-picture conjectural exercise reprised much of the counterfactual logic on which affirmative action programs had justified themselves, but to the majority of justices it seemed overly general in relation to the specifics of the *Bakke* case. Justice Lewis Powell, who did sign on to a few parts of Marshall's opinion, objected to its hypothesis that a particular white individual (Bakke) would have been a comparably weaker candidate *but for* earlier Supreme Court cases fostering racial discrimination, calling it far too broad a "presumption of causality."[58] Objections were made as well to the mismatch between the agents of the injury (previous Supreme Court justices, according to Marshall) and the individual (Bakke) whose aspirations were being sacrificed to the remedy; if the court needed to come up with reparation, should it be allowed to disadvantage, in turn, a nonresponsible party? Of course, Marshall was not really arguing that the previous courts were single-handedly responsible for the current inequality in academic achievement; they were meant to stand for pervasive social forces, but that just made it all the harder to place direct responsibility and tie the cost of the remedy to specifiable wrongdoers. Definitions of the "wrong" and the "wrongdoers" were therefore major conceptual difficulties. And, as Justice William O. Douglas had argued in a 1974 case, relying on "past discrimination" to explain who could benefit from affirmative action remedies had also raised a host of questions about specifying victims:

> The University of Washington included Filipinos, but excluded Chinese and Japanese. . . . But what standard is the Court to apply when a rejected applicant of Japanese ancestry brings suit to require the University of Washington to extend the same privileges to his group? The [University] Committee might conclude . . . that, had they not been handicapped by a history of discrimination, Japanese would now constitute 5% of the Bar, or 20%. Or, alternatively, the Court could attempt to assess how grievously each group has suffered from discrimination, and allocate proportions accordingly; if that were the standard, the current University of Washington policy would almost surely fall, for there is no Western State which can claim that it has always treated Japanese and Chinese in a fair and evenhanded manner.[59]

These were the still undecided issues that the court faced when it took up the Bakke case, issues that exposed the mismatch between normal torts, which had defendants as well as plaintiffs, and affirmative action initiatives, in which benefited parties often did not claim individual injuries and there was no one to blame but "history." It is not surprising that this particular remedial paradigm began to fade from official explanations after the *Bakke* case.[60]

As the Bakke case also illustrated, though, the difficultly of specifying wrongdoers was compounded by the difficulty of exactly delimiting the wrongs. Marshall focused on the culpability of the Supreme Court but did not seriously argue their sole responsibility. In the case of African Americans, the copiousness of wrongs was a special conceptual problem that not only turned "history" into the culprit but also made it difficult to imagine the historical conditions under which the plaintiff would exist absent the wrong. The historical acts that created the people called African Americans—the transportation of hundreds of thousands of Africans into the territories that were to become the United States of America—were themselves to be viewed as injuries, and consequently disentangling the wrongs from the very existence of the wronged presented a conceptual problem. Furthermore, although there had been a brief respite from legal disabilities in the Reconstruction years, debilitating discrimination had been the norm, the consistent historical setting that shaped the culture and even the nature of some of its achievements. The problem, therefore, was not that one couldn't point to past wrongs, but that in the relations between black and white in America, one could point to very little else; consequently the victims seemed to be seeking a remedy for the whole complex of conditions that produced them. If the wrong was described so pervasively as to cover the very identity of the people seeking a remedy, mightn't they be said to protest against their very existence?[61] If, in contrast, it was narrowly identified in a more legally orthodox manner (as in Marshall's but-for argument), it seemed causally insufficient. The tort-law remedial model of historical activism, in short, promised the usual components of alternate history—definable nexuses, responsible agents, and clearly diverging consequences—but it tied them into a tangle of potentially paradoxical conceptual loops.

ALTERNATE HISTORY DURING AND AFTER THE CIVIL RIGHTS ERA

As we'll see in the next chapter, these loops were the very things that attracted many writers of alternate-history novels and short stories, who have a penchant for backward time-travel paradoxes, but the more conventional authors of alternate-history narratives could make very little of them. Indeed, the nonnovelistic form was virtually suspended between 1960 and 1990. It reappeared during a wave of interest in historical counterfactual scenarios of all kinds, which was stimulated by the huge and unexpected turns in contemporary world history—the collapse of the Soviet Union and conclusion of the Cold War—and by the spread of computer technology, which made the pleasures of historical war games known to a new generation. The late twentieth century revived on a vastly magnified scale the impulses toward military counterfactual play that, as we noted in chapter 1, originally arose in the late eighteenth century. Of twenty-six Civil War short-form alternate histories appearing between 1997 and 2006, most confine themselves to developing alternative military possibilities, often expanding on counterfactual suggestions already in the military-historical literature.[62] They are exclusively nexus stories, without any interest in exploring the aftermath of the changes they imagine. Aimed primarily at Civil War buffs, whose sympathies might lie with either side, they are studiously neutral. Eighteen are entirely silent about the probable impact of a reversed outcome on the slaves, whereas eight make perfunctory allusions to the commonplaces we encountered earlier: the already expiring institution of slavery dies a natural death within a few decades of the war's ending, which normally occurs in 1863. Thus, when they do imagine the aftermath, they imply that, from a moral, social, or political viewpoint, the outcome was practically indifferent.

Apolitical as these stories try to be, they also clearly reflect the changes wrought by the civil rights movement in the South. Since contemporary Southern institutions no longer publicly sanctioned segregation, the differences between the regions seemed to have disappeared by the late 1980s, making it much easier to imagine the War between the States as a completely finished historical phenomenon, without a long tail of consequences over which we still trip. To Tourgée, Crosby, Mencken, and even Churchill, late nineteenth- and early twentieth-century race relations in the South seemed so bad that they thought things couldn't have been worse if the South had won the war, so, they imagined, things just might have been better. In the late twentieth and early twenty-first centuries, alternate-history writers seem to think that race relations are so much the same throughout the country that it couldn't have mattered much who won the war. Consequently, they tend to represent the Civil War as a no-fault conflict, even sometimes implying that the causes of the two sides were equally worthy.

Kenneth Burns's enormously popular PBS television series on the war, which was first aired in 1994, signaled this Civil War neutrality and probably also had a role in stimulating the interest in military counterfactuals. With its ambitious racial and sectional inclusiveness wrapped in a languorously elegiac style, the production emphasized the completeness of the past and its inscrutability before the inquisitive eye of history. A repeated voice-over underscored the mysteriousness of the conflict, almost ritually intoning the sentiment that, "between 1861 and 1865, Americans made war on each other and killed each other in great numbers—if only to become the kind of country that could no longer conceive of how that was possible."[63] Just a generation earlier, though, during the turmoil of the civil rights movement it had not seemed "inconceivable" that Americans had killed each other over the issues of the Civil War. The deadliness of the conflict was not hard to imagine when the Klan reemerged after World War II, when black churches were bombed and burned, when Medgar Evers was assassinated, when Northern freedom riders were attacked by mobs as modern-day carpetbaggers, when James Chaney, Andrew Goodman, and Michael Schwerner were lynched, when federal intervention was needed to insure the safety of voting-rights demonstrators marching from Selma to Montgomery. Like most successful social transformations, the civil rights movement might be said to have erased its own tracks and thus to have made the Civil War inconceivable, so that Kenneth Burns found it necessary to produce an epic historical documentary telling us why the conflict was central to our identity as a nation but without hinting at any invidious regional distinctions. These developments freed alternate-history writers as well to divorce the war from its social and political consequences.

Considering this context, we should not be at all surprised by the fact that only one of the alternate histories appearing after that documentary made race a central issue: Peter Tsouras's intriguing 2006 short narrative of counterfactual emancipation, titled "Confederate Black and Gray." Tsouras, a former army officer, is a prolific contributor to the form and his 1997 *Gettysburg: An Alternate History* helped revive its popularity as a means of exploring Civil War counterfactuals. This earlier book stuck exclusively to the military history, but the story he published in 2006 explored the social possibilities folded into the extraordinary actual narrative of Major General Pat Cleburne's early 1864 proposal that the Southern states, facing ruinous shortages of troops and supplies, "immediately commence training a large reserve of the most courageous of our slaves, and . . . guarantee freedom within a reasonable time to every slave in the South who shall remain true to the Confederacy in this war."[64] In actuality, Jefferson Davis suppressed the document only to find himself forced in the next year to try a similar remedy, conscripting slave soldiers but leaving the issue of manumission to the individual states. The point of departure from actuality in Tsouras's alternate history takes place just as Cleburne's manifesto arrives at the White House of the Confederacy: Lee intervenes and convinces Davis to implement Cleburne's plan immediately, large numbers of soldier slaves are freed, and the South wins its independence, vindicating Cleburne's actual assertion that "as between the loss of independence and the loss of slavery, we assume that every patriot will freely give up the latter—give up the negro slaves rather than be a slave himself" (207). With some cajoling and plenty of money from the British to compensate slaveholders, universal emancipation is granted in March 1864, and Tsouras then expounds his own fantasy of affectionate Southern race relations, this time based on the camaraderie of arms: "The United Confederate Volunteers became a leading exponent of the black franchise [passed in 1896]. The bonds of shared hardships and danger had altered many attitudes" (221).

The elements of the early twentieth-century hypotheses are all present, but Tsouras's narrative reverses their order. Here, instead of emancipation following the Confederate victory, freedom and British support not only precede but also *cause* Southern independence; instead of passively receiving liberty from their masters, the slaves actively fight for it, although they do not fight their masters. No longer interested in upholding segregationist policies by demonizing "enforced amalgamation," this counterfactualism subscribes to the commonplace that slavery was on its way out by the very language in which it emphasizes that progressive forces have always been active in the South ("Clearly Cleburne was thinking deeply into the future"), although they had been stifled by "those who would lash themselves to a dying past" (208). Emancipation becomes the sine qua non of an alternate outcome, and the odd twist that places slaves at the sides of their former masters rather than against them in battle makes Tsouras's story a post–civil rights era allegory for the newest "New South," especially the prosperous states of the southeastern seaboard, whose chambers of commerce were busy in the 1980s trying to encourage black migration back to the South as a return "home" (214). Instead of being forced to choose between their natal place and freedom, Southern blacks choose both in this scenario and escape the "shock" of "Northern racism" (215). Moreover, with its emphasis on the bonding power of common military service, the scenario echoes an opinion frequently heard in the 1990s: that the U.S. army was the best integrated and most racially progressive institution in the country.

The story, like many post-1990 histories and alternate histories of the Civil War, registers a knowledge of the history of Southern race relations, and yet, since the contemporary North and South seem alike in their degrees of equality and integration, it wants to place that history in abeyance and imagine how this newly "normal" state of affairs might have been reached much earlier. Tsouras wants his readers to accept three hypotheses that even Winston Churchill would never have ventured: (1) that given a choice between emancipated status in either the North or the South, most African Americans would have chosen the South, (2) that the latent conditions for racial harmony had always been there in the South, and (3) that they might have been activated as early as 1864. Oddly, all of these ideas were also present in the proslavery alternate-history novel *Hallie Marshall* in 1900, which gives us some idea of their staying power. Both in what it repeats and in what it revises from the alternate-history scenarios stretching back to the turn of the century, Tsouras's story reminds us that it is once again possible to argue that the shortest route from slavery to racial equality would have been through the defeat of the USA in the Civil War.

⁂

By the first decade of this century, the counterfactual-historical methods first developed in econometrics had been adapted to a number of other academic disciplines, and counterfactualism was also spreading in the popular-history book market, where Civil War military historians began publishing anthologies of alternate-history scenarios for a mass market.[65] One academic historian of the Civil War, Roger Ransom, combined these trends in an original synthesis of the two forms we've been examining in this chapter. In his *Confederate States of America: What Might Have Been* (2005), Ransom not only urges academic historians to cultivate their counterfactual imaginations but also suggests that they might learn from the narrative varieties of alternate history and even alternate-history novels.

Indeed, Ransom is the only academic counterfactualist to view the three genres that the present book covers as a set of closely related thought experiments. His openness to the nonacademic modes of writing seems especially unusual for a historian trained originally as an economist, and it may owe much to his boyhood reading of Ward Moore's *Bring the Jubilee* (1952), an alternate-history novel I'll discuss at length in the next chapter.[66] Ransom assesses the strengths and weaknesses of each genre. What he calls "new" alternate military history ("alternate history" in our terms), where the writers expand on a single scenario "as if they were dealing with real, not imaginary, events in the past" (7) has imaginative power, but, judging by recent examples, it seems to him limited by the fact that it's *only* military history, with no ambition to consider consequences in the social, political, or cultural realms.[67] The novels, in contrast, provide the kinds of temporally long-range and socially far-reaching speculation he wants to achieve, but they often lose themselves in the private plots of their fictional characters. Finally, the cliometric use of counterfactuals proper to his own professional training, which involves taking the existing historical data as the foundation of a model, the factors of which are varied to produce other possible states, is too rigid to give a broad vision; it is especially limited by its commitment to the "ceteris paribus" rule, "the dictum that 'other' things do not change" (15). Ransom suggests using these modes in tandem to overcome the limitations of each, and sets out to answer a very large question—what if the South won the Civil War?—by linking together a series of smaller counterfactual inquiries. Militarily, how might the South have achieved a negotiated peace? Economically, how might it have survived? Politically, what would the long-term domestic and international ramifications have been?

Ransom produces a unique hybrid of the counterfactual genres we've identified. He declares that he took his world-making ambition from the alternate-history novel; he borrows alternate-history scenarios from both narrative forms, and he organizes his own book by interspersing analytical and narrative discourses. He begins each of his three sections in the conditional mood, surveying the possible options available at various nexus points, and then follows up on individual alternatives in the past indicative, occasionally inserting footnotes to serve as a "reality check" and to explain why the changes he makes are in fact reasonable (122). The academic counterfactual sections analyze and assess the likelihood of several hypotheticals, not making much narrative headway, whereas the alternate-history sections spin out one continuous thread of fictional-narrative cause and effect. Chapters of counterfactual military history therefore give way to alternate histories with familiar patterns, and when Ransom turns to the topics of politics and international relations in a later chapter, he follows the same itinerary. After surveying and analyzing the options, he chooses one and presents it "as if it actually took place, with notes to point out the divergence of the counterfactual narrative from reality" (232). Ransom's book seems to demonstrate that the histories of war, politics, and international relations both invite counterfactual speculation and provide easy transitions from academic analyses to single timeline narratives.

However, in his section on the possible *economic* history of the independent CSA, the transition is not so smooth. Indeed, he never switches into the indicative narrative mode in that section of his book; he sticks to conditional verb forms even after he has chosen his most likely scenario. Ransom uses statistical modeling in all of his analyses, so economic history's resistance to alternate-history narrative cannot be explained solely on the basis of its tropism toward quantifiable data. Instead, it seems to stem from the lack of appropriate historical agents: that is to say, agents who can sustain the role of *characters*. To be sure, this does not mean that economic history is independent of human behavior, either individual or aggregated, only that when markets act, motivation (economic benefit) tends to be taken for granted and is built into the algorithms of the neoclassical models that allow for the counterfactual analysis in the first place. The various economic players—cotton planters, farmers, entrepreneurs, businessmen, agriculturalists, and so forth—have different interests, but they cannot be said to have different *characters* because they lack differentiated motives. We see them interacting in the arena of the general economy, but the result looks more like a weather pattern than a drama of interacting agents. We might say that the abstraction we call "the economy" often plays an important role as a setting, condition, or circumstance in a narrative but does not usually make room for complex characters.

In contrast, Ransom and most other historians have no difficulty attributing humanlike consciousness and personality traits to other abstractions, like nations: "While Britain and the Confederacy were busily gobbling up the Spanish possessions in the Caribbean, the Americans established themselves as a major power in the Pacific, and together with other Western nations they began to cast a covetous eye on the disintegrating Chinese Empire" (234). Literary historians know that characters can be made out of almost anything—the eighteenth century gave us characters in the shapes of banknotes and hackney cabs—but usually novelists, narrative historians, and alternate-history writers prefer agents with consciousness, subjectivity, and some ability to make decisions and take unpredictable actions.[68] Whether they are individuals, political parties, corporations, cities, governments, races, armies, or nations, they have their "own" ambitions and emotions, strengths and weaknesses, cultural constraints and opportunities; most importantly for alternate-history writers, they have good and bad luck, and they can foresee multiple future options. In liberal capitalism, of course, the economy as a whole must have none of these traits; it is conceived of as a headless system. But even the actors inhabiting it seem to lack differentiated motives. Ransom's experiment on the borderlands of the various counterfactual forms thus indicates that, although the econometric revolution gave historical counterfactualism a new methodological legitimacy, it remains situated far from the narrative demands of both traditional history and the alternate-history imagination.

Ransom's book also helps us to see where the counterfactual Civil War discourses we've tracked from the 1850s through the twentieth century had arrived by 2005. Which aspects of the earlier works seemed vital to his extraordinary compilation of Civil War alternatives and which seemed to have faded? Most obviously, the polemical dimensions of the earlier works had almost entirely disappeared. There is no sense here, as there was in Crosby, Mencken, and Churchill, that some contemporary national or international problem—lynching, mob rule, prohibition, sectional poverty, or world war—would have been avoided if the Civil War had never been fought or the CSA had won; neither is there a suggestion that such claims any longer needed refuting. As one might expect of a practicing academic counterfactualist, Ransom conducts his inquiries as independently significant historical exercises, with no overt immediate social or political agendas. Moreover, he is certainly more interested in testing the various nexus points for continuing viability than any of the previous writers were, and he declares several of them historiographically moribund. Could the war have been avoided? No. Could it have been fought so differently that the South could have won? Probably not.[69] Would an independent CSA have continued to allow slavery? Not past the 1880s. Would it have been better for the former slaves if abolition had come through some process internal to the CSA? No.

The topics that have the strongest currents of significance running through them in Ransom's book are not these traditional ones concerning American society but, rather, are questions regarding the world-historical consequences of the war, its widest and most long-term ramifications. Churchill had, to be sure, alluded to the international ramifications in his fantasy of English-speaking global hegemony, but Ransom—situated at the end of the American century—has a much better vantage point from which to envisage recent world history in which a much smaller and less powerful USA competes with a hostile CSA on its southern border, while both find themselves subordinate to European powers. Ransom tells the biggest story of any we've seen so far precisely because he is released, both historically and polemically, from the domestic preoccupations of the earlier writers. We've seen that throughout the late nineteenth and twentieth centuries Americans had pressing reasons for imagining that the USA lost the Civil War, and Ransom demonstrates why we should continue to carry on this hypothetical enterprise: only by imagining all that would have been lost, he argues, can we understand the significance of the victory.

CHAPTER FOUR

Historical Activism and the Alternate-America Novels

Time-travel plots in which characters are transported back into the past to make changes in history that will alter the present have been staples of American popular culture since the 1980s. But they were relatively unusual in 1953, when a writer named Ward Moore combined backward time travel with alternate-history speculation in his novel *Bring the Jubilee*. It was the first American alternate-history novel published since *Hallie Marshall*'s obscure appearance in 1900 (discussed in chap. 2), and like its predecessor it imagined a world in which the Confederacy won the Civil War. *Bring the Jubilee*, though, was a novel in tune with the emerging civil rights movement; we could think of it as the novelistic equivalent of the revisionism in Civil War historiography, which we examined in the last chapter. While the revisionists were changing our understanding and interpretation of the past, the novelist indicated that to change the status quo in the present, we should try to imagine what sort of past could have led to a present we'd like to inhabit and a future we could wholeheartedly desire.

Bring the Jubilee was the first of some thirty novels published in the last half of the twentieth century to construct imaginary Americas, where the changes in our history lead to significantly different interracial arrangements. Not all of these alternate-America novels change the outcome of the Civil War, but—as in most alternate-history narratives—wars and rebellions provide the nexus points: the American Revolutionary War, the Mexican-American War, John Brown's rebellion, the Civil War, or the subsequent U.S. campaigns against Native American nations. Thematically and formally, these novels vary widely; among them we find utopias and dystopias, nexus and aftermath settings, social satires and hero glorifications, war stories, murder mysteries, spy thrillers, and cross-time adventures. But they all make interracial relations the crucial index in their implicit comparisons between the alternate Americas and ours.

This chapter explores the interactions between these novels and the various civil rights federal programs and international justice movements that also used historical-counterfactual reasoning in the late twentieth century. It became common in the political culture of the time to look back at what happened—as well as what might have happened instead—for guidance about how to move forward; examining previous historical options was a way to escape cycles of repetition determined by past injustices. These programs share what I'm calling historical activism in that they attempt to amend past wrongs and mitigate their present effects, viewing history as a reparable continuous process in which we might consciously and actively intervene to undo or reverse some regretted course of events. Historical activism itself underwent changes throughout the last half of the twentieth century, first taking the form of general remedial welfare programs, then affirmative action, and finally appearing in demands for reparations; and the novels were transformed in each phase as well. This chapter situates the novels in this shifting legal-political landscape, but it goes further to demonstrate that the fiction reveals things about the last century's attempts to accelerate racial equality that are not otherwise apparent. Their personalization of the desire to improve the present by changing the past gave form to some of the most elusive hopes, fears, and frustrations entailed in our attempts to remain the *United States of America*.

BRING THE JUBILEE, POST-WWII SOCIAL CRITICISM, AND THE APPEAL OF "IMPROBABILIA"

I'll begin my analysis with an extended discussion of Ward Moore (1903–78) and his fiction because, for all practical purposes, *Bring the Jubilee* launched the American alternate-history novel. Its only predecessor (*Hallie Marshall*) lacked readers and sank immediately into well-deserved oblivion in 1900, whereas *Bring the Jubilee* has had a lasting effect on the form it reinvented. It behooves us to look in some detail at the book, its creator, and the post-WWII milieu that encouraged him, especially since his addition of backward time travel to alternate world making became a staple of the genre and led to its categorization as a type of "science fiction." Ward Moore was not happy with that categorization, his attitude toward the label being at best ambivalent. On the one hand, he feared that it implied mindless adventure tales, on a par with what he contemptuously called "space operas," and he complained that lumping all nonrealistic fiction into the category would bury serious speculative, avant-garde, and experimental works under a pile of commercial sensationalism.[1] On the other hand, he recognized the contemporary vitality of a community of writers who referred to their own work as science fiction, and he included several of them in a competing category of his own invention, which he called "improbabilia." It was an obscure term with a learned sound, which he took from eighteenth-century aesthetic theory and used to raise the cultural profile of nonrealist prose. Its authors included writers of utopias and dystopias ("from Plato and Sir Thomas More through Dean Swift to H. G. Wells and George Orwell"), uncanny speculative fiction (Edgar Allan Poe, Karel Čapek, Aldous Huxley), and high-quality contemporary science fiction (Ray Bradbury, Isaac Asimov, John Campbell).[2] All of these authors, he claimed, departed from common reality in order to test new political ideas and experiment with alternative social possibilities. "Improbabilia," according to Moore, was "the ideal form for displaying not only the shortcomings of the civilization . . . but the remedy, or the disaster if some remedy is not applied."[3] He wanted to combine the "literature of ideas" with that of the "marvelous" in the service of social criticism, and science fiction could be a means to that end, but only in rare cases.

Moore had not begun his career producing improbabilia. He had spent his youth on the radical outskirts of bohemia in Chicago, and (after 1929) California, where he began writing under the auspices of the Federal Writers Project of the Works Progress Administration in the 1930s.[4] From the 1940s until his death in 1978, he wrote essays and reviews for left-wing journals like the *Nation* as well as for more mainstream periodicals like *Harper's Bazaar* and the *San Francisco Chronicle*. In 1942 he published an autobiographical novel, which centered on labor organizing at the outset of the Great Depression and self-consciously imitated Frank Norris's and Jack London's naturalism. His turn to improbabilia began directly after the war, when he published a quirky and acerbic parody targeting popular science-fiction adventures and the chemical industry's environmental irresponsibility (a biologically altered grass takes over the world).[5] And in the early 1950s, he started promoting improbabilia as a vehicle for introducing "ideas" into commercial culture and stressing its political provocations: "Improbabilia authors represent all shades of politics . . . all convictions from atheism to piety, and only the least accomplished leave their opinions behind when they sit down at the typewriter." [6] They were out to shock their readers into thought by recommending "polygamy, or a planned economy," as Jonathan Swift had, ironically, "advocated cannibalism." In 1953, the year that *Bring the Jubilee* came out, Moore claimed improbabilia was under attack from McCarthyite "Senators and Congressmen who equate political purity with intellectual sterility," and he then predicted that when the medium is "respectable" again, it will generate novels that are "political primarily but also philosophical." He clearly wanted his readers to have his improbabilia alternative to science fiction in mind as the proper category for *Bring the Jubilee*, whose political nature he was advertising in advance.

One last point to note about the milieu that produced *Bring the Jubilee*: Moore saw it as a field where readers and writers interacted incessantly. He lovingly described the fanzines—"multigraphed, mimeographed, or hectographed"—produced by the numerous readers' clubs and societies that were "devoted to discussion and analysis of the medium." "It is these 'fanzines,'" he declared, "which give the clue to the peculiar attitude of the enthusiasts . . . ; they are all potential yet unfrustrated writers."[7] With this audience in mind, a writer could give real weight to abstract thought, for his readers would respond with matching conjectures and commentaries. Whereas realist forms reproduce the already known, leaving their fictional premises implicit, improbabilia are obliged to foreground their hypotheses, often creating occasions for explicitly articulating their leading ideas in the fiction itself. Thus, the motivating concepts come to the forefront of the work, inviting critical examination. The general field of improbabilia was thus something like an immense cerebral game, attracting players rather than mere consumers.[8]

All of these features of Ward Moore's political and cultural habitus came together in *Bring the Jubilee*. Its eclectic form combines several types of improbabilia: alternate-history dystopia, episodic quest, utopian experiment, political dialogue, social satire, and lastly—almost incidentally—science fiction. The backward time-travel episode sits like an afterthought at the end of the novel, and it is the hardest part to explain in political terms. At first it might seem just a nod to a community of readers-cum-writers that Moore had invested with peculiar nonconformist vitality, but a closer look will reveal that time travel imports its own set of political themes, which partly accord with the novel's other political engagements and partly sound a note of discord that will reverberate through the genre's subsequent history. To hear its full resonance, we have to separate the alternate-history and time-travel components, an operation the novel makes easy by leaving the time travel for the very end; I will follow the novel's lead and describe first what the book accomplishes simply as an alternate-history novel before delving more deeply into the use it makes of backward chronology.

As if directly refuting the many early twentieth-century fantasies that a victorious South and a defeated North would have been kinder, gentler places, Moore portrays both alternate Americas as dystopias, although their miseries are differently distributed, with the defeated North bearing a disproportionate load of postwar suffering. As in the majority of Civil War alternate histories, the alternate world is constructed on the structural principle of reversal, but instead of preserving the best features of each region (as in the counterfactuals of Crosby, Mencken, and Churchill), the reversed outcome in this novel turns each into an even worse version of the actual other. By the early twentieth century of the novel's initial timeline, economic pressures in the CSA have led to the slaves' manumission, and their descendants outnumber those of their former owners by five to one; but they have never been granted full citizenship and continue to be held in a perpetual state of social and political subordination. Even worse racial horrors, though, have occurred in the defeated USA, for the South has at least reaped the benefits of victory in the form of economic progress, industrial development, and full employment, whereas the North has sunk into a slough of backwardness. It lingers in a twilight state of postwar depression for generations, becoming a nightmarish mirror image of the worst aspects of the *actual* Southern states in the first half of the twentieth century, and it is in this reversed and inverted alternate reality that the protagonist tries to make his way from poverty and ignorance to enlightenment.

The transposed similarities between the alternate and actual Americas form the groundwork of the novel's social criticism. The alternate USA is a rural society in which most farmers are sharecroppers; indeed, to perfect the inversion, most people are not truly free but have descended into indentured servitude. The country is obsessed with racial separation, a fact that one character explains as the natural consequence of having "lost a war, the most important war in our history" to end black slavery; African Americans are therefore viewed as the source of all the impoverished whites' misery.[9] Lynching and other forms of racial violence and exclusion are common; the country is isolationist and narrowly provincial. Politically, its voters veer between electing oligarchic "gentlemen" who sell them out and demagogic "populists" who cater to all of their prejudices. There is even a terrorist organization, like the Ku Klux Klan, which abducts and murders blacks and interfering foreigners, and the educational system lags far behind the standard of the industrial South, where the wealthiest families send their sons to college. To be sure, the alternate "Northron America" is not intended as an exact replica of the actual South, but as a satirical exaggeration, just as the novel's "Southron America," with its emancipated but disenfranchised blacks, its advanced technologies, military and industrial imperialism, and growing international power, is a caricature of the North.

Reversal in the form of regression also characterizes the alternate historical world's social and political position; indeed, *Bring the Jubilee* recalls Tourgée's *Fool's Errand* in its insistence on temporal reversal or devolution to a previous stage of civilization and moral understanding. Carefully described details of the alternate world's 1930s–40s New York—its horse-and-buggy transportation (only the very rich can afford the steam-driven automobiles), deteriorating roads, gaslights, broken railways, continued reliance on the telegraph for long-distance communication, as well as its ruined and disappearing middle class—indicate that there has been degeneration even from the social and political conditions of the mid-nineteenth-century. And the deterioration of the nation's moral condition is one of the novel's major themes, introduced in the narrator's opening self-presentation, when he explains his descent from a notorious man, "Grandfather Backmaker," who had failed to devolve in the required way:

> I got the impression my father's father had been . . . a man who kept on believing in the things for which [the war was] fought after they were proved wrong. I don't know how I learned that Grandfather Backmaker had made speeches advocating equal rights for Negroes or protesting the mass lynchings so popular in the north, in contrast to the humane treatment accorded these non-citizens in the Confederacy. Nor do I remember where I heard he had been run out of several places before finally settling in Wappinger Falls or that all his life people had muttered darkly at his back, "Dirty Abolitionist!"—a very deep imprecation indeed. (4)

The name "Backmaker," the protagonist's patronymic, obviously foreshadows the time travel to come, but it also emphasizes that the chronological movement along the alternate timeline has been a backward movement of decline from the progressive moral standards of the past.

Reversal—in both geographic and moral-chronological terms—is thus the pattern of alteration differentiating this possible North America from ours and emphasizing the clear superiority of the actual outcome. But it is not that simple, for much in this altered reality is designed to make us recognize it as our own, including the very fact that Northron America looks so much like the contemporary Deep South. The rhetorical effect of this geographical transposition of social realities is to suggest that the racial hatred still visible in America's actual South after World War II was not necessarily the legacy of a slaveholding society but might have occurred even in a formerly abolitionist region of the North if the social and economic conditions had been ripe and the political system sufficiently perverted. White racism, the novel seems to claim, is a ubiquitous American trait, which can be exploited in either region. The reversals are designed to disturb our complacency about the direction of history and to make Northerners wonder if their sense of superiority to white Southern racists might not be just winner's arrogance. We had the moral luck to win, it strongly implies, but we might have been worse than they if the outcome had been reversed. We must therefore be on guard against our own tendencies toward provincialism, isolationism, racism, distrust of foreigners, penchant for conspiracy theories, purges of suspected subversives, and all the other symptoms of what Richard Hofstadter would later call the "paranoid style of American politics."[10]

Like many alternate-history worlds before it, this one asks to be read as a warning about contemporary and future conditions not only through such large-scale social allegories but also by introducing specific and noticeable satirical allusions to more local real-world current events. The numerous pointed descriptions of the alternate world's general anti-intellectualism, and especially its self-destructive attacks on its own universities, for example, are clearly intended to have specific cross-world relevance. In the late 1940s and early 1950s, right-wing politicians throughout the country demanded that public universities require their faculties to sign "loyalty oaths" in hopes of producing political conformity. *Bring the Jubilee* was published at the height of the loyalty-oath controversy at the University of California, where legislators had pressured the university's regents into mandating the firing of any faculty member who refused to sign an oath, and Moore's satire of the contemporary situation is overt in the narrator's descriptions of Northron America's disdainful attitude toward higher education. Depicting the state of alternate-world opinion in terms that would have been completely familiar to his readers—"the average man asked what the United States needed colleges for anyway; those who attended them only learned discontent and to question time-honored institutions"—the narrator mocks misguided attempts to bring the faculties under control: "Constant scrutiny of the faculties, summary firing of all instructors suspected of abnormal ideas, did not seem to improve the situation or raise the standards of teaching" (9). So even though the alternate USA is often coded as the actual South, it also defines the direction in which the entire country might be moving in 1952. The dystopia, in short, is not a stable geographical or temporal location but a continuous potential, unfixed in space and time, yet holding particular relevance for Americans in the McCarthy era. By bringing to life the alternate dystopian condition of a nation mired in a prolonged post-defeat malaise and by stressing its surprising similarities to post-WWII America, *Bring the Jubilee* creates the sense that Americans in the early1950s are actually disconnected from their own historical reality. The early 1950s should be years in which Americans bask in the afterglow of an enormous victory; they should feel self-confident, secure, and generous. But instead they are gripped by anticommunist hysteria, stumbling into yet another war, in Korea, and witnessing the revival of racism and isolationism in domestic politics. In short, Moore's alternate world suggests, we were behaving "as if" we'd lost.

Bring the Jubilee thus repeats the theme we explored in the last chapter's alternate histories: in many respects, our world looks surprisingly like one in which the USA lost the Civil War. Moore's estrangement techniques reinforce the uncanny sense of being between realities. Even the bildungsroman narrative form—its hero's alienation from the social norm, intellectual ambition, encounters with competing mentors, enclaves of enlightenment, lists of books, lengthy theoretical conversations and lengthier disquisitions about his ideas—keeps us on the margins of the alternate reality. Indeed, the narrative form serves the purposes of dystopian world making very well, since it uses the picaresque career of a natural outsider—Hodge, an alienated intellectual—to explore the contours of the strange reality. Hodge is the sort of native informant common to travel and ethnographic writing as well as to utopias and dystopias. He seems a stranger in his own world to begin with, and his discomfort in it only grows with wider knowledge. The subjective intensity of the first-person narration, moreover, reinforces the sense that the alternate world's burdensome social and political conditions are less determined by history than by some mysterious will to be miserable, some collective psychological resistance to change. Finally, as in many novelistic dystopias, the plot discovers a community of like-minded souls, a commune of scholars. There Hodge is able to become a historian and also to meditate at length on the puzzles of historical causality that have fascinated him throughout the book: Is history determined or accidental? Is it fated to repeat itself, as Nietzsche claimed, or is it open to our exertions? Thus Moore gradually merges the personal and psychological issues of the quest with the abstract conceptual preoccupations of improbabilia.

The novel's concluding swerve into time travel might be seen as a device that allows the abstract thematic concerns to take over the plot. The story veers away from Hodge's personal history, which is overwhelmed by the very intellectual ambition that had fueled it, and heads toward a climactic moment of history itself. Hodge had become a well-known military historian by publishing a book on the battles leading up to Gettysburg, in which he asserts that the turning-point battle itself might have ended differently if the Confederate troops had not occupied the hills called the Round Tops on July 1 (before the arrival of Lee). He is challenged to prove his thesis conclusively by a Southron historian, who insists that the victory turned on no such "fortuitous" circumstance but was instead the result of the "supreme genius of General Lee," and Hodge loses confidence in his ability to marshal the necessary evidence. After months of hesitation, Hodge (the narrator) reports that he could no longer tolerate his uncertainty about the nature of historical processes; so when his former lover—a psychologically unstable but extraordinarily brilliant physicist—suggests that he use her newly built time-travel machine to visit the battle itself, he agrees. He is careful to "do nothing" to change the outcome, and it is precisely by doing nothing, remaining silent when asked a crucial question about whether Union troops have moved up to the Round Tops, that Hodge starts a panic among the Confederate soldiers, who were just about to occupy that high ground themselves. They not only beat a disorderly retreat from the place, leaving the little hills available for the Union forces, but also cause the death of their commander, who happens to be the grandfather of the physicist. So no physicist, no time machine, and Hodge is stranded in the "elsewhen" he created. He is professionally vindicated—he has proven the power of the merely fortuitous—but it does him no good since he is a nonperson in this new past and inhabits it as a melancholy exile. Hodge's passivity, especially his inability to seize the initiative against perpetrators of social injustice, has been thematized throughout the novel, so when it reappears at a moment of world-changing hesitation, we recognize that the motif has resolved into a message: even if we try to achieve historical neutrality, our very inaction will have consequences.

This is not to say that *Bring the Jubilee* ends on a politically triumphant note. The conclusion is instead split between the narrator's melancholic personal reflections and reminders that the North has still not definitely won the peace. In the first of many such episodes in these novels of historical activism, we are given plenty of time to take in the incongruity of scales in the two levels of action that are brought suddenly and apocalyptically into collision. This is not merely another instance of the "Cleopatra's nose" trope, in which tiny personal motives have huge historical effects, for those older *petite cause* stories (as we noted in chap. 1) concerned private lives of historically powerful persons. Here it is the personal crisis of an insignificant historian that has world-changing effects, and thus the usual novelistic relation between private fictional and public historical plots, the direction of cause and effect between them, and even their chronological synchronization are disrupted. Indeed, *Bring the Jubilee* invents a special kind of narrative anachronia. The time of the events narrated (what Gérard Genette calls the "histoire") is chronologically progressive, since it tracks the biography of the protagonist, from childhood to middle age and through the transformation of the world in which he lives to his old age, which is given in a postscript.[11] But the narrating time (the "récit") is supposed to take place forty-four calendar years *before* the protagonist's date of birth. This much is conveyed in the novel's opening puzzler: "Although I am writing this in the year 1877, I was not born until 1921" (1). Thus the *récit* is said to precede its *histoire* in calendar time, an innovation in novelistic temporality. Drawing on alternate-history understandings of dual timelines we tend to resolve this contradiction by locating the first half of Hodge's life in one timeline and the second in the other, but the solution begs the question of how we are to imagine their articulation. Do they inhabit parallel universes? The melancholy narrator, cut off from those he loves, wants to deny the possibility:

> Are they really gone, irrevocably lost, in a future which never existed, which couldn't exist, once the chain of causation was broken? Or do they exist after all, in a universe in which the South won the battle of Gettysburg and Major Haggerswells founded Haggershaven? . . . I would give much to believe this, but I cannot. I simply cannot.
> . . . And once lost, that particular past can never be regained. Another and another perhaps, but never the same one. There are no parallel universes—though this one may be sinuous and inconstant. (192)

We'll soon look more closely into the pool of time-travel melancholy that this passage is drawn from; for now, we should just note that there is no perfectly coherent way of making historical activism and backward time-travel theories compatible.

Moore's vocabulary sometimes encourages us to imagine simultaneous twin worlds; using the language typical of alternate histories, he describes the "peculiarly frustrate and disinherited world" (1) into which he was born, and later remarks that "this world is a better place than the one into which I was born." The "elsewhens" are thereby analogized to "elsewheres," and yet there is an explicit rejection of their simultaneous existence. Instead, the alternate-history *modal* contrast remains in the formulation of the paradox: Hodge's natal world *would have* come into existence if he had not ridden Barbara's time machine to the Battle of Gettysburg and destroyed the very condition of his time travel in the process of changing the outcome. The paradox reminds us that novels are different from alternate histories; when reading Churchill's or Ransom's narratives, we stand on the heights of a temporal mountaintop beside the counterparts of world-historical players in a gargantuan game, and we are continually reminded of the priority of the alternative actions of their real-world models. The stories are not designed to solicit any psychic investment in the counterpart personnel or their destinies. But the novels try to give us the ground-level view, the lived experience of a possible alternate-historical world. As we've seen, they have to build that world in some detail and populate it with characters who have no real-world counterparts. They aim to give the alternate world an uncanny familiarity and solicit interest in the characters' fates. In a dystopia like *Bring the Jubilee*, we share the protagonist's estrangement from the alternate world and we might therefore look forward to the moment when he leaves it for ours. But it cannot work that way, partly, to be sure, because Hodge has already taken refuge in a utopian enclave, but mainly because, like any novel character, he is not really conceivable outside of his fictional world. Especially in a first-person novel, the diegetic world is realized in represented interaction with the character, and vice versa. So no matter how negatively the fictional character judges his world, he cannot choose another in preference to it, for that would be choosing against himself. Giving in to his merely might-have-been nature, Hodge does nothing in our world except write the "autobiography" that is the novel diegesis and hang around near Gettysburg waiting to die.

What *Bring the Jubilee*'s cross-time plot brings to alternate-history narrative, therefore, is an exploration of the incommensurability of the "objective" historical perspective and the personal one: if a person could move from a world in which his country lost the Civil War to one in which it won, how could he possibly be ready for that change, how could he actually live it? And since the novel leaves us suspended between those two possible worlds, especially by wondering if Our Timeline really did play out as that of the winners, it raises the question of how well prepared *we* are to function in a world where full emancipation is a reality. And finally, by bringing the alternate future that produced Hodge into being and then consigning it to the status of a past memory, Moore calls our attention to the similarities between the alternative futures that confronted the country in the supposed year of the "autobiography's" composition, 1877, when Reconstruction was ended and the country started down the wrong track, and in the actual present of the novel's publication in 1954, when we may be able to get back on the road to the Jubilee. Of course, Hodge is not supposed to know what our future holds in 1877, and his optimistic ignorance allows both the author's admonitory irony and his call to historical action.

Once trapped inside Our Timeline, which is his alternate past, and writing the last pages of his autobiography, Hodge cautiously ventures the opinion that he may unwittingly have created a superior reality: "That this world is a better place than the one into which I was born, and promises to grow still better, seems true" (192). But the hopeful comparison soon opens yet another temporal viewpoint, the present of the novel's writing (in narratological terms, the "author's present") in 1952. As Hodge looks forward from the late 1870s, he sees continuing progress, but his point of view is designed to contrast with the view from the early 1950s: "The Negro is free; black legislatures pass advanced laws in South Carolina; black congressmen comport themselves with dignity in Washington." We are being reminded in this sentence that 1877—the year when the fictional Hodge is supposed to have written it—was the last in which such an optimistic assessment could have been made; it was the final turning point away from "Reconstruction" and back toward white supremacy. The next paragraph makes the impending reversal explicit: "There are rumors of a deal between northern Republicans and southern Democrats, betraying the victory of the Civil War . . . in return for the presidency. If this is true my brave new world is not so brave. And it may not be so new either" (192). With these literary allusions to Shakespeare's *Tempest* and Aldous Huxley's *Brave New World*, both works about mistaken expectations of a utopia, the narrator acknowledges that the new world he inadvertently made may already be turning back into the one he left. Hodge is a "Backmaker" in several senses: he travels back in time to revive the possibilities for which his ancestors had fought, bringing the "Jubilee" of the title, the day of liberation that had been lost in his own timeline; but he also ends his narrative at a second crossroads in Our Timeline that will undo his accomplishment and produce a regression in racial relations. As in *A Fool's Errand*, the reversal (Northern victory) is about to be reversed.

In 1953, when the novel appeared, it would probably have seemed remarkable that Ward Moore's protagonist praises Reconstruction and stresses the malign and conspiratorial nature of the Compromise of 1877. The "deal," as the narrator calls it, resolved the disputed presidential election of 1876 when the Republicans agreed to withdraw the remaining federal troops from the South, definitively ending Reconstruction and paving the way for the disenfranchisement of the black freedmen, in exchange for the Democrats' acquiescence in the Electoral College's selection of Republican presidential candidate Rutherford B. Hayes. In 1952, the reference to that bargain would have had obvious contemporary significance, for that year marked the beginning of an alliance between conservative Republicans and the states-rights Democrats, known as Dixiecrats, who had revolted against the national Democratic party to punish President Truman for appointing his President's Committee on Civil Rights, which proposed several measures repugnant to segregationists: antilynching legislation, an end to the poll tax, a permanent Fair Employment Practices Commission, and integration of both interstate transportation and the armed forces. When Truman in 1948 announced his intention to seek implementation of all of the recommendations through a combination of executive order and legislative initiative, the Dixiecrats fielded third-party candidates in the South. Although the third-party effort was spent by 1952 (when their main antagonist, Truman, decided not to run again), many Dixiecrats supported the Republican candidate, Dwight Eisenhower. The year 1952 saw the beginning of what would eventually become a wholesale transfer of the political allegiance of segregationist white Southerners to the Republican Party, so there are strong parallels between the time of the narrating inside the story and the time of the writing outside of it.[12]

Thus, the novel takes full political advantage of the time-travel plot by pairing 1877, when Hodge writes his autobiography, with 1952, when Moore writes his novel, emphasizing that contemporary America had once again reached a crossroads, a nexus, when it might either again betray the goal of emancipation or finally realize it. Replete with allusions to the turning point in North/South and black/white relations taking place at the moment of its production, Moore's novel issues a warning that we will have to be vigilant lest history repeat itself by *again* reversing itself and turning away from the new federal initiatives. The title of the book, *Bring the Jubilee*, is an exhortation to take action, to complete resolutely the trajectory toward liberation that Hodge's time travel accidentally launched. Here we are again, the novel tells us, back at a similar moment of moral decision. The history-changing time-travel plot is, therefore, used to release certain social dynamics from their particular coordinates in time and space, allowing us to see the similarities between the readers' present options and those of historical actors. The device reinforces the lesson that Hodge learned when mastering the historian's craft: "That the past is past becomes ever less important. Except for perspective it might as well be the present or the future or, if one can conceive it, a parallel time" (117). Numerous such reflections on the unfinished state of history combine with the time-travel plot and the hortatory overtones of the title to suggest that the last campaigns of the Civil War are just beginning in 1952. Hodge's "victory," Moore emphasizes, was later "betrayed" and needs to be re-won. And hence, in the decade before what we call the civil rights era, *Bring the Jubilee* marked another turning point in the history of the trope we traced in the last chapter—the lament that the USA lost the Civil War—by converting it into a call for action.

TIME TRAVEL'S BACK STORY

Here I will interrupt my account of the relation between alternate-America novels and historical activism in the late twentieth century in order to explain how earlier backward time-travel narratives had addressed the issue of historical causation. Considering the background of the device will give us a fuller understanding of its connections to alternate history, especially to hypothetical speculations about the counterfactual destinies of genealogical groups, like nations and races. Backward time-travel stories had been elaborating genealogical puzzles for decades by the time Ward Moore introduced them into the alternate-history novel.

An 1881 *New York Sun* story by Edward Page Mitchell—"The Clock That Went Backward"—seems to be the first in which backward time travel and speculative history were brought together through a genealogical knot. In that story, a young descendant of Dutch settlers from New York, who is studying military science at the University of Leyden, finds himself transported back to a dramatic episode in the city's history, where he organizes a successful defense of the besieged Protestant community against the Imperial Hapsburg invaders. The plot opens in nineteenth-century New England, where one of the protagonist's relatives, a surprisingly long-lived aunt, makes it a condition of her legacy that he study at the University of Leyden after her death. Once in the Netherlands, he is prepared for his destiny by a description of the seventeenth-century battle, in which he discovers its "decisive moment" and learns that the principle of national self-determination, the United States of America, and his own personal existence all depend on the actions of a mysterious man who defended against a sudden breach in the city's fortifications. Using the familiar rhetoric of counterfactual conjecture, his mentor enjoins:

> Consider some of the consequences had he failed. The fall of Leyden would have destroyed the last hope of the Prince of Orange and of the free states. The tyranny of Philip would have been reestablished. The birth of religious liberty and of self-government by the people would have been postponed, who knows for how many centuries? Who knows that there would or could have been a republic of the United States of America had there been no United Netherlands? Our University, which has given to the world Grotius, Scaliger, Arminius, and Descartes, was founded upon this hero's successful defense of the breach. We owe to him our presence here today. Nay, you owe to him your very existence. Your ancestors were of Leyden; between their lives and the butchers outside the walls he stood that night.[13]

The story is an early instance of circular historical causality: the time traveler saves his own ancestors, who then set in motion the conditions under which he will save them, bringing himself into existence. Like many subsequent time-travel stories, this one has a professorial guide, a putatively "Hegelian" philosopher, who explains that, from a purely dialectical "metaphysical" point of view, "before" and "after" are reversible; all exists simultaneously, and hence causes might succeed as well as precede effects. The time-loop pattern of causality is one of the most common backward time-travel plots; it usually entails no contradictions of consistency between past and present, and it possesses a satisfying economy, in which teleology and instrumentality coincide and causes serve simultaneously as effects. All elements of the past are included in the present, so there is only one timeline, although it must curve back on itself to form a circle. The time traveler causes the history we know, but, precisely because he is himself the result of that history, it is impossible that he might have changed it to produce an alternate present in which he might not have existed. There is a kind of historical activism at work in this plot, but it is limited to affecting through affirmative preservation, rather than changing, one's own genealogy and the historical world to which it belongs.[14] In the end, the professor states the "moral":

> We hear much of the influence of the sixteenth century upon the nineteenth. No philosopher, as far as I am aware, has studied the influence of the nineteenth century upon the sixteenth. If cause produces effect, does effect never induce cause? Does the law of heredity, unlike all other laws of this universe of mind and matter, operate in one direction only? Does the descendant owe everything to the ancestor and the ancestor nothing to the descendant? Does destiny, which may seize upon our existence, and for its own purposes bear us far into the future, never carry us back into the past? (86)

Past and present are interdependent, and so, although there can be no alternate history in this story, it nevertheless contains one crucial element of historical activism: we are answerable for the history that produced us.

This moral, though, also allows us to see why time travel could serve as an excellent vehicle for purposeful (if ultimately futile) rebellion *against* history, which was just how the Dadaist poet Jacques Rigaut used it in 1922, when he published a short satirical piece titled "Un brillant sujet." The subtitle is simply "roman," but the story is actually more like a précis for a thought experiment in which the hero goes on a chaotic quest in a backward time machine to undo creation itself. Palentête is the hero's name, perhaps a play on the word "palindrome" (a phrase that says the same thing whether read forward or backward) to imply that the hero has the same *tête*, or head, whether facing the future or the past. He soon learns, though, that backward-orientation changes the very nature of actions, and in the course of this tiny narrative, Rigaut outlines the three most prominent backward time-travel puzzles, which would soon become the common property of science-fiction writers. Seeking to retrieve a lost mistress from his past, the protagonist encounters his younger self as a rival; his attempt to repair his personal past thus multiplies him and puts him at strife with himself. He then moves back another twenty-three years, commits incest, and "has several reasons to believe that he is his own father," producing a time loop of self-generation.[15] Having violated two elementary laws of singular personhood and inaugurated a pair of standard tropes, he sets off on a manically destructive spree, the ultimate goal of which is the prevention of creation, which would obliterate everything, including himself. However, he then confronts the inconsistency called the "grandfather paradox," in which a time traveler destroys the conditions of his time travel, leading to the logical conundrum that he can only perform such an act if he exists, but if he performs the act, he will never have existed. "Doubtful of encountering God and powerless to modify a past of which he is the progeny, Palentête applies himself to creating new versions."[16] He creates alternate-history pandemonium, revisiting and reversing well-known counterfactual nexuses, cutting short Cleopatra's nose, for example, and bestowing the use of gas and electricity on South American indigenous civilizations before their European discovery. These "new versions" are the result of the protagonist's thwarted desire to bring about complete nothingness, and the narrator tells us that they are designed to "confuse the men of his own period who might try to follow him into the past and would no longer find that it conforms to history."[17]

Changing history for Rigaut was thus a subsidiary ambition to destroying it altogether. True to its origin in the absurdist literary environment of Dadaism, Rigaut's time travel is an expression of a nihilism so extreme that it borders on self-satire. He was one of several Dadaists who celebrated suicide, publically announcing his intention to commit the act and meticulously executing it in 1929 at the age of thirty. His time-traveling protagonist's suicidal impulse extends outward to include everything. If he could destroy himself by preventing creation, he not only would obliterate the universe but would also cause it never to have been at all. In identifying the absurdity of such an ambition, the story implies that even suicide is not the radical *acte gratuit*, the superbly free act, that the Dadaists imagined it to be, for it involves the acknowledgment that one's ability to act relies on the unwilled past of which one is the progeny. Thus, although Mitchell and Rigaut are on opposite ends of the spectrum of time-traveling historical activism, the former demonstrating dutiful execution of one's role in the maintenance of one's ancestry and the latter fantasizing defiant negation, both highlight the hero as a contingent effect of his own genealogy. Rigaut's hero may try to cover his tracks by alternate history, but he must still submit to the impossibility of being the agent who destroys the conditions of his being: Palentête can inhabit none of the diverse realities he tries to create. Instead he dies of old age inside his time machine.[18]

These earliest stories of backward time travel thus seem certain that characters are powerless to change history in any way that would change the present and that trying to do so would be self-annihilating. The remarkable thing about them—and about single-timeline time-travel stories after them—is their fixation on the traveler's back story; the main action is usually the discovery that he has one and is unable to take any action that would cancel it, which often means that he cannot take any action leading to an alternate history. We could read the tales as chastisements of modern ambitions to disregard the past either as individuals or as a society, to conceive of ourselves as self-generated, unbeholden to and radically disconnected from our predecessors. But we should also notice that they follow a general rule of historical fiction: fictional characters seldom rise to the level of public importance that would allow them to make changes in the historical record. In these backward time-travel fables, that generic rule comes into the foreground when the personal history of the fictional being prevents him from tampering with the historical world as we know it.[19]

Another French narrative, the full-length novel *Le voyageur imprudent* (1944) written by René Barjavel (1911–85) in Vichy France, makes this point explicitly. Barjavel, like Rigaut, worked in the tradition of French absurdist literature, and *Le voyageur imprudent* shows the strong influence of Alfred Jarry, especially in its visions of future worlds in which the search for self-gratification leads to masses of men, shaped like Jarry's illustration of his antihero Père Ubu, rushing madly toward lustful self-extinction. Only in the last episodes of the book does the protagonist, whose name is St. Menoux, begin traveling into the past, where he finds that—in a slight modification of the formal rule—he can make small changes in the destinies of private persons but truly historic changes are beyond his power. Barjavel's stubborn protagonist, though, insists on testing his ability to bend the rule. Plagued by an irrepressible longing to know for certain whether he can change History with a capital *H*, which he conceives as a desire to know if History is predetermined or contingently and spontaneously made, he attempts to kill the young Bonaparte at the battle of Toulon in 1793: "Napoleon was not set in motion by other men, but imposed himself on them. His personal genius drove his ventures. If he succumbed at the beginning of his career, if a stray bullet killed him at the siege of Toulon, what would History become?"[20] Paradoxically, in order to carry out the experiment, the protagonist must imagine that there is at least one historical agent, namely, Napoleon, whose historical activity is unconstrained, and the book thus makes it explicit that the plot in which a time traveler tries to change history is a parable of the self-assertion of the *common* man (symbolized by the fictional nobody) against historically significant men. The novel equates the categories of fictional persona and private, subhistorical person, and pretends to test whether a random sniper (played by the time traveler) could have killed Napoleon. Predictably, St. Menoux shoots his own ancestor by mistake, so his attack against *l'Histoire* backfires, and he is erased from existence along with his time machine. Fourteen years after the publication of the novel, Barjavel acknowledged that the grandfather paradox rendered the ending absurd, for "if St. Menoux does not exist, and he never did exist, he could not have killed his ancestor!"[21] But, logical or not, his novel, like Mitchell's and Rigaut's stories, demonstrates that when history is conceived of as a single timeline, backward time-travel plots do not generate alternate-history outcomes, even if their timelines take circuitous paths or undergo small perturbations and changes in details.[22]

The use of the grandfather paradox to foreclose possibilities of historical change follows formal constraints on fictional characters and draws on the ironic counterfactual pattern in which attempted historical reversals have unintended consequences that lead back to the original outcomes, chastising our tendency to imagine superior pasts or different presents. This particular device also, though, tells us something about alternate-history fictions that might not otherwise be apparent, for it emphasizes a rupture between the fictional past and the writer's and reader's present that is easy to ignore when the narratives take place entirely inside an Alternate Timeline. To be sure, we are aware of the implicit contrast with Our Timeline when reading alternate histories like Geoffroy-Château's or Churchill's, and yet we are not prompted to wonder if the person imagining the alternative could have come into existence within them. Furthermore, as we've noticed, the relevance of the collateral timeline to our own is maintained in alternate histories by the continuity of historical personnel, which strengthens the reader's impression of an overall identity of human inhabitants between the worlds. But when alternate-history novels and short stories add imaginary personnel, instead of merely reshuffling a constant set of human actors, they frequently raise the specters of biological loss and potential generation. They emphasize that persons are not the given data of history, fixed and prior to events, but are instead its contingent products.

The novels featuring the grandfather paradox take the insight a step further by using fictional genealogies to turn the rift between optional timelines into an utter contradiction; they stage it as a moment in which the creator of the alternate world must go out of existence to bring it into being and therefore cannot complete the creation, or (if the timing is right) cannot survive to enjoy it even if the alteration is made. When reading them we are not asked to compare and judge alternatives impartially but instead to experience the dilemma of a character whose historical wishes contradict his very existence. This is the theme of a little-known science-fiction novel that was published in 1970, John Jakes's *Black in Time*, which explores racial identity through the conventions of the grandfather paradox. As alternate history merged with affirmative action discourse, the number of racially themed alternate-history *novels* increased. Of the fifteen written in the late 1960s through 1980s, *Black in Time* is the one story that takes the urge to change present race relations by altering history as its explicit theme. John Jakes became fairly well known as a writer of popular historical novels later in the decade, but he was publishing mainly in fantasy and science-fiction venues when he wrote this time-travel tale. Its protagonist is a mild-mannered African American academic, a classicist who has the use of a time-travel machine (called a Nexus apparatus) as one of his research tools for studying ancient Roman theater. The book is set in the near future (1977), and our hero unwittingly becomes embroiled in a conflict between warring gangs of black and white extremists. Forced by black nationalists to transport them to various interracial nexuses in the time machine, he reluctantly embarks on a search through history for the most effective "attack point" from which to change the relative conditions of the races in the United States. The white supremacists also hijack a time machine, and the plot takes on the pattern of a cross-time chase, in which the jockeying extremists seek to change history and the hero plays the role of a history policeman, trying to preserve the general continuity of OTL. The hero has the grandfather paradox in mind from the outset, and at each turning point he tries to explain to the black nationalists that their changes might end up "obliterating the whole damn black race!"[23] The goal for the black nationalists is to find an ATL in which Africans settled America instead of being transported in as slaves, and after a great many historical blunders, fights, and last-minute escapes in the Nexus apparatus, the prize is won. A change (the assassination of Muhammad) allows the Songhay Empire (western Sudan, ca. 1375–1591) to survive and thrive unmolested by the Moors, so that when the time travelers return to the Washington DC of 1977, they find New Songhay, a country run by the powerful majority of people derived from African settlers. But there is no racial peace, because the descendants of the European slaves imported in the seventeenth century are rioting in all the major cities. Even worse, no sooner does the little band of time travelers begin to explore the reversed-world racial arrangements than a great lethargy overtakes them; they lose their vitality, becoming perilously weak. On the verge of death, the protagonist recognizes that they are disappearing as "Time" corrects the anomaly of their existence, for the African Americans of Our Timeline have no reality in New Songhay, which descended through an entirely different genetic line. "None of us ever existed," explains the hero; "This isn't our promised land" (148).

Black in Time is a light concoction, with no pretentions to literary merit, but it presents the overlap between the backward time-travel trope and contemporary ambitions for racial historical activism in the form of affirmative action. As we saw in the last chapter, affirmative action programs justified themselves on premises that were borrowed from tort law, seeking remedies for the present consequences of past wrongs. The time travelers in the novel also follow that logic by viewing history as the field in which to seek a different present by exploring crucial historical junctures where revisions would have ameliorated (or worsened) the subsequent condition of some significant group of Americans. Published in the midst of affirmative action's spread, *Black in Time* might be thought of as a fantasy about turning the past into a battlefield on which warring parties seek strategic advantage. "We can change things. I know we can," the black nationalist leader insists; but only if "the right attack point" can be found (61). And, as in *Bring the Jubilee*, literalizing historical activism by introducing time travel exposes their parallel internal tensions. For example, the efforts to reverse the past can too easily themselves be reversed again, a problem signified in the novel by the competing quest of the white supremacists and in the affirmative action debate by demands that "reverse discrimination" be ended. Second, in both the time-travel fantasy and the affirmative action debate, it proves difficult to insure that only actual wrongdoers, those responsible for history's injustice, would be sacrificed to make the change. In the novel, for example, the black nationalist leader notes the irony of blaming Muhammad—"May my Muslim brothers at all those defunct U.S. mosques forgive me! This black [Songhay] empire would've thrived if it hadn't been for one man: The Prophet" (58)—but he assassinates him nevertheless. And finally, both encounter some racial version of the grandfather paradox: in the novel when the historical activists go back in time far enough to make a fundamental change, they preclude not just their own existences but also those of the people who were supposed to be saved.

The novel thus raises the question of a possible conflict between repair and preservation that could also apply to historical activism. Speculating, for example, that the world would have been a better place without the black Atlantic slave trade, do we then have to acknowledge that the existence of African Americans in the present USA would have been unlikely? Doesn't the historical-activist impulse to envision the undoing of the slave trade bear an unpleasant resemblance to the sentiments of white racists like Thomas Dixon, who lamented slavery as the root cause of biracial America? This is not to claim that the novel exposes some logical conundrum at the heart of historical activism. Identifying past injustices to racial and ethnic groups, tracing present inequalities to those sources, and designing programs to eradicate the inequalities is obviously not intrinsically illogical, and even asserting that the injustices were necessary to the existence of the wronged people need not undermine the legitimacy of the programs. The tension between repair and preservation only fuses into an impasse under the pressure of the grandfather paradox.

Lest we be tempted to conclude that applying the paradox to racial themes was primarily a way of foregrounding potential incoherences in historical activism, though, I want to look at the way a subsequent novel used it to explore the pain of the indistinction between injury and origin. Octavia Butler's 1979 novel *Kindred*, is probably the best-known exploration of this theme. *Kindred* is not an alternate-history novel because its time travel occurs inside a self-consistent loop where no divergence arises, and yet that very concentration on the singular genealogical thread running through the history of slavery makes it a powerful literary allegory of the psychosocial drama inspired by the civil rights era's emphasis on African American history. Time travel is an apt, even obvious, metaphor for what was coming to be viewed as the moral imperative to revivify in imagination the anonymous lives of the slaves. The 1970s saw the republication of dozens of long-neglected slave narratives, the development of African American history curricula in schools and the founding of black studies programs at universities; in 1976, the nation established an annual Black History Month; in the same year Alex Haley's novel *Roots: The Saga of an American Family* spent twenty-two weeks at the top of the *New York Times* "Best Seller List," and in the next year its enormously popular television adaptation appeared. *Kindred* can be read as a meditation on the intensity of this new hunger for African American history.

Its first-person narrator and protagonist, Dana, is an involuntary time traveler, a young African American writer living in Los Angeles in 1977, who is repeatedly transported to an early nineteenth-century Maryland plantation, in every instance arriving just in time to save the life of the same person, a boy named Rufus, who grows to manhood in the course of the plot. Although the time passing in 1977 is merely a matter of days, the time spent in the nineteenth century grows longer and longer, and the protagonist becomes increasingly entangled in the plantation's life. She realizes quite early in the novel that the child she saves, the son and heir of the plantation owner, is her great-great-grandfather and that a young girl on the plantation, a free black at the novel's beginning, is her great-great-grandmother. Dana is, moreover, aware that she is caught in a time loop, where she must enable the mating of her great-great-grandparents by insuring their survival. She acknowledges that they must already have survived if she is alive to travel to the past to save them: "His life could not depend on the actions of his unconceived descendant"; and yet it does appear that "he would have died without me." Thus it seems that "if I was to live, if others were to live, he must live. I didn't dare test the paradox."[24] The grandfather paradox is thus established early as the premise of the narrative: at once untestable within the confines of the story to follow and all-determining.

Knowing that she must not make any changes that threaten the lives of her ancestors or set any large-scale alternate historical processes in motion, Dana determines to make the most of her repeated visits to the Maryland plantation. She even imagines that she might intervene locally to improve life on the plantation, literalizing the desire for historical activism, but her attempts often backfire, and the plot works instead to enslave her great-great-grandmother, putting her entirely at the mercy of the young master who has grown up to be a typical specimen of his class. The critical turning point of the novel arrives when Dana's great-great-grandfather asks her to persuade her great-great-grandmother to submit to him sexually. Butler thus turns the grandfather paradox into a moral dilemma: either Dana helps her great-great-grandfather sexually coerce her unwilling great-great-grandmother (who detests him for killing the slave she loved) or she and her entire family will never have come into existence at all. Far from being the heroine who goes back in time to right wrongs and dispense justice, realizing the ambition of historical activism, Dana concludes that she must become complicit in one of slavery's most infamous practices. The narrator, of course, defends her decision as the least of the available evils, and the novel is, in that regard, a defense of slave women who were coerced into becoming their masters' concubines, bearing their children, and thus propagating the system. Indeed, the novel is something of a rebuke to later generations, whose very existence might have depended on such sacrifices, for thinking that they would have acted more rebelliously under the same conditions. Without living as a slave and experiencing the terror and brutality of the system, such retrospective judgments, the novel implies, are merely a form of ignorant arrogance. Moreover, by sending Dana's white husband on several of her time voyages, the novel stresses that even being a white man would be no adequate protection against a system that required constant vigilance against all forms of dissent. Immersing the reader in a detailed representation of that place and time while simultaneously commenting, through Dana's own incurable shock at its harshness, on our inability to realize it, *Kindred* asserts that modern Americans in general are unprepared to recognize themselves as the products of that abhorred past. Precisely insofar as we reject that stage in our national past, we suffer from a dread of our own kin, and this is a dread that no amount of historical knowledge can cure.

The conclusion of *Kindred* tries to balance the needs to protect the history and to avenge it. The narrator delivers her great-great-grandfather's ultimatum to her great-great-grandmother as a choice of options, only one of which, the one she chooses, is really compatible with her survival. Thus, without either actively dissuading or persuading her, the protagonist merely lets her slave ancestor follow the path of least resistance, which is also the one that generates her descendants. Two children, including Dana's great-grandmother Hagar, are born of the union, and when the existence of the entire extended family-to-be seems to have been insured by the matriarch's unwilling mating, Dana returns to 1977. But, like an eruption from the heroine's unquiet conscience, the slave ancestor's rebelliousness flares up again, resulting in her suicide and the last of the narrator's mysterious re-callings to the plantations. In a gesture that might itself be read as suicidal, Rufus (her great-great-grandfather) tries to rape Dana, and she kills him in self-defense. This sketchy plot summary cannot do justice to the oddness of the novel's last chapter, in which the modern African American woman and the nineteenth-century white slave master, now as familiar to her as a brother, sympathize in their mourning for the woman they had both loved. That the deep sympathy between these two relatives should suddenly turn into Rufus's desperate, grasping attempt to control his elusive descendant and result in her equally violent resistance can be read as yet another illustration of the novel's dominant thematic refrain: the injuries of slavery are at once systemic and deeply personal, routed through the longings of intimates as often as through the calculations of strangers. And yet, the swiftness of the justice, after all of the protagonist's efforts at controlling her anger in order to keep Rufus alive, also seems to follow simply from the script of the organizing trope: the slave master lived because of the grandfather paradox, and once it no longer operates, he immediately suffers the consequence. Moreover, when we see the patricide as built into the structuring trope, we might also recognize it as another instance of the historical poetic justice we've encountered frequently in this study: when we moderns take revenge on the slave master, he is put into the position of a slave who has become dispensable after fulfilling his role as a breeder.

Octavia Butler, though, is too good a novelist to settle the issues so neatly; instead of leaving the injury-origin equivalence behind on the plantation, she literalizes it as a permanent disability: when the heroine returns for the last time to the present, her arm fuses with the wall of her house, not the arm with which she stabbed Rufus, but the arm to which he held fast as she faded away. The grotesque concreteness of this image of historical mutilation—of literally having to cut herself away from a limb of her body that had merged with "something cold and non-living"—emphasizes the impossibility of recovering from the injury of origins. Dana is "still caught somehow" (261). *Kindred* thus reflects on a number of paradoxes endemic to the civil rights movement's historical turn. The impossibility of separating origin from injury is connected to the impossibility of keeping black history exclusively black while also resurrecting the sexual dimensions of slavery. Moreover, at a time when the main task was to set the record straight about the history of African Americans, speculation about possible alternatives to their history was limited mainly to imagining what might have happened if Reconstruction had continued. The direction of historical thought in the period was double valenced: on the one hand, a better history is presented as the unfinished business that a second reconstruction will accomplish; but on the other hand, the integrity of the actual history must, as in *Kindred*, be protected as the necessary foundation of current action.[25] Thus Octavia Butler shows us both that the backward time-loop plot would not generate alternate-history fiction and that it could be an excellent vehicle for navigating the crosscurrents of the civil rights era's historical imagination.

Both Octavia Butler and John Jakes thematized the tension between preserving a people and changing its past, but Butler's protagonist explicitly forgoes the temptations of alternate history by choosing to stay in her time loop, whereas Jakes's enacts a quest for alternatives enabled by the multivalence of time in his novel. It seems that, by the 1970s, writers knew that the backward chronotope best suited to alternate-history speculation was that in which nexus points radiate multiple timelines and different possible "worlds" occupy the various trajectories. In the literary history of the twentieth century, this chronotope was made famous by Jorge Luis Borges's "Garden of Forking Paths," in which a "web of times, divergent, convergent, and parallel" is described.[26] Borges's story was not the first to specify the ramifying-timeline idea; even before its 1941 publication, a few American science-fiction writers in the 1930s had experimented with it, proposing that time might be likened to a tree with many branches or a railroad network with radiating tracks. Time includes our own history and also others that took different directions at particular points of disjunction. This conception of time as inclusive of mutually exclusive trajectories was well designed to accommodate backward time travel and historical activism without running headlong into necessary self-contradiction.

Nevertheless, like the time-loop model, it inspired both optimistic and melancholic stories. In 1938, a mathematician by the name of William Sell published his one and only piece of fiction, called "Other Tracks," in which a young engineer makes several trips to the past, where he does trivial things, each time returning to a slightly modified present. At the end of the story, which is obviously just a theoretical illustration, the scientist he works for explains the discrepancies among the various 1938s, drawing elaborate charts to keep them straight: "You started from 1938a. That was when you first came here to try out your battery.... You inadvertently... went back to Point P in 1936 and talked to the watchman.... This threw a switch and you returned to 1938b."[27] The lesson: "If you tamper with the past you cannot expect to find the present unchanged.... Time seems to be like a railway track on which we travel" (89). None of this seems to worry the characters, though. When the scientist and his machine disappear a few days later, his assistants "hoped he had found a world to his liking, on another track—and rather suspected he might have gone to leave a book on functional equations on some Newton's desk" (91). The outcome of historical intervention would thus be accelerated scientific progress.

Describing the same chronotope in a 1939 novel, *Lest Darkness Fall*, science-fiction writer L. Sprague de Camp used the metaphor of a tree on which there are "slippery" places, through which someone might slide down the "trunk" to different branches: "When they stop slipping, they are back in some former time. But as soon as they do anything, they change all subsequent history," explains an Italian archeologist at the opening of the book. And yet, he continues, "the trunk continues to exist ... a new branch starts out where they come to rest. It has to, otherwise we would all disappear, because history would have changed and our parents might not have met."[28] This seems to be the first explicit statement that the branching-time concept would obviate the grandfather paradox. De Camp's archeologist thinks of both time and "history" as "a four-dimensional web. It is a tough web. But it has weak points. The junction places—the focal points, one might say—are weak. The backslipping ... would happen at these places" (5). Of course, the protagonist, an ingenious Yankee, happens to be in such a slippery place, Fascist Rome, and he falls back to another moment of Roman historical crisis in late antiquity. Having already learned that his time travel must have started a new line of development, he determines to take advantage of his accident, spends no time regretting the world he has lost, and hastens to reinvent the machinery of the Enlightenment in order to save and reform the Roman Empire before the Goths can invade and bring the Dark Ages. The book is part Renouvier's *Uchronie*, part Defoe's *Robinson Crusoe*, and part Mark Twain's *Connecticut Yankee in King Arthur's Court*, and it definitely contains a plot of successful historical activism, but it also clarifies a disconnection between the branching-time cosmology and plots of historical improvement, for in *Lest Darkness Fall*, the time traveler's separate temporal shoot is less a comparable alternative, with a clear nexus and set of historical consequences, than a fantastic parallel past, with anachronistically modern technologies.[29]

However, from the very first instance of the forking-timelines plot, it also inspired a sense of futility, for the chronotope imagines such an explosive proliferation of timelines that the project of retrieving a superior version of our world at the end of the narrative is defeated. Just as the grandfather paradox had its beginnings in an early 1920s absurdist story, the unintended proliferation of timelines idea seems to have been invented by an avant-garde Polish writer, Antoni Słonimski, who imagined time travelers setting out to modify the Napoleonic Wars so that they would have produced less suffering but instead only cause different forms of misery.[30] History constantly moves sideways across numerous versions, producing a reality in which all effort seems unavailing because all possibilities are actualized. Even the insouciant stories I've mentioned hold that backward time travel will automatically result in uncontrolled track changing, the assumption underlying *Bring the Jubilee*. Its melancholy implications seem to have been first spelled out in English in a short story from 1935 by D. R. Daniels, "The Branches of Time," which features a protagonist who wanted to "go back to make past ages more livable," but found that instead he only started other lines of development, "other whens," while leaving this "world-line" intact.[31] Daniels has his time traveler, lost in time like Hodge, complain, "I had an idea to . . . go back to make past ages more livable. Terrible things happened in history, you know. But it isn't any use. Think, for instance, of the martyrs and the things they suffered. I could go back and save them those wrongs. And yet all the time they would have known their unhappiness and their agony, because in this world-line those things happened. At the end, it's all unchangeable; it merely rolls before us" (366).

The forking-paths time-travel plots thus seem powerless, like the single-timeline plots, to represent positive historical change in any unique world; change occurs only as a time traveler moves across worlds. Time-travel fantasies of historical activism start new histories, but they do not repair *our* history. This pattern of variation is, of course, similar to Auguste Blanqui's vision of a universe in which all possibilities are realized in an infinity of possible worlds, and it brings to mind as well Franz Kafka's reported remark that "our world is only a bad mood of God, a bad day of his," so there is "plenty of hope, an infinite amount of hope—but not for us."[32] The avant-garde imagination of the late nineteenth and early twentieth centuries seems replete with these scenarios, so no matter which brand of time-traveling improbabilia one chooses, personal loss and a sense of the melancholy persistence of the past tend to haunt the endings. When explaining the continued use of backward time travel in alternate-America novels, we should factor in its tendencies to preserve the damaged past while insistently maintaining "hope, infinite amounts of hope." The time-travel knots that tie science fiction, alternate history, and historical activism seem enduring not because they solve problems but because they destabilize solutions.

ALTERNATE-AMERICA NOVELS AND THE DISUNITED STATES

Most alternate-America novels of the civil rights period, though, are innocent of both time-travel fantasies and cosmological speculations; like the first nine-tenths of *Bring the Jubilee*, they emphasize the qualities of their imagined possible worlds and the historical nexus that might have produced them without evincing any of that novel's curiosity about their ontological status. Nevertheless, in their own ways they also question the contemporary historical activists' project of searching for a past that might have led to an America in which the races live together in peace and equality. To be sure, they share with the affirmative action alternate-history scenarios the method of reimagining race relations by beginning from counterfactual-historical hypotheses, but their social visions depart radically from the integrationist ideal. Fourteen novels published between 1970 and 1990 investigate the possibilities of alternate race relations: eight of the fifteen explore other possible African American histories, half a dozen envision alternative resolutions of the conflicts between European settlers and indigenous Americans, and one thematizes the conflict between Mexicans and Anglo Americans.[33] And yet none depicts the sort of counterfactual history Justice Marshall seemed to have had in mind in the Supreme Court opinion we quoted in the last chapter: a better past in an integrated nation that might have been ours if only we'd lived up to our ideals more fully. Instead of going back to find a better way forward, these novels often feature heroes who struggle just to keep things from getting much worse. Of the eight alternate African American history novels, for example, five result from changes in the outcome of the Civil War and are largely dystopian. Of those presenting ostensibly preferable histories, one depicts the success of John Brown's raid on Harper's Ferry and the rise of a "Nova African" nation, and four others reverse the Native American fortunes of war and imagine independent sovereign states for indigenous people. Rather than visualizing a shared, integrated polity, these novels as a group explain how the United States might have come apart in the nineteenth century, for worse or for better.

To understand why the novelistic alternate-history imagination of these decades moved toward visions of national *dis*integration, rather than toward dreams of greater unity and equality, we should start by remembering that the period was marked not only by significant civil rights efforts but also by high levels of American civil unrest and aggressive confrontation. Affirmative action itself was often accused of divisiveness and was met by reactionary white racism that took violent as well as legal forms. As a group, the novels are far more in sync with the busing riots, black urban uprisings, and "national liberation" rhetoric of the late sixties and early seventies than with the integrationist ambitions of affirmative action programs. They often fantasize extremes of murderous discord between the races, or between different racial systems, and imply that violence—either covert or overt—is the inevitable vehicle of change. Hence they use the wars of the nineteenth century to figure the actual political and ethnic fissures of the late twentieth: the War between the States is a version of the perceived cultural divide between a tolerant, secular North and a repressive, religiously orthodox South, while the "Indian Wars" stand in for a host of internal national liberation movements: black nationalism, Chicano independence activism, and the Autonomous American Indian Movement. In the alternate-America novels of these decades, the United States loses not only the South, as in earlier alternate-history narratives, but also the Great Plains (Martin Cruz Smith, *The Indians Won* [1970]), the Old Northwest Territory (Kenan Heise, *The Journey of Silas P. Bigelow* [1981]), and the Southwest (Ron Montana, *The Sign of the Thunderbird* [1977]). These are the Disunited States, the dismembered polity in extremis, of the period's political unconscious.

There are, additionally, formal reasons for this consistent pattern of imagining, not only the dismemberment of the USA, but also the separate development of the country's different populations as autonomous entities. First, the alternate-history novel often reaches maximal divergence, whereas those who pursued the goal of equal opportunity were careful to reassure the country that integration would not make radical changes in its basic social structure. Even though higher percentages of blacks, Chicanos, Native Americans, Asian Americans, and women would be in trade unions, universities, professions, board rooms, and so on, those places would be basically unaltered. Indeed, it was considered reactionary to claim that fundamental changes would result, since to do so indicated a belief in intrinsic racial and gender differences. The integrated future would be one in which racial difference had ceased to be a salient social or economic category, but in all other regards it was designed *not* to seem different from our reality. Consequently, the vision did not have significant enough divergence to stimulate a lengthy alternate-history novelistic exploration. Especially in contrast to the competing ethnic-nationalist visions—which appeared to arise organically from energetic grassroots movements outside the established professional and political hierarchies—foregrounding the importance of cultural uniqueness and creating vibrantly mythic imaginary pasts, the integrationist aspirations looked anemic.

The ethnic-nationalist visions also intersected with the alternate-history aim of resurrecting not only an unrealized historical potential but also a potential, or "entelechy," that once inhered in some organic being.[34] We last encountered the idea of an organic entelechy in the second chapter of this book, when noting that the nineteenth-century French writer Geoffroy-Château described Napoleon's actual history as a radically "unachieved" version of his proper history, as a failure to realize the emperor's destiny and fulfill his essence. The alternate history, Geoffroy-Château explained, was necessary to complete the arc of the hero's true telos. Several of the racial alternate-history novels of the 1970s and 1980s enact a similar desire to complete the developmental lot of a particular entity, but instead of focusing on a heroic individual, they try to trace out the story lines of whole populations, ethnic and/or cultural organisms, as they would have developed if left to themselves. If the treaty that ended the War of 1812 had provided for a demilitarized Indian nation in the Old Northwest Territory, what sort of country would they have made (*The Journey of Silas P. Bigelow*)? If a successful slave revolt had started at Harper's Ferry and spread throughout the South, what kind of nation would the former slaves and revolutionary abolitionists have created (*Fire on the Mountain*)? There are two kinds of difference that attract us to such fantasies: (1) the difference between the alternate world and ours, and (2) the differences among the various parts of the alternate world, where uniqueness instead of forced subordination or accommodation has prevailed. In these Disunited States stories, the reader's interest is focused on how well the novel *realizes* an improbably achieved state, which has come about in accordance with impulses and energies imagined as proper to a particular people.

So these alternate-America novels, even when set many generations after the separation of time lines, are linked formally to the alternate histories that retain cross-world identity through shared persona, except that the "character" held in common is not an individual but a genealogically descended ethnic group. The break in cross-world identity created by the time-travel historical activism of *Black in Time* is what foils the alternate-history project in the end; the novel's 1977 African Americans could not have been the progeny of settlers from the Songhay Empire, and consequently the ethnic equivalent of the grandfather paradox comes into play. Thus, although the novelists are free to invent new persona, they are limited to the available gene pools, and they even have a tendency to magnify the distinctions among them, returning them to more pristine and homogeneous states. This trend in turn reinforces other common features of these novels: for example, territorial rupture is an easy way to insure that a population maintains genetic continuity through national-spatial isolation. And, finally, as always in alternate-history narratives, war is the obvious way to change the territorial map and superimpose a different past and present onto our familiar geographic world.

The possible narrative choices in this game were quickly standardized, and we can see them already in the first three Disunited States novels to appear, all published in 1970 and all written in the late sixties: *Black in Time*, as we've seen, is a metanarrative exploring what the author took to be the counterfactual premises of African American separatism; Martin Cruz Smith's *The Indians Won* and Robert Stapp's *A More Perfect Union* focus on single slipping points; each chooses a nineteenth-century territorial armed conflict inside the current United States. Neither is a time-travel novel with the option of inserting modern-day characters into the past, so they seek other ways of advancing two stories in one novel: telling the nexus reversal story and developing a separate plot set in the Alternate Timeline at a moment roughly parallel to that of the readers. *The Indians Won* and *A More Perfect Union*, like several Disunited States novels to follow, are each split into a pair of plots, one belonging to the nexus and the other belonging to the aftermath, and the narrative alternates between them. Those two books also illustrate a commonplace of the genre in non-time-travel and time-travel versions alike: some new, contemporary crisis point has been reached in the balance of power that resulted from the reversal, so the aftermath plot is one in which the very viability of the planet is at stake. They therefore borrow heavily from international espionage novels as well as from dystopian and (less often) utopian fiction. Many later novels follow *A More Perfect Union* in depicting a nuclear crisis between the USA and a fascist CSA; others are patterned on *The Indians Won*, which casts the USA as the twentieth-century aggressor in border disputes with Native American nations.

The formulas for these Disunited States novels were thus set early, which makes it all the easier to analyze them as a group, and when we do, we see that they provide both beneficent and malevolent modes of disunity. The alternative of a divided America is depicted as superior to ours if the disunity arose from the struggle of some racial group to live separately in an autonomous (and largely utopian) state. They tell national liberation tales, which were inspired by widespread opposition to the Vietnam War and (later) antinuclear sentiments; Native American history is the usual subject, although Terry Bison's *Fire on the Mountain* applies the pattern to African American history as well. In contrast, when national disunity is imagined to be the result of Southern secession, the alternate world is inferior to ours; the USA is plagued by a CSA where, even after the disappearance of slavery, a dystopian state forces segregation on the black minority as a means of insuring continued exploitation. These contrasting clusters of novels, with their oppositely valued modes of disunity, together yield a simple guide to judging the types of racial separation that were then on offer, and they might have helped readers to sort out the difference between the separatist movements that were purporting to speak for minorities and the segregationists who continued to seek white supremacy. As a contrasting set, they present an acceptable (because chosen by a minority race) version of what we obviously have—a nonintegrated America—while also denying and banishing into a region imagined as a foreign land the historical responsibility for the unacceptable (because imposed) version.

AFTER THE COLD WAR: ALTERNATE AMERICAS AND THE RIGHT SIDE OF HISTORY

The separatist national-liberation cluster petered out in the late 1980s, and then, in the wake of the actual disintegration of the Soviet Union, which seemed to many to be history's judgment on its brutally imposed amalgamation, it became rare to imagine American disunity in positive terms. In 1990, for example, a time-travel alternate-history novel about the battle of Little Bighorn (Kevin Randle and Robert Cornett's *Remember Little Bighorn!*) tells us on its back cover that, "if General Custer survives, present-day America will be devastated—divided into separate and distinct nations."[35] This is a far cry from the insouciant Native American separatism of Martin Cruz Smith's 1970 *The Indians Won*.[36] In contrast to the dismantled and delegitimized USSR, the USA was the prototypical voluntary union where people could keep their ethnic and racial identities while mingling freely. The country, we were told, had even outgrown old-fashioned racial prejudice and had therefore progressed beyond the need for affirmative action, which was sometimes accused of causing racism by keeping the wounds of the past open. What was wanted instead was "race blindness." Even liberal politicians consequently started downplaying remedial discourse and promoting instead the idea of "diversity" as a positive goal not based on compensatory grounds.[37] In the 1990s, both the remediation argument for affirmative action and the racial separatism of the Disunited States moment seemed quaintly out of date, as retro as Afros and bell-bottoms.

Although affirmative action remediation seemed no longer viable, other features of post–Cold War historical discourse obviously continued to stimulate the alternate-history imagination, for both the novelistic and the nonnovelistic forms took off after 1989, in keeping with the period's vibrant awareness of history's motility. Several well-known characteristics of the post–Cold War state of mind favored the kinds of historical speculation conducive to both future conjectures and past hypotheticals. To name just a few of the most obvious: the turning point of 1989 had seemed abrupt; its swiftness, unstoppable dynamism, and enormous scale were unexpected; it had released the world from the tense balance of power that had been in place for over half a century, ending the grand narratives that had given history its coherence for generations; and people had little idea of what might happen next. A general sense of standing on the threshold of some unforeseen new world order pervaded public discourse, and the awareness of being at a crossroads encouraged many to look back at other such transitional junctures.[38] With the ending of the Cold War, attention was focused on the period of its commencement and, in counterfactual imaginings, was especially riveted by the question of how things might have been different had World War II not created the conditions under which the political globe had been divided into Western and Eastern Blocks. Thus, as we'll see more clearly in the next two chapters, the end of the Cold War increased the popularity of WWII counterfactual narratives, which already comprised the majority of alternate histories and alternate-history novels.

Another prompt for the historical counterfactualists was the spike in reparations and transitional justice discourse following the termination of the Cold War, which created an international context for considering the possibilities of historical activism. One modern precedent for making restitution for historical injustices was famously set by West Germany (the German Federal Republic) after World War II, when it signed a restitution agreement with Israel to help compensate victims of Nazi genocide.[39] The two countries were acting as "descendant" entities of the perpetrators and the victims. The German Federal Republic freely took on responsibility for the crimes against the Jews by the Nazi government, recognizing a moral obligation to make amends to both individual victims and some entity representing the Jewish people as a whole. Israel, for its part, recognized the attempt at atonement without "forgiving" the crimes or implying that they could ever be adequately compensated. Several important principles were established by this agreement: first, that collective culpability for historical injustices committed by one regime could descend to successive instantiations of the same nation; second, that compensation might be paid to a "descendant" group even if that group did not demonstrate direct biological lineage with the original victims; third, that reparations might be made without exact calculations of damages incurred; and, fourth, that reparations might be accepted without implying that the injustice was somehow erased, undone, or "made whole."

These principles distinguish the model of reparations from the tort-law model of remediation on which affirmative action programs tried to establish themselves.[40] To be sure, tort law did play an important role in the 1990s by forcing reluctant states and financial institutions to return property held in Eastern European countries to individual Holocaust victims and their families.[41] But the larger-scale reparations movements worked through political rather than legal processes. Both are forms of historical activism, which set out to amend past wrongs and mitigate their present effects, but reparations relax many of the requirements of tort-law remediation, such as the identity of payers and wrongdoers or beneficiaries and victims. In the 1990s, this kind of restitution was widely pursued in many parts of the world, with varying outcomes. Restitution movements in Central and Eastern European countries, for example, tended to consolidate singular national identities by returning land to small landowners, who had been expropriated by communists, and restoring church property, but they often excluded the claims of minorities. In contrast, simultaneous movements on the part of indigenous peoples in democratic English-speaking countries, especially Canada, Australia, and New Zealand, were being met by programs to restore land, and postapartheid South Africa also had a restitution program designed to transfer farms cheaply from whites (who would sell them to the government) to blacks (who would buy them at a discount). The 1990s also heard numerous claims for reparations brought on behalf of more specific groups: those whose artworks were plundered by the Nazis, families and survivors of Argentina's and Chile's dirty wars of the 1970s, the Korean "comfort women" victimized by the Japanese in World War II, people belonging to groups whose cultural artifacts had been removed from their homelands and placed in Western museum collections. Even when land and monetary compensation were not sought, many nations, races, and ethnic groups simply wanted to set the record straight, asking that historical wrongs be acknowledged and that official apologies be made.

Within this international framework, various African American groups and individuals proposed that the U.S. government should offer reparations for slavery, citing domestic precedents, such as the 1980 federal Supreme Court ruling that the United States should compensate the Sioux with $122 million for having dispossessed them of the Black Hills in 1877 and the 1989 federal legislation giving cash payments to Japanese Americans incarcerated during World War II.[42] The Japanese Internment Law was the immediate trigger for slavery reparations proposals; in 1989, Representative John Conyers Jr. of Michigan introduced a bill to establish a national committee to study the possibility. Unlike affirmative action, the idea of reparations for slavery never gained much support outside of the African American community, but it was nevertheless widely debated in the early 1990s, reminding Americans that their nation, too, had unforgiven historical debts. Reparations proponents sometimes used the familiar but-for logic to explain their proposal; in the words of Robert S. Browne, reparations might "provide the black community with the share of national wealth and income which it would by now have had if it had been treated as other immigrant communities were, rather than enslaved."[43] However, the debate put new emphasis on parts of black history that had not been previously stressed, underlining the intercontinental nature of the transatlantic slave trade, the horrors of the "middle passage," and the continuities among African diasporic cultures as a way of demonstrating that the uprooted people were trying to preserve their identities even in exile.

The message was that white Americans had benefited from a larger injustice perpetrated by Europeans and their descendants against Africans, and thus the wrong was not solely the inherited responsibility of those who had actually owned slaves. After Congress passed a bill in 1993 apologizing to indigenous Hawaiians for the overthrow of their royal family in 1893, pressure also built for an apology for African American slavery, which proved problematic because many believed it to be a first step toward the payment of reparations. Five years later, addressing the general wrongs of the transatlantic slave trade, President Clinton apologized for it in Uganda, but his action was met by angry claims from the right that African leaders had benefited from the trade, caustic suggestions from the left that the president should have apologized instead to the descendants of people who were slaves in the United States, and reminders from both that Uganda is nowhere near the West African Coast from which slaves departed for the Americas. Missteps like Clinton's raised the question of where a single nation's historical responsibilities began and ended. Post–Cold War redress efforts thus embedded America's interracial history more deeply in world history and international relations than the civil rights movement of the post-WWII era had. And in that larger world-historical perspective the wrongs could seem, on the one hand, more commonplace and, on the other, graver because linked to the whole process of European imperialism and the colonization of other continents as well as to the twentieth-century growth of racist ideologies and policies, including the Holocaust and the only recently defunct apartheid system in South Africa.

The 1990s alternate-America novel that resonates most fully with this new context was Harry Turtledove's extremely popular *Guns of the South* (1992), a book that places an alternate CSA in the context of world history and asks which side of the long struggle to spread democracy, equality, and the rule of law the CSA would have been on. *Guns of the South* is one of those time-travel novels in which a team of fighters take modern weapons into historical wars to try to change their outcomes; André Blandin and the pacifist poet Théo Varlet wrote the first of them, *La belle Valence*, in 1923, and at least two of the alternate-America novels, *Sign of the Thunderbird* (1977), and *Remember the Alamo!* (1980), were also in the subgenre. But the thrill of battles in which new weapons are pitted against old ones lasts only for the first part of *The Guns of the South*, and then political issues with obvious contemporary parallels come to the fore. The novel, for instance, dwells on the topics of nation making and state building in the CSA's transition to independence; it explores the international pressures to meet standards of "civilized" internal arrangements and the threat of further secession struggles within the Confederacy. These topics had all been explored by other Civil War counterfactualists, and Turtledove is careful to maintain the specificity of the 1860s while dramatizing them, but their relevance to world politics in the early 1990s, when new nations were emerging all around the globe, was also notable. The alternate CSA in this novel seems an allegory of the post–Cold War places (Somalia, for example) where national liberation had left people struggling to bring sovereign states out of loose coalitions of armed groups.

It is the time-travel plot, though, that refers most directly to the issues of post-1989 transitional justice, for it features South African white supremacists, relicts of its apartheid regime still hoping to return the white minority to power in 2014, who transport AK-47s to Lee's Army of Northern Virginia in 1864. Their purpose is to create a history in which "the white man" achieves permanent global dominance. Turtledove is explicit about the real-world identity of the group: they have "AWB" printed on their supplies, which they tell General Lee stands for "America Will Break," but which at least some readers in 1992 would have recognized as the initials for the Afrikaner Resistance Movement (*Afrikaner Weerstandsbeweging*, in Afrikaans). Turtledove inserts a line drawing of their emblem (a three-legged adaptation of a swastika) in the text, describes their uniforms, and uses a Dutch translation of their leader's name, Eugene Blankaard for Eugène Terre'Blanche, all of which seems designed to remind us of recent newspaper accounts of AWB extremism. The actual group had for years been advocating civil war in South Africa to maintain white minority rule, and in 1991, as the country prepared for its first multiracial elections and President de Klerk negotiated with the African National Congress, the AWB made a pair of violent assaults on the negotiators and the negotiation site, killing and injuring in their first attack, and taking over the proceedings in the second. In *The Guns of the South*, the fictionalized AWB men regard the American Civil War as a precursor to the war they hope to start in South Africa and see the Confederacy's cause as an earlier version of their own. They thus raise the question for us of the accuracy of their interpretation: were the Confederate rebels the AWB of their day, or would it be anachronistic to liken the two, as anachronistic as likening a repeating rifle to an AK-47? Both are meant to kill, but the ruthless efficiency of the AK-47 might also be said to put it in a different category of destructiveness. The novel sets up a parallel linking the military and political plots: repeating rifles are to AK-47s as the Confederacy might be to the AWB. If the AK-47s inevitably overwhelm the rifles when the two are placed in simultaneous battlefield action, the novel asks, will the AWB persuade the Confederacy to adopt its totalitarian model of fanatical white supremacy organized in a police state? Or will the Confederate leadership—in the person of Robert E. Lee—refuse to become the ancestor of the AWB and instead renounce slavery?

Of course Robert E. Lee saves the CSA from anticipating and precipitating the future horrors of twentieth-century racism and genocide, and he becomes the great emancipator, a standard formula of Civil War alternate histories, as we saw in the last chapter. Indeed, Turtledove's novel seems to have an even older model: it resembles Geoffroy-Château's *Napoléon et la conquête du monde* because it is a paean to an actual historic hero, an attempt to exonerate his character and keep him in the role of might-have-been savior. The historical injustice that Turtledove and Geoffroy-Château seem to want to remedy most urgently is the supposed injury done to the hero's reputation by other historians.[44] This Lee, though, is a more interesting character than most idealized alternate-history heroes because he faces a Faustian dilemma: although he distrusts the time-traveling strangers, he knows the Confederacy will lose the war unless he becomes beholden to them by accepting their weapons as well as their knowledge of Union military plans, and so he gives them a prominent place in the Army of Northern Virginia and allows them to establish an outpost of their own in North Carolina and a headquarters in Richmond. Predictably, victory, peace, and the transition to nationhood soon reveal the moral and political gulf between Lee and his benefactors; the former general runs for president on a platform of gradual, compensated slave emancipation, and when he wins, the AWB attacks the inauguration, is repelled, but continues to lead an insurrection against the new national government. Thus instead of becoming the precursor to the AWB, the CSA's history becomes a nineteenth-century version of South Africa's transition out of apartheid.

The most unusual part of this plot is the role given to the judgment of history in determining the future of the new nation. Through a cross-dressing former confederate female soldier-turned-prostitute who has clients in the AWB, Lee receives access to twentieth-century history books from Our Timeline, which are found in the AWB headquarters and uncover the "truth" not only about the time travelers but also about posterity's verdict on the Confederacy's intention to maintain chattel slavery. The books are yet another convention of alternate-history narrative—going all the way back to *Napoléon et la conquête du monde*—in which the events of Our Timeline are brought into the diegesis as texts within the text. And they carry the melancholy of the "lost" world, familiar from time-travel fiction and here redoubled since Lee's South would have been lost had he not changed history and won the war: "[Lee] encountered himself, old, grim, and defeated, standing on the back porch of the rented house in which he and his wife had lived in Richmond" (432). But the books in this novel are more than metacommentary; they also determine the plot. Lee reads them only after he has already become a proponent of emancipation, but they confirm his moral instincts about the natural direction of history. Having interrupted that direction with one anachronism—the AK-47—Lee seeks to restore it with his own anachronistic knowledge of history's future trajectory, while at the same time accusing the AWB of being out of "accord with the spirit of the future" (435). His first act as president of the CSA is to have the members of Congress read the books in order to win their support for his emancipation plan; each must confront "the verdict of posterity" and, as the narrator comments, "few men were brazen enough to withstand their great-grandson's scorn" (486–87). Lee sounds like Hegel in his summation of the case against slavery, which is a version of the philosopher's "world history is the court of world justice" argument: "We can see for ourselves the verdict which history has brought in against us. . . . We have the verdict of posterity, which condemns us for maintaining the ownership of one man by another and is convinced that that system, if ever it were justifiable, had in our time long since outlived such justification" (487). That last reminder, that slavery was itself an anachronistic injustice in the 1860s, is the clincher, for it anticipates and obviates the argument that by imposing a judgment from the future on their current behavior, they would be "at strife with the world of their own time" (486).

Nevertheless, Lee's equation of the judgment from the future with definitive moral truth remains open to all of the objections normally brought against the Hegelian formulation: it confuses historical success with moral superiority; it presupposes a history of progressive enlightenment that will encompass the world; it accommodates no further revolutions of opinion. And, perhaps most obviously, because there are no end points in history, it is impossible to imagine in what place of neutral objectivity Hegel's court of world justice could be convened for the purpose of delivering ultimate ethical verdicts. For all of these reasons, Lee's pronouncements ignore the very hindsight bias that alternate histories usually set out to correct. No one in the novel's CSA leadership points out that the books are not exactly the verdict of *their* posterity because they were written in an already defunct reality. Elsewhere the novel makes jokes about winner's history, but at the plot's political climax, the judgment of history is presented as unanimous and final, creating a sort of "great-grandson paradox" in which the grandfathers must change their behavior to align themselves with the judgment of progeny who may otherwise never have come into existence. In *Kindred* the grandfather paradox bent all emerging deviations back toward Our Timeline; in this story, the great-grandchildren, in the guise of future historians, minimize the alteration, partially undoing the intervention of the time travelers.

Another way to analyze Lee's revised Confederacy would be to think of it as the formal equivalent of a transitional justice attempt, in which two possible futures for the new nation, two opposing "sides" of history, are presented. Having been tricked by the AWB men into one possible trajectory, which would link the victorious Confederacy with Fascism (the novel quotes the actual AWB leader's praise of Hitler) and neo-Nazism, Lee then discovers history's other side in the history books, with their confident Whiggish belief in inevitable humanitarian progress and racial equality. In choosing emancipation, Lee and his confederates choose not only one set of grandsons over another but also one "side" in an ongoing history. They thus partially repair the continuity in Our Timeline that they earlier broke, electing to subscribe to the norms by which the historians will judge them positively. The conclusion thus takes a forking-path narrative pattern and diverts it back into a modified time loop. Like the Dutch ancestors in Edward Page Mitchell's "The Clock That Went Backward," Lee struggles to generate the future that will save him. Turtledove thus grapples with the ironic tendencies inherent in the backward time-travel device in order to reach and stabilize the final reversal on which we've seen so many Civil War alternate histories come to rest: the South wins, only to emancipate the slaves. And, although the novel acknowledges that the freedmen will be forced to struggle for actual citizenship, it ends on a note of hope that voluntary and "gradual change would lead to less long-range disruption" and prevent "periodic explosions of hatred" (555).

This wish—that emancipation had been negotiated rather than imposed on the slave states—was a founding retroactive desire of Civil War counterfactuals, as these chapters have amply demonstrated. We should also note, though, that its reappearance in the 1990s, after several decades of disuse, may be partly explained by the way in which it harmonized with some transitional justice movements of that decade. The difference between the new idea of restitution—whether in the form of reparations, apologies, or programs to benefit the descendants of victims—and earlier concepts of historical justice was that restitution asked both sides to acknowledge the wrong of the injustice and agree to a remedy. American Reconstruction might not, therefore, have qualified, because it tried to repair injuries against the wills of the wrongdoers, solidifying resentment in the chastised perpetrators. Some transitional justice efforts, first and foremost the South African Commission for Truth and Reconciliation, went even further in compromising with wrongdoers to elicit acknowledgment of the injustices from all sides and to establish consent among the parties about the necessity for social, political, and cultural change. To be sure, unlike the South African transition, the negotiators in the novel do not include the real victims, the former slaves, and the only reparations mentioned by Turtledove's Lee would be to compensate the loss of their property to slaveholders, for the emancipation imagined in *Guns of the South* is modeled on the process that freed the slaves in the British Caribbean in 1834. In several ways, then, the novel's proposed emancipation seems a far cry from the historical justice movements of the late twentieth century. Nevertheless, we should recall that the South African Truth and Reconciliation Commission (TRC) was similarly problematic when judged by those standards; indeed both Amnesty International and Human Rights Watch claimed in the early 1990s that, as a nonprosecutorial way of treating the apartheid regime's offenses, the planned TRC would violate a positive duty that states have (under international law) to prosecute and punish perpetrators of crimes against humanity.[45] The TRC's process, which automatically granted amnesty to those who voluntarily confessed committing crimes in support of the apartheid regime, was the price demanded of the African National Congress by F. W. de Klerk's government for a peaceful transition to democracy, and it marked the difference between, on the one hand, a criminal court whose primary aim would be to punish past misdeeds and extract compensation and, on the other, an accountability process whose purpose was to obtain a public record of self-confessed wrongdoing, consequent social, political, and cultural transformation, and national reconciliation.[46]

Although *Guns of the South* came out several years before the TRC's proceedings began, the novel breathes the same air of cautious optimism about the possibility of overcoming racial injustice through nonpunitive historical accountability. There is a striking parallel between the way in which the leaders of the CSA in the novel reluctantly accept the metaphoric verdict of posterity's court of world justice against their cause and the way South Africa's apartheid government in the years between 1989 and 1993 capitulated to the international condemnation of their system. Like the real de Klerk government, the imaginary leadership of the CSA begins the political process of ending the wrongful system without further violence and in the hopes of uniting their new nation. The time-travel plot reinforces the parallels by giving the real and imaginary countries a common enemy (the AWB) during their crucial transitional moments. And by linking the negotiated—rather than imposed—cessation of racial injustice to the reformation of South Africa, the book's plot seems to give implicit approval to reconciliatory, nonpunitive historical activism. In doing so it might also be said to endorse some of the old criticisms of Reconstruction's transitional strategy, especially the accusation that it was ineffective because imposed on a vanquished people. Not that *The Guns of the South* simply revives the pre-WWII consensus that Southern victory (or uncontested secession) would have been better for African Americans because it would have given the CSA the opportunity to free its own slaves. After all, the South only achieves independence by the intervention of the infernal AWB agents, and the novel's CSA must struggle to erase the taint of its origins. Turtledove's novel, though, allows for a split decision about the desirable past: it would have been unfortunate if the slaveholders had prevailed; but if by some strange turn of events they had, the stage might then have been set for better race relations in the future. Turtledove is thus able to follow lightly in the footsteps of such liberal thinkers as Ernest Crosby, who ninety years earlier suggested that interracial relations were damaged by Reconstruction, without seeming to imply that secession would have been a superior option.

Turtledove's novel, like Ward Moore's *Bring the Jubilee*, resists the conclusion that America's interracial history could have been solely determined by the outcome of the Civil War. Both the post–Cold War backward-time-travel novel and its post-WWII equivalent remind us instead that it is no easy task to stay on the right side of history. Moore's story ends with rumors of the betrayal of Reconstruction in 1877 (a reversal of the novel's time-travel reversal), and in a clear reference to U.S. Supreme Court decisions of the late nineteenth century; Turtledove ends his with Lee's speculations on whether a Confederate Supreme Court, once established, might overturn his newly passed emancipation legislation, reversing his reversal of the Afrikaner time travelers' reversal. In both novels, backward time travel serves as a metaphor for our ceaseless revisions of the past in our attempts at atonement, but it also renders all roads insecure and thereby sows distrust of the ultimate usefulness of those attempts. By giving the possibility of intervening in the past a fantastic literalism, time travel has a built-in tendency to play with multiple, reversible outcomes until it exhausts the very ideas of historical causality and responsibility, rendering them illogical. From this perspective, the device might be said to be always on the verge of commenting skeptically on historical activism and, by extension, on the use of counterfactuals in social and political criticism.

And yet because the device underscores the merely fantasmatic nature of endless new pasts, authors can rein in its structural skepticism and direct attention to thematic political messages. Both *Bring the Jubilee* and *Guns of the South* use the device to stress the difficulty of staying on track toward justice and equality, implying the need for constant vigilance and leaving us on the brink of further changes. Moore concludes by indicating that his 1953 readers confront yet another crossroads in the shape of a new national struggle, whereas Turtledove points his 1992 readers toward the challenges of increasingly chaotic and uncontrollable international events.[47] The admonition to be alert takes different specific forms, marking the distance traversed in the fifty years between the two novels. Each is an allegory for its time: Moore asks readers to get back on the right path and resume the struggle that was left unfinished, whereas Turtledove seems to want to reassure us that because we are inherently a freedom-loving people, even in the event of a CSA victory the new country would have lined up on the right historical side. We are shown that if America *did* break politically, its values would nonetheless have coalesced and merged with the progressive historical stream. As in so many Civil War counterfactuals stretching back to the late nineteenth century, successful secession in this tale mainly gives the South the chance to show that it, too, is on the side of historical justice. In Turtledove's allegory, unlike Moore's, die-hard racism and inhumanity are shipped offshore: they belong not to Northern or Southern Americans but to a fanatical group of terroristic foreigners from South Africa, who trace their ideological roots to the Nazis. A politically disunified America can thus be a tolerable consequence of regional differences because the real enemy lives elsewhere.

CHAPTER FIVE

Nazi Britain: The Invasion and Occupation That Weren't

World War II, we are frequently reminded, was America's good war, the one we are happy to remember: the one that was fought by the Greatest Generation and ended the Great Depression, that made America the leader of the free world and placed it at the summit of global power. The one in which we triumphed almost unconditionally over our enemies. In the seventy-some years since the war's end, historical research has only deepened our sense of our enemies' perniciousness, especially when recollecting Nazi Germany's brutal and horrendous crimes. In hindsight, the Third Reich looks even more like evil incarnate than it did in December 1941 when America entered the war. The historical studies inspire certainty rather than doubts about the significance of the contest and the comparative moral values of the participants; they do not make us wonder if the world would have been substantially the same in the event of an Axis victory or stimulate second guesses about the importance of having joined the effort.

Thus, World War II seems to occupy the polar opposite position from that of the Civil War in the American historical imagination. Civil War memories, which we examined in the last two chapters, are steeped in regret, and they cause continuing divisions, while memories of World War II are filled with pride and celebrations of our common commitment to democracy. Instead of forcing us to face America's history of slavery, World War II allows us to imagine ourselves as the saviors of enslaved peoples. And in no way was the war our fault; it was "over there," a foreign international conflict into which we were compelled by an unprovoked act of blatant aggression against us. We are thus free to think of ourselves as innocent victims of a genuine axis of evil and heroes of its overthrow. In short, Civil War history, always threatening to expose the latent fractures under our unity, divides us, while WWII history unites us again.

And so, inevitably, the American counterfactual discourses surrounding the two wars show an equally stark contrast. Civil War counterfactuals make us debate the sincerity of our nation's motives, and they continue to inspire feelings of futility as well as charges of hypocrisy, especially when we confront the quick reinstatement of the racial status quo ante. Civil War alternate histories have consequently run the gamut from idealizations to demonizations of a victorious South. Seventy years after the end of the Civil War, in 1935, the implicitly counterfactual-historical consensus declared it to have been largely unnecessary and perhaps counterproductive. Contrast that with the judgment of World War II seventy years after its end; in 2015 historians still believed in the validity of the Allies' future conditional assertions: if Britain had capitulated, if America had not entered the fight, if the Soviet Union's resolve had broken, then our world right up until the present would have been a much worse place to live for most of the planet's people. Of course this is not to say that WWII historiography lacks counterfactual controversies, some of which cast doubt on the morality of specific Allied actions; but unlike the Civil War suppositions, the WWII questions do not challenge the rationale for going to war. They do not raise such questions as: Should we have fought? Should the other side have won? Did any of it matter in the long run? For Americans, the most extreme WWII counterfactual—without U.S. intervention, European civilization would have perished—has certainly been part of the foundation of national identity since 1945.

In this chapter, however, I will shift our attention to the British national point of view not only because the American perspective is (as I've been implying) rather flat but also because the British discourses can tell us more about counterfactualism in general. Officially the two countries have shared both the pride of victory and the certainty that without them World War II would have resulted in a Nazi triumph. Moreover, they derived complementary lessons from their early postwar counterfactuals: Britain should stay heavily armed, maintaining its aloof superiority to the rest of Europe, and America should intervene early and often in military conflicts around the globe.[1] Such shared understandings seem to make the countries equal victors, and yet Europe's World War II belongs to Britain far more than to America. Britain paid a much higher price for it in casualties, as well as in wealth, in the perils and hardships suffered by civilians, and in the empire's long-term decline. It was also, of course, their struggle against Germany before it was ours, and through the crucial year of June 1940 to June 1941—when the other European allies had fallen, neutral countries had been subdued, and the United States and the USSR stood aside—it was theirs alone. This chapter will concentrate on the counterfactuals surrounding that critical period and deriving from the perceived threats of a German invasion and/or occupation of the island. Those fears, although short-lived in actuality, have survived in the British historical literature and are especially active in its counterfactual imagination.

World War II belongs to Britain in yet another sense that has contributed to the prominence of the might-have-been invasion and occupation stories. At the outset of the country's most isolated and vulnerable period, many Britons believed that the crisis could have been avoided if they had made different decisions during the previous decade. To be sure, the avoidance of a second world war had been the guiding principle of British foreign relations throughout the 1930s, and yet the very actions (and inactions) taken to preserve the peace in Europe were censured as inadvertent causes of the conflict as soon as the war broke out. Until late in Germany's career of military aggression, the British saw themselves as playing the decisive role in averting a European conflict, so the very fact that there *was* a war stood as a constant rebuke to the foresight and judgment of virtually the entire political establishment. British WWII counterfactuals consequently assume a high level of national responsibility, and we will shortly see how these features—the belief in a might-have-been Nazi-occupied Britain and the recollection of the follies of appeasement—come together to produce counterfactual discourses in Britain that are peculiarly intense, complicated, multidimensional, and politically freighted.

These particular past hypotheticals also highlight issues that have larger implications for the general study of counterfactual history. First is the issue of character in relation to counterfactual history. Many times in this study we've examined the split between what individual historical actors did and what their "characters"—as abstracted assemblages of individuals' most salient and consistent patterns of behavior—do in alternate histories, and we've noticed that historical people are often said to have been acting "out of character" when their real historical behaviors diverge from an expected pattern. Reestablishing character consistency, we've seen, is a typical motive for constructing historical counterfactuals. The WWII British counterfactuals, though, place special pressure on the concept of *national* character and the question of how such a concept affects our sense of historical probabilities. National character is a concept that no longer seems coherent to us, and even those who used it during the war years admitted its semantic slipperiness. Does it refer to the ways in which a political entity—the nation—acts in relation to its own members and conducts itself among other nations: pacific or bellicose, placating or demanding, responsive or imperious, cooperative or wayward, firm or vacillating? Or does national character refer to personal characteristics of citizens and subjects that are stimulated by particular national political, social, and cultural patterns: self-reliant or dependent, rebellious or subservient, proud or humble, lawful or unruly, narrow or liberal, fair or unfair, self-confident or insecure, determined or irresolute, confiding or distrustful?[2] Or might national character instead mean the typical ways in which a "people"—a more inchoate aggregation than the institutionalized nation—create and experience their own collectivity, especially during times when it seems threatened or otherwise requires assertion? Do they take responsibility for their common life or shirk it; do they cohere or disintegrate, adhere to their values and traditions or abandon them, trust in their ultimate triumph or expect defeat?

The British invasion and occupation stories may be said to serve as revelatory illustrations of the need for counterfactualism when such questions of national character in any of these senses arise. History, with its uncontrollable contingencies, must concentrate on how some actor (a state, a people, certain individuals) behaved under a certain set of conditions and is consequently insufficient to the task of defining *character*, a word we use to describe all sorts of inherent aptitudes and potentials that circumstances might never have actualized; it is the idea of what historical actors were *capable* of doing, not just of what they did. On the one hand, British WWII counterfactuals compensate for history's shortfall by examining what the nation, its people individually or collectively would have done under different circumstances. But, on the other hand, out of the varying and generally competing counterfactuals, especially as they develop through the decades, a number of versions of national character have emerged, and my effort here will be to explore them as responses to a succession of particular challenges in defining Britishness. Counterfactuality, indeed, might be seen as increasingly unrestrained as the idea of national character declines and even begins to look intolerant in its assumption of cultural homogeneity. Historical counterfactuality seems, therefore, to be stimulated by a desire for national character that it ultimately finds itself discrediting.

The second issue is one we've often encountered in this study: the problematic status of history's nonevents, episodes that are expected, perhaps even planned and partly executed, but then, after a time of waiting, simply abandoned rather than either accomplished or decisively thwarted. There are, of course, plenty of such nonevents in military history, moments that are seemingly marked by stasis and inactivity, and we've seen several in the course of this study—for example, Napoleon's indecision amid the ruins of Moscow—that are magnets for conjectural alternatives. The conjectures are fed, moreover, by the increasingly complete records and remnants of unrealized plans, failed trials, and abandoned operations that survive modern wars, obliging historians to incorporate efforts toward unachieved goals into their actual histories and further opening the already porous boundary between actual and counterfactual military history.

The standoff between Britain and Germany in the summer of 1940 both fits that model and stands out from it because of the extraordinary visibility of the German preparations that led most of the world to anticipate an amphibious invasion, which never materialized. Following the eight-month period of inactivity at its start, World War II became such a fast-paced, expansive phenomenon, spreading so rapidly and continuously throughout Europe and Asia, that the several months during which the Wehrmacht halted were in themselves exceptional in their protracted suspensefulness. Germany's blitzkrieg across Western Europe had taken it to the brink of the British Channel, and there it paused, confronting a nation that refused to make peace despite the defeat and retreat of the British Expeditionary Force from the Continent. The geographical narrowing of the potential action to the two sides of the channel and the limitations of duration imposed by other natural factors—the tides, the weather—made that particular space-time nexus an object of fascination for those who experienced it. And we might say that it was experienced the world over, for the Germans made no secret of their preparations, and the British were equally public about their defensive and offensive rearmament efforts. After the war, the space-time nexus of the British Channel in the summer of 1940 provided a vivid instance of a crucial juncture in world history: Hitler's war machine was stymied, providing hope for its ultimate defeat. The substantive outcome of that phase of the Battle of Britain, though, seemed to owe less to British resolve than to Hitler's postponement of the invasion plan: the ships never launched, so the event never occurred. In short, its absence, which preserves it as an unrealized possibility, was the historically significant phenomenon. We will see why the questions this poses for historians can only be answered by explicit counterfactual hypothesizing.

GUILTY MEN, RECRIMINATION, AND
POLITICAL COUNTERFACTUALS, 1938–40

A few weeks after the legendary withdrawal of the British Expeditionary Force from Dunkirk, while the country was still thanking God for the miracle of its deliverance and praising the heroism of the thousands of civilians who had helped carry the army home across the channel in a flotilla of small boats, a bitter little book appeared in London's newsstands and immediately became a sensational best seller. Titled *Guilty Men*, it purported to expose the causes of the expeditionary force's failure by placing the blame on fifteen British leaders—including former Labour prime minister Ramsay MacDonald and Conservative prime ministers Stanley Baldwin and Neville Chamberlain. The guilty men, it claimed, were responsible for the defeat of Britain and its allies as well as for the suffering and humiliation of its soldiers. The book begins by asking: "How was it . . . that the bravest sons of Britain ever came to be placed in such jeopardy? How was it, that, though the best soldiers in the world, they were driven back from Belgium?"[3] And it goes on to explain that the army was doomed *"before* they took the field" (11), betrayed by the political leaders who had failed to arm them sufficiently.

Guilty Men peppers its narrative with references to alternative courses of action and thus makes rhetorical use of counterfactual arguments. The alternative it conjures, however, remains quite general, consisting mainly in the idea that preparations for war with Germany should have started years earlier and been much more extensive. The usual lack of specifics about those preparations, though, is no mere mistake, for it points to a general dilemma faced by most writers at the time of the crisis. The search for villains, or at least bumbling dupes of the enemy, became a national psychological priority in the aftermath of Dunkirk, even though all political parties and most public commentators needed to develop amnesia about their own recent attitudes in order to articulate their charges. That included two of the three authors of *Guilty Men*, who were on record in the previous five years as opposing British rearmament and supporting appeasement. The writing team had one journalist from each of the major parties. The principal author, Michael Foot (later a member of Parliament and leader of the Labour Party), had first run as a Labour candidate in 1935 on an anti-rearmament platform; he even went so far as to support unilateral British disarmament. Peter Howard, the writer from the Conservative Party, had been tolerant of German aggression several years earlier and had flirted for a time with Oswald Mosley's British Fascist organization.

Only the Liberal member of the team, Frank Owen, had actually earned the right to censure others for placating Hitler, for he had been outspokenly anti-appeasement in the late thirties. But the public was unaware of the authors' individual inconsistencies, for they were hidden under the joint pseudonym of "Cato," a reference to ancient Rome's Cato the Elder, sometimes called Cato the Censor for his rigorous exercise of the office that held public men to a scrupulous code of duty. Nor could readers have known that at the time of the writing all three journalists worked for Lord Beaverbrook, the press magnate who had been one of the most loyal advocates of Neville Chamberlain's policies right up until the outbreak of war. Indeed, the slogan of his *Daily Express* was "There will be no war." The book was the first to define "appeasement," which formerly had just meant a policy of seeking peace, as a "deliberate surrender of small nations in the face of Hitler's blatant bullying."[4] It argued that fifteen "appeasers" from previous governments should be forbidden to serve in the current coalition national government, which had been formed under Winston Churchill in early May of 1940.

To appreciate fully just how shockingly abrupt this change in national direction was, we should note that *Guilty Men* uses images and rhetoric repurposed from the antiwar literature of the last years of World War I, as if the culture couldn't quite adjust to the recent turn of events. In the opening chapter, we see the familiar figures of brave and innocent soldiers returning from the front, many of them only silently accusatory but all with the consciousness that they have been betrayed by the politicians who sent them there: "All that courage and discipline could do[,] they had done. They were unbeaten and unconquerable. But all, it seemed, was of no avail. For they were now stumbling back, footsore, eyes red with weariness, sleepless for days . . . stumbling back, aching in every limb" (3). The book's portrayals of aging and callous national leaders were equally familiar from twenty years earlier. The persistence of these stereotypes in *Guilty Men*, though, doesn't quite hide the fact that the old antiwar attitudes had contributed mightily to the very lack of military preparation that the book was intended to indict. Unlike in 1918, the guilty old men in 1940 are not warmongers and profiteers but instead leaders who did too much to mollify the country's future enemies while discounting the likelihood of war. They acted not in opposition to but in accord with the pacifist upsurge that had followed the First World War, and the youth of the country were believed to be especially antiwar until at least the middle of the 1930s, as evidenced by the notorious triumph of the Oxford Union debate motion of 1933: "that this House will in no circumstances fight for its King and Country," which was carried by 275 votes to 153. This was a generation that insisted on contrasting itself to that of the previous war, refusing to be seduced by patriotic clichés or to be used as cannon fodder, and they were certainly not advocates of building new cannons. One tactic of *Guilty Men* was to divert the former antiwar rhetoric into antiappeasement, and therefore pro-war, channels.

That was a delicate maneuver because all British governments and political tendencies in the interwar period supported appeasement. Liberal, Labour, Conservative, and coalition governments sought multilateral disarmament, resisted expanding or updating their own arsenals, tried to mitigate what they saw as the overly harsh conditions imposed on Germany by the Versailles Treaty, and—even after Hitler had come to power—attempted to contain German territorial expansion by negotiated compromises. Historians now tend to concede that these were, at least up to 1937, reasonable and relatively uncontroversial strategies for the leaders of a country contending with a world-financial depression, an overly extended empire, and a larger share of global responsibility than it could comfortably discharge. Besides, as one recent historian has noted, "A policy of mediation and pacification fitted well with the view that the British have of themselves, as the embodiment of fair play and decency."[5] Criticism of the policy of seeking negotiated accommodations with Hitler did, to be sure, increase after Neville Chamberlain became prime minister in 1937 and the Labour Party's pacifist wing began to shrink, but the majority of people still supported the conciliatory efforts right up through the Munich Pact, which was signed at the end September 1938. Hence when Britons found themselves isolated and at bay in June 1940 they needed to disown their earlier, mistaken policies by claiming that they had been misled. Since all political parties had been equally "misleading," there was hardly any limit to the number of potential culprits. Politicians of every stripe disowned the word "appeasement"; even Neville Chamberlain had stopped using it by the time *Guilty Men* portrayed the policy, not as the broadly supported one that it had been, but as a highly controversial path pursued by a minority of irresponsible and unusually wrong-headed politicians.[6] The fact that the vast majority of voters and their leaders had all been wrong together only increased the jolt of the new reality and the anger about it. *Guilty Men* was a symptom of the nation's need to revise its own history quickly by identifying and purging a few scapegoats, and it was also an instance of bald-faced hypocrisy. It does, however, help us to see why and how a set of earlier future conditional scenarios, articulated most forcefully by Winston Churchill in the period between 1934 and 1939, were revived during the summer of 1940 as counterfactual possibilities. In chapter 3 I noted that the counterfactuals used during the American Civil War were taken from the prewar debate, and the same pattern is repeated in Britain during World War II. The difference, though, is that the British debate had been immensely lopsided, so almost all of the dire speculations about future disasters came from a single previously ignored source. The tricky thing was to remind readers of the warnings without also reminding them of the general disregard in which they were previously held.

Recrimination was the order of the day, and *Guilty Men* makes the project explicit by using a quote from Winston Churchill as its opening motto: "The use of recriminating about the past is to enforce effective action at the present" (xiii). Recrimination in June 1940 was needed to enforce all that would be necessary to cure the weaknesses in military preparation that had been so dreadfully exposed by the war in France and Belgium. And recrimination, of course, requires counterfactuals; in order to convict the accused, the book had to prove that they were knowledgeable and powerful enough to have judged and acted differently. Hence it includes a chapter called "They Had Been Warned," which reviews the widely known indications of Hitler's intended aggression:

> Hitler himself had written it in *Mein Kampf*; the million speeches delivered by the Nazi leaders on the hustings of Germany; the denunciation of Versailles; the institution of Conscription in Germany; the murder of [federal chancellor of Austria] Dollfuss; the murder of [French foreign minister Jean-Louis] Barthou; the Rhineland; Spain; Austria; Czechoslovakia; Munich; Prague—these and countless more. How many more proofs were needed? Hitler gave the last supreme warning in the devastation of Poland. . . .
>
> All the facts of Germany's prodigious capacity for war were known. Mr. Churchill had reiterated them to the House of Commons over the previous years. No room was left for doubt. (111–12)

Churchill had also computed the difference between Germany's and Britain's total arms expenditures and made that information public in the years just before the war, so the government, the book insisted, could not claim that it did not know how far its own preparations were falling short (115–18). The need to place blame on some created an equally strong necessity to find others blameless and, thus, recalling Churchill's exceptional behavior was an integral part of proving that the guilty men had stubbornly chosen to ignore the peril into which they were leading the country and its soldiers. The counterexample of his conduct completes the case for convicting the accused, and the book draws the counterfactual conclusion: "If Mr. Churchill had been in office before the war there would have been no question of any unreadiness in the Forces" (126).

When it does use specific historical counterfactuals, *Guilty Men* thus follows the lead of Churchill himself. Always prone to speculative imaginings (as we noted in chap. 3), Churchill had long predicted future scenarios combined with striking images of coming disasters as a way of chastising the governments in power. Between 1934 and 1939, his Parliamentary speeches marked each new phase of Hitler's progress with a barrage of reproachful might-have-beens and reminders that the Nazis were emboldened by successive indications of Britain's reluctance to fight.[7] His speech objecting to the Munich Agreement in October 1938 is typical. First he contrasts the latest misstep in British foreign policy with a preferable unrealized alternative:

> France and Great Britain together, especially if they had maintained a close contact with Russia, which certainly was not done, would have been able in those days in the summer [of 1938], when they had the prestige, to influence many of the smaller states of Europe; and I believe they could have determined the attitude of Poland. Such a combination, prepared at a time when the German dictator was not deeply and irrevocably committed to his new adventure, would, I believe, have given strength to all those forces in Germany which resisted this departure, this new design.[8]

Then he goes on to survey the trail of error that led to the current pact—"the most grievous consequence of what we have done and of what we have left undone in the last five years"—and laments the loss of the peace with honor that might have been. He identifies the nexus point—1933—at which actual history departed from the right course: "When I think of the fair hopes of a long peace which still lay before Europe at the beginning of 1933 when Herr Hitler first obtained power, and of all the opportunities of arresting the growth of the Nazi power which have been thrown away, when I think of the immense combinations and resources which have been neglected or squandered, I cannot believe that a parallel exists in the whole course of history!" Next he measures the distance between the state that might have been maintained if Britain had been committed to "arresting the growth of Nazi power" and that to which the country has been reduced:

> We have been reduced in those five years from a position of security so overwhelming and so unchallengeable that we never cared to think about it. We have been reduced from a position where the very word "war" was considered one which could be used only by persons qualifying for a lunatic asylum. We have been reduced from a position of safety and power—power to do good, power to be generous to a beaten foe, power to make terms with Germany, power to give her proper redress for her grievances, power to stop her arming if we chose, power to take any step in strength or mercy or justice which we thought right—reduced in five years from a position safe and unchallenged to where we stand now.

Finally he moves to the probable calamities of the near future, in which Germany, he predicts, will quickly dominate middle and eastern Europe and then turn its aggression toward France and Great Britain: "What," he asks ominously, "will be the position of that Western front of which we are in full authority the guarantors?" Britain's own folly, he concludes, has rendered it as open to Nazi incursion as any unprepared Continental European nation, unless—there is always a concluding "unless"—the government begins "to regain our old island independence by acquiring that supremacy in the air which we were promised, that security in our air defences which we were assured we had, and thus to make ourselves an island once again" (6:6013).

This rhetoric of counterfactual recrimination, which squarely put a large part of the blame for Nazi gains on British governments, is Churchill's legacy to *Guilty Men*, and like many other statements in the summer of 1940, the book explicitly associated itself with Churchill's previous position by stressing his warnings and regretting that so little heed had been paid to them. It certainly helped the new prime minister ascend to the level of a prophet who might have saved the country *if only* he had been in the government earlier. Churchill thus benefited from the book, which saved him the trouble of having to say "I told you so" while reminding the public of just how many of the previous two years' disasters he had foreseen. Hitler had invaded Czechoslovakia in March of 1939, as Churchill warned he would, violating the terms of the Munich Agreement and capturing all the equipment of a well-armed nation. Then even after Chamberlain had abandoned appeasement, Britain's weakness had prevented it from effectively defending Poland, which fell in a matter of weeks, as Churchill had said it would. Next, after Britain had declared war, there was the successful German invasion of Norway, the first action in which British forces fought and the first in which they were defeated. And finally came the battles in France and Belgium, where Churchill (by then prime minister) had not predicted defeat, but where the insufficiency of arms and men that he had been railing against for years was a factor. In the months before *Guilty Men* appeared, he was already perceived as the only national leader who had been consistently critical of the old policies, and hence his replacement of Neville Chamberlain as prime minister and the substitution of a coalition national government for the Conservative Party leadership went some way toward refocusing a disoriented nation. His leadership was an instance, we might say, of compensatory counterfactual undoing—the country could retroactively make up for not having followed him earlier by trusting his leadership now. And even though the most recent episodes in the country's descent into defeat and vulnerability had occurred on his watch, those losses were not seen as his fault but were instead the inevitable result of policies he had opposed. The popularity of *Guilty Men* should serve to remind us that the high level of Churchill's individual credibility was built on a more general impression of having been betrayed by "the rulers" (as Cato called the previous governments) and a widespread suspicion of those in power.

CHURCHILL'S FUTURE CONDITIONALS AND THE SHAPING OF NATIONAL CHARACTER

Churchill had thus risen on a wave of popular anger, and yet he immediately needed to stem that tide. *Guilty Men* was yet to find a publisher when, on June 18, in his "Finest Hour" speech, the prime minister chided the "many who would hold an inquest in the House of Commons on the conduct of the Governments—and of Parliaments, for they are in it, too—during the years which led up to this catastrophe."[9] Seeking "to indict those who were responsible for the guidance of our affairs," he declared, would be "a foolish and pernicious process." Being acutely aware of how few had publicly stood out against such guidance, he warned his fellow members of Parliament: "There are too many in it. Let each man search his conscience and search his speeches." He also rebuffed suggestions that he should remove ministers of former governments—especially Neville Chamberlain—from their current coalition posts, repelling in advance the calls to "let the guilty men retire" that the book's publication would soon amplify:

> I cannot accept the drawing of any distinctions between Members of the present Government. It was formed at a moment of crisis in order

to unite all the Parties and all sections of opinion. . . . It is absolutely necessary at a time like this that every Minister who tries each day to do his duty shall be respected; and their subordinates must know that their chiefs are not threatened men, men who are here today and gone tomorrow, but that their directions must be punctually and faithfully obeyed. Without this concentrated power we cannot face what lies before us. (6:6232)

"I am quite sure," he told the nation, "that if we open a quarrel between the past and the present, we shall find that we have lost the future."

A few months later, when Chamberlain died of cancer, Churchill made an even more extended argument for mending the "quarrel between the past and present," this time emphasizing that the nation's trustworthiness and international credibility were at stake. Speaking to the House of Commons, he asked his listeners to rise above the passions of the moment and imagine what later generations might say about "these terrible, tremendous years."[10] Future historians should understand "that Neville Chamberlain acted with perfect sincerity according to his lights and strove to the utmost of his capacity and authority, which were powerful, to save the world from the awful, devastating struggle in which we are now engaged." Chamberlain and the policies he pursued are reimagined as stages in the nation's continuous pursuit of a just peace: "What were these hopes in which he was disappointed? . . . What was that faith that was abused? They were surely among the most noble and benevolent instincts of the human heart—the love of peace, the toil for peace, the strife for peace, the pursuit of peace, even at great peril." Whereas in 1938 Churchill had denounced Chamberlain's "five years of eager search for the line of least resistance," now he presents a Chamberlain whose "toil," "strife," and "peril" integrate him into the ranks of the country's currently embattled citizens. Because Churchill was trying to create an overall idea of national character in this speech, the policy of appeasement was less important than the underlying intentions that motivated it. Trying especially to redeem the nation's reputation in the eyes of the Americans, he frankly stated that it would be "a help to our country and to our whole Empire" to reclaim Chamberlain's integrity, for that would be the basis on which Britons could claim "we were guiltless of the bloodshed, terror and misery which have engulfed so many lands and peoples, and yet seek new victims still." Finding the "guilty men" innocent, in other words, had become the prerequisite to placing blame for Europe's war exclusively on Hitler: "It fell to Neville Chamberlain in one of the supreme crises of the world to be contradicted by events, to be disappointed in his hopes, and to be deceived and cheated by a wicked man." Completely suppressed is Churchill's condemnation from two years earlier, in his Munich Agreement address, when Chamberlain's government was portrayed as remiss, neglectful, and undoubtedly responsible for the coming crisis: "So far as this country is concerned the responsibility must rest with those who have had the undisputed control of our political affairs. They neither prevented Germany from rearming, nor did they rearm themselves in time" ("A Total and Unmitigated Defeat," 6:6008). That rhetoric not only made Britain look responsible for its own danger but also implied that the nation had trouble fixing a steady course, that it had been tacking about for a direction and was perhaps incapable of forming a durable resolve to fight. By the summer of 1940, Churchill wanted all Britons to be regarded as equally the victims of the Nazis, and thus taking up the position of a future historian, he concludes that, although "long, hard, and hazardous years lie before us, . . . at least we entered upon them united and with clean hearts." This assertion of British historical guiltlessness—"clean hearts" is very close to "clean hands"— forms the core of the national *character* that Churchill composed in 1940.

Churchill saw clearly that he must construct a story for this character that could accommodate appeasement rather than suppress or anathematize it. Britain had to appear to be a nation whose methods had adapted to changing circumstances but whose goals had not changed radically over the previous decade. Potential allies could trust this nation because deficiencies in its previous policies had arisen not out of any cowardly fear of fighting but, instead, out of its frank and open nature and its belief in fair play—manly virtues exploited by a devious enemy.[11] Neville Chamberlain typified Britishness in his heroic willingness to exhaust every opportunity for peace, and he typified his countrymen as well in the alacrity and wholeheartedness with which he went to war as soon as he realized his good faith had been abused and betrayed. Britons, in the person of Chamberlain, were as free of changeability as they were untainted by war responsibility, for they had continuously sought peace with honor.

The national character, in short, was being given a plausible past that would square with recent memory, and regretful counterfactuals were put aside in this narrative, which concentrated on the spotlessness of motives rather than the unfortunate consequences of actions. Indeed, it was precisely because the appeasers had done what turned out to be the wrong thing for the right reasons that they became stages in a self-correcting national destiny. Generally speaking, national character resembles the classical model of heroic character that we've often encountered in this study:

it unfolds through time and is an expression of an abiding entelechy, an Aristotelian purpose. It does not fully manifest itself in any particular moment but only in the overall trajectory that dynamically registers the invisible guiding principles. Churchill's specific use of this pattern, though, seems more romantic than classical. Like a Walter Scott hero, the national protagonist who emerges in these speeches goes through quixotic episodes of foolishness in pursuit of a praiseworthy goal, and the episodes are an indispensable chastening prelude to the climactic realization of the nation's true nature.

British character, Churchill kept stressing throughout the summer and fall of 1940, was on the brink of a trial by fire, in which its essential mettle would be displayed. No matter what the immediate future brings, he kept reminding his listeners, *this* was to be the moment of national destiny. Indeed, *because* Britons were making themselves ready for all hazards, they had already begun their trial, and so Churchill replaced the past what-ifs with future conjectures, as in this famous conclusion from the speech of June 4:

> Even though large tracts of Europe and many old and famous States . . . may fall into the grip of the Gestapo and all the odious apparatus of Nazi rule, we shall not flag or fail. We shall go on to the end, we shall fight in France, we shall fight on the seas and oceans, we shall fight with growing confidence and growing strength in the air, we shall defend our Island, whatever the cost may be, we shall fight on the beaches, we shall fight on the landing grounds, we shall fight in the fields and in the streets, we shall fight in the hills; we shall never surrender, and even if, which I do not for a moment believe, this Island or a large part of it were subjugated and starving, then our Empire beyond the seas, armed and guarded by the British Fleet, would carry on the struggle, until, in God's good time, the New World, with all its power and might, steps forth to the rescue and the liberation of the old.[12]

The series of battlegrounds in this oft-quoted peroration is clearly not just a list, but a narrative of stages in a hypothetical invasion and occupation. First, the Britons are still fighting in France, which had not yet surrendered in early June, then they are relying on the navy and air force to protect the island, then the perimeter of the island is breached by sea (the beaches) and the enemy invades from the air (the landing grounds), then the countryside (the fields) and the cities (the streets) are scenes of battle, until the fighters seem driven into the hills, and the worst imaginable outcome of total subjugation is reached, requiring that troops from the empire and America come to the rescue. The swiftness of this suggested sequence might give the impression of an unstoppable advance if it were not for the anaphoric incantation—"we shall fight"—at every juncture. Each deeper stage of penetration into the island thus becomes part of a swelling heroic battle. The passage, indeed, is so entirely focused on what Britons will do in every eventuality that the enemy is never even mentioned: the phrase is not "we shall fight *them*" (as often misquoted) but only "we shall fight." Hence, although the grammatical structures of the peroration are conditionals ("Even though . . . , we shall. . . . And even if . . . , then our Empire . . . and our navy . . . would carry on . . ."), certainty about the future course of British action pervades it.

The passage is thus explicitly speculative in its presentation of future contingencies and confidently predictive about national behavior come what may: "We shall fight." Inside the grammatical conditional mood, there is the declaration of unconditional warfare: there are no circumstances under which we would consider surrendering to, or compromising with, Nazi aggression. In all of his speeches of the summer of 1940, Churchill maintained this message: because the Battle of Britain is radically unpredictable, we must respond consistently to all eventualities. Out of the very uncertainties of the summer of 1940, the national character—the reliability of behavior in unsettled situations—would be forged. By stressing that the enemy may or may not invade, may or may not occupy the island, Churchill created the national character as a pure potential, independent of actual history and in that sense noncontingent. And yet contingencies were also its element. Whether the Nazis ultimately invaded, British character consisted in what the people *would do* in every possible configuration of the crisis. In its paradoxical relation to contingency, character generally is not really amenable to proof, for the opportunities that actually present themselves are always shadowed by those that do not materialize.

The threatened Nazi invasion and occupation have thus been consistent shadow events in the history of the actual Battle of Britain. To be sure, in the autumn of 1940, Londoners' stoic endurance of the Blitz and the successes of the Royal Air Force (RAF) and the Royal Navy became actual proofs of national bravery, so gradually the imaginary projections of close-range combat with would-be invaders and occupiers became less necessary to the concept of the heroic nature of the people. Churchill's future perfect conditional phrase from the June 18 speech—"if the British Empire and its Commonwealth last for a thousand years, men will still say, 'This was their finest hour'" (6:6238)—came to refer to victory in the real Battle of Britain. However, we must recall that the battle was at the time conceived as a struggle to repel an invasion; Churchill's speech on the September 11, four days after the beginning of the London Blitz, made the context explicit: "These cruel, wanton, indiscriminate bombings of London are, of course, a part of Hitler's invasion plans. He hopes, by killing large numbers of civilians, and women and children, that he will terrorize and cow the people of this mighty imperial city, and make them a burden and anxiety to the Government and thus distract our attention unduly from the ferocious onslaught he is preparing."[13] The calm fortitude and independence of London's people, along with their willingness to fight actively, began to emerge as the bedrock of their character: "Little does [Hitler] know of the spirit of the British nation, or the tough fibre of the Londoners, whose forebears played a leading part in the establishment of Parliamentary institutions and who have been bred to value freedom far above their lives" (6:6277). Until the end of September, the bombing raids on cities were not seen as an alternative to an invasion but a prelude to one, and even though Churchill had told them on September 11 that the Germans would probably not invade at all if they did not do it by the end of month, 53 percent of Britons persisted in expecting an invasion any day until as late as February 1941.[14]

Many writers have commented on what Elizabeth Bowen called "the heady autumn of the first London air raids," linking it to the expectation that a great collective vindication was at hand. Peter Stansky, for example, quotes letters from prominent Londoners written in the second week of September: "We are all rolling up our sleeves for an invasion and we hope for *this weekend*, at last," wrote Diana Forbes-Robertson almost gleefully, and the Reverend John McKenzie echoed her eagerness: "The invasion is supposed to be starting today. They have got a lovely day for it, but that is all they will find lovely about it."[15] Even Churchill later admitted to feeling a thrilled anticipation during the month of September: "One could not help being inwardly excited alike by the atmosphere and the evidence of Hitler's intention which streamed in upon us." The War Cabinet was spoiling for "the chance of striking a blow at the mighty enemy which would resound throughout the world," and many, he reported, "on purely technical grounds, and for the sake of the effect the total defeat and destruction of his expedition would have on the general war, were quite content to see him try."[16] In retrospect, all agreed that the Battle of Britain was an important turning point in the war, and yet many also seemed to think that their finest hour might have been even finer if only there had been an invasion.

That sentiment outlived the war, becoming one of the primary inspirations for early postwar alternate histories and alternate-history fictions. We'll take a longer look at those later in the chapter, but a single conversation from Noel Coward's 1946 alternate-history play, *Peace in Our Time*, so succinctly sums up the lingering regret over the missed opportunity to display Britain's true colors that I want to quote it here. Explaining why she's glad the English lost the Battle of Britain and were consequently invaded, which is the play's counterfactual premise, the most patriotic of the characters insists that the lack of an invasion would have wrecked the national character: "We should have got lazy again and blown out with our own glory. We should have been bombed and blitzed and we should have stood up under it—an example to the whole civilized world—and that would have finished us. As it is—in defeat—we still have a chance.... We can be united now—we shall have to be—until we've driven them away, until we're clean again."[17] This is certainly a bizarre moment: instead of reveling in the fact that his countrymen won the Battle of Britain and that their national resistance had provided the staging ground for the liberation of the Continent, the playwright uses alternate history to accuse his countrymen of smugness while imagining a more heroic story of armed civilian resistance. And yet this fantasy flows smoothly from Churchill's stirring insistence that "we shall never surrender . . . even if . . . this Island or a large part of it were subjugated and starving." Only by *losing* the Battle of Britain and suffering the invasion could such an epic of national character have been enacted.

CREATING A HOLE IN HISTORY: COUNTERFACTUALISM AND THE INVASION THAT WASN'T

According to the historians, however, getting invaded would not have been such an easy thing to do. There are over a dozen book-length histories in English of the invasion that did not happen in the summer of 1940, and many shorter essays treat the topic as well. Some are critical military histories, in which the line between what did occur and what might have occurred is necessarily very thin, some are broader cultural analyses of the impact of the threatened invasion on war sentiment in Britain and/or Germany, some are institutional histories of Hitler's armed forces at that decisive turning point in the war, and some take up the topic of Britain's countermeasures. There has been plenty of controversy in these studies, but one thing the historians tend to agree about is that *even if* the Germans had won the air war, they could not have succeeded in Operation Sea Lion, as they called their projected cross-channel invasion. Air dominance was not the key to victory, but only one of many factors; a Luftwaffe victory would have been a necessary but by no means sufficient condition for an effective sea landing. The historians point out that the Royal Navy had more than enough flexibility and fire power to prevent a German armada from getting across and could swiftly have cut off from their supply lines any forces who did manage to land, essentially trapping them. No serious historian credits the possibility of a reversed outcome, in which German armored divisions storm out of landing craft onto beaches and take over the island. There weren't any real landing craft at the time, and the Germans' hastily modified barges and other river boats were not and could not be made suitable for crossing the channel and delivering a vast armored force. To be sure, the impossibility presupposes the *actual* Operation Sea Lion, the planning of which began only after Dunkirk. Several historians have gone to great lengths to come up with more plausible scenarios, but they have needed to completely revise the history of the German campaign in the spring of 1940 as well as their preparations for a naval battle. In doing so, they have shown that a cross-channel invasion would have been possible only if it had been one of the top priorities of Hitler's war in the West, instead of the afterthought it actually was.[18] We should certainly be interested in the motivations behind such wholesale revisions, but the point to stress here is that, in the summer of 1940, the island was not in danger of invasion.

Historians, especially military historians, have been explaining these facts since the mid-1950s and growing increasingly irritated by the enduring myth of the almost-invasion from which the RAF single-handedly saved Britain. The myth of "the few" they call it, alluding to one of Churchill's August speeches, where the defensive importance of the bomber and fighter pilots is summed up in a memorable phrase: "Never in the field of human conflict was so much owed by so many to so few."[19] In 1958, for example, one historian complained that the Germans themselves had certainly learned the lesson that no enemy could "invade these islands without first defeating our maritime forces," and yet Britons still seemed ignorant of "that undeniable proposition" since they went on celebrating the pilots every Battle of Britain Day (September 15), while the navy's role remained "in total eclipse."[20] In 1974 the historians' consensus was even confirmed by a war game conducted by the Royal Military Academy at

Sandhurst (with both British and German umpires) to determine the probable outcome of Sea Lion if it had been launched as planned. Their conclusion was also that Germany's relatively weak navy rendered the operation untenable.[21] Nevertheless, thirty years later, a 2005 book opens with the usual complaint, "These confident and unambiguous statements [about the singular importance of the RAF in staving off the imminent invasion] are written as if the Channel and the Royal Navy did not exist."[22]

Sea Lion seems to be one of those cases in which memory and history are at odds. The myth of "the few" survives the facts because it comports well with the need to remember the operation as a near miss, a catastrophe averted at the last minute. It harmonizes equally well with the idea that the British were collectively "the few" who saved European civilization. The phrase alluded to the Saint Crispin's Day Speech from *Henry V*, in which the king rallies his outnumbered British army against their enemy by asking them to think of a future time when those soldiers who stood their ground at Agincourt would be celebrated: "We few, we happy few, we band of brothers" (act 4, scene 3). Remembering the summer of 1940, one contemporary wrote, "there was more than a touch of the address before Agincourt in the air, a secret satisfaction that if it was coming we were to be the chosen, we few, we happy few, and all the other happy few round the coast of an impregnable island."[23] Moreover, there was no definitive moment when the exciting danger of the heroic moment was authoritatively declared past; no "all clear" sounded for the invasion. The official silence about the matter invited rumors that the Germans had actually launched an invasion in which thousands of enemy soldiers had been killed and washed ashore along the southern coast. As Churchill later explained, "We took no steps to contradict such tales, which spread freely through the occupied countries in a wildly exaggerated form and gave much encouragement to the oppressed populations."[24] In fact, the British government was by no means passive in the rumor mill; sensational stories were spread through the propaganda activities of His Majesty's Special Operations. For example, one unit undertook a disinformation campaign to demoralize the enemy by circulating reports in the foreign press that a German invading force had tried to cross the channel but was consumed by a "wall of flame" from oil tanks placed in the water and detonated by RAF planes; not surprisingly, these reports made their way back to England. In 1941, Special Operations also put out pamphlets for home consumption with titles like *Bomber Command*, in addition to planting articles in a popular aviation magazine, all stating that invasion flotillas had been launched and destroyed by the RAF.

And throughout the war there was, of course, an official attempt to engage people imaginatively in what we might think of as nationwide invasion scenario planning. There were the explicitly fictional movies like *Went the Day Well*, with a screenplay by Graham Greene, in which the civilian population of a village heroically fights off Nazi radio engineers disguised as British soldiers in 1942. But perhaps even more deeply effective in keeping people imaginatively focused on an invasion while they went about their daily lives were the omnipresent "stand fast" leaflets, the frequent Home Guard exercises, and the activities of Parish Invasion Committees (established in the summer of 1941), which drew up and continually revised plans for local action in the face of an advancing enemy force. Since people were steadily encouraged to envision such contingencies, to think about where they would go, what they would take, how they would act in encounters with enemy troops, it's little wonder that Britons later had trouble putting the episode in perspective. To give just one more indication of the wartime confusion about the reality of an invasion: as late as the summer of 1944 Churchill was asked in Parliament to clarify "whether the enemy ever set in motion apparatus of a sea-borne invasion," and he answered somewhat evasively: "I do not know what my honourable and gallant friend means by 'set in motion.' 'Set in motion,' in the sense of crossing the Channel, no; 'set in motion,' in the sense of making very heavy concentrations, both of troops and ships, to cross the Channel, yes."[25] He was then, oddly, asked, "If such an attempt was made, at any rate, was it successful?" and although he flatly answered no, he still gave the impression of holding back information. Many Britons consequently went through the war believing that the enemy had very nearly reached their shores alive and had certainly reached them dead, and they had no pressing reason to revise their opinion afterward. Indeed, Britons were so loath to give up the idea of an invasion foiled mid-channel by the RAF that as late as 1992 a revival of the "wall of flame" stories spread through the British press again, purporting to be revelations of a closely held WWII secret.[26]

Resonating as it does with the whole complex of finest-hour emotions and the heady sense of facing the national moment of truth, the myth of an almost-invasion strongly resists the facts. Indeed, without it, Sea Lion might not seem worth remembering at all. And that poses a problem for its historians. Their narratives attempt to puncture the inflated assessment of the threat and thereby to create a kind of hole in history. Of course, there are no holes in history, and the events surrounding Sea Lion are as real as any in the actual war; indeed, historians often explain that its planning and abandonment did represent something of a turning point but not because it could easily have succeeded. Already ontologically precarious as an invasion that was never launched, Sea Lion had to find its meaning in its *failure* to materialize. The RAF legends were far more daring and dramatic than the Royal Navy's story of deterrence through constant, diligent, long-term readiness, and therefore they made the threat seem more substantial. The myth compensated for the anticlimactic narrative, in which the story tapered off into mere nothingness, by providing battles and plenty of dead enemies. Next to the counterfactual event of a successful invasion, even the myth of a close call looks like a mere foothill on the historical landscape; but if that too disappears, the episode begins to resemble a crater. When historians deliver the news that instead of daring raids by bombers and fighters, the mere existence of the status quo in the channel dissuaded the wary enemy and saved the day, they necessarily seem to reduce the reality of the menace itself, perhaps even making it into just one in a long series of never-to-be-implemented plans. Is it history at all, or is it an instance of eventlessness itself, which necessarily defies Narrative? "Eventlessness has no posts to drape duration on," John Steinbeck wrote in *East of Eden*, and we might think of the Sea Lion historians' insistence on the importance of the episode they narrate as attempts to place posts in a desert of eventlessness.

Furthermore, the perception, which arrived fairly early, that Sea Lion was not fully integrated into German strategy also eroded the perception of its actual significance. In popular memory, a belief in the probable success of the invasion—and thus the momentousness of its thwarting—rested partly on its consistency with the relentlessness of the German war machine up to that point. An English invasion was seen by most of the world as the nearly inevitable sequel to the Battle of France, and that appearance suited the purposes of both the Germans, who relied on a sense of inexorability to enhance the threat, and the British, who exploited their position as the only potential obstruction in the path of an all but unstoppable Nazi juggernaut. As is so often the case in counterfactual logic, the meaningfulness of this nexus had lain in how likely the "original" course of history—the Nazi westward drive—seemed to be and therefore how *im*probable its diversion or cessation. The effort in bringing about the actual outcome, its occurrence despite the odds, is what made the spoiling of Sea Lion real and exciting. However, since the end of the war and the capture of German archives, historians have reported that the invasion plan was initiated in a remarkably haphazard fashion and that it trailed off just as nonchalantly. It was not on Hitler's original itinerary, and after the fall of France, when Admiral Raeder, the head of the German navy, raised the possibility with Hitler, he did so merely to cross it off his list of future options. It seemed superfluous to Raeder, but to his surprise and chagrin, he was told to make a plan. The very inception of the operation, therefore, seems a mere historical accident. But this view, as Churchill explained in his 1947 history of that summer, is only possible in hindsight. According to Churchill, since future generations will be able to see that the Germans had hardly any chance of crossing the channel, a Nazi defeat will appear to be the stable, predictable course of a history that had been on the British side all along. However, he continues, 1940 was a year in which it would have been imprudent not to expect the unexpected: "Twice in two months we had been taken completely by surprise.... What else had they got ready—prepared and organized to the last inch? Would they suddenly pounce out of the blue with new weapons, perfect planning, and overwhelming force upon our almost totally unequipped and disarmed Island at any one of a dozen or score of possible landing-places?"[27] In this first historical analysis of Sea Lion, Churchill saves the reality of the phenomenon: first he stresses the War Cabinet was obliged to prepare for all eventualities; second, he shows that the Germans had already proven that they were the very people from whom improbable actions were to be expected. Thus, no matter how it ended, the episode was bound to confound our common sense of what normally happens.

It should not surprise us, therefore, that the perennial issue at stake in the historical studies is the ontological status of the planned invasion, and the different opinions about the reality of the threat are based on varying interpretations of its devisors' intentions. Historians argue over what the Germans could possibly have been thinking in mounting such an unpromising operation, and their views tend to fall into three overlapping categories: (1) Sea Lion was mere theater, mounted to intimidate Britain into a separate peace; (2) it was partly theater and partly an exercise to test the feasibility of an invasion; (3) it was a definite attempt at mounting an invasion, abandoned only after Germany had realized that air superiority was beyond its grasp, that its makeshift troop transports could not negotiate the tricky channel currents, safely delivering tens of thousands of troops, and that the Royal Navy formed an impenetrable barrier. These are not separate phases in a developing understanding of the facts but are, rather, three interpretations that were staked out in the 1950s or 1960s and are still held. Consequently, I'll discuss the historiography not in chronological order but in what might be thought of as an ascending ontological order: from Sea Lion as pure pantomime to Sea Lion as a sincere attempt at invasion.

Historians adhering to the first interpretation argue that Hitler never really intended to invade Britain, so the whole operation was a feint. Peter Fleming described this as a typical German view in 1956; the invasion was considered "a mild aberration of Hitler's strategy, a cross between a daydream and a hoax."[28] Hitler was always, they tend to insist, focused on the east. Those holding this view cite the haphazardness, tardiness, and incompleteness of the plan, its lack of coordination, Hitler's distraction, delays, and the casual abandonment of the operation. They explain the extent and elaborateness of preparations by noting that in order to be convincing the charade had to be kept up even in the German camp. Thus Hitler's commanders were assigned the tasks of planning and preparing the invasion, and they went about their work unquestioningly, regardless of whether they believed their leader to be in earnest.[29] The second group of historians attributes a higher level of reality to Sea Lion. They agree that it might have been initiated as a merely threatening gesture designed to enhance Hitler's bellicose image, but they also acknowledge that the German army and navy took Hitler's command to examine the possibility of a cross-channel invasion very seriously. What may have started simply as an intimidating show, thus evolved into a genuine experimental effort. Like the historians who consider Sea Lion to have been pure fakery, these writers spend a good deal of time discussing all the reasons Hitler had for *not* invading, indeed not even fighting Britain. In one of the earliest Sea Lion histories, Peter Fleming explains that "Hitler did not want, nor did he need, to conquer England" (305). He had strong strategic reasons for wanting Britain to keep her empire; he admired the British and hoped for a noninterference pact with them; he did not see them as a serious staging ground for further warfare in Western Europe; and he was already planning to invade the Soviet Union and desperately wanted to avoid a war on two fronts. Hence, when it became clear that the invasion was not feasible, he simply abandoned it and gave himself wholeheartedly to his war against the real enemy in the east. Many Sea Lion historians follow this line of analysis, although they tend to disagree both about how deeply Hitler was ensnared in his own Sea Lion bluff, how decisive the outcome of the air war seemed in the German camp, and whether the total impracticality of the plan (as opposed to its mere riskiness) ever became fully apparent in 1940.[30]

These two interpretations—that the operation was mere playacting and that it was a mixture of serious but faulty preparations, experimentation, and bluster—tend to foreclose counterfactual questions about what might have happened if the invasion were launched in late September as planned. The main proponent of the charade view, for example, simply dismisses the Sandhurst game exercise out of hand: "The premise of the games was unfounded, since Sea Lion was never planned to be implemented."[31] The conclusion of the Peter Fleming's book is almost as categorical: "When half the pieces on the board have to be redeployed in order to ensure victory for the loser, the business becomes tedious." Even the designer of a 1974 *Seelöwe* board game, apologizing for his subtraction of the Royal Navy from the game's historical premises, explains that "if the British Navy were to intervene, Seelöwe would not be a game. It would be merely a brutal exercise in how to exterminate troops on the beach."[32] Counterfactual history needs better odds than that, which is why so many of the books that argue for the futility of the actual operation conclude by asking if there might have been other plans or other prevailing conditions in which a German invasion would have been feasible. Suppose the Germans had captured the British Expeditionary Force at Dunkirk instead of letting it escape across the channel? Suppose the Luftwaffe had kept up its bombardment of the RAF's airfields and the airplane factories instead of bombing British cities, which allowed the air force to rebuild? Suppose the German air force, navy, and army had been forced to work in close cooperation beginning in early June? But all of these questions seem to stray outside the boundaries of the historical Sea Lion episode, raising the question once again of its ontological status.

The authors of the earliest critical military histories on the subject—those produced in the mid-1950s from the German records that had been captured in 1945 and slowly digested and declassified during the subsequent decade—felt compelled to argue explicitly for the importance of their subject on the grounds that the threat of the invasion was something more than a fantasy, while also detailing the reasons for its probable defeat if launched.[33] They fall into that third category of historians who stress the concrete *reality* of the operation. Although a number of factors combined to make the project ultimately futile, they repeatedly tell their readers, the "threat" in the summer of 1940 was "very real," and hence they help us answer the question of just what the "reality" of an unaccomplished—as opposed to a merely imaginary—invasion might be. Duncan Grinnell-Milne's response to the question in *The Silent Victory* is typical of the lot, and it points to the uses critical military histories routinely make of counterfactuals:

> Interest in [Sea Lion] is not purely academic; it contains lessons which may well be valuable in the future. . . . But as an attempt to conquer

these islands by seaborne invasion it must take its place with the other unsuccessful attempts of the past.

For "attempt" there was—not just a plan—from the moment when the transports steamed from German harbours to assemble in the Channel ports, just as much as when the Armada sailed from Corunna towards Parma waiting in Flanders or as when, with Napoleon's Army encamped at Boulogne, the French Fleet sailed from Toulon on the first leg of the Trafalgar campaign. It is the purpose of the present work to show how this latest attempt was frustrated, and by whom. (9)

Because an *attempt* has a much higher level of phenomenal reality than a mere *plan*, you can learn something from it, and there is much to be learned from Sea Lion. The historical gravity of the operation inheres, the critical military historians tend to argue, in its very failure to materialize and in the variety of lessons to be gleaned from the failure. For example, as an experimental test of the conditions that underlay the continued deterrent effectiveness of the channel barrier, it was a huge success, and its usefulness for that purpose derives from the extent and elaboration of Sea Lion's actual physical preparations: the immense effort at collecting, building, modifying, and improvising troop and equipment carriers and landing craft; massing of ships, weapons, and men; and the troops' training exercises, which although never truly rigorous or adequately repeated, revealed the difficulty of both crossing the Channel and delivering an army, with all of its equipment and supplies, on the other side . In short, it was real because of all the time and resources the Germans expended on it and their evident futility. Even though an invasion itself remained only a historical latency, the abandonment of the effort was a real setback. Also, they argue, instead of being merely unlaunched, the invasion was actively thwarted. Indeed, the point of these books is that there was an actual contest and that by maintaining general sea-power dominance, and undertaking small-scale clandestine actions against the invasion forces in the Continent's Channel ports, in which some ships and transports were sunk, the Royal Navy saved the day. One should, therefore, recognize the likeness of Sea Lion to its historical predecessors, and that very continuity reveals the folly of imagining that the dominance of air war in World War II created a definitive break with past wars.

The reality of Sea Lion rests also in the world-historical *consequences* of its attempt and failure, which were first spelled out in the 1950s and have been subsequently recognized by most historians. The Germans did not just make a cheap, inconsequential experiment, from which they then pulled back at the last minute without cost. Instead, they made a huge and expensive strategic error. Truly ignorant about naval combat and the logistical problems of getting armored divisions across the channel and keeping them supplied, they requisitioned every barge and tugboat in every river and bay under their control, which amounted to thousands of boats, causing considerable harm to their coal transport and hence their munitions industry. Moreover, the abandonment of their attempt, although not as catastrophic as a defeated invasion would have been, was nevertheless the first major check to the Nazis' war machine and a definitive sign to the world that they had lost the Battle of Britain in the air. It kept the western front active, precipitating Germany into a two-front war. The British were seen as having successfully defended their nation and their empire, as well as foreclosing the possibility of an effective German blockade. As we've already seen, both the attempt and its failure strengthened the resolve of the British, for whom it was, in the words of Peter Fleming, "both a tonic and a drug: It braced the islanders to exertions whose necessity seemed beyond question, and it expunged from their minds the memories of the disasters they had suffered" (307). It stoked Britain's munitions industry as well as its morale, especially accelerating the development and production of fighter planes, bombers, troop carriers, and landing craft for a reverse channel crossing. Just as importantly, the thwarted invasion quelled doubts in the United States, which stepped up its munitions industry and shipments, and made it far more likely that America would enter the war. Hence, the historians repeatedly tell us, the invasion that never happened was a very real episode in the war; indeed, it was a major turning point.

A final way to substantiate these actual historical consequences of Sea Lion's default was to imagine the operation's complete nonexistence: suppose some smarter way of dealing with Britain after Dunkirk had been found. This question calls for further assessments of German options, and several counterfactual scenarios arise from it. For example, what if, instead of pursuing further conquest, Hitler had simply declared victory on the western front and slowly eliminated Britain as an active opponent by blockading and containing the island. Peter Fleming was one of the first—but by no means the last—historian to speculate that Hitler might even have gradually gained ascendency over Britain by *not* fighting the Battle of Britain.[34] Noting how completely Hitler's "fee-fi-fo-fum bluster" backfired, he supposes that "instead of bringing [Britons'] patriotic instincts to the boil, [he] left them to stew in their own juices." Among the "immense advantages" Germany might have gained "if in June 1940 [Hitler] had turned his back on England instead of shaking his fist at her" (307) would have been devoting the German navy's energy to blockading the island; a much slower pace of development of the RAF; a British army losing energy and draining resources while training for no imaginable engagement; Americans losing interest and withdrawing their concern and support from a country that was not actively beleaguered; and British war aims beginning to drift, as a future of nothing but "boredom, bankruptcy and blockade" became the only thing on the horizon. Fleming reminds us, too, "that some 40,000 British prisoners of war had fallen into German hands" and asks, "If Hitler had made a contemptuous offer to send them home, could any British Government have refused it?" (308).

This narrative of how Britain might eventually have yielded to Nazi domination if Hitler had been more imaginative, patient, and far-sighted works on the opposite principle from that of the counterfactuals of either a successful or a catastrophically wrecked invasion, for instead of imagining actual battles, it deepens the void of eventlessness. Fleming even suggests that his substitute narrative exposes the deficiency of the actual summer of 1940; in the absence of the invasion threat, "Britain . . . would not have been tempted to remember as her finest hour a summer in which swift disaster had been followed by protracted anticlimax" (309). True, the historians who contemplate this enormous strategic alteration conclude that it was not in Hitler's character to accomplish—he was too unoriginal, impatient, impulsive, and egomaniacal—nor would it have been popular with Germans to abandon the aggressive tactics that had hitherto proved so successful. For our purposes, though, the likelihood of such noninvasion options is less important than the imaginary routes they open. They might be said to fall outside of the boundaries of military counterfactualism by revising German strategy so fundamentally as to seem inconsistent with the underlying historical dynamics, but that just makes them all the more suitable for shifting the emphasis from military to political history. They let the counterfactual imagination dwell on Nazi-occupied Britain without having to pass through the narrow aperture of an impracticable invasion, and they therefore make it possible simply to disconnect the questions of invasion and occupation. To be sure, Sea Lion is a lingering presence in works that are primarily interested in what Britons would have done under Nazi rule (a fact that reminds us once again how little historical plausibility is needed when the impulse behind a counterfactual exercise is strong), but as the weight of historical evidence against a possible successful invasion has mounted over the last seventy years, writers have increasingly either skipped the historical turning point altogether by taking it for granted as the premise of the exercise or giving it only vestigial space. After all, the full test of the unique qualities of British character, especially when matched against that of the French, could only occur after the Germans arrived, especially since the natural protection of the channel already gave Britons an unfair advantage in comparison with their former allies. The continuing discussions of national character therefore seem to require imagining Nazi-*occupied* Great Britain, the forms of which change in response to the specific predicaments of national identity that inspire them. The next section of this chapter will look at the counterfactual imagination in two periods of intense British self-scrutiny: first, as the nation came to grips with its postwar loss of imperial and international power, and second, as it explored its option to become European.

NAZI OCCUPIED BRITAIN: RESISTANCE AND COLLABORATION

The first two decades of Britain's postwar experience were demoralizing. By the sixties, the irreversibly deleterious effects of the war on Britain's economy and status in the world had become clear. Their erstwhile allies, the United States and the USSR, seemed to divide the world between them, and Britain was no longer a major international power. The United States proved a rather unreliable ally in the fifties, devoting enormous resources to rebuilding the West German economy, while the British suffered a prolonged period of postwar austerity. America also forced their withdrawal from Suez in 1956, dealing a humiliating blow to Britain's military forces. Ironically, their "special relation" to the United States then proved a barrier to their bid to join the European Community in 1961, for the French considered them a mere Trojan horse for American interests. In the meantime, of course, they had lost their empire and were subjected to a loud chorus of criticism from the anti-imperialist and nonaligned Commonwealth nations. When the British compared their prewar status to their postwar experience, therefore, they saw little but deterioration. The empire that had been their far-flung power base was dismantled, their former colonies disowned them, the United States took them for granted, their former enemies were flourishing, and they had been locked out of the most dynamic economic alliance on their own continent. The British occupation books resonate with this collective sense of dissatisfaction, and they do so in a pair of opposite registers, expressing the suspicion that they somehow *had* been defeated despite their victory and providing relief by contemplating how much worse things would have been if they had actually lost the war.

Holding these two views—that Britons were justified in feeling bitter about their injuries and that they should remember the even worse alternative they escaped—became all the more important as right-wing anti-immigrant organizations began to appear, some with overt neo-Nazi affiliations. Small but highly visible neo-Nazi groups were active across northern Europe—in Austria, Belgium, Denmark, and the Netherlands—and by the middle of the sixties, the phenomenon was spreading to Britain as well. The National Front, for example, with its outspoken racism and (at the outset) imitation Third Reich regalia, was founded in 1967 and had notoriously alarming growth in the seventies. Fomenting and riding a far wider wave of anti-immigration sentiment—most audibly articulated in Enoch Powell's "Rivers of Blood" speech of 1968—the far right tried to hijack British nativist patriotism, and as economic conditions worsened, it appealed especially to young people in the country's decaying industrial north. We'll look in greater detail at these developments in the next chapter, but suffice it to say here that the topic of the true character of Britain was once again up for debate. The right, of which self-proclaimed neo-Nazis were only a small percentage, defined it as a genealogical entity, comprising the descendants of a mythically homogeneous original island people; the center and left spoke of it as a political tradition committed to representative government and liberal individualism and, thus, capable of integrating new immigrants. Both tended to appropriate Churchillian language: the right complaining that the centrist governments were opening the island to another "invasion," and the left maintaining that anti-immigrant racism betrayed the principles of liberty and equality before the law that distinguished Britons from their former enemies.

The neo-Nazis, who had the stupidity to dress themselves in the costumes of the erstwhile foe, were no doubt something of a godsend to the center-left side of the debate, for they could be used to indicate the brutal and traitorous essence of the entire anti-immigrant movement. Moreover, they exposed a deplorable and frightening ignorance of recent history; young people, it was said, should be taught to "remember" what would have happened to them at the hands of the real Nazis. But how, exactly, could the country remember what had not happened? The very fact that they had triumphed by repelling an invasion and occupation meant that they obviously had no experience of the alternative, no resistance heroes or collaborationist villains, no tales of local Nazi atrocities or patriotic self-sacrifice. In the case of the counterfactual invasion, the wartime generation had at least the recollection of living for years with the bombings that appeared to be a prelude and the ongoing defensive preparations, but the arrangements made to combat a post-invasion occupation were carefully designed to be invisible. Teaching the new generation to imagine the nightmare of a Nazi occupation thus seemed to *require* a detour into historical counterfactualism.

In 1960 a journalist named Comer Clarke wrote the first counterfactual occupation book explicitly in response to a perceived resurgence of National Socialism, asking his readers to take the report of his historical research as "a chastening reminder [of the true nature of Nazism] now that . . . sections of youth are daubing on walls in Germany their wretched slogans and evil swastika symbols."[35] Clarke made his postwar career tracking down and confronting former Nazis, and he was well known for having obtained and published, in 1958, a confession from SS-Sturmbannführer Alfred Naujocks, who had led a group of SS officers posing as Polish partisans in the raid on the Gliwice radio station, which provided Hitler with an excuse to invade Poland.[36] Clarke thus claimed to have found and obtained an admission of guilt from the man who had started World War II. He was outraged that the process of denazification in the German Federal Republic seemed to have stalled in the late 1950s, and he was on a "mission," as he described it, to interview the Germans who had been most deeply involved in planning an occupation of Britain in the summer of 1940 as part of the Sea Lion operation. Hoping to remind Britons of Nazi malice so that they would not prematurely forgive their former enemies, he attempted to interview both those who had drafted the occupation plans and those who had been slated to administer them. The plans—twelve Wehrmacht orders describing how the army should set up and administer the occupation and a separate Gestapo handbook—had been found in archives and warehouses in 1945, taken to London, and archived again. Clarke used them to interrogate the Germans in 1960 about their intentions in 1940, and then drew on the plans and the interviews to "answer the question, What would have happened to us—every man, woman and child in Britain—if the invasion, planned by Nazi Germany in 1940, had succeeded?" (7). Documenting just how "satanic" the occupation would have been, though, was not Clarke's only aim; he was equally interested in demonstrating that "it would not have been part of the British temperament to have taken it lying down" (9). To prove this claim about national character, he turned to the archival records of a hitherto unacknowledged official British Resistance movement, which was "carefully formed and recruited in readiness for the worst" (9), and he enhanced those records with interviews of the Resistance leaders. Having put in place the two sides of the counterfactual but nevertheless historically documentable occupation struggle, Clarke then supplemented his account with records of other occupations, especially those of France and the Channel Islands. This template—featuring (1) the German plans, (2) the British Resistance organization, and (3) the putatively analogous occupations—has been used by all subsequent television documentaries, articles, and books that purport to describe Britain's might-have-been occupation.

Only a few of these works are full-length counterfactual-history *books*, but despite their small number, the three that came out between 1960 and 1972, starting with Comer Clarke's, are worth our attention, for they clearly show how the interpretations of the historical evidence changed over the period to suit developing contemporary needs. Looking first at the formal similarities that derive from the kind of counterfactualism they share, I'll then go on to trace an arc of development in which the concept of national character becomes increasingly problematic. Although they belong in the counterfactual-history category (as opposed to alternate history or alternate-history fiction) these books are very different from the Sea Lion histories. To begin with, they are not written by professional historians but by journalists and freelance writers who specialized in popular history aimed at the general public. Second, the Sea Lion books analyzed the historical causes of a military operation that was begun and then abandoned, using counterfactual scenarios to illuminate the reasons for the failure of the project. In the case of the occupation, though, planning on paper had not gone beyond a rudimentary stage when Sea Lion was jettisoned, and, of course, the sketchy occupation plans were contingent on the completion of the invasion. These books therefore start with a deeper reality deficit—two degrees of separation from actuality—and (perhaps to compensate for the precariousness of their project) put very little skeptical pressure on their documentary base. Whereas the Sea Lion books scrutinized the German plans and judged them implausible, thereby undermining the belief that Britain could have been invaded in 1940, these books are bent on creating belief in the plausibility of an accomplished occupation. When reading the Sea Lion books, the alternate world in which an invasion occurred becomes increasingly unreal; when reading the occupation books, the world of Nazified Britain becomes increasingly substantial. Rather than "Could it have happened?" the occupation books ask "What would it have been like?"

Comer Clarke's *England under Hitler*, we've seen, starts with that question, and the next book, *The Last Ditch* by David Lampe (1968) begins with it as well: "I wanted to know what the Nazi occupation of Britain would have been like."[37] Lampe devotes far more space to the British

Resistance plans than had Clarke and makes a more extensive use of the *Gestapo Handbook*, but the project of alternate-world modeling remains the same. And that project carries over into the third book, *If Britain Had Fallen*, written by the journalist and popular-history writer Norman Longmate in 1972 as a sequel to a three-part BBC series of the same title. Longmate also promises to describe "in an entirely non-fictional way, what German occupation would have been like."[38] The three books thus combine counterfactual history and alternate-world modeling, and into this mixture they fold the styles of investigative documentary journalism, presenting their elaborated syntheses as a kind of news. Although they appeared over a twelve-year period, each author insists that his view of Nazi Britain had only recently become visible because the German plans, as well as the records of British counter-occupation and resistance projects, had been officially unavailable before. To be sure, the documents did go through several changes of official status over those years, but even in 1960 it was an exaggeration to say they were news, since much of their contents had been previously reported in the midfifties. The trope of recent historical discovery, like references to an emerging neo-Nazi threat, gave these books a shared tone of urgency and heightened intensity: each announces that here, for the first time, is the definitive news about British life under Nazi rule, which proves that Britishness and Nazism were always utterly incompatible. By extension, they imply, right-wing racist exclusionism has no legitimate place in the spectrum of British politics. And not only did they claim to present the latest factual news about the alternative past, they also depicted how miserable the lives of Britons would surely still be, decades later, if the Nazis had had their way. Bad as things have been since the war, they imply, this would have been immeasurably worse. In short, they appeal to the desires for novelty and contemporary relevance and promise shocking exposés of the foreign Britain that the readers might have been forced to inhabit.

It is not surprising, therefore, that the books tend to emphasize the most ruthless aspects of the German plans. Beneath the documents' neutral bureaucratic language they wanted their readers to see the pervasive cruelty of the intentions and the manner in which they would have been made routine. They dwell on the suffering that similar occupation measures had caused average civilians elsewhere. Hence, although they explain how the Jews and political undesirables would have been systematically separated from their fellow countrymen before being deported to death camps, they do not linger on that already-established centerpiece of German crimes. Instead they stress that the stated purpose of all Nazi occupations was to subjugate totally the entire conquered people and to make use of them in the German war effort. They explain how the island's human and natural resources would have been exploited, how large portions of the food supply would have been commandeered, industry appropriated and redirected, and labor forced into the channels of the German war machine. They highlight the orders to summarily execute any civilians who attempt to subvert or otherwise interfere with the German military administration, and they dwell repeatedly on an order allowing civilian hostages to be taken and executed in reprisals for acts of sabotage. They tell their readers that Nazi rule in Britain would have been at least as bad as it was in other conquered nations: an unfeelingly and universally applied system of horrendous mistreatment. The documents, in short, were the proof that Hitler's Germans were the enemies of humanity in general and that had the British not stopped them when they did, civilization itself might have perished.

They also try to jolt their readers with the news that, within this generally horrific context, Britons might have been subjected to unusually vicious treatment. They single out some unique sections of the plans for Great Britain to prove their point: those calling for the relocation to the Continent of the entire adult male population between the ages of seventeen and forty-five (in the *Orders concerning the Organization and Function of Military Government in England* and *German-Occupied Britain: Ordinances of the Military Authorities*) and orders to dismantle Free Masonry and the Boy Scouts (in *Gestapo Handbook for the Invasion of Britain* [*Informationsheft G.B.*]).[39] Clarke used obvious shock tactics: "REVEALED AT LAST—THE SECRET NAZI PLANS FOR THE RAPE OF ENGLAND," screams the jacket copy of *England under Hitler*, and he also retailed unsubstantiated rumors in a tabloid-history style: there would have been brothels full of Aryan-featured English girls, where a new population of Anglo-German children would have been bred. And yet alongside such self-discrediting sensationalism, he also reports some illuminating comments from the former German officers he managed to locate and interview. For example, Admiral Karl Dönitz (released in 1956 from his ten years in prison for war crimes) justifies the Nazi's unusually harsh counterinsurgency policies: "The plans for Britain may sound hard, but they had to be. We realized we were up against a determined enemy. Our task was to beat Britain, and war knows few scruples" (43).

David Lampe, in *The Last Ditch*, makes the same point about the special severity of the orders for Britain: "If the Germans had been able to follow the pattern of occupation laid down in their orders, their presence in Britain would have been as repressive as it was in the Eastern European countries" (151). Reinforcing this theme, all the writers mention that Franz Alfred Six, who was slated to head the Gestapo in London, was later convicted at Nuremberg of war crimes on the eastern front. In descriptive passages the authors use the techniques of defamilarization, uncanniness, and estrangement of the accustomed to register the eerie sense of an alienated homeland. When they do carry episodes from Western European occupations into their accounts of what would have happened in Britain, moreover, they usually choose atrocities. Clarke's first chapter narrates in a novelistic manner the infamous massacre of the civilian population in the French village of Oradour-sur-Glane, which he relocates to Buckinghamshire. And in 1972 Norman Longmate's *If Britain Had Fallen* tells an Anglicized Oradour-sur-Glane story in an early chapter as well. The consistent message is that their British readers should recall the worst features of other occupations to envision what they would have endured.

The reader, however, soon becomes aware of a conflict between making the occupation hellish and creating it as a possible environment for the emergence of British virtues, a conflict that appears most insistently where one might least expect to find it: in the descriptions of the official British Resistance movement. All the books argue that the British determination to resist would have played an important role in triggering the most brutal aspects of German rule. To begin with, it was because they anticipated fighting in the fields and in the streets and in the hills that the Germans made their unusual (and no doubt unenforceable) plan to ship the fighting-age males out of the country. And at a later stage, assuming the Germans had routed the regular army and the Home Guard had collapsed, an official Resistance operation, the secret Auxiliary Units, was to have gone underground—literally into burrows that were actually built and standing ready in wooded and rural parts of the country—emerging only to carry on guerilla and commando raids against German bases. The British were the only European country to prepare such a force, and although obviously never deployed, it proved useful in testing weapons and tactics for the actual resistance movements on the Continent (which were all supplied and supported by the British throughout the war), as well as for the Allied Special Operations carried out in German-occupied territories. The United Kingdom was particularly well prepared for such maneuvers because it had extensive experience in putting down guerila insurgencies in its colonies; the officers in charge of training and leading Auxiliary Units were often drawn from the ranks of former anti-insurgency fighters in Ireland and India. The two later books, Lampe's and Longmate's, provide full descriptions of how the units were structured and would have operated, but there is no attempt to pretend that the Resistance could have done serious damage to a full-scale occupying force or even have survived many months after a German conquest. Instead it was intended to harass the enemy behind its lines while a battle for the country was still undecided, keep it off balance until regular troops arrived, or blow up as much German equipment as possible. This Resistance could not have been supplied from abroad, as the French had been; they would have needed to live entirely off the land, thus draining local resources. The books thus note that an occupied Britain would have choked off the channels of support for the other national resistances, and they would probably have proved a fatal liability to the communities among which they lived; as Longmate explained, the German orders directed forces to select hostages "in whom the active enemy elements have an interest"—meaning the families, friends, and neighbors of the Resistance men. His example of Oradour-sur-Glane illustrates that whole villages might frequently have been destroyed in reprisals.

So instead of imagining a heroically victorious Resistance movement, these writers describe its quick demise and worry about its ultimate effect on the enemy's behavior and the solidarity and character of the British people. Lampe and Longmate wrote during the years when the French Resistance was just beginning to come under new, demythologizing scrutiny. Following that lead, Lampe eschews Clarke's earlier practice, which had been to spin stories about possible daring raids, and instead soberly proposes increasingly vicious reprisals and the imposition of "tighter and tighter restrictions until, as a number of former Auxiliary Units Intelligence Officers today admit, great numbers of ordinary, decent Britons would have begun to co-operate with the Germans in putting down the Resistance just to bring about a sort of peace" (152). Even worse, Resistance fighters would ultimately have turned their weapons "on any neighbors whom they judged to be collaborators." He concludes on a thoroughly antiheroic note that "to invite men into any armed underground movement is in a sense to invite them to place themselves above the law, especially when they must be trained to murder and must be armed with the weapons of assassins" (153). Five years later, Longmate's book sees the Resistance as equally problematic. Indeed, the critic Clive James, who reviewed the TV version of *If Britain Had Fallen*, regarded the programs as obvious British counterfactual imitations of Marcel Ophüls's documentary film, *The Sorrow and the Pity*, a movie that so thoroughly deflated French claims to widespread and continuous resistance that French television had refused to air it in 1969.[40] To be sure, Longmate, like Ophüls, admires the men and women who stood ready to resist, but he also documents how such resistance would have put them at odds with the rest of their countrymen's desire to survive. He takes a skeptical view of one of the former Auxiliary Unit men's assurances, when asked if the certainty of reprisals against his friends and family would have caused him to desist, that he was sure they would have preferred death to living under Nazi rule. The protective attitudes of peacetime, he comments, "offer little guide to one's feelings in such a situation" (211). In general the interviews with former Auxiliary Units men tend to blur any simple moral contrast between patriotic Resistance fighters, who defend Britons, and renegades providing pretexts for their slaughter. As Longmate admits, "Even the most loyal patriots [on the Continent] sometimes urged the resistance men to go away and cause trouble elsewhere" (211).

The more dystopian the alternate world, the more it precludes the continuity with the values of civil life, and the more the resisters come to resemble the enemy in their willingness to sacrifice their own community, continuing a cycle of violence without any visible escape route. The failure of resistance seems to spell the impossibility of passing the national character test, and so these counterfactual exercises end up depriving their readers of the very distinctiveness they set out demonstrate. The depictions of the occupation did not give them a way of imagining their vindication and, instead, yielded visions of endless defeat. As Clive James noted in 1972, the exercise was motivated by the lack of a rigorous enough trial, "As it happened, the nation's heroism in the grip of the oppressor was never tested, reinforcing the perennial, guilty suspicion that Britain's liberties are dependent on innocence [of an actual trial]—the suspicion out of which programmes like this arise."[41] The connection between the missing trial to vindicate Britishness and the need to keep reimagining it was thus recognized at the time, and so was the self-conflicted nature of these particular thought experiments.

The books show no way for the British to emerge triumphant or, indeed, to emerge at all. Only Longmate—whose image of the occupation is the most complex, the least consistent, and often the mildest—attempts one: "In the [atomic] bomb seems to have lain Britain's best—if not only—hope of rescue. . . . But [Britain] would surely have survived, to quote Churchill's phrase, 'if necessary for years, if necessary alone'" (262). In contrast, Clarke's and Lampe's occupations are essentially unending; instead of becoming concluded imaginary historical episodes (and therefore definitely defunct current possibilities), they expand into nightmarish atemporal conditions: "Once occupied, Britain might have had to go on alone—forever" (Lampe, 153). These books thus display a common feature of the literature dealing with Nazi atrocities: they tend to lose their historical orientation and dissolve into perpetual dystopias: "Hitler's hell on earth, permanent in its systematic organization of death, abject slavery and horror, which could have been holding us in thrall today" (Clarke, 143). When revived, of course, any superseded possibility might be said to be more present than the actual past, because it was always conjectural and still is; counterfactual events do not seem to undergo ontological transformation as they pass from plans about the future to speculations about the possible past. As thought experiments on the intensification and prolongation of *the* twentieth-century nightmare, they seem doubly resistant to historical closure and suggest a more general affinity between counterfactualism and atrocities. In both their content and in their form they might be said to epitomize the construction of a past that refuses to become the past: the uncanny presentness of this particular historical material, already deterritorialized by its transposition into a location where it did not take place, is intensified by the counterfactual mode.

In short, the dystopian form refuses to yield a dynamic collective narrative, let alone one of national vindication. These books do, though, find a strategy for submerging the difficulty; they dissolve the issue of national character into speculations about *particular* historical characters. Moreover, in the course of breaking the collective down into individuals and small groups, Longmate's book at last comes up with acceptable examples of British character under occupation, but those examples are at a very far remove from Churchill's imagined fighters. As we've seen repeatedly in this study, counterfactual histories and alternate histories tether themselves to the actual by importing historical personae and excluding fictional characters, and these books follow that pattern by mining the documents for the names of individuals—British and German, but primarily British—whose fates would have been changed by the occupation. The names of might-have-been victims and heroes are especially prominent. Who exactly were the men of the secret Auxiliary Units that would have been Britain's own indigenous resistance? Who were the most prominent British antifascists scheduled to be arrested and immediately eliminated by the occupiers? Clarke reports on an interview he conducted with Walter zu Christian, a former SS officer who claimed to have prepared the *Gestapo Handbook* and the notorious "Blacklist" of "Britons who would have been arrested immediately." That list of twenty-seven hundred names had, in fact, been circulating since the end of the war and certainly contained no surprises by 1960. Every member of Parliament and many government officials were in it, as were Jewish leaders, suspected Free Masons, Labour activists, left-wing journalists, and prominent cultural figures like Noel Coward, Virginia Woolf, H. G. Wells, and Bertrand Russell. Throughout the late forties and fifties, indeed, people had bragged about being on Hitler's most-wanted list. David Lampe's book lists thousands of names in forty pages of appendixes, including a facsimile of the entire blacklist, a list of British regional commissioners in the early years of the war, and the Auxiliary Units civilian group leaders. The point of these lists is to give specifically British historical substance to the Germans' most obvious might-have-been victims and conspicuous foes, to move from the plane of an abstract collectivity's lot to the fates of individual persons. They form a counterfactual roll of honor of the people who would have been most likely to die for their country very soon after the establishment of an occupation. Of course, simply having martyrs would not have set the country apart (every occupied nation had them), and in actuality tens of thousands of civilians were killed by the Germans in bombing raids; the names of these individuals take on special significance because they would have been martyred specifically for their projected active opposition to Nazi rule. Still, built into the elegiac style of these lists we once again see the stasis of the models, for the potential heroes immediately become the projected martyrs, a point put wittily in 1945 by the liberal anti-Stalinist writer Rebecca West when commenting to Noel Coward on the number of Communist Party members on the blacklist: "My dear—the people we should have been seen dead with!"[42]

Clarke and Lampe seem to rely on the names of the conjectural victims and resisters to give British specificity to their models, but they refuse to give the names of likely collaborators. They name only the convicted traitor William Joyce (Lord Haw-Haw, to his radio public), who was actually an American although he'd been active in Oswald Mosley's British Union of Fascists. When Clarke interviewed zu Christian, the former SS officer claimed to have compiled a list of Nazi "friends," but then he names only those political prisoners, like Oswald Mosley, who had been rounded up at the beginning of the war and placed in a concentration camp on the Isle of Man. Otherwise, zu Christian speaks vaguely of the Germans' ambition to find "a pacifist or a conscientious objector" who might have persuaded the archbishop of Canterbury to caution patience under a German occupation in order to prevent bloodshed. He also mentions Nazi plans to make use of the Duke of Windsor (revealed in the memoirs of another former SS officer, Walter Schellenberg), but instantly exonerates the former king of any

Nazi sympathies. He even enlists the authority of his German source to vouch for the special loyalty of the British: "My knowledge of the British people told me that we were not likely to find many traitors in Britain" (Clarke, 62). The very fact that the German planners named so few likely collaborators is treated as evidence that there would not have been any.

In Lampe's book the issue becomes a bit more complicated. Just as structural pressures lead to the emphasis on the individual names of anti-Nazis, the formal commitment to the documents weighs against speculating on the *identities* of collaborators as well, but the *activity* of collaboration is an entirely different matter: "No doubt if the Germans had occupied Britain, they would have employed any Quislings who offered their services," writes Lampe, but there was no German list of candidates, and so the topic of persons cannot be pursued. Lampe's insistence here on the documentary nature of these books—records of other occupations and official plans determine the limits of their speculation—apply as well to the other two. Since we know from other occupations that collaborators emerge when summoned, it is therefore safe to say that they would have been part of Nazi Britain. However, unless they are on some prospective list (Mosley and company were on the list of Nazi sympathizers), their identities are forever obscured by the lack of the event that would have made them visible. We are assured simultaneously of the certainty of the activity and unknowability of the agents. So in these two books of the sixties, when British subjects take the stage we see, on the one hand, would-be agents (anti-Nazis) cut off by death from effective activity and, on the other hand, activity (collaboration) devoid of individual agents. Fredric Jameson has recently argued that war writing generally produces such dismemberments of agency, especially in the representation of collective entities; the lives of the people become unnarratable because the pervasive environment or "scene"—made up of atrocities, foreign occupations, blasted landscapes, resistance and reprisals—is the overwhelmingly active element.[43] No doubt Jameson's rule applies with even greater force to books like these, which are nonnarrative exercises in alternate world making. Whatever the structural causes, these books leave no room for British agency, whether rebellious or cooperative.

Longmate's book, though, goes into the topic of what Britons would have done in much greater detail, and it shows signs of being under considerable pressure to dwell on the issue of likely collaborators. By the early 1970s, historians had learned far more about the extent of complicity with German occupiers in other nations, and analyses of the topic had called for distinctions between kinds of cooperation, degrees of culpability, and modes of coercion.[44] For example, the most shocking and original part of *The Sorrow and the Pity* was the second half, which dealt with the normalization of collaboration in France. Mimicking this emphasis in late 1960s' European historiography, several British alternate-history fictions (literary works, television dramas, films) had explored the moral quandaries and incentives to work within the newly established order that would have confronted a range of representative British characters: a civil servant, a nurse, an ambitious TV producer, a patriotic politician, and so on, and we will examine these fictions in the next chapter. Longmate's book and the BBC One programs on which it was based followed the trend, letting their focus on national character drift away from the question of how Britons would have resisted to that of how they might have collaborated, but, true to their documentary promises, they also kept their speculation tethered to historical evidence. Some new names are introduced: Longmate claims to have seen the "white list" of plausible collaborators and declares it not newsworthy, just a bunch of nonentities. In an interview on the television program, which was expanded for the book, Oswald Mosley vouches for his counterfactual self, insisting that he would never have served as a puppet head of state but would have committed suicide instead. In the book, Longmate maintains that the Germans would have wanted a more influential surrogate than Mosley in any case, and points—on flimsy evidence—to Sir Samuel Hoare (a former foreign secretary who spent the war as ambassador to Franco's Spain) as the kind of politician the Germans would have sought for his establishment reputation and pro-appeasement credentials. In a follow-up show on BBC Two, other politicians, sensing that their characters, too, might be impugned by the hunt for a counterfactual Vidkum Quisling or a Philippe Pétain, testified to their own might-have-been conduct. Enoch Powell—then leader of the Ulster Unionists and widely credited with tipping the balance in favor of the Conservative Party in the 1970 parliamentary elections—appeared on the BBC Two show to dissociate himself from racist skinheads and insisted that if he had been forced to collaborate with the Nazis, he, like Mosley, would have committed suicide. As a contemporary put it, Britons wanted to know "*who* would have resisted and who would have collaborated" (James, 35), but all of the witnesses from the war generation maintained that there was no one in the latter category. The spectacle of public figures appearing on television to make up alternate-history destinies for themselves seems bizarre, but we should take it as the sign of a moment when the character-making and -breaking capacity of historical counterfactualism became unusually personal.

Typification rather than individuation, though, is Longmate's main method of representing collaboration, and he makes an undisguised political use of it. Considering the big question of a British quisling, for example, he reaches back to the politics of *Guilty Men*, which had been revived in Labour Party rhetoric immediately after the war and deployed continuously ever since. Ruling-class appeasers, the argument went, bore partial responsibility for the war and therefore for the national decline and economic difficulties it caused. It was but a small step for Longmate to infer that they would also have been the readiest to cooperate with the enemy. "Potential traitors," he confidently asserts, were to be found "among the upper classes," for "it was in comfortable country houses by the Thames and in the Home Counties that pro-German sentiment, masquerading as a desire to do justice to Germany, and the gangrene of appeasement spread fastest" (117). His social profile of the appeasers-collaborators, he claims, is taken from the records of actual occupations: "In every country enslaved by the Germans it was the rich who found it easiest to come to terms with occupation, not least because Hitler had destroyed the spectre of Communism and provided a stable order of society where strikes and demonstrations were banned." Next comes a more specific speculation about the kinds of British families likely to have produced the homegrown quisling: "Somewhere among the noble families which feared a revolution and which had fawned upon von Ribbentrop or been entertained by Göring at his hunting lodge, there may have been someone ready to persuade himself that it was his duty to interpose himself between the invaders and the British people and become head of a 'caretaker' government." This is specific enough to bring to mind representative individuals, such as the Cliveden set, a group of aristocrats who often met at the home of Viscountess Nancy Astor, or the members of the Anglo-German Fellowship, or even diplomats like Halifax and Neville Henderson, but Longmate aims to identify the culpable social-political milieu rather than the persons, a tactic that spreads the guilt around in a fairly large class. The *type* of the ruling-class conservative appeaser becomes the archetypical collaborating figurehead.

Just as the list of culprits in *Guilty Men* provided scapegoats for all of the ordinary Britons who had supported appeasement before the war, Longmate's use of the same type provides cover for all of the common people who would have been forced by circumstances into various forms of complicity with the occupation. He emphasizes that the German documents assume the cooperation of a British civil authority by delegating most of the administration of civilian (i.e., *British*) life to it: the entire legal system was to remain intact, as were the functions of teaching, policing, mail service, even customs administration. Indeed, he points out that the documents assume the French model of occupation by referring to "occupied" and "unoccupied" zones and reminds us that the Germans' invasion force was projected at only 250,000. They would have needed not only a compliant figurehead and government ministers but thousands of Britons as well, willing to continue running their own country once some form of normal daily life was reestablished. In this alternate world, cooperation between German and British authorities would have been unavoidable, so Longmate never even suggests that every judge, lawyer, district nurse or doctor, mailman, teacher, tax collector, mayor, or city clerk would have been guilty of collaboration. A new form of limited but innocent British agency begins to take shape in which active resistance is downplayed and a determination to carry on at one's post becomes the norm.

Longmate's alternate world is thus a far cry from Clarke's, whose model for British behavior had been Major Colin Gubbins, the head of the Auxiliary Units, assassinating Nazi perpetrators after a village massacre. Twelve years later, Longmate's exemplary Briton is the anonymous civil servant, "a good mayor or, perhaps even more, a good town clerk," bearing the day-to-day burden of carrying out German orders and consequently "likely before long to be unpopular all round" (167). Although hardly fulfillments of the Churchillian prophecy, such stoical and internally divided men and women, acting as the buffer between the foreign occupiers and the general population, had enormous narrative potential. Indeed, by 1972 they had already served as protagonists of alternate-history fictions in the late 1960s; *If Britain Had Fallen* did not so much create them as give them historical substance, legitimating them as the most complex registers of the totality of the alternate world and as the inevitable embodiments of its most acute moral dilemmas. Obviously Longmate's world is more morally ambiguous than Clarke's, but the point to be emphasized here is its superior dynamism and narrative generativity, for it is those features that provide the point of contact between the counterfactual history of the occupation and the many alternate-history fictions it continues to germinate.

Before looking at a few of those fictional works, though, we should briefly examine one later stage in the counterfactual-history speculations about British national character, if only to dispel an impression that this chapter might otherwise leave. Up until now, we've been analyzing the use of counterfactuals to assert or discover distinctive national characteristics, but the next phase demonstrates that counterfactuals can be just as important for writers who want to deny such distinctions. Between 1972 and 1990, the topic attracted very little interest, but a combination of events brought it back into public consciousness in the early 1990s. The decade began with the coincidence of a pair of contrasting events: Britain's commemoration of the fiftieth anniversary of the summer of 1940 and the start of the post–Cold War German unification process, the first triggering the usual patriotic rhetoric about having stood alone against the enemy and the second inspiring wry comments about Germany's increasing European preeminence. In this year when "the few" and their pivotal role in winning the war were constantly celebrated but the lasting benefits to Britain of their sacrifice were being questioned, skepticism about the popular version of the history was expressed in revisionist and counterfactual assessments.[45]

For example, in 1990 Adrian Gilbert's *Britain Invaded* used ironic reversal to pursue the hypothesis that winning the Battle of Britain had been futile, for defeat would have resulted in the same long-term fate for the United Kingdom. Gilbert's book is an alternate history, rather than a counterfactual history, like the three we've just been examining, because it invents a narrative persona who inhabits the alternate world. The narrator, memorializing an achieved invasion fifty years later, declares that "the invasion of Great Britain in 1940 was one of the most decisive moments in modern history. Germany's victory—no matter how short-lived—signalled the end of Britain as a major power on the world stage and ushered in a new era where for the next five decades global influence was concentrated in the hands of the two superpowers, the United States of America and the Soviet Union."[46] The year 1990 in this world is identical to the actual present, for the reversed outcome would only have brought the United States into the war earlier. Britain's international power really ended, we learn, when it lost the Battle of France and became militarily dependent on the future superpowers. In 1990, the United Kingdom is just another European country. And, the book pretends to demonstrate, during their occupation Britons had behaved like all the rest. *Britain Invaded* is a mock photo-documentary book, in the mode of the many pictorial histories of World War II that were published for the fiftieth anniversary of the war's onset. Its pictures are actually drawn from prewar and wartime archives, especially from those of the Channel Islands' occupation, and the alternate history is given in the titles and short descriptions of the images. They show some heroes, like Lord Lovat (in reality leader of a commando unit that operated in Norway and France) identified as the head of the Scottish resistance movement, and the usual suspects as collaborators: the Duke and Duchess of Windsor meeting with Hitler (photo actually taken in 1937); Oswald Mosley ostensibly celebrating his release from prison in the autumn of 1940 (in a goose-stepping image also from 1937). And from the Channel Islands' archive come photographs that were less familiar in 1990: German soldiers parading past a Lloyd's Bank branch, actually on Guernsey but identified as Tunbridge-Wells in Kent. Even more perplexing, when purposely taken out of context, are the many images of Britons going about their daily lives under Nazi supervision: the cooperation of British bobbies and German soldiers; uniformed SS officers getting help from local authorities; and British civilians with German soldiers casually sharing a moment of relaxation at an open-air band concert. The implied lesson: like other Europeans, Britons would have counted among them a few resisters and a few treasonous collaborators, and most of the population would have done what was necessary to survive while waiting to be liberated.

This emphasis on Britons' normal Europeanness, which continued in other counterfactuals throughout the 1990s, registered the contemporary controversy over the changing nature of Europe and Britain's place in it. Europe's evolving unity, often under German initiative, reached a critical juncture with the 1992 Maastricht Treaty, and Britons engaged in a complex and many-sided debate over whether to sign on to the new terms of consolidation. That year they opted out of many provisions (including the adoption of the euro), but meanwhile the old arguments about national distinctiveness had been revived. Moreover, they were intensified by another, totally unrelated development: the Public Records Office coincidentally released a large collection of previously secret documents on the Channel Islands' occupation. The British press immediately seized on the documents and made a scandal of them, reporting their contents under sensational headlines like "Secret Files Accuse Island Leaders of Collaboration" and "Channel Island People Profited from Nazis."[47] The headlines proved to be exaggerated distortions of the verifiable facts, but they revealed how much patriotic indignation could still be roused by the news that those few Britons who *were* put to the test had not all remained immaculately loyal, independent, and uncompromised. The press tended to stigmatize them as an unusually corrupt group whose actions were unworthy of the heroic behavior of their mainland peers. And, indeed, there is evidence that the British government immediately after the war had refused to let the islanders prosecute collaborators and black marketeers for fear that the national reputation might be besmirched by news of their activities.[48] Other writers, though, claimed that these were just representative Britons who had undergone a trial and many of them had failed to behave in a way that could sustain the popular myth of unusual national virtue; therefore the myth should be abandoned.

During the next few years, the counterfactual occupation of Britain, the real occupation of the Channel Islands, and the question of Britain's place in Europe became increasingly entangled in the public mind. Journalist and historian Madeleine Bunting's *Model Occupation* (1995) was based on hundreds of interviews with Channel Islanders following the kerfuffle over the released documents, and its opening paragraph makes the connections as explicit as possible:

> What if Hitler had invaded Britain? Who would have plotted resistance? Who would have made a handsome profit selling guns and uniform cloth to the Germans and trading in black market whisky? How would the majority of the British people have muddled their way through? A German invasion so nearly came to pass that such questions have intrigued every generation since the war. The Channel Islands were as close as Hitler got; they were the one bit of British soil he conquered. That is why those blurred black-and-white photos of the Channel Islands' Occupation are so riveting. . . . This is what life could have been like in Britain. . . . What happened on the Channel Islands could have happened in the rest of Britain.[49]

Bunting defended the Channel Islanders against the English press's "moral indignation," which, she argued, stemmed from "the myth of the distinctiveness of the British character from that of Continental Europeans" (6). The islanders were reviled because their occupation exposed the groundlessness of Britain's belief in its wartime exceptionalism, the rhetoric of which, she claims, was still being used by politicians who wanted to keep the United Kingdom out of Europe: "Fifty years after the war's end, the echo still reverberates in contemporary politics of Churchill's oratory that the British alone had fought—like David to Hitler's Goliath—an evil dictatorship from beginning to end. Only Britain had sought no compromise and had 'an unblemished record' in standing up to Nazism" (6). Hard line Eurosceptics, she claims, had resuscitated the national myth and mobilized it against the Maastricht Treaty. The Channel Islanders had innocently been caught up in that debate and served as a convenient magnet for anger against those who would question the wartime record and the idea of British uniqueness it supported.

Bunting even sometimes gives the impression that counterfactual speculation had been rendered obsolete by the Channel Island documents; since there really had been an occupation on British soil, we *know* what would have happened on the mainland.[50] Usually, though, her verb tenses indicate that her extrapolations are as counterfactual as the myth she debunks: if the mainland had been occupied, Britons there *might* also have acted like the islanders. Moreover, the only thing that makes her extrapolation more likely than similar analogies, based on the behavior of the French or the Danes, is the underlying assumption of a shared national character: because Britons in one circumstance would act like other Europeans, Britons in all circumstances would do the same. To be sure, her aim is to create solidarity between Britons and Continentals: "Islanders compromised, collaborated and fraternised just as people did throughout occupied Europe" (6). However, the very basis of that solidarity would be the identification of one set of Britons with another: because some Britons were occupied, all Britons "have a chance to gain an understanding of an experience shared with Continental Europe" (6). This reasoning does not dispense with the idea of national character but instead supports a different construction of it; counterfactualism and national-character creation continue to go hand in hand.

Of course, numerous later historians have refuted Bunting's claims, pointing out how little any occupation of the mainland could possibly have resembled the Channel Islands', where there was a minimum of one German soldier for every two civilians, and the civil authority had been explicitly instructed by the British government to cooperate with the occupiers in order to protect the civilians, most of whom were women and children. In the first historiographical essay on the counterfactuals of Nazi Britain, Andrew Roberts delivered the definitive rebuttal and then went on to erect his own counterfactual occupation, with many arguments supporting the historical uniqueness of Britons.[51] And so it goes. As the critic Clive James wrote in 1972, continually building and demolishing various models in which Britain is successfully invaded seems "a national characteristic," and probably the only one that can be deduced from these works.

CHAPTER SIX

The Fictions of Nazi Britain

NATION AND (ALTERNATE-HISTORY) NOVEL

When we turn to the *fictions* of Nazi Britain, a different character becomes prominent: the nation-state of Great Britain, which is not to be confused with the "national character" of Britons that we explored in the last chapter. National character can refer either to the typical personality traits of the country's people or to their collective morale and cohesive force. Great Britain, in contrast, is the sovereign authority, the state to which the people owe allegiance; it comprises, among other things, its territory, official history, institutions, laws, modes of governing, the structure and relation of its parts, officially sanctioned religions, customs, and languages, and its norms of interaction with its own citizens and with other nations. Like all nation-states and their subjects, Great Britain and the British obviously overlap and yet remain distinct. The nation-state may be thought of as the people's representative or their oppressor, the agent of their will or the force that binds and constrains them, the personification of their fortune or their ruin. But whether acting for or on the people, the state is usually the active part of the national couple, for it must have the authority to participate in the larger system of sovereign states. Modern world history is essentially the history of the actions and interactions of nation-states, and it thus seems natural to say that they, rather than their people collectively, are the main characters in the historical narratives of the twentieth century.

For all its historical agency, though, we seldom think of Great Britain or any other state as a character in a novel because, unlike the people, who sometimes have a collective character function, the state does not obviously qualify as a living entity. We recognize nation-states as geopolitical constructs resulting from centuries of struggle and compromise, whose boundaries, foundations, and legitimacy are frequently contested. For example, the historical variability of Britain is written in the changes to the country's official name: "Great Britain" was first used only after 1603, when James I of England (James VI of Scotland) became the sovereign of the entire island, although the two Parliaments remained distinct; in 1707 the "United Kingdom of Great Britain" came into existence with an Act of Union that merged the two Parliaments; and in 1801, another Act of Union dissolved the Irish Parliament, yielding the "United Kingdom of Great Britain and Ireland," which was then amended to the "United Kingdom of Great Britain and Northern Ireland" after the Government of Ireland Act (1920) provided for separate Parliaments in Dublin and Belfast. We call all of these entities "Great Britain" or just plain "Britain" for short, understanding the substantial changes in the territories and populations while also tracing some degree of persistence of geopolitical identity on one island since the seventeenth century. The variations, combined with the whole sorry history of enforced subjugation to the crown in various parts of the country, keep us aware of Britain as an artificial arrangement, merely metaphorically alive. This is only to say that Britain, like all nation-states, is a self-evident contrivance, which helps explain why it is usually relegated to the deep background of novelistic representation. Even in historical novels, nation-states tend to appear mainly in the allegorical guises of founders or saviors; at best they are animating ideas, but not characters.

In the alternate-history novels, though, they often do something that catapults them onto the plane of living actors: they die. Their deaths are a central theme not only in the novels of Nazi Britain but also in the vast majority of the narratives we've examined in this book. In fact, the destinies of nation-states, not individuals or even peoples, are often the central things at stake. In the first full-blown alternate history, Geoffroy-Château's *Napoléon and the Conquest of the World*, all of the actual states of the early nineteenth century are submerged in the worldwide French Empire; in the many Disunited States novels, the USA is repeatedly dismembered; and in the counterfactual speculations about the German occupation of the British Isles, Great Britain becomes a political and military nonentity, shorn of sovereignty, unity, and control over its empire. To be sure, these books have a range of outlooks toward the state destructions they portray, from the gleefulness and triumphalism of *Napoléon and the Conquest of the World*, to the utopian idealism of several of the Disunited States fictions, to the outright horror of the Nazi Britain conjectures. And yet they are similar in their willingness to imagine the dismemberment, demolition, or decay of states, a tendency that can also be seen in the books' penchant for spatializing the historical changes they describe through maps with altered geopolitical boundaries. The emphasis on the nation-state as *the* perishable element might be said to follow from the fact that states fight the wars and make the world history that readers want to imagine differently. But of course world history might have been significantly altered, even through warfare, without Great Britain or the USA losing their territorial integrity or sovereignty. Indeed, historians seldom push their counterfactual scenarios to the brink of threatening the very existence of well-established states; the tendency is confined mainly to the long alternate-history forms, where collapsing states are the favorite spectacle.[1]

In the novels of Nazi triumph, though, we can see with peculiar clarity why British—and sometimes American—writers have repeatedly depicted the deaths of their own states. In the collective historical imaginations of the former Allies, Nazi Germany has the distinction of posing a unique existential threat, so revising the outcome of that war is the quickest route to state death. In the last chapter, I argued that British counterfactualists envisioned a Nazi occupation in order to put the people, as a whole, through a hypothetical test of character. Those conjectures, though, made only minimal efforts at portraying Britons dispossessed of their nation-state; they made daily life in occupied Britain seem unimaginable, and so the works fell back either on recounting actual Nazi atrocities in European countries or identifying historical British individuals who would have been likely to resist or collaborate. Since their authors labored under the contradictory imperatives of maintaining world continuity by using historical personae, on the one hand, and avoiding libelous statements about actual persons, on the other, their impressions of the inner experience of a nation's people being stripped of their state remained thin and nebulous. The occupation *novels*, in contrast, are devoted to the task of exploring both the psychosocial losses and the potential revelations of such an ordeal. The novel's traditional subject matter is that of individual consciousness in close interaction with its social world, and as we've often had occasion to note, the accessibility of fictional consciousness, its openness to our perusal, is what makes that exploration possible. The alternate histories could speculate gingerly about individuals or make sweeping statements about social types, but without actually turning into novels, they could not follow the subjective dramas of particular characters as they lose their state and grapple with the realization that they had become what was left of the nation.

That revelation is at the heart of these novels, in which the ghost of the former state is a constant presence. To conceive the discontinuance of the state even as the people who should owe it allegiance live on is, paradoxically, to create the perfect conditions for overcoming the difference between the nation's people and its official state forms. The nation-state is killed—often by committing suicide—so that the nation can emerge as nothing but an entity inhering in the minds of the people, where it lives all the more vibrantly because it no longer has existence as an external sovereign entity. The novels do not, to be sure, depict the reemergence of the nation on the subjective level as automatic; indeed, the suspense of the plots relies on its continual hindrance. But by imagining the loss of the usual locations of sovereignty—the monarchy, the executive cabinet, the armed forces, Parliament, the police, the civil services at Whitehall, even the BBC—all are reimagined as nodes of collective identification where Britons might yet incarnate the spirit of the nation and revive it. By dismantling the institutions and suspending the life of the sovereign nation-state, they make it seem, in hindsight, to have been the central vital element of the nation. The nation-state's apparent ability to die thus gives it not only a lifelike but also a life-giving character, and as the individual characters watch it dissolve, they have the opportunity to realize that they are the bearers of its newly unbound vitality. The central question of these plots is whether that transfer of national esprit will take place.

The pattern, indeed, seems designed to test a particular idea of the nation: that it inheres in a "daily plebiscite," which under normal circumstances takes place subliminally in the minds of the citizens. The phrase "daily plebiscite" was coined by the French philosopher and historian Ernest Renan, one of the most influential late nineteenth-century theorists of nationality, who claimed all modern nations are kept alive through a largely unconscious but constantly renewed subjective desire for belonging.[2] Unlike national concepts based mainly on genealogical consanguinity, religious uniformity, or strictly coercive centralized power, Renan's model accommodates considerable diversity in the population. We might think of it as a "civic" rather than an "ethnic" national model, suitable to the liberal political foundations of twentieth-century Britain because of its inclusivity, but nevertheless subjectively demanding, for it requires persistent individual identification with the nation.

The thought experiments of the occupation narratives indicate that this nation-in-the-mind might be optimally observed under conditions of outward state dissolution, for then the nation and its people might become entirely one and the same, a truly identical whole. Ironically, these Nazi-occupation novels reveal the ordinary nonsimultaneity of the nation-as-state, a sovereign entity, and the nation-as-people, for when the state is in full force, the people have fewer reasons or opportunities to manifest themselves as the nation. Normally a functioning state relieves its citizens of the necessity of acting as the nation. When we look at the occupation narratives through this lens, we can see why Britain, as a character struggling for realization, must be reduced to the individuals who think themselves British before it can rediscover its primary nature. And we can also see why the struggle of this character to come back into existence takes precedence over all others.

The prominence of that struggle, moreover, both intensifies the connection between the novel form and national consciousness and strains against the usual modes of integration. The novel has long been recognized as an important cultural element in the rise of the modern nation-state, and historians have given various accounts of the entanglement between the two phenomena: they emerge and develop together, the novel allowing people to visualize the norms, habits, and extent of their "imagined community"; novels often provide historical versions of foundational moments—independence, differentiation, merger, unity, war, revolution, compromise—that make the sovereign polity seem both natural and hard-won to succeeding generations; in new nations, novels help forge and naturalize emotional bonds; in older ones, where they are less often explicitly thematized, they reinforce the assumption that the nation's boundaries are the self-evident horizon of the social, political, cultural, and linguistic totality.[3] To be sure, in historical novels, the nation is also often imperiled; Russia's national history, for example, is an active element rather than a mere inert setting in *War and Peace*. Nevertheless, it is because we know the outcomes of the Napoleonic conflicts with Russia in 1805 and 1812 that our interest can be centered on the individual lots of the fictional characters.

Alternate-history fictions, in contrast, make the nation a character by *undoing* its predetermined history and putting it in play along with the fates of the fictional characters. Both take shape only within the confines of the narrative. The fact that there was no actual Nazi occupation of Great Britain, that the imaginary events rest, at most, on the remnants of abandoned German plans, is the primary thing that sets these books apart from normal historical novels. The closest analogues are the future-conditional novels, which imagine that a Nazi occupation might yet occur, and this chapter will begin by analyzing one such novel in detail, along with the patterns of its surrounding discourse, especially as they are refracted in the work of George Orwell.[4] As we saw in the last chapter, future conjectures are often revived in counterfactual-history forms, and alternate-history novels try to re-create not only scenarios from before-the-event texts but also the affective uncertainty about the fate of the nation.

In many ways, then, the alternate-history Nazi occupation novels turn the novel form inside out. Instead of existing as the social world's horizon, the self-evident thing that is taken for granted, the nation-state becomes a longed-for ideal, at once mourned and aspired to, around which the identities of the characters might, or might not, consolidate. Because the characters are no longer in the nation, the nation must lodge itself in the characters. Whereas in many novels the nation-state is naturalized, in these it is forbidden and thus comes to seem an almost miraculous achievement. Indeed, even their mode of world making often consists mainly of world dismantling, describing not so much what the occupiers impose as the gradual disappearance of what was formerly in place. In many of these books, the Nazis carefully reverse engineer Britain rather than simply shattering it, stripping away the outer layers first before grasping more vital functions. The nation-state in this view is like the half-destroyed buildings so frequently described in the novels: the collapse of the outside wall exposes not only the interior but also the hidden structural supports that had allowed the edifice to stand and will soon, in their damaged state, let it fall. Even the intact physical environment, the stable backdrop of "setting" in most novels, moves menacingly into the foreground through its estrangement: Wehrmacht soldiers goose-stepping down the Mall toward a Buckingham Palace festooned with swastikas.[5] And, perhaps most importantly, the individual characters seem to have only one acceptable destiny: to shoulder the burden of being the stateless nation. Thus they animate normally inert novelistic elements and collapse the form's individual/collective distinction.

At moments when national revival is needed in order to protect or regain sovereignty, the benefits of such novels are easy to see. Animating the nation gives it emotional dimensions, and depicting the gradual elimination of all the things it gives its citizens—laws, courts, markets, security, newspapers, schools, transportation, etcetera—helps them to understand the high stakes of the conflict. But in this chapter, we'll look beyond the immediate propaganda value of these novels to the features that gave them staying power in postwar Britain. Indeed, even the future conjectural examples are more than mere patriotic nationalist propaganda, and perhaps the most interesting thing about the form is just how complicated it makes the idea of the nation. At first blush, the basic lesson might seem simple—we cannot know about the nation until we begin to lose it—but when the novels start to unpack that formula narratively, its paradoxes quickly become apparent. To begin with, there is the obvious epistemological problem: characters' hyperawareness of their responsibility to the nation is a sign that the state is faltering, and conversely the nation-state is healthiest when its citizens can largely ignore it and concentrate on their private lives. And yet, the novels cannot wholly valorize that prelapsarian insouciance, for in addition to being a sign of the state's health, it is sometimes also the cause of its fall. Indeed, a craving for peaceful "normality" is often exposed as the nation's Achilles heel; in some novels it seems the cause of a fatal laxness that allowed for the occupation; in others, it is merely recognized as an inevitable barrier to any effective resistance. Even the most propagandistic of the books thus raises the question of just what kind of nation-state could avoid these contradictions and be worthy of the sacrifices required to save it. They normally imagine less the restoration of the old social and political order than its purification through the spontaneous actions of ordinary people. The "character" of the nation that becomes the object of desire in these novels, whether considered as state or people, is therefore not identical to the empirical historical entity. Its death and rebirth seem to require both the dissolution of the institutions into the people and the transformation of the people into a collectivity worthy of the dematerialized—and thereby idealized—nation, an entity destined to self-rule through popular sovereignty.

Many of these dynamics belong to alternate-history fictions generally; the following chapter, though, will trace the specific variations that developed inside wartime and postwar Britain. Throughout these decades, fundamental issues of national identity and the role of the state were publicly debated, and alternate-history fictions are not only permeated by these controversies but also shape them in patterns that clarify the counterfactual assumptions at the core of the debates. The fictions of Nazi Britain, as we'll see, appeared across a range of media, so this chapter will examine films and television dramas, as well as novels. In tracing their roles in the national conversation, moreover, we will discover how they absorbed and perpetuated their surrounding literary and intellectual currents: George Orwell, Hannah Arendt, and Primo Levi are only a few of the thinkers who were enlisted as collaborators in these thought experiments.

THE SUMMER OF 1940: LOSS OF EDEN

In the first widely read portrayal of a Nazi-occupied Britain, though, the vital transformation of the nation emphatically fails to occur. The novel, titled *Loss of Eden*, came out in the suspenseful summer of 1940, while the British were still getting used to the idea that they would have to "fight on alone" and were trying to imagine, before the London Blitz, what that might entail. It warns against a species of national peril seldom mentioned in studies of the "invasion summer": a fatal division between the state and the people. As its title suggests, this novel concentrates on the *loss* of British sovereignty, measuring the depth and extent of the consequences of state destruction and the seeming impossibility of its recovery. The title resonates with the Christian myth that state sovereignty derives from God's bestowal on Adam of power over the rest of creation. Coauthored by the journalist Christopher Serpell and an unknown Douglas Brown (probably a pseudonym), it is a future-conditional novel, a cautionary tale directed against what it takes to be the most serious threat to the nation: not invasion but a softening of the people's desire for victory, a gradual popular inclination toward compromising with the enemy even though the state is committed to war.[6] Probing the systematic distinction between the people and the state, widening it into a mortal wound, and plotting the frustration of various attempts to heal it, the novel uncovers the foundational problems that the later fictions will try to solve. Indeed, quite unexpectedly amid all of the better-remembered patriotic rhetoric of those months, it gives us a unique window onto Britons' self-doubts and the ruminations on nationhood they generated. The German threat—with its showy massing of troops on the channel, its war of nerves between Churchill and Hitler, and its easy spin into heroic narratives—has obscured our view of this perceived internal danger, and the novel helps us reimagine it.

Loss of Eden's plot has the stark simplicity of a parable. Britons fight stoically until the winter of 1941, enduring air raids and inflicting damage on German cities, but faced with a standoff, they tire and begin to lose their single-mindedness. The novelists make it clear from the outset that the state's resolve does not falter; instead, the people abandon their leaders. Hitler makes a speech proposing a cease-fire, and although officially the proposal is dismissed out of hand, the idea appeals to the island's weary population. The narrator of these events, who is a New Zealand journalist on assignment in London, tells the story after having been expelled from Britain by the new German rulers, and he insists on both the normality and the inconspicuousness of "the slow evaporation of England's fighting spirit."[7] Motivated "not by any real cowardice or lack of resolution, but by a queer blend of simple humanity and sheer weariness of discomfort and anxiety" (11), ordinary Britons turn away from the national war purpose in stages so subtle that the country's leaders do not even register that the mood has changed. "The Government, the Services, the trade unions—all that complex of ruling elements which had taken charge of the British war effort—heard little of these whispers; and they were too closely engaged in the struggle to entertain these doubts themselves" (11). By the time "Parliament began to reflect the new movement a fissure rapidly revealed itself" (12). This rupture between the state's war effort and the people's desire for peace leads to the election of a new government, willing to negotiate a cease-fire and a "Peace of Nuremberg," after which the British armed forces are hurriedly demobilized, without waiting for the Germans to reciprocate. Of course, the Germans never disarm or reduce their fighting forces, and soon the Nazis impose further treaties, including one that makes them responsible for Britain's "security." An Anglo-German cooperation treaty ("Treaty of Saint James") is thrust upon a divided Parliament, which provides for the gradual Nazi occupation and subjection of the island. Thus Great Britain begins to die an eerily quiet death in *Loss of Eden*, and its demise is a kind of slow-motion suicide; the mechanisms of the annihilation are worked by the Nazis, but the original instigators are the British people.

As the plot proceeds, moreover, the entities that deeply matter remain the nation-state and the people, a pair whose complex interactions with their German nemesis dominate the novel throughout. To be sure, *Loss of Eden* also has a few individualized characters; it narrates the action through a fictional persona, and it constructs instances of representative types: the narrator and his wife, who are on the margins of the national plot by virtue of their Commonwealth status but have some official access to events as members of the foreign press corps; their friends who live in the countryside; a couple of other reporters; a German press-liaison officer; Jewish neighbors; and a sprinkling of would-be insurrectionists, whom we'll examine momentarily. Our interest in these characters' individual fates is seldom solicited, though; they are mainly just conduits for information about national events. Even the short-lived antiwar leaders who arise to do the peoples' bidding, the novel takes pains to emphasize, merely actualize an impulse that arose spontaneously in all classes and regions, and it is to the collective character of the people that the novel directs our attention, speculating frequently about its nature and describing its complex psychodynamics. The people, we learn, were neither deluded nor misled into wanting the cease-fire that resulted in new elections and the fall of Churchill's government; their behavior at the outset is described as typical, innocent, even predictable. But as Nazi perfidy becomes obvious, Britons are stunned into passivity by the realization that they had compromised their way into subjection. The narrator contrasts them with the nations the Germans had conquered by force, which therefore "had little to reproach themselves with, while the British had everything" (111). A profound sense of national shame and regret thus makes it impossible for the vast majority of Britons to hold the "fierce inward flame of patriotism that still burned . . . among the Czechs and the Poles" (112). Britons are too guilt-ridden to muster the indignation needed to resurrect themselves. Thus each stage of subjection, instead of inspiring rebellion, makes Britons more morose and apathetic. The plot does include a few, quickly suppressed, public displays of rebellion, but mainly it catalogs the internal divisions born of the people's consciousness of guilt, consequent lack of self-confidence, and the loss of any collective identity of which they can be proud. Ironically, even the Germans come to despise the Britons' declining morale, for their listlessness renders them inadequately energetic allies. As one Nazi complains, "Instead of being quickened into life, [Britannia] swoons and faints. Germany has allied herself to a corpse" (118). The plot thus repeatedly makes its main point: the nation dies if, and only if, the people kill it. And once the people have lost the moral strength to save the nation, they collectively fall into a fatal decline. They try to shield themselves from their guilt by adopting various psychological defenses: cynical nonchalance on the part of the educated classes; scapegoating of "foreigners," especially Jewish refugees, among the working class; and a generalized indifference to the Nazi's first victims. We can see enacted here the obverse corollary of the idea that the nation ultimately lives in the minds of the people: if their esprit is its life source, then their despair is its death.

The other main character, the sovereign state, comes into view as it is dismantled bit by bit. Quietly the royal family goes into exile; Parliament ceases to meet after an acrimonious session on the Treaty of Saint James; the cabinet is replaced by a figurehead council; the press is censored; the police are discredited and disbanded; even the politicians who had been in favor of the Peace of Nuremberg are eventually deposed and jailed; local officials are replaced by German bureaucrats and engineers; property is expropriated, the banking system is destroyed, sterling is declared no longer legal tender, and the economy becomes purely extractive; education, courts, and even leisure activities are all conducted under German supervision. The Nazis finally insist on doing official business in their own language and begin the Germanization of the cultural and educational establishments. In a process that is both gradual and relentless, the people's passive complicity in turning their state over to the enemy results in their inability to be a People, and they devolve into a mass of isolated individuals. The loss of sovereignty leads directly to the loss of national identity.

This novel seems a far cry from the summer-of-1940 texts we analyzed in the last chapter, but it is also in conversation with them. When describing the relapse into conciliation of the enemy, for example, it eschews the scapegoating and vengefulness promulgated by that attack on individual appeasers, *Guilty Men*. The two books, which came out within a few weeks of each other, are recognizably of the same moment since they both seek to stiffen the country's fighting resolve, but whereas *Guilty Men* demonized and disowned prominent leaders associated with the former policy, *Loss of Eden* acknowledges both the misguided idealism of appeasement and the possibility of its continuing mass appeal. It stresses that in a democracy politicians are mere figures for the people at large; when the new prime minister returns to London after negotiating the ill-fated peace, for example, "the popular reaction was less one of relief than of guilty satisfaction. Here was what we had asked for, and it was for us now to make the most of it" (13). Blaming leaders, it stresses, is counterproductive, for the people should be reminded of their responsibility, not absolved of it. *Loss of Eden*'s alternative method is to toughen its readers against war weariness and the longing for peace and normalcy by getting them to recognize these traits, not just in their former leaders but in themselves. In this regard, the novel anticipates Churchill's recognition of Neville Chamberlain's pacific virtues as typically British. Indeed, at its outset, the British people seem like a collective Chamberlain, so straightforward and trusting that they cannot sustain a realistic suspicion of the enemy's intentions. Like their former leader, they endanger themselves through their gentleness, demonstrating, to quote Churchill's later eulogy, "the most benevolent instincts of the human heart—the love of peace, the toil for peace, the strife for peace, the pursuit of peace, even at great peril."[8] The message, of course, is that Britons might work their own destruction through characteristics that they normally value, might be tricked into a ignominious peace through the manipulation of their "simple humanity." Thus, although it is at odds with Churchill's louder, more self-confident and combative rhetoric of that summer, the novel's depiction of the people's characterological vulnerability was also one of the summer's more widely discussed themes.

It was, in fact, an element of the total war mobilization, especially apparent in the efforts to close any developing fissures between the state and people. There were, after all, plenty of reasons to doubt that the mass of civilians enthusiastically supported the decision to fight on alone after the fall of France; they might instead have been hoping for peace after the British Expeditionary Force was withdrawn from Dunkirk. The threat of invasion certainly made outside observers of Britain's predicament think it would soon sue for a negotiated cease-fire, and negotiations had been on the agenda of the British War Cabinet as late as the end of May 1940, when it became clear that the French were collapsing. Even in June, an undersecretary in the Foreign Office made inquiries about what Hitler's terms would be.[9] It was reasonable, therefore, to think that many Britons were still expecting some compromise that would avert the coming crisis rather than bracing themselves for an attack. Witness, for example, George Orwell's complaint in August of 1940 that, after their swift action in the evacuation from Dunkirk and their initial alarm at the possibility of invasion, the majority of Britons had promptly relapsed "into sleep."[10] Orwell, as we'll soon see, expressed the same fear that animated the other novelists, that apathy rather than military defeat would lead to compromise: "One need not doubt that a 'peace' movement is on foot somewhere . . . ; probably a shadow Cabinet has already been formed. These people will get their chance not in the moment of defeat but in some stagnant period when boredom is reinforced by discontent. They will not talk of surrender, only about peace; and doubtless they will persuade themselves, and perhaps other people, that they are acting for the best" (90).

The summer's propaganda campaigns were targeted at reversing this widely imagined popular indifference. At that point, it was apparent that the war would have an active home front and that civilians would be vital to its success, and yet the whole concept of civilian morale was relatively new and undefined, since morale had traditionally been a military concept describing the esprit de corps of the fighting forces. It was only when the Ministry of Information set out to measure public morale in 1939 that it needed to define the object of its investigations. A February 1940 description called it "the amount of interest people take in the war, how worthwhile they feel it is," but after the fall of France, the focus shifted to the population's determination to undertake action and make sacrifices based on a "reasonable awareness of the true situation, and absence of complacency and confidence that are not based on fact."[11] Efforts, in other words, had to be made to prepare people for active involvement in a long struggle against an adamant foe with whom no honorable settlement was possible. As part of the emphasis on raising morale by acquainting the masses of people with the facts, the Ministry of Information waged what it called an anger campaign to inspire loathing for the Nazis. The Ministry of Information distributed pamphlets detailing the crimes of Germans against the occupied peoples of Europe and also, anticipating *Loss of Eden*, predicted what life would be like for ordinary Britons under Nazi rule: "If Hitler won you could not make a joke in the pub; . . . you could not talk freely in front of your children; . . . you would be at the mercy of your employer about hours and wages, for you would have no trade union."[12] Obviously, the pamphlets were rudimentary, but they demonstrate the government's fledgling attempts to direct war propaganda at the civilian urban working class, who would have to bear the brunt of the inevitable German bombing campaign.

The government's diligent monitoring of civilian morale was another sign of the widespread worry. The Ministry of Information formed its Home Intelligence Division, which was charged with keeping track of the public's opinions, its hopes and fears, and its general mood. They mounted an anti-rumor campaign and asked people to report persistent offenders who might be sapping the community's morale by raising unrealistic expectations of imminent peace. The Gallup Poll, an arm of the British Institute of Public Opinion, was founded in 1937, and it also began keeping tabs in 1939 on British public morale, using modern social research techniques. Its data were collated with information from numerous other sources: school inspectors; chambers of commerce, trade unions and professional organizations; branch managers of W. H. Smith stores; librarians; managers of Granada Cinemas; officials of political parties; postal censors and telephone listeners; rotary clubs and workers' educational associations were all asked for information about the people's determination to persist in the war effort. Mass Observation, a private research group founded in 1937, was commissioned to conduct opinion polls, start "spontaneous" discussions in pubs, and ask informants to keep diaries of their own feelings and those of their families. They got people to tell them candidly how they felt about the war and what they thought of the rationing, blackouts, travel restrictions, and other government policies; they learned what people found most onerous and what they thought might be unnecessary. In short, the state made a massive effort to uncover potential sources of alienation. All of this information was pooled to measure changes in the people's psychological and emotional readiness to withstand attack as well as its willingness to undertake war-related work (eventually 45 percent of the British workforce would be organized into the war industries). As historian Robert Mackay demonstrates, the Home Intelligence Division "took the public's pulse" during the first two years of the war "in an almost obsessional way," issuing reports on civilian morale in all parts of the country every single day in the summer of 1940. The incessant surveying, polling, and spying attest to a strong suspicion of cracks in the solidarity between the people and the state's war effort.

Nervousness about a rift like the one illustrated in *Loss of Eden* was thus built into routine interactions between the state and the people, and the novel seems designed both to justify the scrutiny and to encourage readers to internalize it, becoming forearmed against their own natural desires, lest in an unguarded moment they find themselves on the slippery slope to unintended treason. Contemporary reviewers had no difficulty recognizing the book's purpose and praised its attention to civilian resolve. The reviewer for the *Times*, for example, emphasized that the essential value of the fiction was not its depiction of what the Germans would do to the people but rather what the people might do to their own nation: "Yet the mere political disasters imagined in this cautionary tale are as nothing to its dreadful account of the collapse of moral. Shame at the terms of peace develops into fear, as the concentration camp and all the other means of repression are introduced, and fear in turn becomes hopelessness and hopelessness utter despair."[13] The *Times Literary Supplement* echoes this judgment: "All this darkening of the life of England might be, could be if—if the citadel of her *soul* were overthrown."[14] There was, of course, plenty of other propaganda characterizing Britons as heroic and indomitable that summer—for example, there were constant reminders that the brave RAF pilots were fighting in the skies and guarding the channel—but *Loss of Eden* took the country's fate out of the hands of the few and gave it to the many. Their immediate war work, it implied, was to monitor their own sentiments, especially to be on guard against harboring hopes "not based on fact" for a peaceful settlement. The novel's intent was thus to encourage readers to adopt the government's vigilance as their own outlook, thereby closing in actuality the state/people discontinuity portrayed in the fiction.

Nevertheless, there is much in this novel that goes beyond the didactic cautionary tale. Because it was written to warn rather than reassure, its authors were free to explore thematically the problems inherent in Britain's liberal model of nationhood. Thus, as it proceeds, *Loss of Eden* increasingly becomes an inquiry into the nature of nations in general. When, at each new stage in Britain's submersion, the narrator reflects on the conditions under which national regeneration might occur, he repeatedly suggests that the very thing they would be fighting for—the civic model of the liberal democratic nation—is unserviceable in the formation of an insurgent resistance. For example, at an early stage before the health of the body politic had been compromised by demobilization and its consequent unemployment, we learn, "centuries of open political discussion and criticism, and the traditions of a free Press, had immunized [Britain] against the poison of seditious propaganda" (31). But once the economic plight of working-class men destroys their faith in democratic constitutional processes, they fall prey to a seemingly homegrown form of fascist paramilitarism, the "Greyshirts," and their patriotic sentiments are channeled, with the help of German operatives, into anti-Semitic riots, led by a deluded Irish rabble-rouser named Patrick Rosse. Their own political traditions of tolerance, which included offering refugee status to European Jews fleeing Nazism, seem to these men to have betrayed their native interests, and their former rallying cry—fighting for democracy—begins to sound hollow. At an early stage in this history, therefore, the Nazis reduce the most explosively disaffected part of the population—the industrial working class—to their own moral level of racial nationalism, eroding a significant difference between the principles of British national identity and theirs.

But the novel does not simply present the dawn of homegrown fascism in England as another mistake, for it gives lengthy and unresolved consideration to the possibility that it might somehow point the way to national resurrection. This is not to say that the novelists are ambivalent about fascism, only that they imply its dynamics of resentment might be helpful once the habits of civil nationalism fall into disuse. Renan identified a belief in continuity as one of the key components of the act of affirmation that binds otherwise quite disparate groups into a nation, so if that awareness of continuity is broken and the habit of the daily plebiscite is lost, how can the people find the will to create the nation anew? Might some less rational, more instinctual, appeal to collective passions be necessary to galvanize them in such an emergency? The fact that the only character in the novel who knows how to turn Briton's shame into angry action is Patrick Rosse, the Greyshirt leader, suggests that the sort of nationalism needed to inspire an uprising would not rest on principles of liberal toleration but on the memory of common injuries, the blame for which could be placed on convenient scapegoats:

> He made the injustices done to ex-Servicemen sound like some huge and legendary crime which must make the world weep. He created bloated giants of oppression, which the feeblest Jack of all longed to

rise up and slay. He surrounded us with a labyrinthine web of corruption and inefficiency and then led us sword in hand to slash our way out.... Throughout the whole speech he played subtly on the sense of shame which secretly beset so many consciences—a war unwon, a job half-finished, a nation disgraced in the eyes of the world, betrayed by its own half-heartedness and the leaders it had produced. (37)

The narrator certainly condemns the deflection of the people's anger and shame away from the Germans and toward the Jewish émigrés, and the anarchic violence that follows only deepens the rioters' subjugation, for the Germans blame it on their victims and use it as a pretext for taking over the island's police forces. And yet Rosse is nevertheless surrounded with the aura of a great leader. He is created as an enigma, a figure comprising contradictory rumors and perceptions: perhaps an Irish Republican Army operative, or a genuine war hero, or a German tool; the veil of mystery behind which the authors keep him allows him later to metamorphose into an anti-German rebel "on the run in the hills of Connemara" (123). The novel does not tell us whether this is the desperate last act of the charismatic demagogue or the beginning of an effective resistance, but it does strongly imply that the kind of leader who was good at forging fascist paramilitary groups would also be likely to spearhead an uprising.

And that point is reiterated in the authors' next portrait of a possible British resistance leader, an English character named Stephen Mallory, who, "it must be confessed, was no democrat. Rather, he was *fascigeant*, believing that Britain, suddenly finding herself plunged into such a state of shame and self-pity as marked the Weimar Republic, needed the counterpart of the National Socialist movement to restore her self-respect" (62). Mallory's fascism, though, is to be based on Christian principles, stressing a "purified nationalism" in which the people take responsibility for their fate: "There was to be no talk of stabs in the back, or international Jewish machinations, or of a gallant war lost on the home front. To the moral surrender the whole country had been party, the people as well as the leaders. No one was to blame but ourselves" (62). The narrator explains that the "fascist" part of Mallory's thought was manifest in his plan for a putsch that could take over the government (at this stage in the plot, there is still a titular British government), proclaim martial law, disband the German-infiltrated Greyshirts, remobilize the remnants of the British fighting forces, and direct the spontaneous uprising that would inevitably follow. All of this was based on the character's belief in a "politics of power ... that was latent ... in the spirit of the [British] race, co-existent with the race itself, which any resolute political engineer could transform into successful action" (66).

It is typical of *Loss of Eden*'s narrator that he follows this rousing sentence with the comment that "this seemed to most of us pretentious nonsense, like Hitler's or Rosenberg's," and then undercuts even his own skepticism with yet another reflection on its probable inefficacy: "But it is impossible to fight a war without some suspension of disbelief in fallacies about race" (66). The novel's plot follows through on this insight by relying for glimmers of hope along the way on ethnic clichés about the natural rebelliousness of Celts: "What's the good of shooting a dozen Irishmen? . . . You've only created a dozen martyrs in the sacred cause of Irish freedom, and you've inspired a hundred others with the ambition to be shot in similar glorious circumstances" (123). The Scots are less openly defiant, but they also subvert the Nazi occupation with a sullen refusal to cooperate. If the English, still afflicted with "spiritless resignation" by the end of the story, learn to follow the bent of the Celtic Britons—"the stubbornness of the Scots and the fiery resentment of the Irish"—then there may be hope for the nation. In short, racial theories of nationality are of course nonsense, but suspending our disbelief in them frees us to imagine some possible escape hatches from Britain's complete and permanent submersion.

"Suspended disbelief" is, of course, the phrase coined by Samuel Taylor Coleridge to describe the state of mind in which we read works of literature, especially fictions: we do not examine them for their factual truth but instead grant them a form of hypothetical credibility to increase the aesthetic effect. We can read Brown and Serpell's use of this phrase as a sly comment on the fictional compact they have made with the reader, in which we accept *Loss of Eden*'s future conditional premise for the sake of getting on with the story. This self-reflexivity also signals that the novel is more than propaganda because it can admit its role in relaxing our resistance to kinds of rhetoric that might strike us as jingoistic under other circumstances. Readers who recognize the concept of suspended disbelief are reassured that they can maintain their ironic aloofness from crude racial generalizations even if they should simultaneously acknowledge their tactical efficacy. Believing in racial distinctions might be dangerous, but suspending disbelief in them is both harmless (like reading a novel) and necessary to winning the war. The suggestion is that, in wartime, statements about the nation need not conform to a standard of truth; they are not intended to be strictly believed but are rather illocutionary acts designed to motivate their hearers to fight. The context of war thus acts like an operator of fictionality, putting one's rhetoric in implied quotation marks that allow it to be considered just on the grounds of its effectiveness. The idea is similar to what is sometimes now called strategic essentialism. Appeals to an ethnos as the foundation of the national existence, the narrator reminds us, had worked in modern times to revitalize Italy and Germany, just as in the diegetic world of this novel they worked for Patrick Rosse.

Were contemporary readers, therefore, being asked simply to set aside their skepticism because the emergency might demand new—and admittedly "fictional"—ways of arousing national sentiment? Does the novel, while foreclosing the option of a compromise peace, open the possibility of strategically imitating the enemy? Perhaps, but it is just as possible that the authors were trying to imagine a kind of federated civic model that could accommodate the ethnocentric impulse, which at the time seemed subversive. Rosse's example is certainly partly designed to recall that racial models of nationhood had recently been effective in the Irish nationalist movement, then viewed as having resulted in increased British vulnerability to invasion via Ireland, a neutral power. Readers were also likely to know that such appeals formed the basis of other movements thought to undermine the war effort, like Scottish and Indian nationalism. We might, therefore, conclude that authors were calling attention to the power of this alternative model of nationhood inside Britain itself. By making the Englishman Mallory another spokesman for regeneration through racial nationalism, they seem further to be signaling their doubt—not about the truth of the alternative liberal civic model but about its comparative emotional force. The episodes of the novel that center on the characters Rosse and Mallory thus indicate a fear that Great Britain—unlike Ireland, Scotland, Wales, or India—lacked a positive and unified identity, a central raison d'être, with mass appeal.

Trailing this fear, however, is the corresponding wish that great suffering would create a transformation in the social and economic organization of the country. After all, it only takes a slight shift in perspective for the novel's nightmare—the necessity of reinventing the entire nation from the ground up—to reveal itself as a desire for radical change. The perspectival shift comes at the very end of the novel, in an epilogue (supposedly a letter to the narrator, written by a Scot with ties to an incipient underground organization) that describes how the destruction wreaked by the Nazis has uncovered the primary national features, which, it seems, had been partially obscured by unequal social conditions. Staying true to the formal requirement of the cautionary tale, the body of the novel refrains from depicting the discovery of these core principles, but the epilogue outlines them. They have been sustained, we learn, "not by the intellectuals or the thinkers, still less by the politicians and talkers, but by the greatest and most inarticulate section of the population, the working-class" (140). Because the Germans have destroyed the old class system and expropriated everyone's property "the fellowship of the poor has been extended to embrace all classes in Britain, and we are all learning the same lessons together." Social equality, the ironic outcome of German expropriation, is thus the new foundation of the rebounding nation. And from the perspective of this equalized oppression, principles of regeneration emerge, the first of which is "the need for freedom—an equal freedom for every man and every people upon the earth" (141). "The very cause for which we went to war," we learn, "was a belated recognition of the principles of freedom." The "foundation of such freedom" is declared to have been there all along "in the laws and constitution under which we lived," but "private greed and selfish fear" trampled on it. Thus we have a new appreciation of liberty born from an imposed equality; predictably, the last of the three lessons of the occupation is the necessity for the "*brotherhood* of sacrifice." Hence the three French revolutionary virtues—liberty, equality, and fraternity—are at the last minute rediscovered by the people as the redemptive meaning of their suffering and therefore the basis of the state. Viewed from this belated angle, the novel's drama seems to be as much about uncovering Great Britain's obscured vital principles as it is about restoring a lost state.

Obviously, this epilogue reinstates the civic—as opposed to genealogical or racial—model of nationhood, but it also subtly indicates that dismantling the old social, economic, and geographic-ethnic hierarchies would be the key to revitalizing the state. The people must start again from the condition of primitive equality, with the explicit goals of freedom and brotherhood in view. Indeed, by insisting on "an equal freedom for . . . every people upon the earth" the authors seem to be endorsing some sort of self-determination even for subnational groups within Great Britain and perhaps throughout the empire. The contrite Rosse, having gone underground, makes the cause of the "fiery-hearted" Irish one "with that which inspires the quiet English and stubborn Scots" (140). Even the quietness, the characteristic English reserve that had made the people opaque to the government at the outset of the novel, has been taken up as a necessary element in their revolt. "The value of silence," we're told, is now recognized by all. It would appear, then, that the most liberal of all civic nations would be one that accommodates internal national habits as well as ambitions; thus ethnos and demos would cease to be conflicting political principles. The importance of adhering to the right kind of national model comes up again in the epilogue when we are reminded that before the war Great Britain had upheld the promise of an international "brotherhood in the League of Nations," which was destroyed by "national self-seeking" (141). The principles of British nationalism, in short, must be a stepping-stone toward internationalism and decolonization. Behind the fear of the loss of the state, therefore, we can glimpse not only a more revolutionary wish for the transformation of Great Britain but also an attempt to revive and preserve the nation's role as the standard-bearer of liberal values.

THE REVOLUTIONARY POSSIBILITY: ORWELL'S *THE LION AND THE UNICORN*

Loss of Eden was not the only summer-of-1940 book to imagine that the immediate crisis could serve as a staging ground for a British social revolution in which the relation between the state and the people would be reconfigured. To explore the fuller implications of this view, which reemerged in many postwar alternate-history novels, I want to devote some space to its best-known formulation, George Orwell's *The Lion and the Unicorn*. Orwell's book was not a novel but rather a long, future-conjectural essay published as the first of a projected series of works by various left-leaning authors "focusing attention on war-time problems and offering solutions to them" (452). I've already quoted a short passage from it to illustrate that it shared *Loss of Eden*'s fear of a peace movement, but there are many other similarities. Orwell began writing *The Lion and the Unicorn* in the same month that *Loss of Eden* appeared, and his future conjectures overlap significantly with those of the earlier work. For example, here is Orwell considering "in what way England might be defeated":

> The English can probably not be bullied into surrender, but they might quite easily be bored, cajoled or cheated into it, provided that, as at Munich, they did not know that they were surrendering. It could happen most easily when the war seemed to be going well rather than badly. The threatening tone of so much German and Italian propaganda is a psychological mistake. . . . With the general public the proper approach would be "Let's call it a draw." It is when a peace-offer along *those* lines is made that the pro-Fascists will raise their voices. (88)

This passage replicates in extraordinary detail the nexus sequence of *Loss of Eden*, describing the British people's response to Hitler's initial peace offer: "It was such a simple solution," the novel recounts, "—just the 'Cease Fire,' the *status quo nunc*" (11). Orwell copies the motif: "The proper approach would be 'Let's call it a draw.'" In the novel, Hitler's speech touches off "the first spontaneous rumblings of mass pacifism in Great Britain," which are encouraged by those to whom "peace . . . meant dividends, concessions, cartels; it meant escape from the heavy taxation on profits and all the other restrictions which the war effort had imposed on private enterprise" (12). Again Orwell follows suit by imagining the peace movement led by "millionaires quoting the Sermon on the Mount—that is our danger."

Larger thought patterns of the two books also coincide, but the essay form gives Orwell the freedom to explore their common ideas more systematically. Both examine the nature of "patriotism, national loyalty" (97) in general, and both question whether the British people, in particular, have enough of it to keep them fighting a long war with a high toll of civilian casualties. Both books also display some embarrassment about reviving such an old-fashioned topic as national character, even while they defend the necessity of doing so. Orwell helps to put both books in context by noting that "till recently it was thought proper to pretend that all human beings are very much alike" (56). Indeed, he describes a prevailing interwar intellectual atmosphere that, he thought, had discouraged national self-scrutiny during the previous twenty years, especially on the left. British intellectuals, he claims, were "ashamed of their nationality" and they deemed it "a duty to snigger at every English institution" (75).

Orwell's generalizations about the left in this book are undoubtedly exaggerated, but it should be noted that British discourse generally between the wars did emphasize the benefits of internationalism. Even the country's official foreign policy stressed continuity with its self-proclaimed nineteenth-century role as the preserver of world peace and order, and all interwar governments tried to align the country's national interests with international stability. Indeed, its leaders even professed to see a natural evolution from the British Empire to worldwide organizations. Explaining the British commitment to the League of Nations, for example, Lloyd George called the empire the "embryo League of Nations because it is based on the true principles of national freedom and political decentralization."[15] But with the country's international hopes dashed, its empire threatened, and its very existence imperiled, Orwell argues, "it is . . . of the deepest importance to try and determine what England *is*, before guessing what part England *can play* in the huge events that are beginning" (57–58). Here once again, as we've so often observed, historical hypothetical conjectures prompt national characterization.

Thus the first section of this three-part essay describes what Orwell calls "English civilization," with intermittent apologies to the Welsh and the Scots for referring to the entire country as "England" rather than "Britain." Calling the country "England" might seem especially odd in a book titled "The Lion and Unicorn," which refers to the image on the coat of arms of the United Kingdom's monarch, where a lion, standing for England, and a unicorn, standing for Scotland, support an escutcheon containing symbols of all four British groups: English, Scots, Welsh, and Irish. Orwell, though, uses the image to stress the commonality of the British, which, he insists, is most apparent from the outside: foreigners perceive them as sharing a distinctive set of attitudes and way of life. Consequently, adopting the foreign habit of calling them all "English" does not greatly distort the reality. Moreover, the symbol of the lion and the unicorn has another association in the book: the royal coat of arms was stamped on the buttons of conscripted British soldiers and was thus a token of the ordinary British subject's subordination to the state in a time of war. As his argument unfolds, it becomes clear that all of the people are stamped with the insignia of the state for the duration of the war, and the central issue is what permanent changes in the national dyad will arise from this impressment.

Orwell's long essay, though, is by no means a patriotic praise song to his countrymen; indeed, their defining characteristics are wittily and arrestingly negative. The fact that England has a unique civilization is proven by "the dislike which nearly all foreigners feel for our national way of life. Few Europeans can endure living in England, and even Americans often feel more at home in Europe" (56). The dislike, moreover, seems merited. British people are indifferent to art and they have no talent for it; they are incapable of philosophical reasoning and dismiss all other modes of abstract thought; they are anti-intellectual and yet they are also impractical; they refuse to learn foreign languages; they are hypocritical, having subjugated a quarter of humankind while preaching the gospels of peace, freedom, and democracy to others; they spend their leisure time in trivial hobbies; they tolerate enormous inequalities of income and privilege at home and cling to all sorts of outmoded customs and inefficiencies simply because they are theirs. In short, the English are as hopelessly insular, arrogant, two-faced, eccentric, and self-deceived as their detractors claim.

A reader might at first wonder what this description has to do with the role Britain might be able to play in the coming crisis, but soon it becomes clear that because Britons are old-fashioned, xenophobic people, and preoccupied with their private pastimes, they are also immune to fascism. Their disdain for philosophical abstraction makes them equally resistant to most kinds of ideology, and hence the pulsations of left- and right-wing propaganda that swept through Europe in the twenties and thirties made very little impression on them. Simply by virtue of being foreign, moreover, fascism is suspect. The "insularity of the English, their refusal to take foreigners seriously" protects them from the propaganda of the dictatorships: "At bottom it is the same quality in the English character that repels the tourist and keeps out the invader" (65). And the whole bent of British culture, we're told, leans away from the totalitarian tendency toward "being numbered, labelled, conscripted, 'coordinated'" (59). For example, when Britons gather they insist on doing so voluntarily, usually on the basis of their private interests. "Official" groups do not appeal to them, and that goes double for military and quasi-military organizations. The well-known British hostility to a standing army, Orwell notes, is not truly a form of hypocrisy but, rather, the natural result of the country's naval power: "A navy employs comparatively few people, and it is an external weapon which cannot affect home politics directly" (61). There is no military mystique in Britain; the English are not just indifferent to army uniforms but harbor an active "hatred" of them: "The mass of the people are without military knowledge or tradition, and their attitude towards war is invariably defensive. No politician could rise to power by promising them conquests or military glory" (60).

And thus, as an island nation with an empire built on naval power, deploying its force mainly in distant lands, England had developed an unusually pacific home civilization that fostered what Orwell calls "gentleness" in the manners of the people. Furthermore, the state produced by this constellation of historical and geopolitical features—a notoriously eclectic and inefficient conglomeration of modern democracy, impenetrable bureaucracy, aristocratic hereditary privilege, and monarchy—was comparatively unobtrusive in the lives of its people. Indeed, the one idea that unites all the classes in the country is "the belief in 'the law' as something above the State and above the individual, something which is cruel and stupid, of course, but at any rate *incorruptible*" (62). It is this that makes Britain, "with all its sloth, hypocrisy and injustice," "the living contradiction of all the 'infallible' dogmas of Fascism" (107). Their firm belief that the state and the sovereign are *of necessity* subordinate to "the law," Orwell tells us, indicates not only how averse British people are to the fascist ideology of power that makes the state supreme but also how incapable they are of fully understanding such a thing.

This survey of national characteristics, which was made in order to determine what Britain might do in the current historical crisis, does not really answer that question, for the fact it stresses most insistently—Britain's people and its state institutions are incapable of fascism—is double-edged: they may be so incapable of entertaining it that they also cannot effectively combat it. Indeed, the bafflement of the British when confronted with Hitler was, according to Orwell, also the very trait that caused the nation's current peril. British leaders and people alike throughout the 1930s had failed to see the threat because they could not understand this new ideological worldview, and "even when they had begun to grasp that Fascism was dangerous, its essentially revolutionary nature, the huge military effort it was capable of making, the sort of tactics it would use, were quite beyond their comprehension" (71). The very things that make the country instinctively antitotalitarian also make it inefficient and resistant to total military mobilization. Hence, although now the "English-speaking civilization is the only large obstacle in Hitler's path" (107), the problem of how to turn that civilization into an offensive force remains unsolved. Can the country be militarized without sacrificing its liberal values? Can the state's powers be expanded to conscript the massive amounts of labor, capital, and materials needed to defeat the Nazi war machine? And if they were, what social and economic changes could rally the people's enthusiastic support?

This way of framing the problem allows Orwell to conclude, just as Brown and Serpell had, that changing the nation's social and economic order is the only way to protect it. He thus makes a case for democratic socialism as a war measure: "Crudely: The State, representing the whole nation, owns everything, and everyone is a State employee" (79). He argues that nationalization would make Britain's war economy as efficient as Germany's, then immediately goes on to explain that this parity would not turn the country into another fascist regime, for "the idea underlying Fascism is irreconcilably different from that which underlies Socialism. Socialism aims, ultimately, at a world-state of free and equal human beings. It takes the equality of human rights for granted. Nazism assumes just the opposite" (79–81). In outlining the details of this "revolution," Orwell repeatedly tacks between the necessity of matching the enemy's powerfully effective means and that of opposing its goals. The empire, for example, must be maintained as long as the world is "ruled by bombing planes"; "But we must also tell the Indians that they are free to secede, if they want to. Without that there can be no equality of partnership, and our claim to be defending the coloured peoples against Fascism will never be believed" (99). And, of course, on the home front the active assent and participation of the people will be even more important, which is why democratic socialism is the only way to guarantee their commitment to victory: "From the moment that all productive goods have been declared the property of the State, the common people will feel, as they cannot feel now, that the State *is themselves*. They will then be ready to endure the sacrifices that are ahead of us" (97). Thus Orwell argues that the immediate threat of the nation's defeat, the experience of its imminent existential crisis, is the opportunity for the social changes that will bring "the real England to the surface" (109), for it will close the gap between state and people—"the State *is themselves*." Like *Loss of Eden*, *The Lion and the Unicorn* imagines the future conditions under which this truth can be revealed. Both books are pointed toward the moment when the normally nonsynchronous dual structure of the nation—people and state—can be synchronized in the hypothetical future.

The temporality of this future in Orwell's book verges on the millennial, for it promises not only that a new order *will* begin but also that it will divulge a condition that always already existed underneath the distortions of social inequality: the identity of the state and the common people. The inclusivity of the adjective "common" seems designed to merge the various ethnic divisions in a demos defined mainly by its nonaristocratic nature. The current moment of crisis constitutes for Orwell a break in the history of inherited ruling-class domination, beneath which he can show us the broad foundations of the nation. This is, of course, the mysterious temporality of popular sovereignty, which claims to preexist the institutions that guarantee its historical realization. Thus Orwell's rhetoric insists that there *is* a "real England" just below the "surface": "England has got to assume its real shape. The England that is only just beneath the surface, in the factories and the newspaper offices, in the aeroplanes and the submarines, has got to take charge of its own destiny" (86). As these instances indicate, the war has created both the temporal break and the leading edge of the "real" nation we can now see, and so the nation's peril becomes its salvation. The very logic of cause and effect becomes labile at the conclusion of the book: "Compared with the task of bringing the real England to the surface, even the winning of the war, necessary though it is, is secondary. By revolution we become more ourselves, not less" (109). Whereas earlier in the book, the planned economy of democratic socialism was presented as the means to victory, now victory becomes just a means of realizing the "true shape" of the nation, solidifying the identity between the state and common people.

Finally, Orwell again echoes *Loss of Eden*'s scenario while considering the possibility that revolution and victory might be disconnected by future events. "It could happen," he hypothesizes, "that England could introduce the beginnings of Socialism, turn this war into a revolutionary war, and still be defeated" (108). "But," he continues, "terrible as that would be for anyone who is now an adult, it would be far less deadly than [a] 'compromise peace.'" The discourse that surrounds this conjecture is practically a summary of the novel's ostensible lessons, with Vichy France (formed in the interval between the novel's publication and the completion of Orwell's book) standing in as the example of the compromised nation:

> The choice before us is not so much between victory and defeat as between revolution and apathy. If the thing we are fighting for is altogether destroyed, it will have been destroyed partly by our own act. . . . The final ruin of England could only be accomplished by an English government acting under orders from Berlin. . . . The difference between going down fighting, and surrendering without a fight, is by no means a question of 'honour' and schoolboy heroics. Hitler said once that to accept defeat destroys the soul of a nation. This sounds like a piece of claptrap, but it is strictly true. . . . The sort of peace that Pétain, Laval and Co. have accepted can only be purchased by deliberately wiping out the national culture. The Vichy Government will enjoy a spurious independence only on condition that it destroys the distinctive marks of French culture: republicanism, secularism, respect for the intellect, absence of colour prejudice. (108)

But even if Britain should undergo a military defeat, the revolution would protect it against submitting to Nazi orders: "That cannot happen if England has awakened beforehand." If a united, revolutionary nation were overrun, it still would not be "utterly defeated," for "the struggle would continue, the *idea* would survive." "We may see German troops marching down Whitehall," he continues, "but another process, ultimately deadly to the German power-dream, will have been started" (108). At this point in his argument, Orwell invokes the Spanish republicans as the positive model of a people defeated on the battlefield but unbroken in spirit and so persisting as a nation: "The things they learned during those two and a half memorable years will one day come back upon the Spanish Fascists like a boomerang" (108). This last prediction in *The Lion and the Unicorn* blends Orwell's memories of the war for Republican Spain (in which he fought) with a vision of England engaged in the same kind of struggle, a blend that allows him to imagine the imminent English revolution from the vantage point of a more distant future in which it might be temporarily blocked.

These various future conditionals at the book's conclusion are complex, but they can be sorted into several branching paths. The current moment contains only one route to victory, which would lead through democratic socialist revolution, but it also holds two potential routes to British defeat: (1) surrendering without a fight, as in *Loss of Eden*; or (2) "going down fighting." If the first comes to pass, the nation is finished; if the second eventuates, it may do so under two different conditions, the revolutionary and the nonrevolutionary. Military defeat without revolution might result in a puppet government like Vichy, in which further compromises with the Nazis would follow; thus that path seems to lead to the destruction of the national culture. Defeat within the context of revolution, however, would seem to require an outright military dictatorship, as in Spain, and that would be the only path toward eventual national survival. By beginning a revolution, the people will have already learned that they are the state, so they will not be fooled by the claims of any usurping power. They will be inoculated against fascist influences and therefore the struggle would survive. In other words, by viewing the revolution that is supposedly just about to start as also one that might soon be interrupted by foreign conquest, Orwell implies an even longer-range perspective in which the English people might triumph.

And yet, we must note that there is no actual envisioning of a triumphant conclusion, and it is only from the vantage point of the interrupted process that "the struggle would continue, the *idea* would survive." When we reflect that the Orwell who wrote this sentence had already begun his career as a chronicler of the twentieth-century's allegedly successful but ultimately betrayed revolutions, the phrase seems to resonate with uncertainty about sustaining the people's control over the state after the emergency. Of course, we should guard against the temptation to read this 1940 work as a foreshadowing of later stages in Orwell's writing, but we should also note that his determined anti-Stalinism, which stressed the need for revolutionaries especially to be on guard against overweening state power, was persistent in his works. It emerged most visibly in *Animal Farm* (written in 1943 although not published until 1945), but it had already been a major theme in *Homage to Catalonia*. Orwell later insisted that *Animal Farm* was intended as a satire of Stalin's state only and that it was born out of his frustration in 1943 that the British left had ceased to be critical of the USSR's totalitarianism once that country had become an ally against the Germans. It was not to be taken as a conjecture about the necessary fate of all possible postrevolutionary states. Nevertheless, he also wrote in 1944 that "all revolutions are failures, but they are not all the same failure."[16] Bernard Crick, his biographer, argues that Orwell maintained his commitment to democratic socialism until his death, but that his thought also had an anarchist streak, leading to "more than a little ambivalence on whether the State should be strengthened for welfare or diminished for liberty."[17]

It is that ambivalence that seems to emerge in the open-ended future conjectures of *The Lion and the Unicorn*. In addition to writing that book in the summer and fall of 1940, Orwell was serving in the Home Guard, publishing pamphlets encouraging other socialists to join as well, agitating for distributing arms to the people at large, and generally laboring to increase socialist sentiment in defense of the nation. In short, his revolutionary fervor in *The Lion and the Unicorn* was no mere rhetorical flourish; it was the center of his existence. But that very sense of the uniquely momentous present, in which possibilities are expanding, might also be experienced as the highpoint of revolutionary enthusiasm, after which any transition into normal governance would be a deflation. Orwell saw the present, into the immediate future, as a gap in continuous political time, a dislocation from the ordinary, when the people might feel themselves to be the state and might soon be fighting for its survival. By using the Spanish comparison, he manages to freeze that moment in imagination, putting off any conclusion into a still more distant future; the transformative moment seems thereby to become an end in itself. It is the time just before revolutionary realization—not the moment of reviving, but the moment of struggling to revive the people's chosen state—that serves as the apotheosis of the democratic national *idea*.

Throughout *The Lion and the Unicorn*, the insurmountable objection to equating the people with the state is the existence of the empire, which plays havoc with that logic. The empire in this book is an embarrassment, for it puts pressure on the concept of the "people" by adding extraneous overseas populations, "peoples" who were entirely without even a nominal role in the state that ruled them, peoples whom nobody would have argued belonged in the category of the people of Great Britain. To his credit,

Orwell does not ignore the problem; he mentions it frequently, and two of the items in his "six-point programme" for initiating the English revolution concern the empire: "Immediate dominion status for India, with power to secede when the war is over" and "formation of an Imperial General Council, in which the coloured peoples are to be represented." These, he had made clear elsewhere, are merely the first steps in the larger project of gradual decolonization, but as he develops the ideas, especially in relation to India, his ambivalence at parting with the colony comes to the fore. Britain must cease "to stand towards India in the relation of an exploiter," but it must not grant the immediate independence for which Gandhi and Nehru were then campaigning: "If India were simply 'liberated,' i.e. deprived of British military protection, the first result would be a fresh foreign conquest, and the second a series of enormous famines which would kill millions of people within a few years" (99). "We must . . . tell the Indians that they are free to secede, if they want to," he insists, "but it is a mistake to imagine that if the Indians were free to cut themselves adrift they would immediately do so. When a British government offers them unconditional independence, they will refuse it. For as soon as they have the power to secede the chief reasons for doing so will have disappeared" (99). This is followed by the vision of "Englishmen and Indians" working "side by side for the development of India, and for the training of Indians in all the arts which, so far, they have been systematically prevented from learning" (100). Expiation is certainly imagined here, as if Britain could expunge its guilt by reversing India's underdevelopment, and avoidance of the calamitous alternative during wartime is also a strong motive: "A complete severance of the two countries would be a disaster for India no less than for England" (99). But by disposing of the decolonization issue through this future conditional hypothesis—that if it would be made an option, the colonials would voluntarily reject it—Orwell keeps himself from having to face the difference between an English or even a British revolution and a revolution in the empire of Great Britain. The difference would expose the problem of thinking about Great Britain in purely national terms (the same problem suggested by Orwell's stubborn use of the term "England"): it is obviously not *just* a nation. Moreover, because it was an empire the majority of whose subjects were structurally unable to realize that "the State *is themselves*," Great Britain could not have a democratic socialist revolution without ceasing to be what it manifestly was, and Orwell was unwilling to face the question of what the British state would be in the absence of its colonies.

CHARACTERIZING THE STATE IN 1945: WARFARE TO WELFARE

Orwell's prediction that the war would remake the nation proved true, although not exactly in the ways he'd foreseen. He had correctly predicted that the war would require unprecedented state control over the means not only of production but also of distribution and consumption, and yet he was wrong to imagine that capitalism would be unable to adapt to those controls. He was right as well to imagine that victory would require a strong sense of national identification on the part of many who were previously political outsiders but wrong to think that such an identification with the state needed the permanent nationalization of all industry. Instead of requiring revolution, the transformations followed instead from the nature of total war, which reshaped the mere "population" into the politically resonant "people" through complete mobilization. Men and women alike were pressed suddenly and strenuously into a war for national survival, which resulted in a hearty personal identification with the collective effort. German air raids, not revolution, destroyed state/citizen and combatant/civilian distinctions, and Britons lived with the sober reality that they were fighting a people's war, in which many of them would die and for which all were asked to make great sacrifices. Those who were not subjected to bombing endured rationing, separation from loved ones, universal male conscription, and compulsory national service for all adults, which entailed large-scale dislocations and migrations of workers; lands, buildings, homes, and equipment were commandeered in the massive conversion of peacetime to wartime manufacturing. And yet numerous polls and surveys indicated that, despite their suffering, Britons took comfort in the experience of sharing a national purpose and believed that each class was contributing fairly.[18] All of which vindicates Orwell's claim that British morale depended on a perceived "equality of sacrifice" (87).[19]

As Bernard Crick notes, Orwell was also "half-right" to recognize that many of the wartime transformations of the state would be permanent: "He understood the conditions that would give rise . . . to the limited social revolution of the postwar period."[20] The transition from warfare to welfare was by no means automatic or uncontroversial, though, and we should recognize that 1945, like 1940, was a turning point in the life of the British state, a moment of metamorphosis. The change was being prepared as early as 1942, with the publication of the Beveridge report titled "Social Insurance and Allied Services." Commissioned by the coalition government, the report was itself a future conjectural work, which imagined in detail what role the state would play in reconstructing Britain if the country should win the war. Decisions about its implementation were, of course, put off for the duration, but as soon as victory had been declared in Europe, the Labour ministers dissolved the coalition government, over Tory objections, and general elections were called.[21] The people, in the guise of the electorate, were explicitly presented with a choice of state models: (1) the Labour model of a large, strong state that would continue many of the functions of the warfare government (economic planning and national service, for example), take on new responsibilities to provide housing and healthcare, and even nationalize key industries; or (2) the Conservative model, which would decrease the size and responsibilities of the state, restoring their prewar dimensions. The result was an unexpected but decided victory for the Labour Party, indicating widespread support for a larger and more activist centralized state, dedicated to the well-being of the common people. The election of 1945 thus seems to follow the script elaborated in *The Lion and the Unicorn* in which the war leads to socialist national renewal and a closer merger of the people with the state: the emergency mobilizes the people, who take ownership of the state, and in the process the state is redesigned.

There were, however, other ways of conceiving the changes; to Conservatives who believed that a grateful people should have returned the party of Churchill to power after the victory in Europe, the election of 1945 looked like an inexplicable sign of disaffection between the people and the government, one that recalled wartime fears of defeat through internal divisions and insufficient patriotism. The voters, it seemed, had repudiated the very people who brought them their success. After all, the ministers with primary responsibility for the conduct of the war in the coalition government had almost all been Conservatives; the election turned them, Churchill included, out of office and, thus, signaled the people's refusal of their debt to their wartime leaders. This new peace, in short, spelled the end of national solidarity and the outbreak of domestic discord.

The first Nazi Britain alternate-history fiction—not a novel, but Noel Coward's play *Peace in Our Time* (1946)—ironically doubles the idea of peace and multiplies the dimensions of "our time." There had been a few dramatizations of Nazi invasions and occupations during the war; most notable were the propaganda films by Alberto Cavalcanti (*Went the Day Well?* [1942]) and Humphrey Jennings (*The Silent Village* [1943]). Since there was no longer any need to warn the people about the danger they faced, Coward's play seemed remarkable in 1947 for its untimely war nostalgia combined with antipathy toward the country's recent political turn.

For our purposes, it illustrates one way in which the Tory view of the election generated counterfactual ruminations. Taking place entirely inside a London pub, the action spans the war's five years and follows a familiar itinerary: instead of winning the Battle of Britain, the British have lost and were occupied in November of 1940; the Germans are at first polite to most Britons but become increasingly oppressive; the characters (patrons and owners of the pub) sort themselves into collaborators and resisters (no neutrals have speaking parts); finally American forces liberate London with the help of the British resistance fighters. Thus once again we watch the eradication of the normal state/people distinction, the replacement of the state by foreign occupiers, and the promotion of the people to the role of national agents. The play opened in London in 1947 to mixed notices, the *Times* reviewer complaining: "As an imaginative picture of what might have happened in England it is so very nearly a replica of what did happen in France that we cannot help thinking of it as the tired successor of many exciting films based on the French Resistance movement."[22] *Peace in Our Time*, in short, suffers from resistance envy and indulges a fantasy of national unity lost and restored, in which a simple test (resister or collaborator) would separate true patriots from false.

Just beneath the surface of this finer finest-hour daydream, though, is a revenge fantasy prompted by the people's recent ingratitude toward their victorious wartime leaders. The two themes are wrapped together in the patriotic speech, part of which I quoted in the last chapter, where one of the characters explains that "it *wouldn't* have been better for us" if "we'd won the Battle of Britain." Referring pointedly to the current actual British state of mind, she complains that "we should have got lazy again and blown out with our own glory. We should have been bombed and blitzed and we should have stood up under it—an example to the whole civilized world—and that would have finished us. As it is—in defeat—we still have a chance. There'll be no time in this country for many a long day for class wars and industrial crises and political squabbles. We can be united now—we shall have to be—until we've driven them away, until we're clean again."[23] The speech is followed immediately by a discussion of the execution of Winston Churchill. In this other world where the Germans won the Battle of Britain, the people have a chance to save their collective soul by donning the fighting spirit of their dead prime minister and by cleansing themselves through heroic resistance, whereas in their actual reality—the "peace" in *our* time—they never went through such an ordeal and consequently have merely reverted to "class wars, industrial crises and political squabbles." The playwright condemns his fellow countrymen to additional suffering because they have proved themselves unworthy of their victory. Simultaneously, the title's allusion to Neville Chamberlain's phrase describing the Munich Agreement as "peace for our time" serves as a reminder that Britons were ready to make an ignoble peace with the enemy before Churchill led them to a better destiny. Noel Coward thus finds ways of linking the ungrateful Labour voters with the prewar appeasers, while also providing the usual patriotic clichés about a possible finer finest hour, assuring the audience that their resistance would have been at least as valiant as that of the French.

Peace in Our Time was the first alternate-history fiction produced in Great Britain, but no notice was taken of the novelty, and it is easy to see why. The play has very little in common with the form as it was to develop after 1950; the judgments of the *Times* review—"stale," "tired"—stress the plot's indistinguishability not only from the French tales but also from the earlier invasion fantasies, of which there had been half a dozen in addition to *Loss of Eden* and the two films already mentioned.[24] If it weren't for its occasional outbursts of political pique, Coward's play could easily be dismissed as just another—oddly belated—piece of jingoistic propaganda, reaching far into the realms of implausibility to provide occasions for "eloquent patriotic tirades."[25] But it is the play's angry undercurrents that let us see how the wartime depictions of a possible Nazi Britain would be repurposed in the postwar years, when they would become vehicles for contemporary social and political criticism as well as for continuing reflections on the character of Britain.

Before moving on to those fictions, though, we'll look at an additional Tory characterization of the state in the general election campaign of 1945, a characterization made most definitively in Winston Churchill's notorious campaign-opening speech: "There can be no doubt that socialism is inseparably interwoven with totalitarianism and the abject worship of the State. No socialist government conducting the entire life and industry of the country could afford to allow free, sharp or violently worded expressions of public discontent. They would have to fall back on some form of Gestapo."[26] This raising of the specter of Nazi Britain as a warning against voting Labour seemed absurd and tasteless to many listeners, especially since the existence of the Third Reich's atrocious death camps had been exposed just weeks before. Indeed, instead of making Labour look politically illiberal, it made Churchill seem intolerant to equate his Parliamentary rivals with the reviled former enemy. Churchill dropped the Labour-Nazi metaphor for the duration of the campaign, but he continued to vociferate about the totalitarian tendencies of national programs, and the very word "state" became pejorative in his rhetoric. Warnings against overdependence on the state as a provider of goods and services was, of course, an earlier feature of Conservative politics, but Churchill's increasingly negative use of the word in 1945 and after was new and may have been inspired by his reading in 1944 of Friedrich Hayek's recently published *The Road to Serfdom*.[27] Of course, Churchill could hardly present his party as outside of the state establishment, so he eventually split the concept of the national government into bad and good aspects: the potentially tyrannical force wielded by unelected career civil servants in administrative offices, on the one hand, and the freedom-enhancing institution of the representative legislature, on the other: "I stand for the sovereign freedom of the individual within the laws which freely elected Parliaments have freely passed." He went so far as to accuse Labour of actually planning to transfer sovereignty from Parliament to the bureaucratic offices of the executive.[28]

This, too, was a version of a time-honored Whig distinction in British politics between the overmastering executive (royal force, in its early instances) and the representative legislature (the proponents of parliamentary government). Making it a central *Tory* principle may have been a novelty, which we now call neoliberalism, but the operation of dividing the state into positive and negative manifestations was neither new nor restricted to Conservatives. In 1945, Labour had its own versions, accusing Tories of planning to use state power on the side of industrial monopolists and of wanting to waste tax money on far-away imperialist adventures. Using the military or the police for strike breaking and union busting were predicted if the Tories were to win. Some Labour candidates claimed that Conservative civil servants would place administrative obstacles in the path of promised social programs, thwarting the voters' will. And, of course, as British governments oscillated between parties over the following decades, the candidates for the positive and negative poles of the state continually shifted. Labour primarily ran on platforms of maintaining rather than abandoning government programs, and Conservatives promised to reduce taxes and give the people more private discretion over how their money was spent. We might say, therefore, that this stage in the characterization of the nation preserved the people/state distinction and, moreover, made it internal to the state itself.

We'll be looking at Nazi Britain fictions that are shaped by this pattern, works that designate some parts of the state as foreign impositions and others as still precariously British. The fictions allegorize the binary opposition between the good and the bad state, and we'll see that the pattern accommodates considerable changes over the decades as Britons faced a series of fundamental national alterations. The first of these came in the fifteen-year period immediately following the war, when the actual transformations of the state did not match the expectations raised in 1945. To be sure, the Labour government accomplished much of what it promised by greatly expanding the state's reach: it kept up full employment through National Service, built tens of thousands of units of low-cost housing, established new schools and universities, subsidized higher education, created the National Health Service, and nationalized important industries, like coal and steel, as well as public utilities. But, despite high taxes, the state's resources turned out to be far scantier than anticipated and its commitments and debts far greater.[29] Austerity measures were used to pay for the new programs: wartime food rationing was maintained, taxes on the middle and upper classes were increased, and imports severely limited. Objectively, the lasting accomplishments of the Labour government are impressive: indeed, even when the Conservatives came back to office in 1951, they kept many of Labour's Keynesian policies, which allowed the eventual economic recovery of the late 1950s and 1960s to benefit the majority of the people. For three decades there was a consensus that the welfare state was the necessary bedrock of the country, which was an enormous alteration of national identity.

And yet there was also disappointment that the welfare state had not produced a more egalitarian society. People expressed puzzlement at the persistence of class stratification, snobbishness, and social friction. One Labour MP, Richard Crossman, lamented in 1951, when the Conservatives won the general election that "all the obvious things have been done which were fought for and argued about, and yet mysteriously enough, the ideal, the pattern of values has not been achieved. . . . We have created the means to the good life. They all said, if you do all these things, after that, there will be a classless society. Well, there isn't."[30] The naïveté of this statement may seem extreme, but it shows the quasi-millennial expectations of social transformation harbored by some Labourites in 1945, which made disappointment on the left almost inevitable. No matter how vigorously it tried, the state, it seemed, could not fulfill the role that Orwell had imagined for it in *The Lion and the Unicorn* by remaking society into a cohesive brotherhood of "the people." Moreover, the new role of the state as an important manager of personal life also bred contradictory feelings. The kind of housing many people would have, their educational choices and the number of years they would remain in school, the care of their physical and mental health, all relied on government agencies. And in the early years those were often inadequate to meet the needs, slow to respond, hastily organized, and tied up in red tape. The sense of having to depend on administrations that were not always dependable of course brought the Janus-faced character to mind: the good state provided services; the bad state regulated their distribution, collected the taxes to pay for them, and was inefficient to boot.

The most important and unexpected change in the character of the British state, though, was its transformation from a mighty empire to a mere nation.[31] This is not the place to summarize the processes leading to the independence of Britain's colonies during the two decades following the war; suffice it to say that the empire was not purposely and methodically dismantled by the state. In fact, both Labour and Conservative governments went to great lengths trying to retain most of it, for they realized that its end would mean the loss of Britain's international standing.[32] Indeed, despite their fondness for the image of their country as a tiny David that had held out bravely against Hitler's Goliath in 1940, the country's leadership was well aware of their vast empire's decisive role in the victory.[33] Britain's status as a Great Power relied on its sovereign control of a quarter of the world's population (as Orwell had put it); but by the mid-1960s, it could claim sovereignty over just the people of the United Kingdom and Northern Ireland. Of course, those postwar years were the acceleration of a much longer declension; as historian Robert Skidelsky has recently put it, "Britain started the century as Rome and ended it as Italy."[34] Nevertheless, most Britons seemed stunned in 1956 when the Suez Crisis suddenly revealed their lack of international power and influence. Britain and France, in collusion with Israel, attempted to take control of the Suez Canal, which had been nationalized by Egyptian president Gamal Abdel Nasser, and the United States stepped in to end their military intervention. The blow to Britain's sense of international autonomy and power was severe, and the incident was generally credited with ending Britain's imperial ambitions. Thus, within a dozen years, Britain's global role had gone from being a source of pride and self-confidence to being a cause of humiliation. In 1945, the British state seemed powerful, and Britons had expected foreign gratitude for their heroic, solo defiance of Hitler, which, they believed, saved Western civilization. By 1956, they felt dependent on their overbearing American ally and were censured by former and remaining colonials. To make matters worse, they would soon find themselves unwelcome in the new European Economic Community. The limitations of their state's internal resources had been revealed, and concurrently a sense of international powerlessness and isolation were growing. Such developments might naturally make some Britons reflect that it did not seem as if they had truly won the war.

ALTERNATE HISTORY AND POSTWAR PROTEST

Gaps between reality and expectation often open the imaginative space for alternate histories, of both the regretful (things might have been better) and the consoling (things might have been worse) kind. In the postwar years, when Britons looked back resentfully at missed opportunities or roads not taken toward a superior present, they revived the guilty-men recriminations against appeasers, which helped create the Labour majorities of the late 1940s, but they seldom questioned their later conduct of the war or the wisdom of having fought it. Thus fictional depictions of Nazi Britain in the Cold War period, like the nonfictional works we looked at in the last chapter, tended to stress how much worse Britain's historical fate might have been, just as they also bear the traces of the 1950s and 1960s contexts noted in the last chapter: the stirrings of neo-Nazis, increasing race consciousness, the publication of the *Wehrmacht*'s orders for the occupation of Britain and the gestapo's handbook as well as the perception that the postwar generation of Britons was uninformed about how close the country came to defeat and how world altering a Nazi victory would have been.

The fictions, though, seldom stress the horrors of the world the Germans would have created in Britain, nor do they concentrate on how the national character would have borne up under such a test. Indeed, these alternate Britains are not cleanly divided between occupiers and occupied, Germans and Britons, oppressors and oppressed. Instead, they often explore the spaces that would have stayed under the jurisdiction of British subjects, the layers of an occupied state where remnants of Britain would have continued to operate almost normally, albeit under the ultimate supervision of the Reich. There are a few exceptions, but this is by far the most common mise-en-scène because it puts the focus on alternate-state making, on describing how familiar structures would be reshaped under the pressure of foreign forces, rather than on the personal destinies of fictional characters.[35] These narratives, we might say, cope with the actual economic hardships and the unexpectedly abrupt shrinkage of Britain's territory and significance in the world by imagining different changes, which are certainly far worse and yet also, as we'll see, uncannily similar.

Like the interstitial states they inhabit, the protagonists are liminal characters, neither collaborators nor resisters but merely vestiges of the former state under new overlords. Their positions are not really chosen; they simply find themselves in new circumstances to which they stoically adapt. They are, we might say, the characters of the bureaucratic and military state, who are trying to get their jobs done under increasingly compromising conditions. Insofar as their personal trajectories claim our attention, which they do only intermittently, they present case histories of how loyal and dedicated British national servants might be unintentionally transformed into the enemy. Where does duty end and collaboration begin, the works seem to ask, and what moral tests will reveal the difference? Thus the action emphasizes the persistence and vicissitudes of the British state inside Nazi Britain. The state is not murdered, as it was in *Loss of Eden*, and it is not waiting to be reanimated. It is, rather, both intrusive in the lives of Britons and weakened, reduced, subsumed, and therefore in danger of insidious forms of alteration while remaining putatively British. In short, the alternate-history fictions allegorize perceptions of the actual states of the nation. In what follows, we'll track the main stages in those perceptions by looking at a handful of typical narratives, including a movie and two television plays as well as several novels. My point, though, is not only to reiterate that alternate-history fictions always reflect and often satirize their conditions of productions, which should go without saying by now, but also to demonstrate that they are crucial to the project of creating the character of the nation by varying its circumstances.

Take, for example, the earliest of these stories to be conceived, an experimental film by two very young men titled *It Happened Here*, which was inspired by the fact that London in 1956 simply did not look like a victorious national capital. *It Happened Here* was an amateur production that took eight years to make, had no script until it was nearly finished, and was then shown almost exclusively at film festivals, where it became a brief succès de scandale. The filmmakers, Kevin Brownlow and Andrew Mollo, grew up in postwar London and were little more than children—only eighteen and sixteen, respectively—when they began their project. The older, Brownlow, later became a well-known cinema historian, made several documentaries about the silent era, and restored Abel Gance's epic film *Napoléon* to great acclaim, but at the time he was a teenaged London cineaste with a particular sensitivity to the implications carried by filmic scenes independently of dialogue or even sequences of events. The unfathomable and also largely unarticulated meanings of a war he could barely remember were, he thought, built into the physical state of his city, where the bombed sites and the general shabbiness and neglect made its devastation present at every turn. As he later explained in a 1968 book, he had seen a man quickly park a black car one morning, get out, and hail someone in German; Brownlow was struck by the appropriateness of the action to the scene, which retained the appearance of a war zone. The driver's language caused Brownlow to speculate on what might have happened if the Germans had invaded England. Without a script, a story, or any ideas about characters, Brownlow and Mollo were inspired simply by the atmosphere of war that lingered in London and that might be transformed into the landscape of a Nazi occupation by altering a few details.[36]

In the process of trying to "dress" London sites so that they could realize the occupation, the teenaged filmmakers encountered both the shocked disapproval of ordinary Londoners and the distressingly friendly interest, indeed the voluntary participation, of homegrown fascists. An early effort to drape Trafalgar Square in Nazi regalia and shoot a crowd scene, for example, was interrupted by the police; the filmmakers were taken for pranksters, vandals, or neo-Nazis. Such difficulties in making the movie underline how unusual alternate-history fiction was in the mid-1950s and how especially incomprehensible was the desire to see London as it would have looked under Nazi occupation. What could be the purpose of such a visualization? At our historical remove, we might notice that the meaning of the visualization was precisely the ease with which it might be accomplished, which meant that postwar London still looked too much like a city devastated by war, a perception that cast doubt on the completeness of Britain's victory. Had victory truly been realized? If so, why hadn't prosperity arrived, why hadn't economic development cleared the rubble, and why did Brownlow and Mollo need to interrupt shooting so that they could do their National Service?

If the first inkling of the mise-en-scène for a movie about an alternate outcome to the war was provided by the contradiction between victory and London's dilapidation, the story seems to have been partly occasioned by the filmmakers' chance encounters with the city's neo-Nazis and their voluntary participation in the movie, which includes a notorious scene where the neo-Nazis portray themselves explaining their ideas to the fictional characters. At the time of the early filming, the young cineastes had no explanation for their intentions and had to make up rationales for wanting to imagine the occupation as they went along; neither of them seemed to have known very much about the actual history. Nazism, according to Brownlow, was a mystery to them at the outset, and their curiosity left them open to suspicions that they harbored an unconscious admiration for Hitler, an immature prurient interest in atrocities, or an attraction to a cultic Nazi mystique. Reverse alternate histories of World War II have, in fact, never been able to dispel such suspicions completely. Under the insistent pressure of questions from onlookers, permitting agencies, volunteer actors, and prospective funders, though, the film slowly began to take *British* Nazis, rather than German occupiers, as its primary focus.

Indeed, the imagining of an occupied Britain partly run by a British Nazi Party is one of the film's most unusual features, and it gives structure to the story of the protagonist, a district nurse who must join the party to secure employment when she comes to London after being evacuated from an insurgent area of Northern Ireland. When she arrives in the capital, she is told that nurses, like most other civil servants in occupied Britain, are expected to join the local Nazi Party organization, so she does. We see her training and indoctrination, her conversations with English Nazis (those improvised scenes with neo-Nazis playing themselves), her initiation into Nazi ceremonies, and her eventual emergence as a full-fledged party member. The actress is entirely opaque throughout this transformation; she registers no internal reactions, either positive or negative, and she acts only mildly surprised, yet still unflustered, when her party uniform encounters hostility from other Londoners on the streets. She is temporarily brought under suspicion inside the party when a friend of hers, a doctor whom she knew previously in Northern Ireland, is caught treating a wounded insurgent fighter, but even then she remains stoically inscrutable as the doctor and his wife are dragged off by the Gestapo. Indeed, she seems the embodiment of the wartime advice to "keep calm and carry on." Only when she is sent out of London to work at a mysterious hospital and discovers that she has been unwittingly poisoning children with shots that she thought were inoculations does she realize the horrific malevolence of the power she serves and attempt to escape from Nazi control.

The movie thus uses two features of mid-1950s' Britain—London still looks like it might have been invaded and it contains self-proclaimed Nazis—as portals into an alternate historical world. And, as in most alternate-history fictions, these world-bridging elements were intended to carry contemporary satirical messages, although in this case the ironic staging of the neo-Nazis' recruiting pitch was lost on many viewers when the film was finally shown after eight years of discontinuous shooting and editing. Indeed, the American distributor who bought the picture cut that scene. The final episode in the film, though, proved just as controversial; it shows the British resistance forces fighting to liberate the country with American help and implies that their moral state, after years of struggle against Nazism, would have been little better than that of the invaders.

They are depicted unloading a truckload of prisoners in the countryside and slaughtering them, as an American soldier approvingly snaps photographs. The scene mirrors an earlier one in which Germans murdered hostages, and British critics complained that it thereby implied a moral equivalence between the Allies and the Nazis. A French critic at the Cannes Film Festival accused the film of being an attack on the honor of the French resistance.[37] The filmmakers, though, claimed that the scene was not intended to reflect specifically on the behavior of the Allies or the resistance but was instead a warning against the general dehumanizing tendencies of all wars and therefore signaled their own alignment with the contemporary antiwar movement. Nevertheless, the film does imply that, in the event of an occupation, the continuation of total war would ultimately have led to a breakdown of the ethical difference between the two sides. That idea—quite common before the war and revived afterward by critics of the allied bombing campaign against German cities—would become a commonplace of Nazi Britain fictions as well.[38]

The last scene in *It Happened Here* was also the entry point for another theme that became pervasive in alternate-history scenarios: the liberation of Britain from the German Reich depends on and is immediately followed by the liberated country's subordination to the United States. Indeed, the scene in which British freedom fighters murder German prisoners under the supervision of Americans seems an ironic updating of Churchill's resonant prediction: "Even if . . . this Island or a large part of it were subjugated and starving" Britons would await the moment when, "in God's good time, the New World, with all its power and might, steps forth to the rescue and the liberation of the old."[39] By the mid-1960s when the film was finally screened, not only had the full extent of British dependence on its ally been revealed but anti-American sentiment was also growing among young Britons as the war in Vietnam escalated. *It Happened Here* was only the first depiction of a Nazi occupation to reflect on the nation's actual subservience to another power. It creates the double vision in which one simultaneously sees how much worse things might have been and suggests a slew of semifacetious parallels between the reviled Nazis, who might have dominated Britain, and the resented Americans, who actually do.

The movie acts as an echo chamber for depictions of Britain's plight that were widely resonant in postwar culture. It reverberates, for example, with the voices of the mid-fifties' Angry Young Men (a group of mostly working- and middle-class British playwrights and novelists), especially that of playwright John Osborne, whose *Look Back in Anger* (1956) and

The Entertainer (1957) are brutally eloquent complaints against the persistence of class stratification, the hardships of economic stagnation, and the indignity of American domination. Osborne certainly occupies common ground with the filmmakers in suggesting that the fruits of victory had mainly been harvested elsewhere, but the playwright's protagonist consoles himself by blaming Britain's class structure and imagining (albeit feebly) that a different social and economic system could still create a better world. The filmmakers console themselves by imagining that history might have dealt them a worse one. *It Happened Here* does not, therefore, tell us much that we did not already know about the disappointments of the postwar years, but it does indicate how, by telling a story of what the nation did not become, the discontents could be incorporated into implicit narratives of the nation's continuity over time. The British state never was handed over to a Nazi Party, and so there never was a ruthless resistance movement, and so on. And yet, we are shown that the Nazi threat lingers precisely because of a stagnating economy and Britain's subordination to a new military world power. The loss of British supremacy is the very thing that allows a sense of wartime emergency to bleed into the postwar. For Osborne, the war is decidedly over, but for the filmmakers it goes on, side shadowing current events and sustaining an unbroken sense of national peril.

Later postwar Nazi Britain fictions, which continued to be focalized through state functionaries, set up similar dramatic arcs in which the plots seek the limit of change under Nazi pressure beyond which Britain simply ceases to be itself. The fictions thus keep processing the country's actual transformations by imaging other alterations that would truly have destroyed its identity. And it remains the special task of these counterfactuals to find principles of national identity through time by exploring what the nation's history was *not*—which is always *Nazi*—while also maintaining and updating the shadowy survival of that threatening possibility.

I'll use just one more early example to clarify this pattern and explain its postwar political resonance before moving on to later Cold War uses of the form. In 1964, the year that *It Happened Here* was finally released, a far more adept, mainstream, and self-aware example of the genre was aired on Britain's Independent Television network: a television play written by Giles Cooper (the country's preeminent broadcast dramatist), which starred Michael Caine as a British army officer. The play is set in the barracks of an army regiment, which changes geographic locations several times over the years covered in the plot, all the better to emphasize the isolating "barrack mentality" that develops in its officers. The earliest point in the story is the spring of 1940, when the regiment remains in Britain instead of joining the British Expeditionary Force on the Continent. Consequently, its staff has been untouched by combat when Britain makes peace with Germany directly after the fall of France. British and German armies then become allied forces, and we see the British officers entertaining their German "advisers," making fun of their odd peculiarities, like their intolerance of Jews in the officer's mess, while also politely accommodating them. Over the next few years, there are the usual signs of British Nazification: the disappearance of Jewish and politically unreliable officers, rumors filtering into the barracks of trade unionists killed at a demonstration, evidence of slave labor, and the like, but the protagonist, as a loyal British officer, suspends judgment and obeys his superiors. Even as the British chain of command comes increasingly under Nazi control and he begins to feel qualms, he continues to tell himself that his only clear duty is to follow orders. Finally, the predictable moral crisis arrives after the protagonist has been promoted and reassigned to India, where Britons and Germans together are putting down an insurgency. There he is forced to betray an old friend in exchange for the command of a German task force that will build a road through the Hindu Kush mountains to supply the war against Russia. Beset with guilt about his friend, he confronts the full horror of the world the Nazis are making, but his intended expiation is interrupted by a rebel attack, which wounds him severely. He wakes up to find himself literally transformed in a German hospital, where parts of his own body have been replaced by those of "subhumans," and in return for these life-saving transplants, he owes the Germans a tour of duty back in England, where the Reich needs displays of native enthusiasm.

This portrayal of an officer who drifts into inhumanity by floating on the current of events, conforming to the opinions of those around him, and automatically obeying his superiors seems indebted to Hannah Arendt's analysis, in *Eichmann in Jerusalem*, of the dreadful ordinariness of Nazi officials' behavior. Arendt's book was published in Britain in 1963, the year before Cooper's drama was aired, and it immediately sparked a controversy over what the author meant by the phrase "banality of evil," which she used to describe the motives and actions of Adolf Eichmann, the organizer of the mass deportations of European Jews to ghettos and concentration camps. Arendt claimed that Eichmann was neither a sadist nor a particularly zealous anti-Semite but merely a petty-minded careerist whose very shallowness allowed him to be easily led into deeply evil actions. Her detractors claimed that the analysis seemed to lessen the burden of guilt carried by individual perpetrators by shifting responsibility for history's most heinous crime to an anonymous totalitarian system; it thereby seemed to duplicate the defense of the accused that he was only following orders. Arendt and her defenders, however, retorted that the argument neither denied nor mitigated Eichmann's guilt but rather pointed to the horrors and continuing dangers of a modern collectivism that not only provided anonymity and impunity but also encouraged a peculiarly shallow, "banal" subject who became unable to evaluate the authority of his superiors. The argument spilled over into the questions of whether the Holocaust was unique, whether its perpetrators were pathological or normal, whether Nazism was an extreme version of folkish nationalism or altogether off the spectrum, and whether its roots lay in uniquely aberrant social and cultural conditions or in the opportunities for moral irresponsibility presented by modernity more generally. In short, the controversy surrounding *Eichmann in Jerusalem* propagated a view of Nazism's crimes that widened their contexts and deemphasized their specific assignment to a particular past regime; the dangers of Nazism could be said to survive the regime and live on as ever-present possibilities, inherent in modern political structures.

It is just such an out-of-time Nazi threat that *The Other Man* endorses, first simply by representing a time out of time where British Nazism achieves an official stronghold. The drama is a frame tale, and the primary diegetic level structures it as the alternate life of a British brigadier general in the actual present, who begins to reminisce about his wartime adventures but is interrupted by another officer's grumble—"now we're going to have it, our finest hour and all that"—which sends the tale off on a tangent that departs widely from its expected direction.[40] The frame thus drives home the point that if the circumstances had been different and Britain had made peace in the summer of 1940, the very same people who held out against Hitler in the nation's finest hour might instead have served king and country in tandem with the Third Reich. The protagonist's character is consistent in both worlds: his concepts of loyalty and obedience remain the same; his courage, his good humor, his devotion to duty, and his love for country are stable. And, in a strict sense, the state that he serves is the same, for the difference between serving in the British army allied with Germany might not, at first, look very different from serving in the British army allied with the United States. Thus, the point is driven home: the other man is only the same man in a Britain subjected to different circumstances. What is being tested here are the limits of the state, not the individual. The play, indeed, creates several ironic parallels between the actual present of the frame and the alternative present of the tale: in both, British decline is a source of discontent; America and Germany are said to be surpassing Britain economically and technologically; and British foreign policy in both is a response to the threat from Russia. The parallels add an extra level of complexity to the work, but they don't encourage us to think that the war was a pyrrhic victory for Britain, that its outcome was tantamount to defeat. In fact, the parallels seem partly designed to raise and refute such doubts: in the summer of 1940, it seems to insist, Britain's decline might have been unavoidable but its soul was yet to be lost or saved. Thus, despite the cynicism of the postwar generation, "our finest hour and all that" was actually a turning point at which Britain made the right decision, and yet it might have gone wrong.

And this drama also implies that the British state or one of its offspring still might go wrong, for even though in actuality the summer-of-1940 turning point was safely negotiated, the potential for British Nazification persists in the legacies of imperialism. The polemical point of the tale is that Britons and former Britons who would currently use force to retain their dominance over resistant peoples in, for example, Rhodesia or South Africa were behaving as though Nazi ideology had won the day. A short novelization of the play, which also came out in 1964, underlined its anti-imperial implications by stressing that, although the protagonist is not an ideological Nazi, he keenly supports their war because he believes it will preserve the British Empire. The complaints of those around him echo the sentiments of actual Britons—Britain is becoming a second-rate power, losing its international prestige, and falling behind others in productive capacity—but the British soldier focuses on imperial dominion, and the Germans exploit that obsession. As the work's science-fiction style conclusion emphasizes, it is the protagonist's dedication to the empire that turns him into a hybrid creature, with the body parts of colonials and the mind of a Nazi.

To be sure, by 1964 Britain had committed itself to decolonization, and most Britons seemed to accept the judgment delivered by Conservative prime minister Harold Macmillan, in his "Winds of Change" speech, that old-fashioned imperialism was a thing of the past, which was being replaced in a natural progression that had begun centuries earlier: "In the twentieth century, and especially since the end of the war, the processes which gave birth to the nation states of Europe have been repeated all over the world. We have seen the awakening of national consciousness in peoples who have for centuries lived in dependence upon some other power. . . . We must all accept it as a fact, and our national policies must take account of it."[41] The speech signaled a shift in the self-characterization of the British state from a ruling imperial power to a hegemonic leader of a Commonwealth of newly emerging states. The attempt was to create continuity by preserving a base of power independent of both the new European Economic Community and the United States. Cooper's story seems to conform to that version of voluntary decolonial transition; after all, fighting for the old empire in the alternate world is a German-inspired project, whereas granting independence and Commonwealth status to the new nations is the result of the victory over Nazism.

Nevertheless, the out-of-time form spreads the shadow of imperialism over the actual present as well. It reminds us, for example, that the most prominent pro-imperialist organization of the postwar years, the League of Empire Loyalists, was led by a former member of the British Union of Fascists. Even more salient in 1964 were the references to British Africa, for the struggle between the Rhodesian government (which sought independence for a nation ruled by a white minority) and the British government (which was insisting on majority rule for Commonwealth status) was reaching a climax in that year. The atemporality of *The Other Man*'s form allows for the superimposition of the former empire onto the current Rhodesian attempt to maintain white power: the alternate universe's imperialism may be a road not taken by Britain, but it nevertheless resembles the path Rhodesia seemed to be traveling. Furthermore, both routes branch off of one and the same British imperial road. Thus, by 1964 alternate-history fiction was being used not only as contemporary satire but also as a means of opening the actual British past, especially its imperial phase, to critical examination. This complex of references might furthermore be seen as a way of coping with the loss of the colonies: it implies that imperialism was a proto-totalitarian inclination in the British state and that the natural progression of history requires its extinction.

COLD WAR: NORMALIZING THE ALTERNATE PAST AND FEARING A LOSS OF HISTORY

There was plenty in the politics of the late 1960s and 1970s to support the view that Nazism lurked inside British history and culture. As we saw in the last chapter, a series of reactions against immigration from Commonwealth countries, sometimes dominated by explicitly racist organizations using neo-Nazi slogans and iconography, put images of Nazi Britons in the news and generated numerous counterreactions, including the books and television shows we've examined that purported to show what a German occupation would have entailed. But these developments—the neo-Nazi activities and the anti-neo-Nazi counterfactual speculations—worked in concert to make the general scene of an imaginary Britain under Nazi occupation increasingly familiar and ripe for commercial exploitation. Consequently, taking advantage of the automatic *frisson* of the setting, writers from the late 1970s until the present have produced mass-market novels blending Nazi Britain alternate history with the most typically British popular genre, the detective novel—or more precisely the detective-cum-espionage novel. It is a natural coupling because spy novels also tell stories of the state, and the detective/spy genre already featured a split state in its standard plot: a detective routinely investigating a crime stumbles into some international intrigue that exposes both the state's internal tensions and its activities in the occulted nether world of international espionage. The police force, in the person of the detective, represents a form of coercive state power that comes into contact with ordinary citizens in the course of enforcing the law and protecting the law abiding. The secret intelligence services, in contrast, are hidden from the public so that they can gather information and guard the nation against foreign and domestic threats; they thus stand in for all of those shadowy aspects of the state that lie beyond the people's ken. In detective/spy novels, the figure of the visible—and partially controllable—state, the police detective, ventures into the dark state's territory.

During the Cold War especially, the genre's attraction lay in its promise to reveal the penetralia of the invisible state (where interagency conflict thrives) as well as the structure and workings of a vast system of secret interstate and supra-state entities. Thus the detective/spy novel was already structured like an alternate-world novel, for the actual universe of international espionage is so deeply surreptitious that it can be conceived of as a parallel universe. Separated from us by an invisible but also usually impenetrable membrane, the espionage world operates according to its own rules and is a rich source of alternative narratives to the official, public histories of international relations. These similarities between the spy and alternate-history genres remind us, once again, of the centuries-old connections between secret-history and counterfactual-history narrative. Like alternate-history authors, moreover, the writers of the detective/spy genre spend most of their time in world making, tracing out the unfamiliar global networks of spies, counterspies, and non–state agents like multinational corporations, arms dealers, and international terrorist moles.

Mapping all of these features onto a counterfactual-historical landscape like Nazi Britain both magnified the parallel-universe effect and created a novelty item in a crowded generic field.

Len Deighton, the author of numerous earlier spy novels, first transposed the detective/spy plot onto the Nazi Britain setting in 1978. *SS-GB*, as his novel was tersely titled, quickly became a best seller, and almost every Nazi Britain novel since has been in the genre.[42] *SS-GB* features a Scotland Yard detective (an appropriate symbol of the surviving remnant of British government), who performs his routine duties, as he did under the former state, until some unusual features of a murder investigation attract the attention of the Waffen-SS in Berlin. As in most spy novels, the plot turns on internecine conflict: one faction of the SS conspires with the Wehrmacht, a cabal of English aristocrats, and an American spy to steal nuclear secrets. The details of the plot are less important than the reframing of the WWII material inside the Cold War genre, which significantly alters the character of the state. Whereas in the earlier stories and alternate histories of the late 1960s and early 1970s the hazardous life of Britain under Nazi dominion was beset by ideological and moral perils, in *SS-GB* all players—whether representing the British government in exile, the German occupation, or the Americans—seem morally comparable, if not entirely interchangeable, and they pursue their aims with equal ruthlessness.

The detective in this Cold War genre usually serves as the reader's proxy; he learns to live with the understanding that the state he serves can never fully see itself, can never establish control over itself, and will always protect itself through opacity, deceit, and indifference to ideological purity. To be sure, setting these lessons in Nazi-occupied Britain does make them seem unusually disturbing even as it maximizes the distance between the people's nation, lodged in Britain's remnants, and the secret state of arbitrary power and totalitarian Nazi opaqueness. But *SS-GB* goes to great lengths to illustrate that the British government in exile is equally secretive and devious; indeed, one of its agents engineers the death of King George VI in order to bring the Americans into the conflict. And thus it follows the logic of most Cold War detective/spy novels, where British agencies become mirror images of enemy agencies in order to be effective, leading to a world in which all participating states, totalitarian and democratic alike, are riven by alien elements, secret plots, and self-concealment. The Nazi Britain schema of *SS-GB* might be said to reframe that familiar Cold War version of realpolitik by merging it with the earlier British willingness to fight a total war; World War II and the Cold War become blended in one continuous struggle for national survival. In the mixture, the detective/spy-novel form took on some of the nostalgic conviction about the stakes of the conflict that still adhered to the wartime setting. But the genre's commitment to the irrelevance of ideology and the constancy of moral ambiguity tend to mute the self-questioning implicit in other uses of the Nazi Britain trope, which becomes just another setting in this novel.

Indeed, reviewers complained that Deighton's Nazi Britain was merely a backdrop, without any intrinsic relation to the plot, and one recent historian of the form, Gavriel Rosenfeld, sees the book's failure to depict any real "horror" as evidence that the history of the Third Reich was being "normalized" by the late 1970s.[43] In Rosenfeld's view, the earlier, more dystopian alternate-history speculations about the consequences of a Nazi victory emphasized its "abnormality," its singular trauma-inducing terrors, whereas the later ones tended to downplay what would have been its distinctive crimes and to suggest that Britons might have come to live submissively under its yoke.[44] Rosenfeld's analysis may be open to numerous objections, the chief of which is that his idea of "normalization" is so broad and vague that it could be applied to most counterfactual speculations about the possible consequences of a Nazi victory.[45] It could, after all, even be applied to most histories of Nazism that try to understand its sources and dynamics and thereby go beyond what Rosenfeld seems to approve of as a starting point: "a shared belief in Nazism's absolute evil."[46] Moral outrage may be a powerful motivation to historical analysis, but the category of "absolute evil" is ipso facto outside of history.[47] Nevertheless, Rosenfeld is right to notice that *SS-GB* pushes the ideological dimensions of the struggle against Germany into the background and that it was not designed, as the alternate *histories* of the sixties and the seventies were, to inform readers about actual Nazi occupations and the suffering they caused. We can, therefore, agree that Len Deighton's book draws on the familiar setting created by the earlier works and uses it to increase the stakes of an otherwise generic narrative of wartime intrigue; in that sense it can be said to "normalize" Nazism.

There was, though, another, opposite tendency in the fictions of the period: far from enacting "normalization" several of them focused on it explicitly as a problem. Indeed, exploring how alternate norms would have been born out of different historical conditions becomes an increasingly overt and dominant theme. As these writers turned their attention to the processes of adjusting norms, especially to the state's role in revising or erasing the actual historical record, they began to reflect on the growing temporal gap between their present and the nexus moments—the moments of national decision—they were attempting to revive in their fictions. How might a German-dominated Britain have used the mere passage of time and restoration of peace to make an appalling past seem acceptable because inevitable? Turning the process of normalization into an explicit topic is, indeed, built into the Nazi Britain alternate-history project, for any plausible parallel reality must seem at least habitable. If the social order in the alternate world is so brutally dystopian as to be unlivable, then it will cease to qualify as a viable alternative arrangement. Nazi Britain portrayals often thus faced the major formal challenge common to dystopias: how to imagine life going on in a world too oppressive for normal people to inhabit.

One obvious solution is to change what "normal" means; indeed, for British writers especially, dystopias were defined by their techniques for altering subjective standards. The locus classicus for the theme was, of course, George Orwell's *1984* (1949), which imaged subjects who have so thoroughly internalized state authority, via an electronic version of the Benthamite panopticon, that they are incapable of developing individual desires or oppositional consciousness. Moreover, *1984* was an especially apt precedent for the Nazi Britain fictions because it views the totalitarian mega-state that had swallowed Britain, "Oceana," from the perspective of the "Ministry of Truth," where the protagonist, Winston Smith, alters historical records to fit the ruling Party's official version of the past. Orwell's novel thereby stressed the pivotal importance of controlling the historical record in order to maintain the illusion of the status quo's ordinariness. By destroying knowledge of the past, the origins of the existing hierarchy are hidden and, crucially, the notion of any alternative eliminated: "The Party member, like the proletarian, tolerates present-day conditions partly because he has no standards of comparison."[48] The protagonist's mode of rebellion, his "thoughtcrime," is his short-lived refusal to accept the Party's control over both national history and his own personal memory.

The first Nazi Britain fiction to explore this Orwellian theme of normalizing the totalitarian state by censoring its history was a BBC miniseries titled *An Englishman's Castle*, written by the prolific film and television screenwriter Philip Mackie, which aired in 1978, the same year that Len Deighton's *SS-GB* was published.[49] The three-episode program followed Orwell's precedent closely by exploring the re-creation of collective memory and identity in an alternate 1978. Although its world is nothing like the joyless, standardized, oppressive milieu of *1984*, it is in some ways more insidious. The alternate London at first looks like the viewers': it seems prosperous, and the characters we encounter are not pale listless bureaucrats like Orwell's Winston Smith but affluent writers, actors, directors, and BBC studio executives. Gradually we come to see that the state is manipulating the chattering classes by techniques of social control that encourage pleasure seeking and foster the illusion of freedom, both of which, the show implies, would have been more effective in the long run than the intolerable privation and coercion of *1984*'s Oceana. This seems a dystopia informed by the New Left's critique of liberal consumerism. Instead of faceless bureaucrats, there are celebrity members of the culture industry; instead of overt propaganda, there is stupefying popular entertainment encouraging passivity; instead of universal deprivation, regimentation, obtrusive spying, and harsh physical coercion, there is the "repressive desublimation" (to use Herbert Marcuse's phrase) of sexual permissiveness, personal expression, and private luxury. As a consequence, this is not your usual Nazi Britain. Most noticeably, it does not contain any occupying Germans. By 1978, they have become an absent presence because most Britons know their rules and quietly follow them.

It is only slowly revealed that Britain's partial autonomy depends on its ruthless promulgation of Nazi racial policies; the eradication of "non-Aryans" from the population, it turns out, is the historical chapter most deeply repressed in the national psyche. Once again, the contrast with *1984* is telling: whereas the earlier book imagined a vast bureaucracy purging the historical record and forging new documents (the model was Stalin's Soviet Union), *An Englishman's Castle* relies on the psychology of collective guilt: "We cleaned up the West Indian Problem, the East Indian Problem, the Jewish problem, and all the ethnic problems . . . thirty years ago." "People have forgotten," a British Broadcasting executive explains: "They've forgotten because they wanted to forget. They've pushed it out of their minds. You can't remind them." The hero, who is writing a historical drama—we'll get to that in a moment—wants to include a character named "Rosenfeld" among the British troops, a friend who was deported in racial purges, but the studio executive explains that the Germans would be affronted by the appearance of a character with a Jewish name and might use it as excuse to interfere in the operations of British Broadcasting: "They might even take away our monopoly!" The hero's awakening is also occasioned by a romance with an actress who, it turns out, is clandestinely Jewish and therefore in danger of deportation and extermination. Thus, Britain's parallel-universe normalcy relies on the nation's willingness to impose a racial test for inclusion.

The theme of racial violence in the United Kingdom obviously points to its prominence in British politics over the previous decade and a half, when the end of the empire had led to an increase in the number of people migrating to the United Kingdom from former colonies. Even slight increases in the numbers of West Indians and East Indians in the cities were met with alarm, and radical right-wing groups, including some who were openly neo-Nazi, exploited the fear. Many of the newcomers were, officially, already British subjects from the colonies who could not legally be denied entry, and consequently a debate arose over the very meaning of the word "British," in which the dichotomy between demos and ethnos appeared once again. A gap opened between citizenship, or belonging to the state, and "Britishness," or belonging to the body of the people. The Conservative politician Enoch Powell, one of the most persistent and effective leaders of the anti-migrant movement, called attention in the early 1970s to precisely that gap when he argued that an African or an Asian might have British citizenship but that did not make him a "Briton."[50] Thus the state/people dichotomy was aggressively asserting itself anew: the state could deem people citizens whom the majority might still try to shut out from the ranks of the people. These issues became entwined with the history of the war and the meaning of British victory because each side claimed that it was staying true to the values of that effort by protecting national distinctiveness: liberals connected skinhead youths sporting swastikas to anti-migration politicians, while those politicians declared that ethnic Britons had not "won that war only to hand over parts of our territory to alien races."[51]

As the years went on, Labour and Conservative governments made concessions to both sides in this debate over what should constitute the identity of the nation. On the one hand, a series of immigration acts, which effectively restricted the rights of mainly nonwhite Commonwealth subjects to live and work in the United Kingdom, attempted to appease those who feared being "swamped" by immigrants. On the other hand, the passage of a series of race relations acts from 1965 to 1976, which combated discrimination against those already in the country, gave some reassurance to those who feared that Britain was refusing to be an enlightened, inclusive, and multiethnic nation, with an identity based on historical responsibilities, laws, and institutional continuity rather than on genealogy. By the time *An Englishman's Castle* was produced in 1978, this controversy was more muted in mainstream politics, but the previous two years had seen a revival of skinhead neo-Nazi activity that brought it again to national attention. Punk rockers sporting swastikas and pictures of David Bowie giving a Nazi salute were in the press, and one House of Commons Commission reported "deplorable outbursts of racial violence" against numerous minority groups in London's East End.[52]

Newly exposed racist tendencies among Britons were not the only signs that the principled distinctions between themselves and the Nazis were blurring and thus a sense of the moral importance of their wartime victory was fading from memory.[53] There was an even more direct assault on the historical record from the English writer David Irving, whose *Hitler's War*, an exculpatory account of Hitler's motives and actions, had appeared in 1977. The seventies had already seen a number of fringe works denying or minimizing the enormity of the Holocaust, but Irving was the first well-known British writer to promulgate what became known as "negationist views," which although they did not deny the Holocaust outright, sowed skepticism about the records on which its historiography is based. Although Irving's book was strongly criticized and finally discredited by academic historians, it sold very well. These were the most obvious contemporary targets of *An Englishman's Castle*: a world in which characters must struggle to remember the actual historical record is a world in which the Nazis have metaphorically won. And, of course, the logic implicitly casts Irving and his ilk as the representatives in the actual world of the would-have-been Nazi rulers.

All of this helps to contextualize *An Englishman's Castle*, but it does not fully explain the paradoxical logic by which a counterfactual-historical fiction champions actual history. For that we need to return to the normalization theme and trace the ways in which it implicates the viewing audience. The first episode of the miniseries makes the alternate and actual presents indistinguishable by opening with a dramatization of their common historical starting point. The first shot is of the television studio's production booth during the taping of a scene set in the summer of 1940. The episode we see being made takes place on the eve of the invasion, as a middle-class family anticipates history's further unfolding: will their prime minister, the mother wonders, be reasonable like the French and make peace? Her soldier son denounces the very suggestion, and the episode ends with the family in conflict and the invasion still only a possibility. Not until we later see the screenwriter and a studio executive discussing the show's enormous popularity do we realize that we have been watching a historical soap opera being produced in a 1978 where the invasion succeeded. The show within the show at first seems to be a parody of the counterfactual scenarios we know so well, in which brave Britons fight off their invaders. Then, as subsequent episodes unfold, each around a familiar counterfactual node—the loss of the Battle of Britain, the acceptance of a cease-fire—the show within the show seems to invite the viewer to register, first, that depictions of counterfactual invasions have also become a cliché and, second, that these are subtly different from our norm. The premise of a German victory in itself no longer has an edge or the power to shock or outrage us; overfamiliarity has rendered it banal, a judgment ironically echoed by all of the characters in the alternate present, who think the show within the show is a hackneyed potboiler. The characters in the alternate present, however, regard as most clichéd the very things that look unusual to us: the history of 1940 is being delicately edited and revised to foreshadow and justify the acceptance of defeat. The Bible and the English literary canon are rifled to square with its overall quietism. Young soldiers in the field quote Ecclesiastes ("Better a live dog than a dead lion") and Boswell's Johnson ("I would not give half a guinea to live under one form of Government rather than another. It is of no moment to the happiness of an individual").[54] The paterfamilias of the show within the show recommends the stolid virtue of "survival above all" as the key to the national character.

In contrast to *1984*, which starts with a big blast of defamilarization, *An Englishman's Castle* wants viewers to think they are at home, and then gradually introduces hints of the totalitarian underpinnings of this apparent normalcy. The technique is designed to illustrate that reasonable Britons might have been led to regard a Nazi-dominated Britain as routine—not uninhabitable, death-dealing, or unbearably destructive—if the regime had exercised its power indirectly and maintained the trappings of personal freedom for the "Aryan" Britons who survived the postwar racial purges. Advertising the fact that "BIG BROTHER IS WATCHING YOU" is not the sort of thing this regime would do. Instead, its propaganda is summarized in the title: *An Englishman's Castle*, which names both the historical soap opera and the three-episode miniseries about its production. Obviously alluding to the maxim that "an Englishman's home is his castle," it reminds viewers in the alternate world that sovereignty was always based in the personal realm of the home, and because their privacy seems to remain inviolate, they are still free. Like *Loss of Eden* thirty-eight years earlier, *An Englishman's Castle* exposes flight into private life as the source of the national capitulation in the first place, and it then depicts the connivance of the culture industry in the regime's message that nothing very unusual has happened, that they have been faithful to their history and are the same people living under the same values. The war was the break with normalcy, and the cease-fire, followed by general amnesty for the ethnically acceptable, was its restoration. Thus the title also reminds actual viewers that the limitation of the idea of sovereignty to the private sphere serves as psychic compensation for the foreign captivity of the state, and it indicates that the dramatic tension will arise on the borders between the personal and the political, which is exactly where it appears.

Again following and adjusting the precedent of *1984*, the protagonist is the writer of the show within the show, who at first seems ambivalently amenable to representing the 1940 invasion in terms that will not offend German sensibilities: as an inevitable prelude to a peaceful and prosperous German-dominated Europe. Unlike Orwell's hero, though, this writer thinks he will be allowed to draw on his personal transformation from resistance fighter to pacified civilian in order to explore the nation's alteration. "I can't rewrite history," he insouciantly explains to the studio executive. "Of course not," the executive urbanely retorts, "but how are you going to present it?" When the writer slowly explains, "Well, the Germans invaded us and we got beaten," the executive insinuates, "Did we?" "I was there, damn it," the writer insists. "I was a soldier!" But the studio executive blandly muses: "I wasn't old enough to be in the forces, but of course I remember it, too. I look back on it now as a victory . . . a victory for common sense, humanity, decency; a triumph for peace-loving people everywhere." Obviously unconvinced but unwilling to prolong the disagreement, the writer laconically answers: "I suppose that's one way of looking at it." The exchange sets up a memory versus official history dichotomy that resembles the conflict in the mind of Orwell's Winston Smith, but here the specific issue is whether the war was "lost." This writer thus struggles to protect his personal integrity by insisting that the loss he experienced actually happened, whereas the studio executive tries to revise it out of existence, providing a strikingly concrete instance of what psychoanalytic thinkers might characterize as the eventuality of losing loss itself. Despite his general willingness to cooperate with the authorities, the process of writing the series within the series continually puts the writer in touch with different instances of the loss denied by the official version of history. He wants to represent the death of his "romantic, patriotic" self by killing off the resistance-fighter protagonist of the soap opera but faces objections from the cast, who insist that the only reason for writing such "drivel" should be to provide actors with employment; he is censored when he remembers and tries to include his Jewish friend from 1940. *An Englishman's Castle* thus makes explicit an insight that *1984* could not quite articulate: even in the process of *revising* the historical record, memories are stirred and the repressive psychological mechanism begins to fail. But is there any actual history that gets lost in this story of defeat and capitulation? Since there was no invasion, no state subjugation, no racial purging, what has been lost if the nation forgets to remember these nonevents?

Orwell's *1984*, again, helps us to see the answer by stating explicitly that history's main political use is its preservation of alternatives. As yet another cautionary tale, *1984* was engaged in an implicit dialogue with the future-conjectural elements of *The Lion and the Unicorn*, in which Orwell had trumpeted the immediate historical momentousness of 1940 as a national crossroads where Britons would make a choice between futures. His *1984* visualizes in place of the revolution a postwar shift away from deliberative collective choice making and argues that the resulting totalitarianism would rest on the state's obliteration of the people's ability to differentiate between historical situations. That is, the totalitarian world would erase the nation's temporal dimension. For all of their differences, Orwell's two books concur on the importance of the nation knowing the actual narrative, being able to orient itself in the dimension of time so that it can assess the stakes of its present actions. In *1984*, of course, the Allies are supposed to have won the war, for Oceana is formed after America has taken over the old British Empire, the Cold War has turned hot in the 1950s, and then cooled down again in the face of assured mutual atomic destruction.

Alternatively, *An Englishman's Castle* gives a counterfactual genealogy for a more deeply disguised form of totalitarian history loss, but it nonetheless cleaves to this Orwellian premise that historical consciousness is the ground of democratic sentiment because it makes people conscious of the meaning of their past and present actions. History opens a view of the alternatives they once hoped to achieve or avoid. Losing the sense that they had lost the war would mean forgetting what the fighting had been about and foreclosing curiosity about what military victory might have brought, thus disabling judgment of the present arrangement. Orwell stresses totalitarian denial of variation through time—current enemies of the Party must always have been its enemies; current international allies must always have been allies—lest the people realize that the present might be otherwise. The TV series takes a more direct route to asserting the possibility of alternative current realities: instead of seeing variations over time, we are presented with a parallel concurrent versions, suggesting that alternate history is in itself an antidote to authoritarianism. Since the revisions of the history of 1940 inside the show within the show are aimed at cutting off visualizations of a superior present, *An Englishman's Castle* indicates that Nazi totalitarianism would have precluded not history tout court but *counterfactual* history, the hypothetical mode that most strenuously keeps the alternatives alive. What the characters in the alternate world are in danger of losing is therefore an ability to imagine our world, or actual history. The point of the series is to produce the distance from our history that can allow us to see it as extraordinary and desirable precisely because it was not inevitable. Seen from the alternate perspective, it ceases to be the merely given, the self-evident. Thus counterfactuality, far from being opposed to actual history, seems rather a crucial mode of imagining its vitality, consequences, and ongoing significance; it becomes actual history's champion. And yet, simultaneously, the series seems bent on discouraging political complacency. By visualizing this alternate present and noting its uncanny resemblances to our own, *An Englishman's Castle*, like so many other Nazi Britain fantasies, implies that the nexus moment is not really over: the fruits of the victory are still ours to enjoy or to lose.

BEYOND THE NATION: FATHERLAND AND HISTORY LOSS AT THE END OF THE COLD WAR

Robert Harris's *Fatherland* (1992) was the first alternate-history novel to become an international best seller, partly by broadening the scene from Nazi Britain to Nazi Europe in the immediate context of German unification. Nevertheless, its roots in the British dystopian tradition are obvious. Like *An Englishman's Castle*, it builds on Orwell's foundational idea about the totalitarian state's need to control history, but it extends the theme into a more complex understanding of the processes of historical oblivion. Harris had read Deighton's *SS-GB* and followed its formula as well, plotting his alternate history in the form of a detective-spy thriller, although *Fatherland*'s detective-hero is an SS officer working for the criminal police (the Kripo) in 1964 Berlin. A successful blockade of British Isles along with several other small changes in the actual history of the war, we learn, had delivered a German victory, and Nazi Britain, which gets little explicit attention in this novel, is ruled by Edward VIII and Queen Wallis. A few wry allusions to its cultural exports help maintain the continuity between our 1964 and that of the alternative world—Cecil Beaton and the Beatles are on the scene, whereas George Orwell and Graham Greene are proscribed and must be secretly printed—but this alternate world is centered in Berlin, and most points of world convergence/contrast affect the whole of German Europe. There are birth-control pills and an increasingly rebellious antiwar youth movement protesting "the seemingly endless struggle against the American-backed Soviet guerillas, which had been grinding on east of the Urals for twenty years."[55] The early phases of *Fatherland*, like those of *An Englishman's Castle*, feature slight alterations and inversions of the familiar, pointing away from an obviously Orwellian dystopia and toward a subtler totalitarian reality. In keeping with the late Cold War atmosphere in which it was conceived, though, *Fatherland*'s world is redolent of the crumbling Soviet Union rather than the affluent consumerist Britain of *An Englishman's Castle*. Most of its latter-day Nazis practice the "cynical reason" that had been recently described by the German philosopher and cultural theorist Peter Sloterdijk: aware of the distance between their actual social reality and the party's official assertions about it, the Germans nonetheless collude in the falsifications and act *as if* they were true.[56] This state of mind, which has some resemblances to *1984*'s "doublethink," preempts attempts to expose the regime's falsehoods, for the majority of people disbelieve them in advance. "Thoughtcrimes" pose no threat. Despite its war-weariness, overextension, economic stagnation, and the corruption and laxity of most of its citizens, then, the Nazi state still wields immense power. The novel poses the question of whether such a regime could survive the full revelation of its wartime crimes, which it has, thus far, succeeded in suppressing. Thus the telos of the plot is the resurrection of a buried history.

Harris uses the standard device—the police detective entangled in state secrets through a routine murder investigation—to enter the totalitarian labyrinth and recover the history that we already know. Indeed, the "secret" in this book is the very thing readers are expected to consider the metonymic essence of Nazism, the act that reveals its unspeakable depravity: the Holocaust. Hypothesizing that the victorious Germans would have destroyed all traces of the genocide against the Jews immediately after the war and that the regime would later have systematically eliminated the planners and direct perpetrators, the novel asks if they could have succeeded in presenting themselves to the world as a normal, legitimate member of the international community. In 1964, at the opening of the novel, normalization seems the only hope for the regime's continuation: the war in the east is draining the Reich's resources, and Berlin is plagued by terrorist attacks, but U.S. president Joseph P. Kennedy Sr. seems ready to regularize relations with the former enemy.

This is the world in which *Kriminalpolizei* detective, Xavier March, discovers the assassination of Josef Bühler. In actual history, Bühler served as state secretary to Hans Frank, the governor-general of the Polish territories, and attended the Wannsee Conference as Frank's deputy for the planning of the Final Solution in early 1942. He was executed in Poland in 1948, but in the alternate history he lives a prosperous postwar life in Berlin, close to the very site of the conference itself on the shore of the Wannsee. His assassination, unsuccessfully disguised as a suicide by the SS leader Odilo Globocnik (also a historical figure, nicknamed "Globus," who was responsible for operations at the death camps and actually took his own life in 1945), arouses the detective protagonist's curiosity. He thus begins following a trail of other suspicious recent deaths of *Alter Kämpfer*. Since we learn early on that detective March, a former U-boat captain who spent the entire war under the water, is singularly curious about what happened to the Jewish families who previously lived in Berlin, we are also aware that the genocide is a secret. As the protagonist later declares, "We knew, but we didn't have the facts," so his countrymen have pretended that the Jews had simply been resettled in the east (352). Aided by an American newspaper woman, the detective stays on the case despite the objections of his superiors until he uncovers the cover-up, making contact with the last surviving participant in the Wannsee conference, receiving the contraband documentation of the planning and execution of the Holocaust, and passing it off to the American to be perhaps smuggled out of the Reich just in time to disrupt a planned peace conference between Hitler and President Kennedy.

Fatherland may well have owed its unprecedented success to the brilliance of this device, in which the detective form is used to reveal a secret that is known to the reader all along. The structure, we should note, creates the same kind of desire we've seen in most Nazi Britain fictions. We imagine losing an overly familiar piece of our reality, one that we take for granted and even have ambivalent feelings about, so that we can actively want it and participate vicariously in the struggle to recover it. Again, the contrast to *An Englishman's Castle* is instructive. In the television series, the missing object also appeared to be history, but the recovery of its memory was in the service of retrieving a truly independent British state, so state sovereignty was still the ultimate object of desire. The lost object here, though, is not a state but the knowledge of history's most notorious state crime. To be sure, the crime in the alternate world is even more egregious than the one we know; the novel estimates that over ten million Jews, rather than six million, would have died as a consequence of complete German victory in Europe. Thus, at one level, this book triggers the usual response to Nazi-victory counterfactuals: "Thank God we stopped them."[57] But the novel by no means tries to relativize the actual genocide; indeed, the emphasis instead is on the absolute horror of what happened in our own world and, moreover, on the *actuality* of the intention to exterminate even more people. Clearly, the knowledge of these aspects of our history brings no one solace, and yet the narrative incites in the reader a positive desire to find and then disseminate the proof of them.

Murder mysteries usually create narrative desire by hiding the cause of the death at the story's outset, whereas in this novel, the fictional world's mystery early on becomes an open book to us; most readers have no trouble predicting where the detective's work will lead him. Our fascination is held not by wanting to *know* what is behind the crime but by wanting to *realize* it, for in the course of the story we begin to understand that we, like the people in the alternate world, tend to look away from this history. We are unable to acknowledge how important a feature of our mental landscape it actually is. Thus, what we gain by imagining its suppression and then plotting the perils of its retrieval is the knowledge of how much we should want this knowledge. In the diegetic world, to be sure, the possibility of an ultimate victory for the former Allied powers lingers sporadically around the edges, but the central realization exacted here is an acknowledgment that we tend to lose awareness of the enormous loss sustained despite the victory. And yet, by suggesting that the alternate 1964 might have been so cynical and inured to violence that the revelation of the Holocaust could no longer make any difference, *Fatherland* both creates a kind of nostalgia for the actual postwar world, in which it mattered, and also warns that our consciousness of the events is precarious even now.

When Robert Harris began writing *Fatherland* in 1989, he was asking his readers to imagine the suppression of the events that served as the traumatic background of the postwar international order; it was only after several months of writing that the Berlin Wall fell, and he realized that the actual world order was changing rapidly. The novel was published in the context of German reunification, and its popularity is often attributed to contemporary apprehensions about the dominance of a united Germany in Europe. But we need to consider West Germany in the 1980s to understand the novel's inspiration. The Britain that Margaret Thatcher led in the 1980s was dismantling its "postwar settlement" (which had included collectivism, a mixed economy, and the welfare state); the neo-Nazi youth culture was waning in the United Kingdom, and interest in the war's legacy was generally dwindling as the population aged. Perhaps for those reasons, no alternate-history WWII work was published in Britain during the decade. But in West Germany, interest in the Nazi past was growing. The early eighties saw what was called the "Hitler Wave"; as the fiftieth anniversary of National Socialism's rise to power approached in 1983, a topic that had earlier been avoided became newly fashionable. In the middle of the decade, West German conservative politicians attempted to make the nation's past seem relatively normal, insisting that the brief twelve-year period of Nazi rule was a mere aberration, involving only a small minority of Germans, the majority of whom went on living decent lives, untouched by the horrors. West German chancellor Helmut Kohl even tried to enforce that view internationally when he pressured President Ronald Reagan to pay his respects to German war dead at the Kolmeshöhe Cemetery, near Bitburg on the fortieth anniversary of V-E Day. Because forty-nine members of the Waffen-SS were buried there, close to the spot where Reagan was to lay a wreath, the planned ceremony was denounced internationally, and the president later admitted that the incident had opened old wounds rather than closing them.[58] Then, in 1986, the eminent German historian Ernst Nolte ignited the "historians' dispute," or *Historikerstreit*, when he recommended abandoning what he called the "negative myth" of the Third Reich, which cast it as the ne plus ultra of evil, and argued instead that National Socialism was comparable to other forms of early twentieth-century totalitarianism, adding that it learned its brutality from the Bolsheviks.[59] He was immediately accused of downplaying German war crimes, and the debate raged on internationally for three years, leaving the impression that many German intellectuals, although certainly not the majority, were all too ready to draw a "line under the German past," as Nolte put it.

When *Fatherland* appeared, its author was already known as a critic of the new tendency toward minimizing the Third Reich's atrocities. Harris's earlier book, *Selling Hitler* (1986) narrated and analyzed one of the decade's most bizarre attempts to recast Nazism as just another manifestation of totalitarianism, rather than a singularly inhumane and genocidal system: the Hitler diary hoax. In 1983, a petty German con man tricked an illustrious group of organizations and individuals—the German magazine *Der Stern*, the London newspaper the *Sunday Times*, the renowned British historian Hugh Trevor Roper, and *Newsweek* magazine in New York—into believing that a bunch of notebooks he was filling with the pretended daily reflections of the führer (most of them banal and all of them drawn from a single readily available historical source) were actually Hitler's lost and rediscovered diaries. Despite the unlikeliness of the assertion, the publishers of *Stern* paid millions for the notebooks (dealing through a *Stern* reporter, himself fooled, who served as intermediary) and then sold copyrights to the *Sunday Times* and *Newsweek*. But the publishing coup turned into a nightmare when the news conference, which *Stern* had called to announce the serialization of these "diaries," became a raucous public exposure of their fraudulence, followed by a noisy international scandal, acrimonious reproaches, and, finally, criminal prosecutions.

Selling Hitler tells a gripping, sensational story, and Harris, who was the political editor at the *Observer* at the time, worked the material into a mordant critique of the greed and haste of the publishing industry, as well as the disregard for truth of "scoop-happy" reporters. He also made it clear that, although the forged diaries were primarily a money-making scheme, part of their appeal was their portrayal of Hitler as an ordinary nice guy, who was appalled by *Kristallnacht* and shocked by the war mongering of Churchill. In the diaries, Hitler admires Neville Chamberlain, sends Hermann Hesse on a sincere peace mission to Britain, and, of course, has no knowledge of the Holocaust. In short, the phony diaries were an attempt to forge a historical record in which Hitler could still be seen as a legitimate leader, peace loving and innocent of any crimes that other Nazis might have committed. Harris ends *Selling Hitler* with a chilling counterfactual about what might have happened if the forger had been better at his job and had produced documents using period-appropriate materials to thwart expert falsification: "After all, *Stern* and News International stopped publication only because of the conclusiveness of the forensic tests. . . . If those tests had found nothing substantially wrong, the diaries would now stand as an historical source. No doubt they would have been dismissed by most serious scholars, but nevertheless they would have been bought and read by millions."[60]

The links between this counterfactual and *Fatherland* should be obvious. *Selling Hitler* raises the threat of the historical distortion of our own reality, stressing time and again that criminal forgers, like all con men, play on their victims' desires to believe, and the readiness of the editors of *Stern* to participate in their own deception indicated a more general, unconscious willingness to forget and repress the painful facts of the German past.[61] *Fatherland* at once acknowledges this natural inclination to forget—which, we should recall, Ernst Renan placed at the heart of all nation making—and implies that following it in this case would bring a posthumous victory to Hitler: the historical record would come to resemble one that a victorious Third Reich might have invented. Moreover, in researching *Selling Hitler*, Harris had become aware that Hitler himself had created the conditions under which he could escape personal responsibility for the Holocaust by leaving all of the planning and execution of the genocide to others and creating no paper trail leading to himself. The ease with which the forger fooled *Stern* thus appears to confirm the hypothesis that if the Third Reich had been victorious, Hitler's intended cover-up might have worked: the genocide's documentation could have been destroyed, and the people who actively carried it out could have been eliminated if necessary.

Thus the story of the forgery and its exposure in *Selling Hitler* easily transitions into the alternate-history story of the suppression of the documentation of the Holocaust and its discovery. Like other alternate-history scenarios we've examined in these chapters, *Fatherland* was inspired by a current outrage that makes our world look like one the Nazis might have created; it is then only a short step to the inference that the enemy is on the threshold of a deferred victory. We might call these "Hitler wins if" scenarios: if Britain ferociously suppresses independence movements in the colonies, then Hitler wins; if young Britons wearing swastikas beat up immigrants, then Hitler wins; if we forget the enormity of Nazi crimes, then Hitler wins.[62] The alternate-history discourse proper begins with the reversal of the antecedent (if clause) and the consequent (then clause) and the change in the verb's mode and tense: thus "Hitler wins if we are not mindful of the Holocaust" equals "if Hitler had won, we would not have been mindful of the Holocaust."

In this instance, as in *An Englishman's Castle*, the Orwellian threat of history loss—and the responsibility of counterfactual history for preventing it—hovers over the genocide and, through it, the knowledge of the stakes of having won the war. *An Englishman's Castle*, though, implied that people would naturally tend to protect at least their personal memories from the regime's depredations, so that historical events—the loss, as the protagonist puts it, "of the whole Jewish population of the British Isles"—could not easily be obliterated. *Fatherland*, in contrast, warns that the past is easy to lose and extraordinarily difficult to find again. The effort requires not only the forensic and archeological skills of the protagonist but also the help of his trusted friend in the Reich's archive, a maneuver that liberates a cache of documents from a Swiss bank vault, and the wiles of the plucky American journalist tasked with smuggling the evidence out of the Reich. The Reich's steely determination to thwart the effort connects the novel closely to *1984*'s thesis that history is the natural enemy of totalitarianism and might therefore be used to oppose it.

And yet *Fatherland* also stresses the almost inevitable obliteration of the past, repeating *1984*'s speculations about the ontology of the past. Harris makes his debt to Orwell apparent in the torture scenes of *Fatherland*, which reprise the episode of Winston's "reeducation" through electric shock in *1984*.

> "Is it your opinion, Winston, that the past has real existence?"
>
> Again the feeling of helplessness descended upon Winston. His eyes flitted towards the dial. He not only did not know whether "yes" or "no" was the answer that would save him from pain; *he did not even know which answer he believed to be the true one.*
>
> O'Brien smiled faintly. "You are no metaphysician, Winston," he said. "Until this moment you had never considered what is meant by existence. I will put it more precisely. Does the past exist concretely, in space? Is there somewhere or other a place, a world of solid objects, where the past is still happening?"
>
> "No."
>
> "Then where does the past exist, if at all?"
>
> "In records. It is written down."
>
> "In records. And—?"
>
> "In the mind. In human memories."
>
> "In memory. Very well, then. We, the Party, control all records, and we control all memories. Then we control the past, do we not?" (109–10, emphasis added)

Winston finally capitulates to the proposition that the past exists only in the Party's pronouncements, that it literally *is* whatever the Party decrees. He forgets his knowledge of the past that was, and then forgets that he forgets in order to evade pain; history is, quite literally, turned into what hurts in *1984*. The torturer in *Fatherland*, Globus, similarly tells the protagonist (who has been shouting the names of the death camps) that the past is now nonexistent: "'They're just names, March. There's nothing there any more, not even a brick. Nobody will ever believe it. And shall I tell you something? *Part of you can't believe it either.*' Globus spat in his face. . . . 'That's how much the world will care'" (358). Winston's uncertainty about what to believe is copied in March—*"Part of you can't believe it either.* That had been his worst moment—because it was true" (373)—and yet March, unlike Winston, is not defeated by his doubt; instead he abducts his former partner and undertakes a suicidal drive to Auschwitz, where he finds the very bricks—the past existing "concretely, in space"—that Globus denied. Despite Orwell's more pessimistic ending, the two books are equally invested in the idea that the more hidden the past is, the more urgent its resurrection and protection, and through the torture episodes, they heroize the effort. When the torturers claim that indifference is the appropriate response to the nonpresence of the past, we draw the opposite conclusion: presenting it is our responsibility, lest the torturers win.

In *Fatherland*, the lost history is not the past in general but a specific episode whose very atrociousness might consign it to oblivion: the revelation of the Holocaust is particularly threatened, we are repeatedly told, by its supposed unbelievability. Indeed, the novel plays with the idea that its counterfactual premise—German victory—is no less plausible than the actuality of the Holocaust, which, when first revealed, was almost universally declared to be unimaginable.[63] Harris explicitly based Globus's claim that "nobody will ever believe it" on the remarks of an SS officer quoted in Primo Levi's *The Drowned and the Saved*, which stand as the epigraph to the last section of the novel: "However this war may end, we have won the war against you; none of you will be left to bear witness, but even if someone were to survive, the world would not believe him. . . . People will say that the events you describe are too monstrous to be believed" (323). Implausibility is thus yet another level of the genocide's especially precarious ontology, which presents a further paradox: one of the most *remarkable* episodes in history is by its very monstrosity one of the least likely to be credited without extensive documentation.

To be sure, Harris was writing within the growing consensus that, once documented and believed, the mass murder of European Jews had become a watershed in the history of humanity, *the* horrendous event that marked an epoch and has, we're often told, forever darkened our view of human nature, without, of course, darkening it so deeply that we can no longer discern the episode's singular dreadfulness. However, even when its knowledge is firmly established, it is said to be unintelligible—a judgment that tends to place it beyond historical understanding, if not analysis. Isaac Deutscher mused in 1968 that historians will probably never have "a better historical perspective" on "Hitler, Auschwitz, Majdanek, and Treblinka than we do now," but would instead continue to be merely baffled and terrified by the phenomena.[64] Sociologist Jeffrey Alexander has explained that attributions of inexplicability to the Holocaust began to appear more frequently in the 1970s and 1980s and strengthened a tendency toward allegorization of the events as the epitome of wrongdoing. Thus, despite the massive number of historical studies that appeared between the late 1960s and the end of the Cold War, declarations of the genocide's tragic incomprehensibility had become common enough for Harris to echo them in his novel, where the deep unknowability of the events threatens to make them incredible. And yet the novel makes us aware that the inscrutability becomes sacrosanct when the phenomenon symbolizes absolute evil.[65] Primo Levi, for example, insists that it "cannot be comprehended, or rather, *shouldn't* be comprehended, because to comprehend is almost to justify." It is, we are often told, an abysmally sublime event; traumatically suffered, it thwarts representation and coherent remembrance. So, despite the variety of historical explanations of the Holocaust on offer, knowing it in the right way seems to entail also knowing its incomprehensibility.

This odd epistemological status, inside of historical knowledge but outside of historical comprehension, becomes part of the phenomenon's uncanny temporality. Primo Levi, calling for *recognition* of the emotions driving the genocide as opposed to their comprehension, claimed that being able to recognize, or "know again," the signs of such hatred could prevent future genocides: "What has happened can happen again, consciences can again be seduced and obscured: even our own."[66] To recognize it is thus also to anticipate its recurrence, and so the Holocaust (like its Nazi perpetrators) comes to float above the particularities of time and space as the epitome of an unfathomable malevolence that is always looming. However, this mode of knowing in turn seems problematic, since it allows for the dissolution of historically specific guilt into generalizations about the evil inside all of us, and consequently Primo Levi folds these paradoxical issues of historical knowledge back into the basic facts of his personal experience: "I do not know, nor am I particularly interested in knowing, whether a murderer is lurking deep within me, but I do know that I was an innocent victim and not a murderer."[67] *Fatherland*'s invocation of Levi thus complicates the Orwellian theme of history loss by stressing that the impossibility of adequate historical understanding and the temptation of lapsing into universalist clichés are built into the structure of knowing this particular history.

And finally, even if the genocide were acknowledged and believed, as in our own reality, *Fatherland* emphasizes that barriers between knowing and caring remain in place. The novel devotes long passages of dialogue to the causes of such indifference, in which the characters speculate about the probable consequences of their attempted disclosure, thereby projecting our actual experience into the future of the alternate world. Insensibility, the characters tell each other, will paradoxically arise from the vast number of vanished victims, which tends to make the suffering seem abstract and numbs human compassion, and that response will be exacerbated by its placement inside the context of the total civilian war dead in World War II. Moreover, the international propaganda wars will compare the genocide not only to the American atomic-bomb attacks on Hiroshima and Nagasaki but also to Soviet camps and Stalin's mass exterminations. With the passage of time and the winding down of the alternate world's Cold War, they imagine, the disclosure will come to seem even less relevant to the present and would probably become just one more set of statistics underscoring truisms about man's inhumanity to man. Indifference is the modality of loss that *Fatherland* explores most fully because it is the state of mind where the alternate and actual worlds meet. To be sure, Harris invents a plot and setting that give the revelation far greater exigency in the alternate reality than it could ever again achieve in ours—a fact, as I explained at the outset, that structures our desire in this novel—even as he has his characters harp on the threatened unconcern: "Suppose everyone knew all of the details. Who would care? Would it really make any difference?" (288). The insistent questioning, though, is designed not so much to dampen our pleasure in the fictional prospect of punishment for the surviving perpetrators, as to make us reflect on whether knowledge of the Holocaust has made a sufficient difference in our world.[68] We get both a fantasy of impending justice—the accomplishment of which is still just a possibility at the novel's conclusion—and a repeated exhortation to make our own knowledge matter.

Fatherland inaugurated a new phase in the WWII alternate-history novel, and it seems almost, but not quite, to have abandoned the preoccupations of the Nazi Britain fictions. It is, to be sure, still a novel featuring states—mainly Germany and America—as the main historical actors, and yet it would be inaccurate to say that the novel solicits concern about the destinies of these entities. We might think of *Fatherland* as the inverse of the Nazi Britain fictions, which had suggested possible redemption and thereby let us experience the ahistorical side of the concept of the nation, the ways in which it is not synchronous with its actual history. For all of their insistence that Nazism lurks in Britain (in its lack of resolve, class divisions, racism, imperialism, greed), they nevertheless created Britain as revisable and independent of the chronicles of its particular, irrevocable events. False governments may temporarily assume power in the Nazi Britain novels, and yet the character of the imagined community, to use Benedict Anderson's familiar phrase, rebounds because no single destiny defines it. Britain always inhabits a range of possibilities much more capacious than its historical actuality. Just as Nazi Britain fictions reassure us that a true nation might recover from the captivity of its state, *Fatherland* illustrates the inverse premise: the Third Reich was a depraved conspiracy of criminals posing as a state, which will be exposed and expelled from the community of nations.[69] Indeed, the Third Reich is not a genuine nation-state character in the earlier fictions either but only a grotesque simulacrum of one, which haunts the stories of nations as a symbol of radical evil but seems doomed as an entity. So although state execution is the theme that unites Harris's novel with its predecessors, this novel lets us desire it.

Perhaps the most important difference between *Fatherland* and the fictions that preceded it, though, is that the later novel is designed to renew the readers' full cognizance of the horrors of Our Timeline. Harris's novel does not veer toward theodicy, as all of the Nazi Britain fictions from *Loss of Eden* to *An Englishman's Castle* did. It implies the comparative superiority of the actual course of history by depicting a worse one, but it nonetheless explicitly guards against the Leibnizian tendency toward complacent acceptance. By stressing how much of the Final Solution was actually accomplished and how many of its perpetrators went unpunished, as well as by surrounding the account of Nazi crimes with references to numerous other twentieth-century atrocities, it asks us to see that the war against radical evil has had only partial, compromised victories. *Fatherland*'s mode of counterfactualism does not follow the usual pattern of dystopias, which encourage us to write off the actual losses because they pale in comparison to the possible ones but instead stresses that Our Timeline is uncomfortably close to the Alternate Timeline. The plot aims, in both the alternate world and our own, to force a reckoning with past "crimes against humanity" (a phrase coined by the postwar prosecutors of the Nazis) and calls attention to the still open gap between the crimes and the world's response. By citing Primo Levi, Harris joins the Italian writer's entreaty to make a future in which our abiding knowledge of the Holocaust would matter.

Begun at the end of the Cold War, a period during which the precedents set at the Nuremberg trials had laid dormant, *Fatherland* was published just as a worldwide movement for historical criminal justice took off.[70] In earlier chapters, we noted a sharp increase after 1989 in historical justice movements around the world and outlined the structural similarities between counterfactual histories (especially alternate models of race relations in America) and campaigns to compensate groups for historical wrongs. Those chapters focused on legal and political movements for affirmative action and reparations. *Fatherland*, though, directs our attention to a different historical-justice effort: indicting, finding, apprehending, prosecuting, and punishing perpetrators of crimes against humanity. We have been discussing reparations and retribution as complementary aspects of historical justice, but as events in post-WWII West Germany illustrate, they are also often played off against each other. The controversial 1952 pact in which the Federal Republic of Germany agreed to make restitution for crimes against the Jews of Europe by paying reparations to Israel (deemed both the "descendant entity" for the victims and a state where many refugees had settled) was an early precedent for international historical-justice demands.[71] The German Federal Republic took on responsibility for Nazi crimes against the Jews, recognizing a moral obligation to make amends to both individual victims and a state representing the Jewish people as a whole. Israel, for its part, accepted the settlement without "forgiving" the crimes or implying that they could ever be adequately compensated.

Historian Norbert Frei has demonstrated, however, that the international agreement coincided with Chancellor Konrad Adenauer's efforts to obtain amnesty for thousands of Nazi Party members previously convicted of war crimes during the immediate postwar denazification proceedings, which the majority of Germans viewed as foreign impositions.[72] The 1952 agreement repeated the logic of an earlier Adenauer address, in which he accepted the need to compensate the victims while downplaying any complicity on the part of the German people in the crimes. As historian Elazar Barkan wryly notes, "The crimes, it seemed, just happened; nobody was really responsible."[73] The admission of collective responsibility in the reparations agreement was therefore offset by the exculpation and integration of numerous former Nazis, especially in the military and legal professions. The state's action of paying reparations, we should notice, conceded collective liability, as in a tort case, in order to shield particular people from criminal prosecutions. The arrangement also reveals that the two available modes of historical justice, reparative and retributive, have differently defined wrongdoers: the state can take responsibility in a reparative tort action, but only individuals are subject to criminal prosecution. Although it is certainly possible to bring both sorts of legal action, in this case collective national obligation went hand in hand with personal impunity.

That combination formed the status quo in Germany until the New Left in the 1970s began demanding greater historical accountability, but their efforts, too, were seldom directed at bringing specific perpetrators to justice.[74] To be sure, a few notable Nazi war criminals who escaped the Allies, such as Adolf Eichmann, had been tracked down and prosecuted, but the task fell to private Nazi hunters and the state of Israel rather than to Germany. Of the thousands of fugitives who established themselves in South America (as Adolf Eichmann and Klaus Barbie eventually did), only a handful was ever captured. The German-born cultural critic Andreas Huyssen maintains that even after reunification, when rituals and sites of Holocaust memorialization were multiplying in Germany, the identities of the perpetrators drew little attention. Too few seemed interested in the fact that "the crimes of the Third Reich were not [merely] committed 'in the name of Germany,' as Bonn-speak all too frequently has it, but by Germans" (84). This distinction between Germany and Germans reminds us once again of the national pair, the state and its people. In Huyssen's formulation, the German state acknowledges its nominal continuity with its predecessor and thereby admits that it is responsible for a massive wrong, but the admission then suspends further inquiry into the criminal actions of Germans.

When Robert Harris started writing *Fatherland* in 1989, the impunity of former Nazis was beginning to attract international attention. Klaus Barbie's capture in 1983 revealed that both the United States and West Germany had helped him evade the law while their own intelligence agencies made use of his knowledge, and it was widely noted that his case was not unique. The internationally covered Barbie trial in France, which did not begin until 1987, brought the issues surrounding impunity for Nazi war criminals back to the world's attention at the end of the decade, when Marcel Ophüls's academy award–winning documentary *Hotel Terminus* (1988) underlined their urgency. Moreover, by that time another highly publicized set of prosecutions for crimes against humanity—the trials of the Argentine juntas in 1985—had occurred and their results were still uncertain. The Argentine trials were the first such large-scale prosecution since the Nuremberg Trials, the first ever to be conducted by a civilian court, and the first prosecutions by a democratic government of members of a former dictatorship of the same country. They convicted members of three successive military juntas of kidnapping, torture, forced disappearance, and the murder of an estimated fifteen to thirty thousand people during the Dirty War against political dissidents. Eventually the Argentine trials became a model for the global movement for retributive justice against war criminals, but while Harris was working on his novel, it seemed as though the convicted Argentine generals might be pardoned after all. Indeed, the ending of *Fatherland*, in which the American reporter flees to Switzerland with the documentary proof of the Holocaust, bears an eerie resemblance to a secret 1988 trip of the Argentinian judges to Oslo, where they deposited the original videotapes of the trials with the Norwegian parliament for safekeeping. Of course, I'm not suggesting that Harris modeled his ending on the Oslo trip but rather that they share an insight: saving history and prosecuting it are often intertwined.

Thus, although impunity for state officials was still normal during the writing of *Fatherland*, it was becoming more controversial, and human-rights activists in many parts of the world were bringing pressure for prosecutions. The novel clearly participates in that broader desire for retributive historical justice, which rose into a worldwide movement during the next twenty years. The number of trials for crimes against humanity swelled from fewer than fifty in 1989 to more than four hundred in 2009.[75] The prosecutions, moreover, established general principles of historical retributive justice that were codified in international law and underpinned the operations of new international agencies and organizations, like the International Criminal Court. The new norms hold that: (1) crimes violating the most basic human rights (such as torture, disappearance, and summary execution) by definition cannot be legitimate acts of a state and therefore must be the crimes of individuals; (2) no matter what their previous position in the government, the individuals can and *should* be prosecuted; and (3) they are entitled to fair trials.[76] These principles and the institutions that uphold them were certainly not realities when *Fatherland* was written. To be sure, they are unequally and imperfectly recognized and enforced even now, but they have been legally established and most nations pay them lip service. *Fatherland* was intended as an admonition that our world looked too much like a counterfactual Greater German Reich, and it seems fair to say—at least on the issue of impunity for government officials who violate basic human rights—that the resemblance became less striking in the following twenty years. The novel's international popularity over those decades might be partly attributed to that context of reception. This is not to say that the increase in prosecutions by itself indicates a mass conversion to universal human rights or even what Elazar Barkan called a "new international morality."[77] Most trials were parts of national transitions to different forms of government as the Cold War order crumbled, and many others indicate a rise in the number of crimes against humanity in the period, as the massacres in the former Yugoslavia and Rwanda, the harbingers of twenty-first-century slaughters, grimly remind us. Indeed, the premise that prosecutions discourage future crimes has now been widely challenged.[78] Far from making *Fatherland* seem dated, the continuing outrages, as well as the debates to which they give rise, might be said, alas, to keep it all too relevant.

However, as the principles underlying the prosecutions make clear, the *law* still exempts from scrutiny the very thing that *Fatherland* sought to revivify and accentuate: the state's responsibility for the crimes. By clarifying that a legitimate state simply cannot have committed crimes against humanity, the law attempts to prevent individuals from shifting the blame for their actions to the state that employed them. The state thereby becomes incidental, a sort of enabling condition of the actions but not determinative and perhaps not even mitigating if the individual is to be found guilty. For the purposes of such proceedings, agency is lifted from the state, and we might therefore say that the novel's vision and that of the body of law that has developed since its publication are disjunctive. In the novel, the Third Reich is a counterfactual character, identical to the historical entity but with a different destiny, which is still to be completed. The Third Reich, in short, has the peculiar forms of life and death that state characters take on in alternate-history novels. Moreover, as we noticed at the beginning of this chapter, alternate-history novels follow the lead of modern historians by placing the state in the foreground of the narrative, so the law might also be said to depart from the historians' norm. The historiography of the Holocaust, for example, continues to concentrate on how the Third Reich conceived and accomplished the genocide, and historians working on subsequent crimes against humanity have also emphasized the roles of the states. There thus seems to be an important gap between the historical way of understanding the events and the criminal-justice way of prosecuting them. Indeed, when we apply the term "historical justice" to the prosecutions, it seems somewhat oxymoronic, for, in that context, the aims of history as a mode of understanding the past and those of criminal justice as a mode of redressing it have divergent imperatives.[79]

Fatherland, we might say, occupies this gap without exactly bridging it: the novel gives us both an alternative history of the Third Reich and the hint of an alternative collective punishment for the genocide: the outraged nations of the world, suddenly apprised of Germany's crimes, the fiction suggests, would topple the regime. The novel imaginatively resurrects the Third Reich in the hope of seeing it put to death properly, this time not as the result of a mere military loss but instead as an explicit punishment for its crimes. The prospect that the criminal state as a whole might be punished allows us to think of the guilty party not as a collection of individuals but as an enormous entity, sized to fit the colossal buildings so copiously described in the opening chapters. By holding his title character, *Fatherland*, responsible, Harris holds onto the idea of a collective criminal who would be not only proportionate to the crimes but also constitutive of their peculiar horror: the state's meticulous administrative planning and commission of millions of murders.

FINALE: NO END IN SIGHT

During the decades following the Cold War, when Britain tried to become European, a few historians speculated about how the twentieth century might have yielded a different and better result. Could the two world wars, the first seeming to lead inexorably to the second, have been avoided? Niall Ferguson's 1998 *The Pity of War* argued that World War I was not only unnecessary but also the "greatest *error* of modern history."[80] He drew on B. H. Liddell Hart's argument that the nation broke from its historic practice by sending a huge land army to the Continent rather than relying on economic pressure and naval power. A Britain that decided to "stand aside" in 1914, he insisted, would have been a more consistent character as well as a wiser and freer one.[81] Although many critics have criticized the pro-imperialist and Thatcherite aspects of Ferguson's arguments, at least one member of the British left, Doris Lessing, shared his starting point, that Britain should have stayed out of World War I. In her 2007 hybrid of alternate history and memoir, *Alfred and Emily*, we learn that if it had not been for the war, her mother and father could have stayed in England, leading peaceful and prosperous lives, instead of being forced to emigrate to Rhodesia.[82] Ferguson's and Lessing's works are far apart both generically and politically, but both explore the desirable possibilities of a century with fewer, smaller wars, creating alternate Britains that would have been less constrained, richer, and more independent.

The counterfactual possibility of making a better twentieth-century history by choosing peace in 1914 was thus a beguiling alternative at the turn of the twenty-first century; that Britain should have chosen peace in the summer of 1940, however, remained a scandalous suggestion. In 1993 the British historian John Charmley argued that Churchill may have erred in not making a separate peace with Nazi Germany after the fall of France. His book, *Churchill: The End of Glory, a Political Biography*, briefly imagines a world in which Britain opts out of the war early, keeps its empire (which Charmley thinks was a very good thing), and watches from the sidelines as Hitler and Stalin destroy each other. In a rhetorical flourish, Charmley went so far as to question whether Britain could objectively be said to have won the war.[83] The book started a noisy debate, and most of the historians joining it decried the implication that the world would have been a better place had Britain not fought the war. In demolishing Charmley's counterfactual, his opponents reproduce all of the Nazi Britain counterfactual scenarios we have examined here, from *Loss of Eden* up through *Fatherland*: Hitler only pretends to make peace and finds ways of dominating Britain; Britain is forced to unite with Hitler and loses control of its empire; Britain becomes a satellite and finally a collaborator; the United States joins the conflict, and Britain is further marginalized; and so forth. In short, the hypothesis proposed by Charmley—suppose we had made a separate peace—had already been repeatedly played out, starting in the summer of 1940, and the character of twentieth-century Britain had been explicitly formulated in relation to it. Everybody already knows what happens if Britain makes a separate peace: it suffers a just retribution, from which it might rise again redeemed, but only after immense suffering.

The consensus about both the rightness and the necessity of fighting World War II, however, has not kept alternate-history fictions after *Fatherland* from imagining a *better* war. For example, in keeping with the movement toward historical repair, Christopher Priest's 2004 novel, *The Separation*, uses a double-time-track narrative form to materialize possibilities for peace in the early years of the war, with a particular focus on avoiding the Holocaust and preventing Britain's frequently condemned firebombing of German cities.[84] The norm in the later fiction, however, has been to elaborate the patterns set in the wartime and postwar works. The plots tend to imitate *Loss of Eden* by tracing the unhappy consequences of making a separate peace (invasions are no longer fashionable), and the genre continues to be that of the detective-spy novel. The thematic emphases change to accommodate the times—regionalism, gay sexuality, nuclear proliferation—but these remain tales of rescuing the British state.[85] Whatever it does or does not do in the war, the one thing needful is that it try to fight and win. Perhaps it could have prevented Nazism from coming into existence in the first place by taking different actions earlier in the century, but once its nemesis has arrived on the scene, it is, by its very nature, unable to coexist with it permanently and peacefully. Hypothesizing otherwise would change not only the narrative but also the *character*: Britain would simply no longer be Britain.

The point is perhaps best made not by any alternate-history work but by Kate Atkinson's 2014 *Life after Life*, a novel in which the heroine's multiple lives are experienced successively. Each time she dies, she is reborn into a different plot, and yet she, like each character in the book, retains self-identity, even achieving an enhanced realization. The novel is an extended meditation on individual, familial, and national identity under varying circumstances, and only one of its numerous life-endings is repeated exactly. The first chapter, titled "November 1930," is set in a Munich café, where Ursula tries to assassinate Hitler:

> A move rehearsed a hundred times. One shot. Swiftness was all, yet there was a moment, a bubble suspended in time after she had drawn the gun and leveled it at his heart when everything seemed to stop.
> "Führer," she said, breaking the spell. "Für Sie."
> Around the table guns were jerked from holsters and pointed at her. One breath. One shot.
> Ursula pulled the trigger.
> Darkness fell.[86]

Placed at the beginning of the book but without any apparent consequences for the history that follows, the chapter serves as a kind of lure: will the heroine, after realizing that she is continually reborn, direct her energies toward changing the world? In the fourth-to-last chapter, the attempt to kill Hitler is repeated verbatim; this time the reader understands who the character is and how she got there, but the outcome is the same and the subsequent chapters find us back in our own history. This book, according to the author, is "about being English. . . . Not just the reality of being English but also what we are in our own imaginations." For all the variations we see in these characters' lives, all their multiple deaths and births, what seems to remain unimaginable is the possibility of twentieth-century England in a world without that war.

ACKNOWLEDGMENTS

As befits a work on counterfactual history, this book began in pure contingency when a graduate student in a seminar I was teaching at Berkeley happened to make a presentation on Philip K. Dick's alternate-history novel, *The Man in the High Castle*. So, if not for the inspiration of Benjamin Widiss, I might never have taken up this topic, and if other individuals and institutions had not supported my research and writing, I would certainly never have completed a book on it. The School of Criticism and Theory at Cornell gave me the opportunity to explore it with a brilliant group of young scholars from around the world, and in 2005–6, I was lucky enough to share a sabbatical year at the National Humanities Center with scholars whose own research overlapped with mine (Paul Saint-Amour, Mark Maslan, and Sarah Lochlann Jain), which helped me to clarify my inchoate ideas. In 2009–10, similarly generous groups of scholars at the Stanford Humanities Center and at the American Academy in Berlin gave me new perspectives on the phenomenon and an appreciation of its global reach. I might not have been able to carry on the work without the help and encouragement of the many colleagues and friends whose responses to presentations and informal discussions have been both bracing and motivating, especially Hilary Schor, Colleen Lye, James Vernon, and Kim Chernin. Without David Hollinger's, Stephen Best's, and Bryan Wagner's many corrections and suggestions, the chapters on American history and literature might have been anemic, and Kent Puckett's perceptive criticism and buoyant enthusiasm kept up my spirits during the writing of the sections on twentieth-century Britain. My readers will have been saved many errors and much tedium by Thomas Laqueur's extensive and incisive critiques on the draft chapters, and the same can be said for the heroic efforts of the two readers for the University of Chicago Press, Allan Megill and his anonymous colleague. Three young scholars who served as research assistants during the book's gestation—Annie McClannahan, Gina Patnaik, Urmi Banerjee, and Luke Terlaak Poot—left a deep impression on the finished product, and without the endowment of the Ida May and William J. Eggers Jr. Chair in English, I would not have been able to afford their help. Furthermore, were it not for the patience and support of my editors at the University of Chicago Press, Timothy Mennel, Yvonne Zipter, and Alan Thomas—this book might never have seen the light of day.

The most conspicuous sine quo non, though, the person without whom this work would surely not have been possible, is my husband, Martin Jay, who was as always my best reader, toughest critic, and most loving supporter. To him, our daughters Shana Lindsay and Rebecca Jay, and our grandchildren (to whom I've dedicated this book), I give my deepest thanks.

NOTES

INTRODUCTION

1. L. A. Hart and Tony Honoré's book, *Causation in the Law*, 2nd ed. (Oxford: Clarendon Press, 1985), describes the importance of such counterfactual causal reasoning in the law. See, esp., 16. Other theorists of counterfactualism also stress its connection to our desire to place blame and to investigate not the past in general but primarily things that went *wrong*. See Ruth M. J. Byrne, *The Rational Imagination: How People Create Alternatives to Reality* (Cambridge, MA: MIT Press, 2005), 1–14; Philip E. Tetlock and Geoffrey Parker, "Counterfactual Thought Experiments: Why We Can't Live without Them and How We Must Learn to Live with Them," in *Unmaking the West: "What-If?" Scenarios That Rewrite World History*, ed. Philip E. Tetlock, Richard Ned Lebow, and Geoffrey Parker (Ann Arbor: University of Michigan Press, 2006), 14–44. For an account of past counterfactual conditionals that focuses on the legal issues, see Michael S. Moore, *Causation and Responsibility: An Essay in Law, Morals, and Metaphysics* (Oxford: Oxford University Press, 2010).

2. For several helpful discussions of the problems of comparison in history as well as methods of surmounting them, see the essays in *Natural Experiments of History*, ed. Jared Diamond and James A. Robinson (Cambridge, MA: Harvard University Press, 2010).

3. The penchant for catastrophic history among counterfactualists can also be explained by the fact that we normally use past counterfactuals when we're trying to explain how things went wrong. We do not often feel the need to think about alternatives to actuality when things are going well or our routines are uninterrupted. This is a point made repeatedly by the psychologist Ruth M. J. Byrne in her survey of the experimental literature on how people use counterfactuals in daily life, *The Rational Imagination*. Similarly, although all causal statements about history may assume unstated counterfactuals, the explicit declaration of those assumptions tends to be motivated by some prior negative judgment about the outcome.

4. Jay M. Winter, *The Great War and the British People* (London: Macmillan, 1986), 76–83.

5. For discussions of the conceptual relations between historical justice movements and legal paradigms, see Klaus Neumann and Janna Thompson, eds., *Historical Justice and Memory* (Madison: University of Wisconsin Press, 2015). Two historical treatments of the historical justice movements worldwide are Elazar Barkan, *The Guilt of Nations: Restitution and Negotiating Historical Injustices* (Baltimore: Johns Hopkins University Press, 2000); and Kathryn Sikkink, *The Justice Cascade: How Human Rights Prosecutions Are Changing World Politics* (New York: Norton, 2011).

6. Both of these views are on display in a forum on the topic published in the journal *Historically Speaking* in 2004, where Richard J. Evans, "Telling It Like It Wasn't," complains that recent forays into counterfactualism on the part of British historians evince "postmodern helplessness" (12); and Edward Ingram, "Is the Dark Light Enough," insists that every "causal inference" involves a counterfactual (15)—both in "Counterfactual History: A Forum," *Historically Speaking: The Bulletin of the Historical Society* 5, no. 4 (March 2004): 11–32. Two polemical books on the topic demonstrate its capacity for politicization: Jeremy Black, *What If? Counterfactualism and the Problem of History* (London: Social Affairs Unit, 2008); and Richard J. Evans, *Altered Pasts: Counterfactuals in History* (Waltham, MA: Brandeis University Press, 2013).

7. Methodological discussions of the new forms of historical counterfactualism, especially those used in economic history, began appearing in the 1960s, and they usually focused on the issue of causality. Prominent examples are: J. D. Gould, "Hypothetical History," *Economic History Review* 22, no. 2 (August 1969): 195–207; George Murphy, "On Counterfactual Propositions," *History and Theory* 9, no. 9 (1969): 14–38; and T. A. Climo and P. G. A. Howells, "Possible Worlds in Historical Explanation," *History and Theory* 15, no. 1 (February 1976): 1–20. For methodological considerations that are less exclusively interested in causality and more pertinent to the longer narrative forms, see Geoffrey Hawthorn, *Plausible Worlds: Possibility and Understanding in History and the Social Sciences* (Cambridge: Cambridge University Press, 1993); Richard Ned Lebow, "What's So Different about a Counterfactual?" *World Politics* 52, no. 4 (July 2000): 550–85; Martin Bunzl, "Counterfactual History: A User's Guide," *American Historical Review* 109, no. 3 (June 2004): 845–58. Niall Ferguson's introduction to the edited collection *Virtual History* is one of the few that gives some historical background, but its short history of the mode soon gives way to a much longer history of the "historical determinism" to which the author opposes it. See Ferguson, "Virtual History: Towards a 'Chaotic' Theory of the Past," in *Virtual History: Alternatives and Counterfactuals*, ed. Niall Ferguson (London: Picador, 1997), 1–90.

8. Among the works by academic historians that have informed this study are the following on the topic of the history of history: Reinhart Koselleck's *Futures Past: On The Semantics of Historical Time*, trans and intro Keith Tribe (New York: Columbia University Press, 2004); Allan Megill, *Historical Knowledge, Historical Error: A Contemporary Guide to Practice* (Chicago: University of Chicago Press, 2007); and J. D. Gould, "Hypothetical History," *Economic History Review* 22, no. 2 (1969): 195–207. An extremely useful study that includes both analytical and narrative forms of the mode is Gavriel D. Rosenfeld, *The World Hitler Never Made: Alternate History and the Memory of Nazism* (Cambridge: Cambridge University Press, 2005), which surveys

alternate histories of Nazism in the United States, the United Kingdom, and Germany. It has been especially important for the last two chapters of this book.

9. There are three excellent overviews of the issues: Philip E. Tetlock and Aaron Belkin, eds., *Counterfactual Thought Experiments in World Politics: Logical, Methodological, and Psychological Perspectives* (Princeton, NJ: Princeton University Press, 1996); Tetlock and Parker, "Counterfactual Thought Experiments"; and Richard Ned Lebow, *Forbidden Fruit: Counterfactuals and International Relations* (Princeton, NJ: Princeton University Press, 2010), 1–66.

10. The best international overview is Éric Henriet, *L'histoire revisitée: Panorama de l'uchronie sous toutes ses formes* (Amiens: Encrage, 2004). See also Darko Suvin, "Victorian Science Fiction, 1871–85: The Rise of the Alternate History Sub-Genre," *Science-Fiction Studies* 10, no. 2 (1983): 148–69; Karen Hellekson, *Alternate History: Refiguring Historical Time* (Kent, Ohio: Kent State University Press, 2001); Kathleen Singles, *Alternate History: Playing with Contingency and Necessity* (Berlin: De Gruyter, 2013); and Ben Carver, *Rewriting History in Nineteenth-Century Literature: The Uses of Imaginary Pasts in Britain, France and America* (London: Palgrave, forthcoming). Rosenfeld, *The World Hitler Never Made*, also belongs in this category. A very useful archive for the alternate-history narrative forms can be found online at The Alternate History List, Uchronia.net. It is crowdsourced, and so the usual caveats apply, but it lists over three thousand works.

11. The distinction between "constrained" and "exuberant" counterfactuals is made by Allan Megill, *Historical Knowledge, Historical Error*, 151–56. Although Megill is quite tolerant of the exuberant variety, he mainly argues for the usefulness, even the necessity, of the constrained kind in historical explanation.

12. There is a large philosophical literature on "transworld identity" as well as the related but competing idea of possible-world "counterparts." See, e.g., Saul Kripke, *Naming and Necessity* (Oxford: Blackwell, 1981); Donald Davidson, *Essays on Actions and Events* (Oxford: Clarendon Press, 1980); David K. Lewis *Counterfactuals* (Cambridge, MA: Harvard University Press, 1987); and Bernard Williams, "Resenting One's Own Existence," in *Making Sense of Humanity and Other Philosophical Papers* (Cambridge: Cambridge University Press, 1995), 224–32. For an overview, see Penelope Mackie and Mark Jago, "Transworld Identity," in *The Stanford Encyclopedia of Philosophy*, ed. Edward N. Zalta (Fall 2013 edition), https://plato.stanford.edu/entries/identity-transworld/.

13. Of course, counterfactualists often vary the agents who are active in an event to see how it might have been different. Consider, e.g., the question: "If Richard Nixon had been president in 1962, would there have been a Cuban missile crisis?" We assume the person referred to as Nixon is the same as that person in our history. Otherwise we wouldn't be able to gauge how his presidency might have affected the crisis.

14. See Saul Kripke's adaptation of Leibniz's concept of possible worlds into his own possible-worlds semantics in *Naming and Necessity* (Oxford: Blackwell, 1981). David K. Lewis's possible-worlds ontology, *Counterfactuals*, in contrast, would remove the idea of identity and assert a possible world that holds a "counterpart" of JFK.

15. See Kripke, *Naming and Necessity*, 48–49.

16. One piece of evidence that hypothetical speculation is a common mode of making something seem lifelike is that realist novels—long considered the normative fictional form of modernity—tend to imitate it when inventing characters. Three books by literary critics have been especially important in analyzing novelistic narratives' fascination with multiple simultaneous possibilities: Gary Saul Morson, *Narrative and Freedom: The Shadows of Time* (New Haven: Yale University Press, 1994); Michael André Bernstein, *Foregone Conclusions: Against Apocalyptic History* (Berkeley: University of California Press, 1994); and Andrew H. Miller, *The Burdens of Perfection: On Ethics and Reading in Nineteenth-Century British Literature* (Ithaca, NY: Cornell University Press, 2008)—the latter offering a different perspective on this issue.

17. For example, narrators of alternate-history novels sometimes speculate that the incompatible reality comes into existence only at the moment of a world-altering breach so that it would be possible to disrupt or retrieve the singularity of actuality through temporal manipulation. At other times they allude to parallel universes or a multiverse. Quantum physicists and astrophysicists thus seem to have had an influence on how some of the fiction writers imagine the relation between their alternate worlds and our own, and that influence has led alternate-history novels generally to be classed as a subgenre of science fiction. To sample laypersons' guides to the relevant science, see Igor D. Novikov, *The River of Time*, trans. Vitaly Kisin (Cambridge: Cambridge University Press, 1998); and Brian Greene, *The Hidden Reality: Parallel Universes and the Deep Laws of the Cosmos* (New York: Knopf, 2011). Nevertheless, the novels merely use such ideas as fictional premises, making very superficial use of the issues that quantum physicists and analytical philosophers have been debating for decades.

CHAPTER ONE

1. Livy, *Historiae Romanae with an English Translation*, trans. B. O. Foster, 14 vols. (Cambridge, MA: Harvard University Press, 1919–67), 4:227–41.

2. Those who stress the connection between counterfactualism and causal explanation trace the insight to David Hume, who argued that a true cause must be that without which an event would not have occurred. Thus when claiming that A is the cause of B, we are really arguing the counterfactual proposition that if A had not occurred, B would also not have occurred. See, e.g., Martin Bunzl, "Humean Counterfactuals," *Journal of the History of Philosophy* 20, no. 2 (1982): 171–77.

3. Niall Ferguson, e.g., views both Hume and Leibniz as contributors to a scientific revolution that "eliminated contingency from the physical world" and led to "the rigid determinism of Laplace," against which counterfactual history struggles. He quotes Leibniz's sentence "as God calculates, so the world is made," without noticing that God is *calculating contingencies*. *Virtual History: Alternatives and Counterfactuals* (London: Picador, 1997), 26–27.

4. Leibniz, *Theodicy: Essays on the Goodness of God, the Freedom of Man and the Origin of Evil*, ed. Austin Farrer, trans E. M. Huggard [from C. J. Gerhardt's Edition of the Collected Philosophical Works, 1875–90] (Bibliobazaar, 2007), 147. All quotations from Leibniz are from this text and page numbers are given in the body of the chapter.

5. In his treatment of contingency in *Theodicy*, Leibniz was revising Aristotle.

Aristotle's "necessity" involved one kind of truth—the truth of reason—that would have to be the case in any possible world, and the inessentials, or "accidents," involved another kind of truth—the truth of facts—the contraries of which are conceivable and therefore might obtain in other possible worlds. Arguing that history is the realm of contingency, however, did not lead Leibniz to conclude, as Aristotle had, that it was merely a formless chronicle of events that might have been otherwise, lacking philosophical interest. For Aristotle on history, see chapter 9 of *Poetics*, trans. Gerald F. Else (Ann Arbor: University of Michigan Press, 1967), 301–2.

6. Quoted in Isaac D'Israeli, "Of a History of Events Which Have Not Happened," in *A Second Series of Curiosities of Literature: Consisting of Researches in Literary, Biographical, and Political History; of Critical and Philosophical Inquiries; and of Secret History* (London: J. Murray, 1823), 255. See n15 below, this chapter, for a discussion of the original publication date of this work.

7. To make history's overall path visible, Priestley invented the horizontal timeline, on which he traced not only the rise and fall of empires but also the numbers of world-historical figures devoted to various occupations over a three thousand–year span. On his *Chart of Biography*, published in 1765, the names of individual "Statesmen and Warriors" are rather equally distributed across the centuries, but the names in the arts and sciences are thickly massed in modern times. Thus, although the individual names are barely legible, one can see at a glance the relative aggregated weight of the learned professions over time. See the illustrated section on this chart in Daniel Rosenfield and Anthony Grafton, *Cartographies of Time* (Princeton, NJ: Princeton University Press, 2010), 116–28.

8. Joseph Priestley, *Lectures on History, and General Policy* (Philadelphia: P. Byrne, 1803), 81. Subsequent quotations are from this edition and page numbers are given in the body of the chapter.

9. Reinhart Koselleck, *Futures Past: On the Semantics of Historical Time*, trans. Keith Tribe (New York: Columbia University Press, 2004), 115–27.

10. "The famous nose of Cleopatra, which, according to Pascal, changed the face of the world reaches from one epoch to another," Koselleck writes (ibid., 117).

11. *Pascal's Pensées*, trans. W. F. Trotter (New York: E. P. Dutton, 1958), 48.

12. Leibniz was one of many seventeenth-century philosophers, including Descartes and Spinoza, who tried in different ways to make religion more amenable to and consonant with human reason. For relations among these various thinkers, see Jonathan I. Israel's magisterial *Radical Enlightenment: Philosophy and the Making of Modernity, 1650–1750* (Oxford: Oxford University Press, 2001). The phrase "irrationalization of religion" belongs to Leszek Kolakowski, who uses it to describe the fideistic tradition to which Pascal belonged. *Chrétiens sans église: La conscience religieuse et le lien confessionnel au XVIIe siècle*, trans Anna Posner Leszek (Paris: Gallimard, 1969), 250.

13. Koselleck, *Futures Past*, 117.

14. Pierre Bayle was translated into English in 1709. See also Adrien Richer, *Great Events from Little Causes: A Selection of Interesting and Entertaining Stories, Drawn from the Histories of Different Nations* (Dublin: James Hoey, 1768); and Frederick II, King of Prussia, *Anti-Machiavel; or, An Examination of Machiavel's Prince*, with

Notes Historical and Political, Published by Mr. de Voltaire, Translated from the French (London: T. Woodward, 1741).

15. The date of composition is uncertain, but Benjamin Disraeli, the author's son, claimed that the first two volumes of *Curiosities* were in their second edition in 1794. See his preface to the *Curiosities of Literature*, ed. the Earl of Beaconsfield (London: F. Warne, 1881), 1:xvii. There is, moreover, internal evidence for accepting Benjamin Disraeli's judgment that the essay was originally published in the early 1790s at the latest. First, it refers to Priestley's 1788 *Lectures on History* as a recently published book, and second, it draws no examples of chance occurrences from the Revolutionary or Napoleonic Wars, which became the major sources of such examples in the first decades of the nineteenth century. The edition of the essay used here is "Of a History of Events Which Have Not Happened," in *A Second Series of Curiosities of Literature: Consisting of Researches in Literary, Biographical, and Political History; of Critical and Philosophical Inquiries; and of Secret History* (London: J. Murray, 1823), 253–68. All quotations are from this edition and page numbers are given in the text.

16. D'Israeli was certainly a Tory, but he satirizes both Whig and Tory historians in the essay.

17. See Benjamin Disraeli's remarks on his father's intellectual debts to Montaigne and Bayle, both of whom tended to be read as skeptical anti-providentialists in the late eighteenth century (preface to the *Curiosities of Literature*).

18. Koselleck, *Futures Past*, 126–27.

19. Ferguson, *Virtual History*, 26–64.

20. A recent study by Anders Engberg-Pedersen argues that the modern interest in military contingencies arose from new paradigms of warfare created in the French Revolutionary and Napoleonic Wars. See *Empire of Chance: the Napoleonic Wars and the Disorder of Things* (Cambridge, MA: Harvard University Press, 2015).

21. Azar Gat, *The Origins of Military Thought: From the Enlightenment to Clausewitz* (Oxford: Clarendon Press, 1980), 26–29.

22. See, e.g., Jacob Soll, *The Information Master: Jean-Baptiste Colbert's Secret State Intelligence System* (Ann Arbor: University of Michigan Press, 2009).

23. Two works give overviews of the history of military academies in the eighteenth-century: F. Artz, *The Development of Technical Education in France, 1500–1800* (Cambridge, MA: MIT Press, 1968); and Henry Barnard, *Military Schools and Courses of Instruction in the Science and the Art of War; in France, Prussia, Austria, Russia, Sweden, Switzerland, Sardinia, England, and the United States* (New York: E. Steiger, 1872).

24. The British were slow to develop what they thought of as European methods of military training, but by the mid-Victorian period counterfactual history was well entrenched in British officer training. Although maintaining a resolute empiricism, Edward Hamley, e.g., provides numerous counterfactual analyses in his *Operations of War Explained and Illustrated* (Edinburgh: W. Blackwood, 1866), which became the standard textbook of military instruction and was the single textbook that needed to be mastered for the staff college entrance examinations.

25. Tim Travers, "The Development of British Military Historical Writing and

Thought from the Eighteenth Century to the Present," in *Military History and the Military Profession*, ed. David A. Charters, Marc Milner, and J. Brent Wilson (Westport, CT: Praeger, 1992), 26.

26. Henry Lloyd, *The History of the Late War in Germany between the King of Prussia, and the Empress of Germany and Her Allies: Containing the Campaigns of 1758, and 1759*, 2 vols. (London: T. and J. Egerton, 1790), 2:2–3.

27. Gat, in *The Origins of Military Thought*, explains the importance of Lloyd's formulation of the theory of the operational line and its impact on later thinkers (69–137).

28. It is also possible that the sentence refers to the fact that Silesia would remain under Prussian conquest, and in that sense "the war was finished." But then the sentence seems even more out of place in the paragraph.

29. Peter P. Perla, *The Art of Wargaming* (Annapolis: Naval Institute Press, 1990), 17. See also Jorit Wintjes, "Europe's Earliest Kriegsspiel?" *British Journal for Military History* 2, no. 1 (November 2015): 15–33.

30. Perla, *The Art of Wargaming*, 22. The new war game was described in Georg Venturini's *Beschreibung und Regeln eines Neuen Kriegsspiel zum Nutzen und Vergnuegen Besonders Aber zum Gebrauch in Militairschulen* [Description and rules of a new war game for the benefit and pleasure but especially for use in military schools] (Göttingen: Niedersächsische Staats- und Universitätsbibliothek, 1797).

31. Ed Halter, *From Sun Tzu to Xbox: War and Video Games* (New York: Thunder's Mouth Press, 2006), 39.

32. See Wintjes, "Europe's Earliest Kriegsspiel?" 21–23, who also reports that, according to the 1806 publication, the game was originally invented in the 1740s.

33. Halter, *From Sun Tzu to Xbox*, 45.

34. I am using a mid-nineteenth-century American translation of the *Traité* in this chapter: *Treatise on Grand Military Operations; or, A Critical and Military History of the Wars of Frederick the Great, as Contrasted with the Modern System*, trans. Col. S. B. Holabird (New York: D. Van Nostrand, 1865). All quotations from this work are from this edition, and page numbers are given in the text. Information about Jomini's career and the formation of his system come from Gat, *The Origins of Military Thought*, 108–21.

35. Antoine Henri de Jomini, *The Art of War*, trans G. H. Mendell and W. P. Craighill, special ed. (El Paso, TX: El Paso Norte Press, 2005), 12. All quotations from this book are from this edition, and page numbers are given in the text.

36. Rudiger Campe points out that games of chance in general operate according to a logical principle that was dear to the Sophists, for they seek moments in which "what is otherwise normally improbable suddenly appears probable in a particular case," such as the roulette-wheel ball landing on the very number on which you placed your bet. *The Game of Probability: Literature and Calculation from Pascal to Kleist*, trans. Ellwood Wiggins (Stanford, CA: Stanford University Press, 2012), 274–75.

37. Gat, *The Origins of Military Thought*, 125.

38. Azar Gat's magisterial study seats each theorist and historian deeply in his intellectual context and is especially illuminating about Clausewitz's rich intellectual

heritage, which, he makes clear, should not be reduced simply to German historicist romanticism (ibid., 170–200). Gat sums up the abundant evidence for the importance of Kant's *Critique of Judgment* to Clausewitz's thought. For Clausewitz's use of probability theory, see Engberg-Pedersen, *Empire of Chance*, 56–68.

39. Carl von Clausewitz, *On War*, ed. Beatrice Heuser, trans. Michael Howard and Peter Paret (Oxford: Oxford University Press, 2007), 98–101. Subsequent quotations are from this edition and page numbers are given in the body of the essay.

40. Gat, *The Origins of Military Thought*, 179.

41. Ibid., 92.

CHAPTER TWO

1. Charles Renouvier published the work first in 1857 in *Revue philosophique et religieuse*, but the title "Uchronie" was apparently not used until the revised edition of 1873. See Eric B. Henriet, *L'histoire revisitée: Panorama de l'uchronie sous toutes ses formes* (Paris: Encrage, 2004), 17.

2. In *Altered Pasts: Counterfactuals in History* (Waltham, MA: Brandeis University Press, 2013), Richard J. Evans repeatedly and dismissively claims that "wishful thinking" is the dominant impulse behind the counterfactual-historical mode. However, his evidence for this claim seems to be based solely on examples drawn from the British historical profession during the last thirty years.

3. This chapter uses the following translation: Louis Geoffroy, *Napoléon and the Conquest of the World, 1812–1832: A Fictional History* trans. and ed. by Kenneth Berry (Oklahoma City: Campaign Publishers, 1994), 10. All quotations are from this edition, and page numbers are given in the body of the chapter.

4. Stanley Mellon, "The July Monarchy and the Napoleonic Myth," *Yale French Studies*, no. 26 (1960), 70–78.

5. See Christopher Prendergast's analyses of these paintings in *Napoleon and History Painting: Antoine Jean Gros's La Bataille d'Eylau* (Oxford: Clarendon Press, 1997).

6. These terms seem to have emerged among science-fiction fans in an ad hoc way. I have not been able to locate their precise origins.

7. "Close-run thing" is actually a common misquotation of a note by Thomas Creevey, which reports Wellington to have said, "It has been a damned nice thing—the nearest run thing you ever saw in your life." Thomas Creevey, "1814–1815," chap. 10 of *The Creevey Papers: A Selection from the Correspondence & Diaries of the Late Thomas Creevey, M.P., Born 1768—Died 1838*, ed. Sir Herbert Maxwell, 2 vols. (London: J. Murray, 1903), 1:236 (18 June 1815).

8. L. A. Hart and Tony Honoré's book, *Causation in the Law*, 2nd ed. (Oxford: Clarendon Press, 1985), describes the importance of such counterfactual causal reasoning in the law. See, esp., 16. Other theorists who stress its connection to investigating *wrongs*. See Ruth M. J. Byrne, *The Rational Imagination: How People Create Alternatives to Reality* (Cambridge, MA: MIT Press, 2005), 1–14; Philip E. Tetlock and Geoffrey Parker, "Counterfactual Thought Experiments: Why We Can't Live without Them and How We Must Learn to Live with Them," in *Unmaking the West: "What-If?" Scenarios That*

Rewrite World History, ed. Philip E. Tetlock, Richard Ned Lebow, and Geoffrey Parker (Ann Arbor: University of Michigan Press, 2006).

9. The distinction resembles the late medieval monarchial idea of the "king's two bodies," which saw the monarch as possessing two different orders of existence: an individual one and an ideal one embodying the realm as a whole. See Ernst Kantorowicz, *The King's Two Bodies: A Study in Mediaeval Political Theology* (Princeton, NJ: Princeton University Press, 1957).

10. Thomas Rymer was the first to use the English phrase "poetic justice" in 1678, while offering a commonplace defense of "poetry" (or what we now more often call "fiction"): although its incidents are often invented, he explained, it teaches morality by illustrating that good and evil ultimately receive their proportional punishments and rewards. Writers on both sides of the channel had associated the theory with Aristotle, although Aristotle was more concerned with the fitness of events in fiction, their probability and appropriateness to genre and character, than with their moral valence. His famous formulation of what is proper to fiction stresses what is proper to various kinds of characters: "The poet's job is not to tell what has happened but the kind of things that *can* happen, i.e., the kind of events that are possible according to probability or necessity . . . [and] what kinds of thing *a certain kind of person* will say or do." See Gerald Else, *Aristotle's Poetics: The Argument* (Cambridge, MA: Harvard University Press, 1967), 301–2.

11. It should go without saying that Geoffroy-Château's attempt at poetic justice bears little resemblance to the period's dominant romanticism, through which other writers explored a different sense of the appropriateness of Napoleon's actual destiny to his character. In 1840, e.g., Victor Hugo wrote "Le retour de L'Empereur," which made Napoleon's actual historical fate aesthetically satisfying by emphasizing its tragic and mythical proportions. That poem depicted Napoleon as a modern Prometheus in rebellion against the slow pace of God's providence. It drew on what was already a common French image of Napoleon as Prometheus, "chained to the rock of St. Helena, tormented by the British." See Jules Richard, "Preface to the 1896 Edition" of Louis Geoffroy, *Napoléon Apocryphe, 1812–1932* (Paris: Librairie Illustrée, 1983), 21.

12. The book's aesthetic thus conforms to the post-Kantian idealism Philippe Lacoue-Labarthe and Jean-Luc Nancy contrast with romanticism in *The Literary Absolute: The Theory of Literature in German Romanticism* (Albany, NY: SUNY Press, 1988), 33–37. It also draws on the neoclassical concept of the beau ideal, which Christopher Prendergast (*Napoleon and History Painting,* 59) has shown was still alive in early nineteenth-century France.

13. *Uchronie (L'utopie dans l'histoire): esquisse historique apocryphe du développement de la civilisation européenne tel qu'il n'a pas été, tel qu'il aurait pu être,* 2nd edition (Paris: Felix Alcan, 1901), 21. There is no English translation of this work. The passage in question is: "Dès la haute antiquité, les nations de l'Orient obéirent à des prêtres ou à des rois absolus" (21); . . . "Les Grecs, [et] les Italiens, ingnorèrent le pouvoir des prêtres ou le subordonnèrent aux intérêts civils. Au lieu de grandes monarchies, ils eurent des cités libres et furent les inventeurs de la Loi, cette abstraction destinée à devenir une des grandes réalités des établissements humains."

14. "Les philosophies, comme les théologies de tous les temps, à de bien rares exceptions près, quoique importantes, ont penché à l'affirmation d'une nécessité universelle. Le dix-huitieme siècle a fait comme ses devanciers" (*Uchronie*, viii).

15. "Préoccupés avant tout de leur lutte contre les traditions d'intolérance, de superstition et de barbarie, obligés de stigmatiser les crimes historiques, ils auraient eu mauvaise grâce à proclamer la nécessité des institutions et des actes dont ils niaient hautement la légitimité morale" (ibid.).

16. "Nous avons appris à les admirer toutes, chacune sous le bon point de vue" (xi). And the result was that the study of history once again impeded the exercise of historical judgment: "Les historiens ont pris à tâche de vivre de la vie du passé: ils on tout compris, le mal comme le bien, les nécessités du mal, les excuses du crime, mieux encore, sont indispensable utilité" (ibid.).

17. See William Logue, *Charles Renouvier, Philosopher of Liberty* (Baton Rouge: Louisiana State University Press, 1993) for a full account. For Renouvier's exposition of his ideas in the 1850s, see his *Essais de critique générale. Deuxième essai. L'homme: la raison, la passion, la liberté, la certitude, la probabilité morale*, 2nd ed. (1859; repr., Paris: Bureau de la "Critique philosophique," 1875).

18. Charles Renouvier, *Deuxième essai*, as translated and quoted by Logue, *Charles Renouvier*, 210.

19. Logue, *Charles Renouvier*, 91.

20. Renouvier, *Philosophie analytique de l'histoire*, vol. 4 (Paris: Ernest Leroux, 1897), 177. "Rien de moins moral qu'une telle justification de la passion populaire et de ses emportements, rien de moins libéral que cet abaissement de l'individu devant l'instinct de foules." For a longer discussion of Renouvier's relation to contemporary French historians, see Paul Mouy, *L'idée de progrès dans la philosophie de Renouvier* (Paris: J. Vrin, 1927).

21. Karl Marx, *The Civil War in France*, in *Marx and Engels Collected Works* (London: Lawrence & Wishart Electric Book, 2010), 22:307–59, 352.

22. Walter Benjamin, in a letter to Max Horkheimer in 1938, somewhat misreading Blanqui's treatise as asserting merely the proliferation of copies of our world throughout the universe, notes that "the piece has, in its theme, the eternal recurrence, the most remarkable relation to Nietzsche" (Walter Benjamin, *Briefe*, vols. 1–2 of *Gesammelte Schriften* [Berlin: Suhrkamp Verlag, 1978], 740–41). George J. Stack, in *Lange and Nietzsche* (New York: W. de Gruyter, 1983), demonstrates that Nietzsche had read Blanqui by the time he came to write about the eternal return (28).

23. Auguste Blanqui, *Éternité par les astres*, in *Maintenant, il faut des armes*, textes choisis et presents par Dominique Le Nuz (Paris: La Fabrique, 2006), 318–82; 360. All quotations from this work are from this edition and page numbers are given in the body of the chapter.

24. Loc. cit.

25. Blanqui makes various uses of his version of eternal recurrence. For example, he sometimes takes a page from Boethius's *Consolation of Philosophy*, picturing the wheel of fortune to invoke the vanity of ambition: "Here is Pompey, who is about to lose that of Pharsalus. Poor man! He goes away to find consolation in Alexandria with his good friend King Ptolemy . . . Caesar laughs well. . . . But just now he is on his way to receive

the twenty-two knife wounds in the midst of the Senate" (*Éternité par les astres*, 367). At other moments, though, he thinks about repetition in space on planets where history is perfectly synchronized with the earth's, a reflection that gives the prisoner a different kind of solace as he imagines himself multiplied into numerous prisoners looking back at himself from the stars: "If someone interrogates the celestial regions demanding their secret, millions of his copies raise their eyes at the same time, with the same question in the same [train of] thought, and all those looks cross paths, invisibly" (378).

26. On the influence of *Éternité par les astres* on Borges and other avant-garde writers of the interwar years, see Lisa Block De Behar, *Borges: The Passion of an Endless Quotation*, trans. William Egginton (Albany, NY: SUNY Press, 2003), 31–55.

27. Saul Kripke's "rigid designator" theory of proper name reference, on which I am relying, defines a rigid designator as that which designates "the same object" in "any possible world." Saul Kripke, *Naming and Necessity* (Cambridge, MA: Harvard University Press, 1980), 48–49. In *Heterocosmica: Fiction and Possible Worlds* (Baltimore, MD: Johns Hopkins University Press, 1998), Lobomír Doložel asserts that "persons with actual-world "prototypes" constitute "a distinct semantic class within the set of fictional persons . . . ; an ineradicable relationship exists between the historical Napoleon and all fictional Napoleons" (17). However, Doložel wants to see the counterfactual Napoleons as "counterparts" of the historical person, rather than "versions" (the term preferred by Nicholas Rescher), and he also maintains that, "as nonactualized possibles, all fictional entities are of the same ontological nature" (18). I have sometimes used his term "counterpart" for the counterfactual textual referents of the historical proper names.

28. The word "novel" may be losing this precision of meaning, but this study will insist on its retention. In a 1998 *American Historical Review* article, the historian Lynn Hunt complained that her students in a recent introductory course referred to all of the assigned books (including such historical and philosophical classics as Carlo Ginzburg's *The Cheese and the Worms*, Christopher Browning's *Ordinary Men*, and Nietzsche's *Genealogy of Morals*) as "novels." "'No Longer an Evenly Flowing River': Time, History, and the Novel," *American Historical Review* 103, no. 5 (December 1998): 1517–21, esp. 1517. My views on the distinctiveness of the modern novel are given in Catherine Gallagher, "The Rise of Fictionality," in *The Novel*, vol. 1, *History, Geography, and Culture*, ed. Franco Moretti (Princeton, NJ: Princeton University Press, 2006), 336–64.

29. On the semantics of using proper names, see Kenneth A. Taylor, *Reference and the Rational Mind* (Stanford, CA: Stanford University Press, 2003), 167–90. Taylor distinguishes between "full" proper names, which already have semantic values, and "empty" ones, such as those used in fiction, which accumulate content as the text proceeds. On this issue, also see the following: Roland Barthes, *S/Z*, trans. Richard Miller (New York: Hill and Wang, 1974), 67–68; Peter Nesselroth, "Naming Names in Telling Tales," in *Fiction Updated: Theories of Fictionality, Narratology, and Poetics*, ed. Calin-Andrei Mihailescu and Walid Hamarneth (Toronto: University of Toronto Press, 1996); and John Frow, *Character and Person* (Oxford: Oxford University Press, 2014), 181–225.

30. Some theorists claim that all fictional works are in the hypothetical mode and that we construct counterfactual worlds in order to understand them. However, this view misses the distinctiveness of the historical counterfactual mode by not taking

into account its "instead of" structure. There are many different ways of applying possible-worlds theory to fiction. See Doložel, *Heterocosmica*; Marie-Laure Ryan, *Possible Worlds, Artificial Intelligence, and Narrative Theory* (Bloomington: Indiana University Press, 1991); David Lewis, "Truth in Fiction," *American Philosophical Quarterly* 15, no. 1 (1978): 37–46; Thomas G. Pavel, *Fictional Worlds* (Cambridge, MA: Harvard University Press, 1986); and Ruth Ronen, *Possible Worlds in Literary Theory* (Cambridge: Cambridge University Press, 1994). I have argued elsewhere that possible-worlds semantics is highly useful for alternate-history narratives but not for normal novels: "What Would Napoleon Do? Historical, Fictional, and Counterfactual Characters," *New Literary History* 42 (Fall 2011): 315–36.

31. Eugene Nicole, "L'onomastique Litteraire," *Poetique* 54 (1983): 233–53, esp. 236.

32. For the idea of the "facts of the fiction," see Ann Banfield, *Unspeakable Sentences: Narration and Representation in the Language of Fiction* (1982; repr., Abingdon: Routledge, 2015), 216–19.

33. Ryan, *Possible Worlds*, 57.

34. Several critics, including Karen Hellekson in *The Alternate History: Refiguring Historical Time* (Kent, Ohio: Kent State University Press, 2001), claim that Hale's story is the first alternate-history narrative in English, perhaps because Hawthorne's counterfactual biographies imagine no significant historical effect. Éric Henriet, in *L'histoire revisitée: Panorama de l'uchronie sous toutes ses fromes* (Amiens: Encrage, 2004), gives Hawthorne the temporal priority but nevertheless claims that it was Hale who introduced the Anglophone world to alternate history (83). Both mistakenly attribute nineteenth-century dates to Isaac D'Israeli's "Of a History of Events Which Have Not Happened," whereas it was actually written and published in the 1790s. See n15, chap. 1 above.

35. I am using Ryan's idea of a textual modal system here to describe the relation between the parts of *Uchronie*. See *Possible Worlds*.

36. "P's Correspondence" was first published in *United States Magazine and Democratic Review* in 1845 and was included the next year in Hawthorne's story collection, *Mosses from an Old Manse* (New York: Wiley & Putnam, 1846). My quotations are from the Modern Library Classics edition: *Mosses from an Old Manse* (New York: 2007), 287–301. Page numbers are given in the body of the chapter.

37. Edward E. Hale, *Hands Off* (Boston: J. S. Smith, 1895), 25. Quotations are from this edition and page numbers are given in the text. First published in *Harper's*, March 1881.

38. Edmund Lawrence, *It May Happen Yet; a Tale of Bonaparte's Invasion of England* (London: printed by author, 1899), 9. Subsequent page numbers are given in the body of the chapter.

39. I am expanding here on Harry E. Shaw's idea of "disjunctive" historical novels—those in which the direction of the protagonist's story does not align with that of historical developments. See Shaw, *The Forms of Historical Fiction: Sir Walter Scott and His Successors* (Ithaca, NY: Cornell University Press, 1983), 151–211. Shaw notes that such novels conform to what Siegfried Kracauer called history's nonhomogeneous structure, in which "interrelated events at low and higher levels exist, so to speak, side by side." *History: The Last Things before the Last* (New York: Oxford University Press,

1969), 117. My addition to this theory is just to note that the supposed "microhistory" of the protagonist often aligns with the super-macro level of the *longue durée* even when it seems extraneous to the level of the historical events.

40. A passage from a letter by Hegel is sometimes summarized to indicate that Hegel said he saw world history, in the person of Napoleon, sitting on a horse. This is what Hegel actually wrote: "The Emperor—this world soul—I saw riding through the city to a review of his troops; it is indeed a wonderful feeling to see such an individual who, here concentrated in a single point, sitting on a horse, reaches out over the world and dominates it." Hegel to Friedrich Niethammer (13 October 1806), cited in Walter Kaufmann, *Hegel: A Reinterpretation* (Garden City, NY: Doubleday, 1965), 319.

41. See, e.g., William Wordsworth's sonnet on Bonaparte, published in 1815, which concludes:

O joyless power that stands by lawless force!
Curses are his dire portion, scorn, and hate,
Internal darkness and unquiet breath;
And, if old judgments keep their sacred course,
Him from that Height shall Heaven precipitate
By violent and ignominious death.

42. There are, to be sure, a few nondystopian twentieth-century alternate-history novels that are modeled on historical novels and nevertheless branch toward an alternative considered desirable in the terms set by the fiction. In the Italian writer Guido Morselli's 1975 *Past Conditional: A Retrospective Hypothesis*, e.g., a victory by the Austrian Empire in World War I makes World War II unnecessary. Even in this semiutopian novel, though, the change mainly accelerates the pace toward a world resembling the actual present: the outcome of Morselli's alteration is a European Union in the 1920s, with a promise of democratic collectivism to follow. The original title was *Contro-passato prossimo: Un'ipotesi retrospettiva* (Milan: Adelphi, 1975). The English translation, by Hugh Shankland, came out in 1989 (London: Chatto and Windus).

43. For a discussion of the development of this idea in late-eighteenth and nineteenth-century literature, see Catherine Gallagher, "Workers and Slaves: The Rhetoric of Freedom in the Debate over Industrialism" in *The Industrial Reformation of English Fiction: Social Discourse and Narrative Form, 1832–1867* (Chicago: University of Chicago Press, 1985), 3–35.

44. F. P. Williams, *Hallie Marshall: A True Daughter of the South* (New York: Abbey Press, 1900), 101. Subsequent page numbers are given in the body of the chapter.

CHAPTER THREE

1. This chapter discusses the great majority of the counterfactual scenarios published before the 1960s. I have not, in other words, needed to be choosey, since there were few counterfactual or alternate-history essays. The choice of counterfactual histories has been somewhat trickier, since I argue that many mainstream academic Civil War and Reconstruction histories before the 1960s were based on counterfactual premises (e.g., that slavery would soon have withered away by itself even if we hadn't

fought the Civil War) that only became explicit when they were challenged in 1960s and 1970s. I therefore discuss both the most important counterfactualists (Roger L. Ransom and Richard Sutch, Robert Fogel and Stanley Engermann) and the implicit counterfactualizing of their targets, especially James G. Randall and William Archibald Dunning.

2. William Lloyd Garrison, "Dissolution of the Union Essential to the Abolition of Slavery," *The Liberator*, 24 September 1855.

3. Hazel Dicken-Garcia and Giovanna Dell'Orto, *Hated Ideas and the American Civil War Press* (Spokane, WA: Marquette Books, 2008), 84.

4. Dicken-Garcia and Dell'Orto (ibid.) describe at length the struggle for press freedom in the war years.

5. See Brayton Harris, *Blue and Gray in Black and White: Newspapers in the Civil War* (Washington, DC: Brassey's, 1999) for an excellent overview.

6. Crompton Burnton, "'No Turning Back': The Official Bulletins of Secretary of War Edwin M. Stanton," in *Words at War: The Civil War and American Journalism*, ed. David B. Shachsman, S. Kittrell Rushing, and Roy Morris Jr. (West Lafayette, IN: Purdue University Press, 2008), 281–93.

7. Quoted in Bill Hyde, ed., *The Union Generals Speak: The Meade Hearings on the Battle of Gettysburg* (Baton Rouge: Louisiana State University Press, 2003), 4–5.

8. Ibid., 14.

9. Quoted in Gabor S. Boritt, "Unfinished Work: Lincoln, Meade, and Gettysburg," in *Lincoln's Generals*, ed. Gabor S. Boritt (New York: Oxford University Press, 1994), 89. See also Bruce Tap, *Over Lincoln's Shoulder: The Committee on the Conduct of the War* (Lawrence: University Press of Kansas, 1998), 173–92.

10. These and subsequent quotations from the record of the Meade Hearings are taken from Hyde, ed., *The Union Generals Speak*, and the page numbers refer to that book.

11. The following exchange evinces the tension between the professional military men and the congressmen:

> Question. Did not the fact that [Lee] was intending to cross that river afford you a very favorable opportunity to attack him while he was in the act of crossing, and why was it that he was permitted to escape without being attacked?
>
> Answer [Major General Sedgwick]. He occupied a very strong position in front of Williamsport, and he withdrew at night. It certainly would have been very advantageous to have attacked him while he was withdrawing, but not while he was in position there. I believe that if we had attacked him we would have received a severe repulse.
>
> Question. Could not an attack have been made upon him sufficient to ascertain his strength without endangering our force?
>
> Answer [Sedgwick]. I scarcely know how to answer that question.
>
> Question: I will say—without seriously endangering our forces?
>
> Answer [Sedgwick]. It is very difficult to withdraw troops after they have once become seriously engaged, without having them severely handled.

Testimony of Major General John Sedgwick, a West Pointer and a Democrat, ibid., 328–29.

12. The hearings began when the personal motives of several army officers (including General Hooker, whom Meade had replaced) converged with the political motives of the abolitionist Republicans.

13. For example, the committee spent a great deal of time hearing trumped-up testimony in support of the idea that Meade actually planned to withdraw from Gettysburg on the eve of the battle, despite the absurdity of the charge in light of all the evidence that he was marshaling troops toward the battlefield at the time. Only one witness—Brigadier General Howe—gave the committee the sort of overtly political testimony it sought, stating that "there is copperheadism at the root of the matter" (95).

14. William Swinton, *Campaigns of the Army of the Potomac: A Critical History of Operations in Virginia, Maryland, and Pennsylvania from the Commencement to the Close of the War, 1861–5* (New York: Richardson, 1866), 371–72. Swinton had been a war correspondent for the *New York Times* during the war and had at one point been accused of inaccuracy by Meade. Nevertheless, in his role as critical historian, his judgment of the general is largely positive.

15. Under these codes, the freedmen were typically prohibited from work except as field hands, and those refusing to sign labor contracts could be punished; unemployed black men could be seized and forced to work for planters; in some states, black children could be taken from their families and made to work. It should be noted that the Union Army had set the precedent for many of these measures when it occupied the Southern states and imposed harsh discriminatory measures against blacks in the name of preserving social order. It was little wonder, then, that white Southerners called the federal government hypocritical when the black codes were annulled. See Dan T. Carter, *The Failure of Self-Reconstruction in the South, 1865–1867* (Baton Rouge: Louisiana State University Press, 1985), 217ff.

16. Albion Tourgée, *A Fool's Errand, by One of the Fools*, 2nd ed. (New York: Fords, Howard & Hulbert, 1879), 156. All quotations of the novel are from this text, and page numbers are given in the body of the chapter.

17. Michael T. Gilmore, *The War on Words: Slavery, Race, and Free Speech in American Literature* (Chicago: University of Chicago Press, 2010).

18. Ernest Crosby, "If the South Had Been Allowed to Go," *North American Review* 177, no. 565 (December 1903): 869. Page numbers for further citations given in the body of the chapter.

19. Every Civil War Internet discussion group seems to have debated or to be still in the process of debating this question—"What if the South had been allowed to secede?"—and the first thing most debaters say is that "slavery would have died a natural death." More controversial is the proposition that the CSA and USA would have reunited. See, e.g., "Great Debates: What If the South Had Been Allowed to Secede?" Straight Dope Message Board, http://boards.straightdope.com/sdmb/archive/index.php/t-463927.

20. The logic is the same as that reported by D'Israeli when writing about the English Civil War. Had the Royalists defeated the commonwealth men at the Battle of Worcester, they would have hurt their own cause in the long run; only when the rebels were left "at full leisure to complete and perfect their own structure of government" could they be ultimately overcome.

21. Ernest Crosby, *Garrison the Non-Resistant* (Chicago: Public Publishing, 1905), 95. Page numbers for further citations are given in the body of the chapter.

22. H. L. Mencken, "The Calamity of Appomattox," in *A Mencken Chrestomathy* (New York: Knopf, 1949), 196–99; first published in *American Mercury*, September 1930.

23. Alma White, *Klansmen: Guardians of Liberty* (Zarephath, NJ: Good Citizen, 1926).

24. Regarding other contemporary counterfactual reflections published in Northern magazines, e.g., Webb Waldron examined three alternatives for avoiding the Civil War in "If Lincoln Had Yielded" in *Century Magazine* in June of 1926, and the Southern antisegregationist writer Virginius Dabney imagined a better South arising from a Confederate victory at Gettysburg in "If the South Had Won the War," an *American Mercury* story of 1936.

25. In *The Culture of Defeat: On National Trauma, Mourning, and Recovery* (trans. Jefferson Chase [New York: Henry Holt, 2003]), Wolfgang Schivelbusch notes that the two moments when Northern intellectuals entered most deeply into the mentality of the defeated were the turn of the century and the early 1930s; see 88–101 for examples. The production of alternate-history scenarios in the North corresponds precisely to his chronology. See also Lewis P. Simpson, *Mind and the American Civil War: A Meditation on Lost Causes* (Baton Rouge: Louisiana State University Press, 1989).

26. Winston Churchill was given to future conjectural military speculation as well as to past hypotheticals. For example, as first lord of the Admiralty he privately circulated, in April 1913, the story of a possible imperial German surprise attack on the British coast. Titled "A Time Table of a Nightmare," it's an interesting example of military scenario planning, and it is also reminiscent of the novel examined in the last chapter: Edmund Lawrence's turn-of-the-century *It May Happen Yet: A Tale of Bonaparte's Invasion of England*, which had warned of a possible future surprise attack by a Continental power.

27. Winston Churchill, "If Lee Had Not Won at Gettysburg," in *If It Had Happened Otherwise: Lapses into Imaginary History*, ed. J. C. Squire (New York: Longmans, Green & Co., 1931), 175. All quotations are from this edition, and page numbers are given in the body of the chapter.

28. The only 1930s' American writer to present a Southern victory as a worse outcome was the liberal Southerner Virginius Dabney, who speculated in 1936 that if the Confederacy had prevailed, Southern populism in the 1930s could easily have been perverted into fascism. In the subsequent chapters we'll look at other mid-1930s stories, such as Sinclair Lewis's *It Can't Happen Here* (Garden City, NY: Doubleday, Doran & Co., 1935), about how the United States might slide into a totalitarian state with a popular mandate. See Dabney, "If the South Had Won the Civil War," *American Mercury* 39, no. 154 (October, 1936): 199–206.

29. MacKinlay Kantor, *If the South Had Won the Civil War* (New York: Forge, 2001), 91–92—first published in *Look* magazine November 22, 1960.

30. J. G. Randall, *The Civil War and Reconstruction* (Boston: Heath and Co., 1937), 17.

31. William Archibald Dunning, "The Undoing of Reconstruction," *Atlantic Monthly*, 88, no. 528 (October 1901): 449. The reference to "our lately established rela-

tions with other races" may refer to the Asian Exclusion Act of the 1880s or to the Philippine-American War (1899–1902), which was often justified on racial grounds. Both of these developments would have given Dunning ample evidence that racial equality was an entirely discredited idea among white Americans.

32. U. B. Phillips, "The Decadence of the Plantation System," *Annals of the American Academy of Political and Social Science* 35 (January 1910): 37–41, 41.

33. Kenneth M. Stampp, "The Historian and Southern Negro Slavery," *American Historical Review*, 57, no. 3 (1952): 613–24. On the question of slavery's profitability, Stampp cites Lewis C. Gray, "Economic Efficiency and Competitive Advantage of Slavery under the Plantation System," *Agricultural History* 4 (1930): 31–47; Thomas P. Govan, "Was Plantation Slavery Profitable?" *Journal of Southern History* 8 (1942): 513–35; Robert R. Russel, "The General Effects of Slavery upon Southern Economic Progress," *Journal of Southern History* 4 (1938): 34–54; and Robert Worthington Smith, "Was Slavery Unprofitable in the Ante-Bellum South?" *Agricultural History* 20 (1946): 62–64.

34. Alfred H. Conrad and John R. Meyer, "The Economics of Slavery in the Ante-Bellum South," *Journal of Political Economy* 66, no. 2 (1958): 95–130, 101.

35. Stampp's *Peculiar Institution* came out in 1956 (New York: Knopf); his earlier article was "The Historian and Southern Negro Slavery" *American Historical Review* 57, no. 3 (1952): 613–24. Conrad and Meyer's 1958 article had been presented in 1957 at a joint meeting between the Economic History Association and the National Bureau of Economic Research. The bureau had recently assembled a vast amount of historical economic data regarding the nineteenth-century United States, which served as the basis for the first practitioners of cliometrics. My information about the early years of econometrics comes from Claudia Goldin, "Cliometrics and the Nobel," *Journal of Economic Perspectives* 9, no. 2 (Spring 1995): 191–208.

36. North was interested in why institutions like slavery create a kind of insensitivity to whether the elite might potentially have a higher level of income. Under such regimes as serfdom and slavery, he concluded, "there is no assurance that more efficient institutions will drive out less efficient ones." Hence, interventions like the Civil War are necessary. See Goldin, "Cliometrics and the Nobel," 199.

37. This description of the elements of cliometric analysis comes from Robert William Fogel and Stanley L. Engerman, *Time on the Cross: The Economics of American Negro Slavery* (Boston: Little, Brown, 1974), 4. All further references to this book are from this edition and page numbers are given in the body of the chapter.

38. Fogel's first book, *Railroads and American Economic Growth: Essays in Econometric History* (Baltimore: Johns Hopkins University Press, 1964), had familiarized historians with the general idea of the new counterfactual economic history. As we've often noted, historians might be said to use counterfactual logic implicitly whenever they argue that a certain cause was indispensable to a particular outcome, but they seldom put their arguments in the hypothetical conditional form that would make them explicit. Fogel pointed out the historians' inconsistency in this regard and claimed that cliometricians had the advantage of making such claims overt and subjecting them to hard evidence. He thus came on the scene as a reformer who characterized mainstream historians as methodologically naive. Not surprisingly, historians gave *Railroads and American Economic Growth* a mixed reception.

39. See Herbert Gutman and Richard Sutch, "Sambo Makes Good; or, Were Slaves Imbued with the Protestant Work Ethic?" in Paul A. David et al., *Reckoning with Slavery: A Critical Study in the Quantitative History of American Negro Slavery* (New York: Oxford University Press, 1976).

40. This is the position held by Roger L. Ransom and Richard Sutch in *One Kind of Freedom: The Economic Consequences of Emancipation*, 2nd ed. (1977; repr., Cambridge: Cambridge University Press, 2001).

41. See Kenneth M. Stampp and Leon F. Litwack, eds., *Reconstruction: An Anthology of Revisionist Writings* (Baton Rouge: Louisiana State University Press, 1967); and Eric Foner, *Reconstruction: America's Unfinished Revolution* (New York: Harper and Row, 1988).

42. See "Reconstruction as It Should Have Been," special issue of *Civil War History*, vol. 51, no. 4 (2005).

43. For a 2005 reflection on previous and contemporary black reparations claims, see law professor Robert Westley, "The Accursed Share: Genealogy, Temporality, and the Problem of Value in Black Reparations Discourse," *Representations* 29 (Fall 2005): 81–116.

44. Steven F. Lawson, ed., *To Secure These Rights: The Report of President Harry S Truman's Committee on Civil Rights* (Boston: Bedford/Saint Martin's, 2004), 159, first released in October 1947.

45. Quoted in Terry H. Anderson, *The Pursuit of Fairness: A History of Affirmative Action* (New York: Oxford University Press, 2004), 82.

46. See W. E. B. DuBois, "The Counter Revolution of Property," chap. 14 in *Black Reconstruction: An Essay toward a History of the Part Which Black Folk Played in the Attempt to Reconstruct Democracy in America, 1860–1880* (New York: Russel and Russel, 1935), 580–636.

47. President Lyndon B. Johnson's Commencement Address at Howard University: "To Fulfill These Rights," June 4, 1965, http://www.lbjlib.utexas.edu/johnson/archives.hom/speeches.hom/654604.asp.

48. The term "affirmative action" was apparently first used in President Kennedy's 1961 executive order 10925, which said that "the contractor will take affirmative action to ensure that applicants are employed, and that employees are treated during employment, without regard to their race, creed, color, or national origin." John F. Kennedy, "Executive Order 10925: Establishing the President's Committee on Equal Employment Opportunity," 6 March 1961, sec. 301, no. 1.

49. *Milliken v. Bradley*, 433 U.S. 267, 280 (1977); quoting 418 U.S. 717, 746 (1974).

50. David W. Roberson, "The Common Sense of Cause in Fact," *Texas Law Review* 75 (1996–97): 1770.

51. Anderson, *The Pursuit of Fairness*, 116.

52. Ibid., 117.

53. Quoted in ibid., 77. Farmer was testifying in 1963 about JFK's Civil Rights Act.

54. The University of California, Davis, did not use counterfactuals in defense of its admission program, instead arguing that it had a First Amendment right to academic freedom, which allows it to use an admissions system that would improve the learning environment through diversity (at 311–15 of the opinion). A plurality of the U.S.

Supreme Court agreed with this claim, but disagreed with the specific mechanism (a 16 percent set-aside) used to achieve it.

55. *University of California v. Bakke*, 438 U.S. 265, 366 (1978).

56. Ibid., 402.

57. Ibid., 401.

58. In objecting to this line of thinking at the time, Justice Powell insisted it was fallacious to hold "but for this discrimination by society at large, Bakke 'would have failed to qualify for admission' because Negro applicants . . . would have made better scores." The argument, he thought, involved an unwarranted presumption of causality since one might agree that black Americans would have been better qualified without concluding that any particular white candidate would have been unqualified.

59. *DeFunis v. Odegaard*, 416 U.S. 312, 337–40 (1974) (dissenting opinion).

60. A new way of thinking about affirmative action came out of Justice Powell's reasoning. In the Congressional Record Service's Report for Congress titled "Federal Affirmative Action Law: A Brief History," Charles V. Dale explains that Powell's opinion, which became the law, prevented colleges and universities from simply setting aside places for minority students or establishing quotas that would "insulate the individual from comparison with all the other candidates for the available seats" *Bakke*, 317. However, Powell also found a diverse student body to be a permissible goal and concluded that race could be considered as "one element of a range of factors" in considering candidates.

61. Common law tradition now does allow for such suits, since individuals suffering through lives with major disabilities have successfully sued parties who negligently caused them to be born. "The reality of the 'wrongful-life' concept is that such a plaintiff both exists and suffers, due to the negligence of others. It is neither necessary nor just to retreat into meditation on the mysteries of life. We need not be concerned with the fact that had defendants not been negligent, the plaintiff might not have come into existence at all." *Curlender v. Bio-Science Laboratories*, 106 Cal. App. 3d 811 (1980).

62. My sample is composed of twenty-two short pieces published in various anthologies (in addition to the collections listed in n65 below, see Frank McSherry Jr., ed., *The Fantastic Civil War* [New York: Baen, 1991]) and five book-length stories: Peter Tsouras, *Gettysburg* (Mechanicsburg, PA: Stackpole Books, 1997), and *Dixie Victorious* (London: Greenhill, 2006); James Cupelli, *1864: An Alternate History* (West Conshohocken, PA: Infinity Pub., 2006); Howard Means, *C.S.A.—Confederate States of America* (New York: William Morrow, 1998); and Dennis P. McIntire, *Lee at Chattanooga* (Nashville, TN: Cumberland House, 2002).

63. This sentence, from the introductory sequence, is taken from the PBS website for *The Civil War: A Film by Ken Burns*: "About the War," http://www.pbs.org/kenburns/civil-war/war/war-overview/.

64. Peter G. Tsouras, "Confederate Black and Gray: A Revolution in the Minds of Men," in *Dixie Victorious*, 202–24, 207.

65. See, e.g., Brian Thomsen and Martin H. Greenberg, ed., *Alternate Gettysburgs: Original Visions of the Civil War That Might Have Been* (New York: Berkley Books, 2002); Robert Cowley, ed., *What Ifs? Of American History* (New York: G. P. Putnam's, 2003); and James C. Bresnahan, ed., *Revisioning the Civil War: Historians on*

Counter-Factual Scenarios (Jefferson, NC: McFarland & Co., 2006). Unlike the social scientists, the military historians seldom engage in methodological reflection. In the last-mentioned anthology, Keith E. Gibson of the Virginia Military Institute tersely explains their reasoning when he acknowledges that although "what-ifs" are "right up there near the top of the list of things historians are warned—indeed, trained—not to do, . . . military historians . . . are encouraged to speculate—and for good reason: survival" (foreword in *Revisioning the Civil War*, ed. Bresnahan, 1). No need for lengthy methodological explanations.

66. Roger L. Ransom, *The Confederate States of America: What Might Have Been* (New York: W. W. Norton, 2005), xi. It is noteworthy, also, that *The Confederate States of America* was published by a trade—not an academic—press. All further citations of this book are from this edition, and page numbers are given in the body of the chapter. Like those of most cliometricians, Ransom's PhD is in economics, and he taught in the University of California, Riverside, economics department from 1968 to 1984, when he moved to the history department, where he has taught social, economic, and military history.

67. Ransom is referring here only to our contemporary alternate histories and not to works like Geoffroy-Château's or Renouvier's, which we studied in earlier chapters. Our judgment of the limitations of the military alternate histories of the last fifteen years accords with his.

68. On the history of the concept of "character" in fiction, see Deidre Lynch *The Economy of Character: Novels, Market Culture, and the Business of Inner Meaning* (Chicago: University of Chicago Press, 1998). On intentionality and agency in history writing, see Paul Ricoeur, *Time and Narrative*, vol. 1, trans. Kathleen McLaughlin and David Pellauer (Chicago: University of Chicago Press, 1984), 175–230.

69. The only path Ransom finds to a Confederate victory is through the resurrection of Stonewall Jackson. Because Jackson's death was a freakish accident—the result of friendly fire from which he was expected to recover, followed by a bout of pneumonia—it's an easy thing to reverse. Ransom also works hard at his counterfactual military scenarios to make the battles in which Jackson participates into plausible Confederate victories or standoffs, but the single major departure from actuality is a mere matter of chance.

CHAPTER FOUR

1. In a series of self-referential and self-differentiating jokes, the narrator of Ward Moore's 1947 *Greener Than You Think* pokes fun at what he often called "space operas": "Contributors to scientifiction magazines burst bloodvessels happily turning out ten thousand words a day describing their heroes' adventures amid the red grass of Mars or the blue grass of Venus after they had singlehanded—with the help of a deathray and the heroine's pure love—conquered the green grass of Tellus." Ward Moore, *Greener Than You Think* (Rockville, MD: Wildside Press, 2008), 73–74. Note that he uses the interwar term "scientifiction" rather than "science fiction," which was only becoming the norm in the postwar years.

2. Ward Moore, "A Letter from Southern California: Improbabilia on the Rise," *San Francisco Chronicle*, This World Section (9 April 1950), 15 and 18. The term "improba-

bilia" comes from the eighteenth-century German aesthetician A. G. Baumgarten, who made improbabilia a separate category of objects for poetic representation in his 1750–58 treatise *Aesthetica*.

3. Ward Moore, "Improbabilia and Politics," *Nation* (30 May, 1953), 463.

4. Kenneth Rexroth, *An Autobiographical Novel* (Santa Barbara, CA: Ross-Erikson, Inc., 1978), 311–13, gives a portrait of Ward Moore (renamed, in the novel, Bard Major) in the late 1920s: "He was one of the historic eccentrics of American bohemia. He is still around today [1964], an influential, if not very successful, science-fiction writer. His parents were even more eccentric than he was, but his grandmother was the leading *modiste* of Canada and matriarch straight out of G. B. Stern. . . . Bard had been put in the best prep school in America which admitted Jews. In his fifteenth year he read Lenin, Trotsky, and Shaw, and he ran away" (311).

5. Ward Moore, *Greener Than You Think* (New York: William Sloane Associates Publishers, 1947).

6. Ibid. Hollywood, for example, was only just beginning to film works of fantasy because the studios had an aversion to "ideas": "A means of expressing ideas can be an uncomfortable thing to have around a studio—like an unexploded mine." Moore, "A Letter from Southern California," 15 and 18.

7. Moore, "A Letter from Southern California," 18.

8. The need to pause and clue the reader in to the concepts could also trigger self-satire, for narrating and reflecting on the possibility of the narrative are often difficult to synchronize. A 1942 backward time-travel story (i.e., from the future to the present), by Edna Mayne Hull, has the protagonist, an American squadron leader in the midst of a dogfight with the Germans, impatiently query a physicist, who is a passenger and has just been hit by a stray bullet, to account for the presence of a mysterious stranger, who has suddenly appeared in the fighter plane in the place of the copilot:

"The time theory!" [the squadron leader] croaked.

"Oh, yes, the old business of probables—You're the bravest man I ever met, Squadron Leader, to carry on such a conversation [at a time like this]: . . . about . . . time theories, about worlds and men that might have existed if—something hadn't happened. Of course, to the theorist, those worlds do exist; that is, some projection of them, something of the spirit that carried on—."

E. M. Hull, "The Flight That Failed" (first published in 1942), in *Science Fiction Adventures in Dimension*, ed. Groff Conklin (New York: Berkely Publishing, 1953), 117.

9. Moore, *Bring the Jubilee* (New York: Farrar, Straus & Young, 1953), 142. All quotations are from this edition and page numbers are given in the text.

10. Richard J. Hofstadter's classic essay, "The Paranoid Style in American Politics" was the title essay of his 1964 book (New York: Knopf).

11. See Gérard Genette's remarks in the introduction to *Narrative Discourse Reconsidered* for a discussion of the basic distinction between the time of the narrating (what he calls the "récit") and the time of the events narrated (the "histoire"). *Narrative Discourse Reconsidered*, trans. Jane E. Lewin (Ithaca, NY: Cornell University Press, 1988), 13–16.

12. Kari Frederickson, *The Dixiecrat Revolt and the End of the Solid South, 1932–1968* (Chapel Hill: University of North Carolina Press, 2001).

13. Edward Page Mitchell, "The Clock That Went Backward" (first published in the *New York Sun*, 1881), in *The Crystal Man: Stories by Edward Page Mitchell*, ed. Sam Moskowitz (Garden City, NY: Doubleday & Co., 1973), 79–80. All quotations are from this edition and page numbers are given in the body of the chapter.

14. Paul J. Nahin's *Time Machines: Time Travel in Physics, Metaphysics, and Science Fiction* (New York: Springer-Verlag, 1999) is the best overview of the history of the concept of backward time travel. Nahin discusses the difference between affecting the past and changing it in his chapter on time-travel paradoxes, 269–94.

15. Jacques Rigaut, "Un brillant sujet," *Littérature*, no. 2, n.s. (April 1922).

16. "Incertain de rencontrer Dieu et impuissant à modifier un passé dont il est issu, Palentête s'applique à en créer de nouvelles versions."

17. "Juste de quoi déconcerter ceux des hommes de son époque qui s'aventureraient à sa suite dans le passé et qui risquent de ne plus rien y rencontrer de conforme à l'histoire."

18. While Jacques Rigaut was using backward time travel to explore the absurdities of personhood and being, the French fantasy writer André Blandin and the pacifist poet Théo Varlet collaborated on the first novel in which the plot of repairing history—rather than enacting or destroying it—appeared, *La belle Valence* (Amiens: E. Malfère, 1923). This may be the first novel in which the undoing plot of historical activism is broached, but the attempted change is thwarted, and Our Timeline prevails. Blandin and Varlet evince no interest in the puzzles and paradoxes that form the core of Rigaut's story, and they depict heroes—French soldiers who rediscover H. G. Wells's time machine in 1917 and use it to return, with modern arms, to a fourteenth-century siege of Valencia—who try to change history without any fear of undermining their personal existence. They ally themselves with the Moors, who are besieging the city, and temporarily succeed in enlightening those Spaniards who are attempting to establish the Inquisition. Like Twain's *Connecticut Yankee*, though, these heroes are ultimately routed by the forces of historical reaction, and no alternate-history path emerges.

19. The paradox had become such a widespread cliché by the 1940s that Mortimer Weisinger found it ripe for satirical treatment. In a short 1944 story, a beleaguered and bumbling editor of a science-fiction magazine tries to explain why he has placed a ban on any further time-travel stories:

> Now look here, . . . I've told you before that all time-travelling stories were taboo with this magazine office. My readers are too sophisticated. Doctors, lawyers, students and professional men in all different walks of life are enthusiastic followers of my publication. If there is anything at all that disturbs them, it's an illogical story. Why, the last time I printed a time-travelling story, we received dozens of protests from readers. If you went back in time to kill your grandpop, you wouldn't be born to go back to kill—just how would it work out? No matter how ingenious be the plot, the old "grandfather" argument invariably whips the author!

Mortimer Weisinger, "Thompson's Time-Traveling Theory," *Amazing Stories* (March 1944).

20. "Napoléon . . . n'a pas été entraîné par les hommes, mais s'est imposé à eux. Son génie personnel a conduit toute son aventure. S'il succombe au debut de son carrière, si

une balle perdue le tue au siège de Toulon, que deviendra l'Histoire?" René Barjavel, *Le voyageur imprudent* (Paris: Editions Denoël, 1944), 235.

21. Barjavel, "To Be and Not to Be," postscript to the 1958 edition of *Le voyageur imprudent* (Paris: Editions Denoël).

22. Isaac Asimov's *The End of Eternity* (Garden City, NY: Doubleday, 1955) is an exception to this rule. His story imagines a continuous timeline in a world where an elite group of people who live outside of spatial and temporal location make small alterations in history to bring about "reality changes" for the benefit of mankind.

23. John Jakes, *Black in Time* (1970; repr., New York: Bart Books, 1988), 62.

24. Octavia Butler, *Kindred* (Boston: Beacon Press, 1979), 29.

25. Stephen Best has discussed this ethic of recovery as a kind of "melancholy historicism" "that seeks to continue, animate, or complete the political projects of those who were defeated in the past." He argues that this ethical recovery project, especially when applied to the history of slavery, is in many ways politically self-defeating. My analysis here owes a great deal to Best's article "On Failing to Make the Past Present," *Modern Language Quarterly* 73, no. 3 (2012): 453–74.

26. Jorge Luis Borges, "The Garden of the Forking Paths," trans. Anthony Boucher, *Ellery Queen's Mystery Magazine* 12, no. 57 (August 1948): 109. This is the first translation and English language publication of Borges's 1941 story, "El jardín de senderos que se bifurcan."

27. William Sell, "Other Tracks" (first published in *Astounding Science Fiction*, October 1938), in *Science Fiction Adventures in Dimension*, 89.

28. L. Sprague de Camp, *Lest Darkness Fall* (Riverdale, NY: Baen Publishing, 1996), 4. An earlier version of the story was first published in the magazine *Unknown Fantasy Fiction*, in December 1939; de Camp's *The Wheels of If* came out in the same magazine in October 1940.

29. In "Alternate History and Postmodern Temporality," Paul Alkon usefully and concisely distinguishes between alternate history and parallel history. The essay is in *Time, Literature, and the Arts: Essays in Honor of Samuel L. Macey* (Victoria, BC: University of Victoria, 1994), 68. See also Nahin's discussion of splitting universes, in *Time Machines*, 295–303.

30. See Franz Rottensteiner's account of this story in "European Science Fiction," in *Science Fiction: A Critical Guide*, ed. Patrick Parrinder (New York: Longman, 1979), 205.

31. D. R. Daniels, "The Branches of Time," *Wonder Stories* 7, no. 3 (August 1935): 295–303, 366. Other references are to this edition and page numbers are given in the body of the chapter.

32. Kafka's friend Max Brod recalled this remark in a 1921 article on Kafka (in *Die Neue Rundshau*), and it was quoted by Walter Benjamin in "Franz Kafka: On the Tenth Anniversary of His Death," later collected in *Illuminations*, ed. and intro. Hannah Arendt, trans. Harry Zohn (New York: Schocken Books, 2007), 116.

33. The eight novels that explore other possible African American histories are Robert Stapp, *A More Perfect Union* (1970); John Jakes, *Black in Time* (1970); David Poyer, *The Shiloh Project* (1981); Harry Harrison, *A Rebel in Time* (1983); Kevin Randle and Robert Cornett, *Remember Gettysburg!* (1988); Terry Bisson, *Fire on the Moun-*

tain (1988); and Leonard Skimin, *Gray Victory* (1988). The half dozen taking conflicts between European settlers and indigenous Americans as their theme are Martin Cruz Smith, *The Indians Won* (1970); Ron Montana, *The Sign of the Thunderbird* (1977); Kenan Heise, *The Journey of Silas P. Bigelow* (1981); Mack Reynolds and Dean Ing, *The Other Time* (1984); and Kevin Randle and Robert Cornett, *Remember the Little Bighorn!* (1990). One on Mexican and Anglo American conflict is Kevin Randle and Robert Cornett's *Remember the Alamo!* (1980).

34. The term "entelechy" was coined by Aristotle and combines (according to one of his modern translators) the ideas of full-grown completeness or ripeness with the concept of persisting, through continuing effort, in a specific condition and with the notion of having a telos, or intrinsic purpose. See Joe Sachs, *Aristotle's Physics: A Guided Study* (New Brunswick, NJ: Rutgers University Press, 1995), 245.

35. Kevin Randle and Robert Cornett, *Remember Little Bighorn!* (New York: Charter Books, 1990), back cover. Nothing in the ill-conceived plot of the novel actually conforms to this threat, but the idea of a great nation coming apart with devastating swiftness probably seemed like a timely advertising ploy in 1990.

36. Two later Native American nationalist novels (Jake Page's *Apacheria: An Epic of Alternate History* and Pamela Sargent's *Climb the Wind*) came out in 1998.

37. See Terry H. Anderson, "The Demise of Affirmative Action in the Age of Diversity," chap. 5 of *The Pursuit of Fairness: A History of Affirmative Action* (New York: Oxford University Press, 2004), for an analysis of the decade.

38. I use the term "new world order" in H. G. Wells's sense, not in the sense attributed to it by recent conspiracy theorists. See Wells's *The New World Order*, first published in January 1940 and describing a plan for global peace in the post-WWII era.

39. For the history of modern restitution movements for historical injustices, see Elazar Barkan's *The Guilt of Nations: Restitution and Negotiating Historical Injustices* (Baltimore: Johns Hopkins University Press, 2000). See also the anthology of documents edited by Roy L. Brooks, *When Sorry Isn't Enough: The Controversy over Apologies and Reparations for Human Injustice* (New York: New York University Press, 1999).

40. For a lucid discussion of the differences between affirmative action and reparations, see Eric A. Posner and Adrian Vermeule, "Reparations for Slavery and Other Historical Injustices," *Columbia Law Review* 103, no. 3 (April 2003): 689–748. See also Alfred L. Brophy, *Reparations Pro and Con* (New York: Oxford University Press, 2006).

41. Derek Brown, "Litigating the Holocaust: A Consistent Theory in Tort for the Private Enforcement of Human Rights Violations," *Pepperdine Law Review* 27 (2000): 553–95.

42. The best history of the reparations movement in the United States is Brophy, *Reparations*. For a thorough discussion of the efforts at Native American restitution and the complications besetting them, see Barkan, *The Guilt of Nations*, 169–215.

43. Robert S. Browne, "The Economic Basis for Reparations to Black America," *Review of Black Political Economy* 2, no. 2 (March 1972): 67–80.

44. Turtledove specifically disagrees with Thomas Connelly's *The Marble Man* (Baton Rouge: Louisiana State University Press, 1978), which concerns not so much Lee the historical person as Lee the persona in Lost Cause writings. See Harry Turtledove,

"Historical Notes," in *The Guns of the South: A Novel of the Civil War* (New York: Random House, 1993), 559. All further quotations are also from this edition, and page numbers are given in the body of the chapter.

45. For a thorough discussion of the controversy surrounding the TRC's amnesty provisions and international law, see Christine M. Hart, "Learning from South Africa: The TRC, the ICC and the Future of Accountability," *Journal of Public and International Affairs* 12 (January 2001): 19–44.

46. Many studies have been made of the TRC's amnesty policy, its failure to compensate victims monetarily, and its general effect on South African transition. Books and essay collections include James L. Gibson and Amanda Gouws, *Overcoming Intolerance in South Africa: Experiments in Democratic Persuasion* (New York: Cambridge University Press, 2002); Charles Villa-Vicensio and Wilhelm Verwoerd, eds., *Looking Back Reaching Forward: Reflections on the Truth and Reconciliation Commission of South Africa* (Cape Town: University of Cape Town Press, 2000); and Robert Rothberg and Dennis Thompson, eds., *Truth v. Justice: The Morality of the Truth Commissions*, (Princeton, NJ: Princeton University Press, 2000). For a comparative study of two nation's transitional justice processes in the mid-1990s, see M. R. Rwelamira and G. Werle, eds., *Confronting Past Injustices: Approaches to Amnesty, Punishment, Reparation and Restitution in South Africa and Germany* (Durban: Butterworths, 1996).

47. Turtledove's next Civil War alternate-history work, *How Few Remain* (New York: Del Rey/Ballantine, 1998), is the beginning of a long saga, consisting of more than a dozen volumes, which is intent on exploring the international implications of a Southern victory on world history and on picturing a world in which the North American nations become entangled in international rivalries and wars from 1862 onward. This epic work has a far darker vision of history's possible moral trajectories than *Guns of the South* has.

CHAPTER FIVE

1. Gavriel D. Rosenfeld, *The World Hitler Never Made: Alternate History and the Memory of Nazism* (Cambridge: Cambridge University Press, 2005). See esp. chap. 2, 95–160.

2. For a look at how one group of British and American social scientists tried to revive the concept of national character and use it to both win the war and prepare for a multicultural peace, see Peter Mandler's *Return from the Natives: How Margaret Mead Won the Second World War and Lost the Cold War* (New Haven, CT: Yale University Press, 2013).

3. Cato, *Guilty Men*, introduction by Philip Wittenberg (New York: Stokes Company, 1940), 10–11. All further quotations are from this edition, and page numbers are given in the body of the chapter.

4. D. J. Dutton, "Guilty men (act. 1940)," *Oxford Dictionary of National Biography*, Oxford University Press, accessed 15 March 2017, http://www.oxforddnb.com/view/theme/70401.

5. Stella Rudman, *Lloyd George and the Appeasement of Germany, 1919–1945* (Newcastle upon Tyne: Cambridge Scholars Publishing, 2011), 4.

6. Rudman's book gives a detailed account of the term's complete fall from grace in 1938-39.

7. As early as 1934, e.g., Churchill attacked Ramsay MacDonald's National Labour government by asserting that they were ignoring the threats to homeland security that had already been illustrated by near catastrophes in the last war: "Not one of the lessons of the [last war] has been learned, not one of them has been applied, and the situation is incomparably more dangerous. Then we had the Navy and no air menace. Then the Navy was the 'sure shield' of Britain. . . . We cannot say that now. This cursed, hellish invention and development of war from the air has revolutionised our position. We are not the same kind of country we used to be when we were an island, only twenty years ago." Quoted in Churchill, *The Gathering Storm* (New York: Bantam Books, 1961), 84.

8. Winston Churchill, "A Total and Unmitigated Defeat" (House of Commons 5 October 1938), *Winston S. Churchill: His Complete Speeches 1897-1963* (New York, 1974), 6:6004-13, 6:6008. All quotations of his speeches are from this collection (hereafter referred to as *Complete Speeches*), and page numbers are given primarily in the body of the chapter.

9. "Their Finest Hour" (House of Commons, 18 June 1940) in *Complete Speeches*, 6:6231-37, 6232.

10. "Neville Chamberlain" (House of Commons, 13 November 1940) in *Complete Speeches*, 6:6307-8.

11. For the use made by Gregory Bateson and Margaret Mead of "fair play" as the common cultural denominator of the British and American national characters, see Mandler, *Return from the Natives*, 93.

12. "Wars Are Not Won by Evacuations" (House of Commons, 4 June 1940), in *Complete Speeches*, 6:6225-31, 6231.

13. "Every Man to His Post" (Broadcast, London, 11 September 1940) in *Complete Speeches*, 6:6276-77.

14. James Hayward, *Shingle Street: Flame, Chemical and Psychological Warfare in 1940, and the Nazi Invasion That Never Was* (Essex: LTM Publishers, 1994), 101.

15. Quoted in Peter Stansky, *The First Day of the Blitz, September 7, 1940* (New Haven, CT: Yale University Press, 2007), 125.

16. Churchill, *Their Finest Hour* (New York: Houghton Mifflin, 1985); originally published as vol. 2 of his *The Second World War* (London: Cassell, 1946), 264.

17. Noel Coward, *Peace in Our Time: A Play in Two Acts and Eight Scenes* (Garden City, NY: Doubleday, 1948), 47-48.

18. For an overview of the scenarios in which Hitler bends all resources in 1940 toward an invasion of Britain, see Andrew Roberts, "Hitler's England: What If Germany Had Invaded Britain in May 1940?" in *Virtual History: Alternatives and Counterfactuals*, ed. Niall Ferguson (London: Picador, 1997), 281-320.

19. "The Few" (House of Commons, 20 August 1940), in *Complete Speeches*, 6:6261-68, 6266.

20. Duncan Grinnell-Milne, *The Silent Victory, September 1940* (London: Bodley Head, 1958), 176-77. Subsequent citations are given in the text.

21. The exercise is described in Paddy Griffith's, *Sprawling Wargames* (n.p: Lulu.com, 2009), 27–89.

22. Derek Robinson, *Invasion, 1940: The Truth about the Battle of Britain and What Stopped Hitler* (New York: Carroll and Graf, 2005), 3.

23. Margery Allingham, *The Oaken Heart* (Garden City, NY: Doubleday, Doran, 1941), 198–99.

24. Churchill, *Their Finest Hour*, 275.

25. Quoted in Hayward, *Shingle Street*, 97.

26. Hayward's book was inspired by the eruption of these 1992 stories, and the information about the Special Operations disinformation campaigns and their revival comes from *Shingle Street*, chaps. 5 and 6, 75–110.

27. Churchill, *Their Finest Hour*, 143.

28. Peter Fleming, *Operation Sea Lion: The Projected Invasion of England in 1940—an Account of the German Preparations and the British Countermeasures* (New York: Simon and Schuster, 1957), 9. Subsequent page numbers will be given in the text.

29. The most vigorous argument for this point of view is Peter Schenk, *Invasion of England, 1940: The Planning of Operation Sealion*, trans. Kathleen Bunten (London: Conway Maritime Press, 1990); German edition was published in 1987.

30. Walter Ansel, e.g., sees Hitler as proceeding out of a desire to save face despite deep ambivalence about fighting the English, whom he admired: *Hitler Confronts England* (Durham, NC: Duke University Press, 1960). For other books that view Sea Lion as the product of mixed motives, none of which was strong enough to get it launched when the odds became clear, see Egbert Kieser, *Hitler on the Doorstep: Operation "Sea Lion": The German Plan to Invade Britain, 1940*, trans. Helmut Bögler (Annapolis: Naval Institute Press, 1997)—the German edition was published in 1987; Michael Glover, *Invasion Scare 1940* (London: Leo Cooper, 1990); Telford Taylor, *The Breaking Wave: The Second World War in the Summer of 1940* (New York: Simon and Schuster, 1967).

31. Schenk, *Invasion of England, 1940*, 355.

32. *Seelöwe* Designer's Notes (New York: Simulations Publications, 1974).

33. In addition to Grinnell-Milne's *The Silent Victory*, Ronald Wheatley's *Operation Sea Lion: German Plans for the Invasion of England, 1939–1942* (Oxford: Clarendon Press, 1958) falls into this category.

34. Other Sea Lion historians who consider the option of not threatening invasion are Wheatley (*Operation Sea Lion*), Taylor (*The Breaking Wave*), and Schenk (*Invasion of England, 1940*).

35. Comer Clarke, *England under Hitler* (New York: Ballantine Books, 1961), 7. Subsequent citations to this work will be given in the text.

36. In 2009, Bob Graham of the *Telegraph* renewed interest in Clarke's story when he reported that Poland had decided to commemorate the incident as the first action of World War II and honor the hapless Silesian farmer who was killed as part of the plot. See Graham, "World War II's First Victim," *Telegraph*, August 29, 2009, http://www.telegraph.co.uk/history/world-war-two/6106566/World-War-IIs-first-victim.html.

37. David Lampe, *The Last Ditch* (London: Cassell, 1968), ix. Subsequent citations to this work will be given in the text.

38. Norman Longmate, *If Britain Had Fallen* (London: British Broadcasting Corporation; Hutchinson, 1972), [11]. Subsequent citations to this work will be given in the text.

39. The so-called *Gestapo Handbook* was finally published in an edition approved by the Imperial War Museum in 2000. See *Invasion 1940: The Nazi Invasion Plan for Britain* by SS General Walter Schellenberg, intro. John Erickson (London: St. Ermin's Press, 2000).

40. Marcel Ophüls's *The Sorrow and the Pity* was released in London in 1970.

41. Clive James, "Storm over England," *Observer* (17 September 1972), 34. Subsequent citations to this work will be given in the text.

42. Noel Coward, *Future Indefinite* (London: Bloomsbury, 2014), 121.

43. Fredric Jameson, *The Antinomies of Realism* (New York: Verso, 2013), 240–58.

44. An early example of the academic interest in the complexities of collaboration with the Nazis can be found in three articles published in one issue of the *Journal of Modern History* 40, no. 3 (September 1968). They are Henry Ashby Turner Jr., "Hitler's Secret Pamphlet for Industrialists, 1927," 348–75; Stanley Hoffmann, "Collaborationism in France during World War II," 375–95; and John A. Armstrong, "Collaborationism in World War II: The Integral Nationalist Variant in Eastern Europe," 395–410.

45. For a revisionist account of the politics of the invasion, see Michael Glover's 1990 *Invasion Scare 1940*, which argues that Churchill was too knowledgeable to have taken the threat of a German invasion seriously, but he was happy to exploit the German plans and preparation as a means of galvanizing the British people, awaken them from the torpor of their post-Dunkirk demoralization, steel them against air attack, and put them on a firm war footing. Glover thus adds to the arguments that there was never an objective threat by further claiming that the British government artfully fomented the fear.

46. Adrian Gilbert, *Britain Invaded: Hitler's Plans for Britain, a Documentary Reconstruction* (London: Century, 1990), [6].

47. Hazel Knowles Smith, *The Changing Face of the Channel Islands Occupation: Record, Memory, and Myth* (London: Palgrave, 2007), 168. Smith sums up the consensus about the Channel Islands occupation that prevailed before the controversy that erupted in the 1980s and 1990s. She summarizes the conclusion of the official history by Charles Cruikshank, which was commissioned by the islands' governments: "He described the conduct of the Island administrators as 'plainly commonsense,' adding that if they did 'seem occasionally to have leaned too far in the direction of collaboration, it was their judgement that was at fault and not their loyalty'" (*The German Occupation of the Channel Islands* [London: Oxford University Press, 1975], xvi). Cruikshank's history of the military operation is still the standard account.

48. Smith, *The Changing Face of the Channel Islands Occupation*, 163–80.

49. Madeleine Bunting, *The Model Occupation: The Channel Islands under German Rule, 1940–1945* (London: Harper Collins, 1995), 3. Subsequent citations to this work will be given in the text.

50. In this regard Bunting follows a tradition among occupation counterfactualists of claiming that the Channel Islands example can be used to *prove* the writers' thesis. Comer Clarke's 1961 book *England under Hitler*, e.g., concludes with a chapter on the

islands, tellingly titled "It Happened Here," in which he relates only the deportations of the islands' Jews and the activities and punishments of the islanders who defied German orders to stop communicating by radio with the mainland. Longmate, *If Britain Had Fallen*, also turns to the actual Channel Islands occupation to find proof of a peculiar British ability to cooperate innocently, in the interest of protecting one's fellow citizens and restoring civil order, rather than in the interests of "treason." He even tries to quantify the amount of culpable cooperation with the enemy, claiming that 10 percent of the Danish population were collaborators, 10 percent resisters, and 80 percent neither, whereas only 2 percent of Channel Islanders were collaborators.

51. Andrew Roberts, "Hitler's Britain," in *Virtual History: Alternatives and Counterfactuals*, ed. Niall Ferguson (London: Picador, 1997), 281–320.

CHAPTER SIX

1. The theme did appear before the alternate-history fictions. It was first popularized in the pre-WWI stories depicting British national extinction known as "guerre imaginaire." They became international favorites during the decades of intense nationalism and imperial competition among Western European powers between the Franco-Prussian War of 1870 and 1914, but then faded from view until after Hitler's rise to power. The stories of the late 1930s and early 1940s often explicitly allude to the pre-WWI works, especially the 1913 novel *When William Came: A Story of London under the Hohenzollerns* (London: 1913), by Saki (one Hector Hugo Munro). For the history of this literature, see I. F. Clarke, *Voices Prophesying War: Future Wars 1763–3749* (New York: Oxford University Press, 1992), 93–131.

2. "Qu'est-ce qu'une nation?" was a lecture given at the Sorbonne in 1882 and published that year by Calmann Lévy. Ernest Renan, *Qu'est-ce qu'une nation? Conférence faite en Sorbonne, le 11 mars 1882* (Paris: Calmann Lévy, 1882). The original phrase is "un plébiscite de tous les jours" and has also been translated as "a daily referendum." The phrase signifies the need for a continually renewed consent of the nation's people, which he likens to the individual will to live: "comme l'existence de l'individu est une affirmation perpétuelle de vie" (15).

3. The best-known book on the symbiotic relation between the novel and the modern nation-state is Benedict Anderson's *Imagined Communities: Reflections on the Origin and Spread of Nationalism* (London: Verso, 1983). See also Homi K. Bhabha, ed., *Nation and Narration* (London: Routledge, 1990); and Irene Tucker, *A Probable State: The Novel, the Contract and the Jews* (Chicago: University of Chicago Press, 2000).

4. A different kind of analog can be found in a nonhypothetical fiction actually written during and depicting the historical experience of state destruction, while the likelihood of continued national sovereignty remained uncertain. The novel that, perhaps uniquely, fits this description is Irène Némirovsky's unfinished *Suite Française*, which was composed in 1941–42 and describes the immediate aftermath of the Nazi conquest of France. Indeed, the formal structure of that novel seems to demonstrate that in the dissolution of the legitimate state, narrative foci also scatter and dissipate, and this is the effect that the Nazi Britain novels also strive to achieve. Irène Némirovsky, *Suite Française: Roman* (Paris: Denoël, 2004).

5. Fredric Jameson's chapter titled "War and Representation" describes this sinister vitality of the setting as a characteristic of war literature generally. See Jameson, *Antinomies of Realism* (New York: Verso, 2013), 232–58.

6. This point is reiterated in the contemporary reviews, e.g., JS, "If We Made Peace with Hitler," *Times* (London), 17 August 1940, 7.

7. Douglas Brown and Christopher Serpell, *If Hitler Comes: A Cautionary Tale* (London: Faber & Faber, 2009), 12. This edition uses the book's revised title, whereas I refer to the novel throughout by its original title, *Loss of Eden*. Subsequent citations to this work will be to this edition and given in the text.

8. *Complete Speeches*, 6:6307.

9. For a full canvassing of the pressures inside Britain to seek a negotiated peace in the late spring and summer of 1940, see Julian Jackson, *The Fall of France: The Nazi Invasion of 1940* (Oxford: Oxford University Press, 2003), 200–213. Jackson's book is important as well for its use of Britain as a comparison case for testing counterfactual arguments regarding the fall of France: Did it happen because of France's incompetent leaders, political culture, insufficient morale, democratic pressures? In the final analysis, he concludes, only the counterfactuals concerning military tactics and strategy are plausible; the political, cultural, and leadership differences between France and Britain were negligible and cannot account for the capitulation of the former.

10. *The Lion and the Unicorn*, in *George Orwell: The Collected Essays, Journalism and Letters*, vol. 2, *My Country Right or Left*, ed. Sonia Orwell and Ian Angus (Boston: Nonpareil Books, 2000), 66. Subsequent citations to this work will be given in the text.

11. Robert Mackay, *Half the Battle: Civilian Morale in Britain during the Second World War* (Manchester: Manchester University Press, 2002), 1–13.

12. Cited in Anthony Osley, *Persuading the People* (London: HMSO, 1995), 21, quoted in Mackay, *Half the Battle*, 63.

13. JS, "If We Made Peace with Hitler," 7.

14. "If England Fell" *Times Literary Supplement* (London), August 10, 1940, 385.

15. Lloyd George, quoted in Glenda Sluga, *Internationalism in the Age of Nationalism* (Philadelphia: University of Pennsylvania Press, 2013), 35.

16. George Orwell, "Arthur Koestler," in *Critical Essays* (London: Secker and Warburg), 130–41, 141.

17. Bernard Crick, *George Orwell: A Life* (Harmondsworth: Penguin, 1980), 496.

18. Wartime popular culture was full of egalitarian reformist rhetoric from the beginning of the war. In a short film called *Dawn Guard*, from 1941, e.g., a Home Guard character declaims that when peace comes "There mustn't be no more chaps hanging around for work that don't come. No more slums neither. No more dirty, filthy backstreets and no more half-starved children with no room to play in. . . . We can't go back to the old ways of living, leastways not all of it. That's gone forever and the sooner we make up our minds about that the better." Quoted in Mark Connelly, *We Can Take It! Britain and the Memory of the Second World War* (Edinburgh: Pearson Longman, 2004), 118. A similar class consciousness pervades the one film that imagines British villagers thwarting an attempted German occupation of their community, Alberto Cavalcanti's 1942 *Went the Day Well?* And the Ministry of Information reported in 1942 that

"home-made socialism" was flourishing. Home Intelligence Report, 24 March 1942, quoted in Connelly, 119.

19. For a full discussion of how Conservative economic and social policies disintegrated in 1940–42 under the pressures of total mobilization and the necessity for equality of sacrifice, see Paul Addison, *The Road to 1945: British Politics and the Second World* (London: Quartet Books, 1975), esp. 127–63.

20. Crick, *George Orwell: A Life*, 408.

21. For a full discussion of the struggle in the coalition government over projected postwar reconstruction programs and the eventual end of the coalition, see Kevin Jefferys, *The Churchill Coalition and Wartime Politics, 1940–1945* (Manchester: Manchester University Press, 1991), 166–88.

22. "Lyric Theatre," review of *Peace in Our Time* by Noel Coward, *Times* (London), 23 July 1947, 7, Times Digital Archive, Gale Document Number CS119096567.

23. Noel Coward, *Peace in Our Time: A Play in Two Acts and Eight Scenes* (New York: Doubleday, 1948), 47–48.

24. Wartime invasion novels include: Robert Nathan, *They Went on Together* (1941); Gordon Boshell, *John Brown's Body* (1942); David Divine, *Tunnel From Calais* (1942); Margaret Storm Jameson, *Then We Shall Hear Singing: A Fantasy in C Major* (1942); Vita Sackville-West, *Grand Canyon* (1942); H. V. Morton, *I, James Blunt* (1942); Martin Hawkin, *When Adolph Came* (1942); and Anthony Armstrong and Bruce Graeme, *When the Bells Rang* (1943).

25. "Lyric Theatre."

26. Winston Churchill, the first conservative election broadcast, 4 June 1945, quoted in Antoine Capet, Monica Charlot, and Irène Hill, *Civilians in War: Key Documents, 1939–1945* (Paris: Ophrys Ploton, 1996), 201–2.

27. According to Harold Macmillan, Churchill was "fortified in his apprehensions [of a Labour government] by reading Professor Hayek's *The Road to Serfdom*." See *Tides of Fortune, 1945–1955* (London: Harper & Row, 1969), 32.

28. "Have we not heard Mr. Herbert Morrison descant upon his plans to curtail Parliamentary procedure and pass laws simply by resolutions of broad principle in the House of Commons, afterwards to be left by Parliament to the executive and to the bureaucrats to elaborate and enforce by departmental regulations?" The Labour Party, his fantasy continues, would then usurp the functions of the elected representatives and "gather all the power to the supreme party and the party leaders, rising like stately pinnacles above their vast bureaucracies of Civil servants." Churchill here alludes to a feature that he thought set twentieth-century totalitarianism apart from earlier authoritarian forms of government: the monopoly of power held by the party elite. Churchill, the first conservative election broadcast, quoted in Capet, Charlot, and Hill, *Civilians in War*, 202.

29. These included the costs of the war, the expenses of the empire, the failing infrastructure, the worn out equipment of the nationalized industries, the withdrawal of the U.S. Lend Lease funds and consequent need for new borrowing, the expense of helping to occupy and then rebuild Germany, and outlays for continuing to keep a large army (National Service for men continued until 1960), an air force, and, eventually, a nuclear weapons program and participation in NATO.

30. Richard Crossman, *The Charm of Politics, and Other Essays in Political Criticism* (London: Harper, 1958), 67.

31. It is often said that Britain's loss of its empire was accelerated by the war, for some of the same conditions that undermined socialist ambitions at home also weakened its hold on overseas territories. But to put it that way makes it seem as though the empire had been a luxury the country could no longer afford, whereas it had been, in fact, a source of the nation's enormous wealth. Moreover, it was Britain's life-support system during the war, the supplier of huge numbers of troops and munitions, and the location of many essential strategic bases. Thus instead of saying that Britain won the war and then lost its empire, it would be more accurate to say that the British Empire won the war and then its constituent elements came apart.

32. Peaceful and relatively orderly withdrawal from India in 1947 was negotiated only after it became undeniable that the vast majority of all Indians supported the demand for independence, and Burma's independence followed shortly thereafter. But there were both economic and Cold War strategic reasons for wanting to keep territory in South East Asia, the Middle East, and Africa. Indeed, in the early 1950s, Britain launched its plan to amalgamate Southern Rhodesia with two African protectorates, Northern Rhodesia (now Zambia) and Nyasaland (now Malawi), trying to take advantage of a copper boom and provide more room for white settlers. Although the resulting Central African Federation could not withstand the forces of decolonization on the continent and went out of existence in 1964, the project exemplifies the postwar state's continuing commitment to the imperial effort. Until the 1960s, the state continued to present itself as imperial even as it increasingly replaced direct rule with a "British Commonwealth" model of influence and investment. Although peaceful disengagement ultimately became the norm, by the late 1950s Britons were increasingly experiencing the process of decolonization as a long, slow retreat, preceded in such places as Malaya and Kenya by brutal anti-insurgency operations, which injured Britain's international reputation.

33. See, esp., Yasmin Khan, *The Raj at War: A People's History of India's Second World War* (London: Bodley Head, 2015), and *India at War: The Subcontinent and the Second World War* (Oxford: Oxford University Press, 2015).

34. Robert Skidelsky, *Britain since 1900: A Success Story?* (London: Vintage, 2014), 3.

35. The main exception is the earliest Nazi Britain novel, *The Sound of His Horn*, written by John W. Wall under the pseudonym Sarban and published in in 1952 (London: Peter Davies). The work fits less well under the rubric of alternate-history novel than it does under that of fantasy, for reasons outline by Gavriel Rosenfeld, *The World Hitler Never Made*, 44–46.

36. Kevin Brownlow described the inspiration for the film, as well as its production and reception, in *How It Happened Here: The Making of a Film* (London: Doubleday, 1968).

37. Ibid., 189.

38. For the earlier anxiety evinced in wartime films about imitating the ruthlessness of German warfare, see Kent Puckett, *War Pictures: Cinema, Violence, and Style in Britain, 1939-1945* (New York: Fordham University Press, 2017). The bombings, espe-

cially of Dresden, which were late in the war, had always been controversial, but Kurt Vonnegut's novel *Slaughterhouse-Five; or, The Children's Crusade: A Duty-Dance with Death*, published in 1969, renewed the debates in the context of the Vietnam War.

39. "Wars Are Not Won by Evacuations" (House of Commons, 4 June 1940), in *Complete Speeches*, 6:6225–31, 6231.

40. Giles Cooper, *The Other Man: A Novel Based on His Play for Television* (London: Panther Books, 1964), 11.

41. Harold Macmillan, "Winds of Change," speech made to the South Africa Parliament on 3 February 1960. A transcript of the BBC's recording can be found at "Tour of South Africa: Rt Hon Macmillan," BBC Archives, http://www.bbc.co.uk/archive/apartheid/7203.shtml.

42. See, e.g., the trilogy by Jo Walton featuring Inspector Peter Carmichael (*Farthing* [Leicester: Thorpe, 2006], *Ha'penny* [London: Thorpe, 2007], and *Half a Crown* [Leicester: Charnwood, 2008]) and C. J. Sansom's *Dominion* (London: Mantle, 2012).

43. James Cameron, "Damn Near Happened Here," *Guardian*, 27 August 1978, 22.

44. Rosenfeld, *The World Hitler Never Made*, 16; see 68–70 for his critique of Deighton.

45. A helpful overview of the uses of the German term *Normalisierung* can be found in Jeffrey K. Olick, "What Does It Mean to Normalize the Past?" *Social Science History* 22, no. 4 (Winter 1998), 547–71. Olick points out that the term was used by the West German left to criticize the routinized, mechanical fashion in which the nation acknowledged Nazi crimes through annual ceremonies marking, e.g., *Kristallnacht*. The West German right, in contrast, called for an end to such ceremonies in the name of *Normalisierung*.

46. Rosenfeld, *The World Hitler Never Made*, 18. For an insightful critique of Rosenfeld's normalization thesis, see Benjamin Aldes Wurgaft, "Notes on Camps, or Counterfactual Fuhrers and the Structure of the Joke," *History and Theory*, vol. 56 (forthcoming).

47. For a discussion of the problems implicit in positing "absolute evil," see Richard J. Bernstein, *The Abuse of Evil: The Corruption of Politics and Religion since 9/11* (Cambridge: Polity Press, 2005).

48. George Orwell, *Nineteen Eighty-Four* in *Orwell's Nineteen Eighty-Four: Texts, Sources, Criticism*, ed. Irving Howe (New York: Harcourt, Brace, 1963), 94. Subsequent quotations from this work are also from this edition, and page numbers are given in the text.

49. The BBC serial of *An Englishman's Castle* was directed by Paul Ciappessoni and starred Kenneth More. The screenwriter Philip Mackie had earlier written and produced a very popular ITV network historical drama series, *The Ceasars* (1968), and wrote the screenplay for *The Naked Civil Servant* (1975). The Internet Movie Database has additional information on Philip Mackie.

50. Paraphrased in Paul Addison, *No Turning Back: The Peacetime Revolutions of Post-War Britain* (New York: Oxford University Press, 2010), 253. For an account of the far right's exploitation of the immigration issue, see Richard Thurlow, *Fascism in Britain: A History, 1918–1985* (Oxford: Basil Blackwell, 1987), 230–68. See also Kathleen Paul, *Whitewashing Britain: Race and Citizenship in the Postwar Era* (Ithaca, NY:

Cornell University Press, 1997), for the history of postwar governments' actions to reconstruct "British subjecthood" so that (without explicitly mentioning race) it included descendants of white colonizers while excluding those "who had become British through conquest or domination" (181).

51. John Stokes, *Parliamentary Debates*, Commons, 5th series, vol. 914, col. 1066, 5 July 1976, quoted in Addison, *No Turning Back*, 367.

52. *Annual Report of the Commission for Racial Equality: January to December 1978*, HC 128, PP 1979–80 (London: HMSO, 1979), 2.

53. There were also changes in the behavior of West German politicians, who were faced with their own neo-Nazi youth: Federal president Walter Scheel declared that Germany's history, like that of all normal nations, included "highs as well as lows." See Addison, *No Turning Back*, 370; Olick, "What Does It Mean to Normalize the Past?" 552. Before the mid-1970s West Germany was busy atoning for Nazism at the international level; by the late-1970s, it apparently wanted to forget. Deeper in the background was the European Union, increasingly dominated by a West Germany that had weathered the economic crises of the late 1970s better than most developed countries. Britons had recently voted to stay in the European Union, but despite the outcome of the 1975 referendum on the issue, all political parties had substantial anti-European Union factions, and the Labour Party especially became increasingly opposed to British membership toward the end of the decade. By 1979, the party's "manifesto" warned of attempts to turn "the Community into a federation" and vowed to oppose them. Fears of being subsumed in a united Europe under West German leadership were not, in themselves, anti-German, but they might have indicated a skepticism about Germany's apparent desire to forget its earlier international aggression.

54. James Boswell *The Life of Samuel Johnson, L.L. D.* (London: Printed for G. Walker, 1820), 319.

55. Robert Harris, *Fatherland* (New York: Harper Paperback, 1993), 18.

56. See Peter Sloterdijk, *Critique of Cynical Reason*, trans. M. Eldred (London: Verso Books, 1988).

57. Robert Harris in an Internet interview with the *Guardian* ("Robert Harris on Fatherland," April 2, 2012, https://www.theguardian.com/books/video/2012/apr/02/robert-harris-fatherland-video).

58. See Olick, "What Does It Mean to Normalize the Past?" for a discussion of the Bitburg incident in the context of 1980s' normalization attempts.

59. Ernst Nolte, "Die Vergangenheit, die nicht vergehen will," *Frankfurter Allgemeine Zeitung*, 6 June 1986.

60. Robert Harris, *Selling Hitler* (New York: Pantheon, 1986), 381.

61. Henri Nannen was the chief editor of *Stern* when the flamboyant reporter Gerd Heidemann proposed that the magazine entertain former Nazis on Goering's yacht and publish their reminiscences and other table talk; it was out of this scheme that they came into contact with the forger. One of Nannen's subordinates later explained that Nannen (who had worked in various capacities for the Nazis in the late thirties and then in a military propaganda unit during the war) had an unconscious desire to minimize their crimes: "the less bad the Nazi past turned out to have been, the less bad his role in it was" (Quoted in Harris, *Selling Hitler*, 66).

62. I'm borrowing this idea from the discourse of born-again Christians, who use "Satan wins if" scenarios to describe the unendingness of the battle against the devil. See, e.g., Robert Don Hughes, *Satan's Whispers: Breaking the Lies That Bind* (Eugene, OR: Wipf & Stock, 2006) for numerous examples of this rhetoric, including, "Satan wins if he can blind our minds to our spiritual bondage" (26).

63. The trope of the Holocaust's unrepresentability is a variation on the incomprehensibility theme. See Ann Parry, "Idioms for the Unrepresentable: Postwar Fiction and the Shoah," in *The Holocaust and the Text: Speaking the Unspeakable*, ed. Andrew Leak and George Paizis (London: Macmillan, 2000), 109–24.

64. Isaac Deutscher, "The Jewish Tragedy and the Historian," in *The Non-Jewish Jew and Other Essays*, ed. Tamara Deutscher (London: Oxford University Press, 1968), 163. Quoted in Jeffrey C. Alexander, *Remembering the Holocaust: A Debate* (New York: Oxford University Press, 2009), 29.

65. Philosopher Susan Neiman also stresses that its status as an ultimate evil precludes understanding; see her "What's the Problem of Evil?" in *Rethinking Evil: Contemporary Perspectives*, ed. Maria Pia Lara (Berkeley: University of California Press, 2001), 27–45; 29.

66. Primo Levi, appendix to *If This Is a Man*, trans. Stuart Woolf, in *The Complete Works of Primo Levi*, ed. Ann Goldstein, 3 vols. (New York: Liveright Publishing Co., 2015), 1:190.

67. Levi, *The Drowned and the Saved*, in *Complete Works*, 3:2439.

68. Another critic who notices this intention is Gary Weissman in his entry on Robert Harris in *Holocaust Literature: An Encyclopedia of Writers and Their Work*, ed. S. Lillian Kremer, 2 vols. (New York: Routledge, 2003), 1:517–19, 519.

69. For a discussion of the wartime debate over the status of the Nazi regime in relation to the German nation, see Edward Bahr, *Weimar on the Pacific: German Exile Culture in Los Angeles and the Crisis of Modernism* (Berkeley: University of California Press, 2007), 223–41. Bahr details the debate among eminent German émigrés over the issue of whether to try to set up a German organization to serve as a representative of the true nation in exile. The debate came to an end when the Allies' demand for unconditional surrender became firm, precluding "any negotiations with representatives of the 'other Germany' from the outset. From 1943 on, the State Department opposed, therefore, the formation of a German government in exile" (240).

70. Kathryn Sikkink, *The Justice Cascade: How Human Rights Prosecutions Are Changing World Politics* (New York: W. W. Norton, 2011), 5. Sikkink discusses the reasons for the hesitancy of many prosecutors to use the precedents of the Nuremberg and Tokyo trials, especially in national trials. The Nuremberg precedents were revived in those years for the express purpose of applying them to broader movements for human-rights law, as Samuel Moyn has reminded us. The trials, he demonstrates, were not imagined to be part of a larger movement toward "universal justice" until the 1970s and 1980s. Samuel Moyn, *The Last Utopia: Human Rights in History* (Cambridge, MA: Harvard University Press, 2010), 80–83.

71. Derek Brown, "Litigating the Holocaust: A Consistent Theory in Tort for the Private Enforcement of Human Rights Violations," *Pepperdine Law Review* 27 (2000): 553–95. For the general history of twentieth-century restitution movements for histori-

cal injustices, see Elazar Barkan's *The Guilt of Nations: Restitution and Negotiating Historical Injustices* (Baltimore: Johns Hopkins University Press, 2000). See also the anthology of documents edited by Roy L. Brooks, *When Sorry Isn't Enough: The Controversy over Apologies and Reparations for Human Injustice* (New York: New York University Press, 1999).

72. See Norbert Frei, *Adenauer's Germany and the Nazi Past: The Politics of Amnesty and Integration*, trans. Joel Golb (New York: Columbia University Press, 2002).

73. Barkan, *The Guilt of Nations*, 13.

74. For an insightful discussion of the important role played by the New Left in making the Holocaust a central part of the West German historical memory, see Andreas Huyssen, *Twilight Memories: Marking Time in a Culture of Amnesia* (1995; repr., London: Routledge, 2012). Huyssen, however, faults the Germans on the left, both before and after unification, for a tendency toward "post-nationalism" which has allowed them to downplay the idea of *national guilt* while acknowledging the need for memorialization and reparations, 84.

75. Sikkink, *The Justice Cascade*, 21.

76. These three principles are summarized in ibid., 13.

77. Barkan, *The Guilt of Nations*, ix.

78. Sikkink, *The Justice Cascade*, surveys the literature on this topic, 162–88.

79. The gap between the legal and historical discourses may help account for the fact that, as Klaus Neumann has recently noted, "historians have not had a major influence on debates about historical justice." See "Historians and the Yearning for Historical Justice," *Rethinking History* 18, no. 2 (2014): 145–64, 145.

80. Niall Ferguson, *The Pity of War: Explaining World War I* (New York: Basic Books, 1999), 462.

81. Niall Ferguson, "The Kaiser's European Union: What If Britain Had 'Stood Aside' in August 1914?" in *Virtual History: Alternatives and Counterfactuals* (London: Macmillan, 1997), 228–80. For Liddel Hart's argument, see *The British Way in Warfare: Adaptability and Mobility*, rev. ed. (1932; repr., London: Penguin Books, 1942), 29–32.

82. Doris Lessing, *Alfred and Emily* (New York: HarperCollins, 2008).

83. John Charmley, *Churchill: The End of Glory, a Political Biography* (London: Faber and Faber, 1993).

84. Christopher Priest, *The Separation* (Baltimore: Old Earth Books, 2005).

85. For the theme of regionalism in recent Nazi Britain novels, see Owen Sheers's *Resistance* (New York: Nan A. Talese/Doubleday, 2007), which features a war-weary Wehrmacht officer trying to take his small group of men AWOL into an isolated Welsh valley. The theme of gay sexuality is prominent in Jo Walton's trilogy of Nazi Britain London police thrillers (*Farthing*, *Ha'penny*, and *Half a Crown*), where the protagonist is a gay detective. Nuclear war is the centerpiece of C. J. Sansom's *Dominion*, which tries to imagine an alternate history of the bomb.

86. Kate Atkinson, *Life after Life* (London: Reagan Arthur Books, 2013), 4, 515.

INDEX

abolition, of U.S. slavery, 99–100, 109–17, 129–30, 146
action, affirmative, 125, 130, 133–38, 148, 165–67, 174–75, 179–81, 332n48, 333n60, 338n40
activism, historical, 139, 147–48, 153–56, 158–89, 336n18
Addison, Paul, 345n19, 347n50, 348n53
Adenauer, Konrad, 305
agency, collective, 4, 65, 83, 93, 229, 232, 237
Alexander, Jeffrey C., 301, 349n64
Alexander the Great, 16
Alkon, Paul, 337n29
Allingham, Margery, 341n23
alternate history: vs. alternate-history novel, 3, 72–74, 157, 239; as antidote to authoritarianism, 292–93; and collective character, 66, 145, 192–93; and comparison, 62; as contemporary commentary, 48–49, 153–54, 184, 230, 299; defined, 3–15, 48; and fictional characters, 72–77, 144; focus on collectivities, 14, 66, 145, 192–93, 239; and historical personae, 72–75, 82, 176, 192, 227, 230; and judgment, 64–65; and justice, 54–57, 95, 131–39; narrative patterns of, 10, 48, 52, 57, 63, 83, 132, 137, 317n10; origins of, 49–50, 326n34; and revision, 52–53, 58–59, 151; as rhetoric, 63–64; and spy novel, 283; and U.S. race relations, 121–22, 140–43
alternate-history novel: changing history in, 89–90, 95–96, 155–56, 162–74, 184–86, 188–89, 318n17; and characters, 11, 49, 72–77, 88–89, 93; and collectivities, 14, 90–96, 176–77; as critique, 48, 92, 147–48, 151–53, 159–60, 274, 282, 299; defined, 3–15, 48, 84–85; narrative forms of, 80, 83–84, 94, 148, 177–78; nation as character in (see nation: as character); origins of, 83–87; relation to detective/spy novel (see detective/spy novel); relation to historical novel (see historical novel); relation to science fiction (see science fiction); use of time-travel (see time-travel, backward); and utopia/dystopia, 90–95, 175, 327n42; and world-making, 15, 148, 153–54, 276
Alternate Timeline (ATL), 52–53, 56–57, 65, 72–83, 90, 94–95, 134, 152, 165–66, 177, 304
Anderson, Benedict, 303, 343n3
Anderson, Terry H., 332n45, 338n37
Ansel, Walter, 341n30
apartheid, 182–84, 187
appeasement, Nazi, 192–97, 200–203, 231, 247, 269, 273, 288
Arendt, Hannah, 243, 279–80
Aristotle, 56, 318–19, 318n5, 323n10, 338n34
armistice of Leoben, 41–42, 44
Armstrong, Anthony, 345n24
Armstrong, John A., 342n44
Artz, F., 320n23
Asimov, Isaac, 337n22
Associated Press, 101
Atkinson, Kate, 310
Avidius Cassius, 58–59, 64–65, 95

351

Bahr, Edward, 349n69
Bakke, Allan P., 333n57
Banfield, Ann, 326n32
Barjavel, René, 164
Barkan, Elazar, 305, 307, 316n5, 338n39, 338n42, 349n71
Barnard, Henry, 320n23
Barthes, Roland, 325n29
Bateson, Gregory, 340n11
Baumgarten, A. G., 334n2
Bayle, Pierre, 25–26, 319n14, 320n17
Belkin, Aaron, 317n9
Benjamin, Walter, 68, 324n22, 337n32
Bernstein, Michael André, 318n16
Bernstein, Richard J., 347n47
Best, Stephen, 337n25
Bhabha, Homi K., 343n3
Birth of a Nation, 115
Bisson, Terry, 178, 337n33
Black, Jeremy, 316n6
Blandin, André, 336n18
Blanqui, Auguste, *Eternity through the Stars*, 49, 66–73, 81, 324n22, 324n25
Block De Behar, Lisa, 325n26
Boethius, 324n25
Bögler, Helmut, 341n30
Bonaparte, Napoleon, 327n41; as counterfactual character, 14, 46, 74, 78, 80, 164, 323n11, 325n27; and Frederik II, 34–36, 39; invasion of Britain (*see* invasion: Napoleonic); and military actions, 41–47, 56, 69, 103, 194; and unfulfilled potential, 51–57, 176
Borges, Jorge Luis, 72, 171, 325n26
Boritt, Gabor S., 328n9
Boshell, Gordon, 345n24
Boswell, James, 290
Bourbon restoration, 52–53
Bowen, Elizabeth, 206
Bowie, David, 289
Bresnahan, James C., 333n65
Britain, Battle of, 194, 205–8, 216, 233, 268, 290
British Empire, 202–5, 213, 216, 218, 255, 257, 259–60, 264–65, 272, 281–82, 288, 292, 346nn31–32
Brod, Max, 337n32
Brooks, Roy L., 338n39, 349n71
Brophy, Alfred L., 338n40, 338n42
Brown, Derek, 338n41

Brown, Douglas, 344n7; *Loss of Eden*, 244–45, 247, 249–50, 253, 256–57, 261, 263, 274, 290, 310
Browne, Robert S., 181
Brownlow, Kevin, 346n36
Brown v. Board of Education, 137
Bühler, Josef, 295
Bülow, Adam Heinrich Dietrich von, 46
Bunting, Madeleine, 235–36, 342nn49–50
Bunzl, Martin, 316n7, 318n1
Burns, Kenneth, 141
Burnton, Crompton, 328n6
Butler, Octavia, 168–71
Byrne, Ruth M. J., 315n1, 315n3
Byron, George Gordon, Lord, 78–80

Caesar, 324n25
Calhoun, John C., 100
Cameron, James, 347n43
Campe, Rudiger, 321n37
Capet, Antoine, 345n26, 345n28
Carter, Dan T., 329n15
Carver, Ben, 317n10
causality, 17, 24, 32, 137, 154, 161, 315n1, 315n3, 316nn6–7, 318n2, 333n58
Cavalcanti, Alberto, 344n18
Chamberlain, Neville, 195–97, 200–203, 247, 269, 298
chance, 22, 24, 26, 34, 69, 320–21, 334
Channel Islands' occupation, 233–36, 342n47, 342n50
character: collective, 13–15, 90–91, 145, 177, 192–93; counterfactual vs. fictional, 12–15, 36, 49, 54–57, 72–89, 157, 164–65, 227; vs. identity, 12–15, 45–47, 55–56, 144–45, 192, 311; national character (*see* nation: national character); nation as character (*see* nation: as character)
Charles II, 20, 25
Charlot, Monica, 345n26, 345n28
Charmley, John, 309–10
chronology, 25, 47, 151–52
chronotope, backward, 171–73
Churchill, Winston, 196–212, 246–47, 267–70, 277, 298, 309, 340n7, 342n45, 345nn27–28; "If Lee Had Not Won the Battle of Gettysburg," 117–21, 140, 145–46; "A Time Table of a Nightmare," 330n26
Ciappessoni, Paul, 347n49

Civil Rights Act, 108, 132–34, 136, 332n53
civil rights movement, 125, 132, 140–41, 147, 171, 182
Civil War: American, 4, 10, 15, 84, 91–93, 97–102, 107, 111–31, 139–47, 151–60, 175, 182–91, 198, 327n1, 329n19, 331n6; English, 20, 329n20
Clarke, Comer, *England under Hitler*, 220–21, 223–29, 232, 342n50
Clarke, I. F., 343n1
Clausewitz, Carl von, 5–7, 34, 39–44, 46–47, 103, 322
Cleburne, Pat, 141–42
Cleopatra's nose, 23–24, 156, 163, 319n10
Climo, T. A., 316n7
Clinton, Bill, 182
cliometrics, 126–28, 130, 143, 331n35, 331n38
Cold War, 139, 273, 278, 282–84, 293–94, 302–4, 307, 309, 346n32
collaboration, Nazi, 225–32, 234–36, 239, 268, 273–74, 342n44, 342n47, 342n50. *See also* appeasement, Nazi
Committee on the Conduct of the War, Joint Congressional, 101, 103, 267, 329n13
Commodus, 64–65
Compromise of 1877, 130, 159
Confederate States of America, 90–92, 95, 143, 333–34
Connelly, Mark, 344n18
Connelly, Thomas, 338n44
Conrad, Alfred H., 127–29, 331n35
Cooper, Giles, *The Other Man*, 278, 280, 282
Cornett, Robert, 337n33, 338n35
counterfactual history: as analysis, 3, 7, 31, 43, 46, 128, 144, 301, 315n3, 331n36, 385n3; and comparison, 7–9, 19, 25, 28, 30–31, 57, 62, 75, 127–30, 315n2, 344n9; defined, 1–3; and determinism, 4, 17, 21, 23, 26, 61–64, 119, 316n7, 318n3; and judgment, 4–9, 15, 27–28, 40, 62, 66, 119, 184, 292, 315n1; and jurisprudence, 3, 5–6, 49, 54, 56, 132–33, 139, 180, 305
Coward, Noel, *Peace in Our Time*, 207, 228, 267–69
Cowley, Robert, 333n65
Creevey, Thomas, 322n7
Crick, Bernard, 264, 266
Crosby, Ernest, 111–15, 117, 121–22, 140, 145, 151, 188
Crossman, Richard, 271, 346n30

Cruikshank, Charles, 342n47
Cupelli, James, 333n62
Curlender v. Bio-Science Laboratories, 333n61

Dabney, Virginius, 330n24, 330n28
Dale, Charles V., 333n60
Daniels, D. R., 173
Davidson, Donald, 317n12
Davis, Jefferson, 141
Dawn Guard, 344n18
de Bergerac, Cyrano, 67
de Fontenelle, Bernard le Bovier, 67
Defunis v. Odegaard, 138, 333n59
Deighton, Len, *SS-GB*, 284–86, 293
Dell'Orto, Giovanna, 328nn3–4
democracy, 5, 8, 98–99, 190, 247, 251, 258; and socialism, 260–65, 292
detective/spy novel, 283–85, 294–95
Deutscher, Isaac, 301, 349n64
Dicken-Garcia, Hazel, 328nn3–4
Disraeli, Benjamin, 25, 79, 119, 320n15, 320n17
D'Israeli, Isaac, 25–26, 320n16, 326n34, 329n20
Divine, David, 345n24
Dixiecrats, 159
Dixon, Thomas, 114–15, 167
Doložel, Lobomír, 325n27, 325n30
Donald, David, 124
Dönitz, Karl, 223
Douglas, William O., 138
DuBois, W. E. B., 123, 126, 132, 332n46
Dunkirk, 195, 208, 214, 216, 248
Dunning, William Archibald, 124–25, 327n1, 330n31
Dutton, D. J., 339n4
dystopia, 2, 10, 75, 95, 147, 150–51, 154, 157, 227, 286–87, 304

Else, Gerald, 323n10
Engberg-Pedersen, Anders, 320n20, 321n38
Engerman, Stanley L., *Time on the Cross*, 129–30, 327n1, 331n37
Englishman's Castle, An, 286–90, 292–95, 299, 304, 347n49
Enlightenment, 16–17, 21, 23–24, 28, 61–62, 173
entelechy, 56–57, 93, 176, 204, 338n34
ethnos, 176–78, 251–54, 347n50

Europe, postwar, 191–94, 199–200, 204, 213, 219, 234–36, 258–59, 267, 281, 291–94, 296, 348n53
Evans, Richard J., 316n6, 322n2

Farmer, James, 135, 332n53
Ferguson, Niall, 26, 309, 316n7, 318n1
Fifteenth Amendment, 108
First Amendment, 332n54
Fleming, Peter, 213–14, 216–17
Fletcher, Arthur, 135
Fogel, Robert William, *Time on the Cross*, 129–30, 327n1, 331nn37–38
fog of war, 41, 106
Foner, Eric, 332n41
Forbes-Robertson, Diana, 206
Fourteenth Amendment, 108
Franco-Prussian War, 67, 85, 343n1
Frederick II, the Great (king), 35–39, 319n14
Frederickson, Kari, 335n12
Frei, Norbert, 305, 350n72
French Empire, First. *See* Napoleonic Empire
French Empire, Second, 58, 60
French Republic, Second, 60–61, 66
Frow, John, 325n29

Gallagher, Catherine, 325n28, 325n30, 327n43
games, war, 33–35, 139, 208, 321
Gandhi, Mahatma, 265
Garrison, William Lloyd, 99, 112, 114
Gat, Azar, 40, 321n27, 321n34, 321n38
Genette, Gérard, 156, 335n11
Geoffroy-Château, Louis, *Napoléon and the Conquest of the World*, 49–52, 54–58, 60, 64, 71, 87–88, 93, 165, 176, 184, 323n11
George, Lloyd, 257
Gestapo Handbook, 220, 222–23, 227, 342n39
Gettysburg, Battle of, 93, 102–4, 106–7, 109, 117–19, 141, 155–57, 329n13
Gibson, James L., 339n46
Gibson, Keith E., 333n65
Gilbert, Adrian, 233, 342n46
Giles v. Harris, 112
Gilmore, Michael T., 112
Glover, Michael, 341n30, 342n45
Goldin, Claudia, 331nn35–36
Gould, J. D., 316nn7–8
Gouws, Amanda, 339n46
Govan, Thomas P., 331n33
Graeme, Bruce, 345n24, 345n28

Grafton, Anthony, 319n7
Graham, Bob, 341n34
grandfather paradox, 155, 162, 164–70, 172–73, 177, 185–86, 336
Gray, Lewis C., 331n33
Greeley, Horace, 114
Greenberg, Martin H., 333n65
Greene, Brian, 318n17
Griffith, Paddy, 341n21
Grinnell-Milne, Duncan, 214, 340n20, 341n33
guerre imaginaire, 85, 343n1
Guilty Men, 195–201, 231, 247
Gutman, Herbert, 331n39

Hale, Edward Everett, "Hands Off," 75, 81–85, 326n34, 326n37
Haley, Alex, 168
Halter, Ed, 321n31
Hamarneth, Walid, 325n29
Hamley, Edward, 320n24
Harris, Brayton, 328n5
Harris, Robert: *Fatherland*, 293–94, 296, 298–304, 306–7, 309; *Selling Hitler*, 298–99, 348n61
Harrison, Harry, 337n33
Hart, Christine M., 339n45
Hart, L. A., 315n1
Hawkin, Martin, 345n24
Hawthorn, Geoffrey, 316n7
Hawthorne, Nathaniel, "P's Correspondence," 75, 77–80, 326n34, 326n36
Hayek, Friedrich, 345n27
Hayward, James, 340n14, 341nn25–26
Hegel, Georg, 22, 26, 88, 161, 185, 327n40
Heidemann, Gerd, 348n61
Heise, Kenan, 175, 337n33
Hellekson, Karen, 317n10, 326n34
Hellwig, Johann Christian, 33
Henriet, Éric B., 317n10, 322n1, 326n34
Hill, Irène, 345n26
historical novel, 10, 77, 85–90, 95, 164, 238, 241, 289, 326n39, 327n42
Hitler, Adolf, 11, 198–200, 206, 211–13, 216–17, 231, 234–35, 244, 249, 257, 262, 295, 297–99, 311, 340n18, 341n30
Hoffmann, Stanley, 342n44
Hofstadter, Richard J., 153, 335n10
Holocaust, 280, 289, 294–96, 299, 301–4, 306–8, 310, 349n63, 350n74
Honoré, Tony, 315n1

Hooker, Joseph, 103, 106, 329n12
Horkheimer, Max, 324n22
Howe, Brigadier General, 329n13
Howells, P. G. A., 316n7
Hughes, Robert Don, 349n62
Hugo, Victor, 323n11
Hull, Edna Mayne, 335n8
Hunt, Lynn, 325n28
Huyssen, Andreas, 306, 350n74
Hyde, Bill, 328nn7-8

identity: collective, 98, 132, 191, 218, 243, 247, 251, 271, 278, 288; personal, 4, 11-15, 45-46, 56, 70-72, 311, 317n12, 317n14
immigration, 219, 282, 288, 347n50
improbabilia, 148-50, 155, 174, 334n2
infinity, 68, 70, 73, 174
Ing, Dean, 337-38n33
Ingram, Edward, 316n6
invasion, 29, 37-38, 132; Napoleonic, 53, 84-90; Nazi invasion of Britain (*see* invasion summer [1940]); Nazi occupation of Britain (*see* occupation, Nazi)
invasion summer (1940), 192-94, 204-23, 233-35, 244-48, 267-69, 289-91, 340n18, 342n45, 345n24. *See also* Operation Sea Lion
Irving, David, 289
Israel, Jonathan I., 319n12
It Happened Here, 274-75, 277-78

Jackson, Julian, 344n9
Jackson, Stonewall, 334n69
Jago, Mark, 317n12
Jakes, John, *Black in Time*, 165-67, 171, 177, 337n33
James, William, 63
Jameson, Fredric, 229, 344n5
Jameson, Margaret Storm, 345n24
Jarry, Alfred, 164
Jefferys, Kevin, 345n21
Jim Crow, 91, 109, 121, 132
Jomini, Antoine Henri de, 35-40, 42
July Monarchy, 51, 60
justice: historical, 4-6, 8, 49-50, 52, 54-55, 66, 95-96, 189, 304-5, 307-8, 316n5, 349n71; poetic, 56, 78, 116, 170, 323n10; reparations for U.S. slavery, 125, 131, 148, 187, 332n43, 338n40, 338n42; reparative justice or restitution, 6, 180-82, 186-87, 305, 350n74; retributive, 78, 305-7

Kafka, Franz, 174, 337n32
Kant, Immanuel, 40, 321n38
Kantor, MacKinlay, *If the South Had Won the Civil War*, 121-23
Kantorowicz, Ernst, 323n9
Kaufmann, Walter, 327n40
Kennedy, John F., 2, 12, 14, 332n48, 332n53
Khan, Yasmin, 346n33
Kieser, Egbert, 341n30
Kohl, Helmut, 297
Kolakowski, Leszek, 319n12
Koselleck, Reinhart, 22, 24, 26, 316n8, 319n10
Kracauer, Siegfried, 326n39
Kriegsspiel, 33-35, 321
Kripke, Saul, 12, 317n12, 317n14, 325n27
Ku Klux Klan, 111, 115, 117, 140, 151

Lacoue-Labarthe, Philippe, 323n12
Lampe, David, *The Last Ditch*, 221, 223-29
Lawrence, Edmund, *It May Happen Yet*, 84-86, 88-90, 92, 326n38, 330n26
Lebow, Richard Ned, 315n1, 316n7, 317n9
Lee, Robert E., 103-6, 117-18, 120, 141, 155, 183-88, 328n11, 338n44
Leibniz, Gottfried, 6-27, 82-83, 317n14, 318n3, 319n12; *Theodicy*, 17-19, 23, 45, 67-68, 318n5
Lessing, Doris, 309
Levi, Primo, 243, 301-2, 304
Lévy, Calmann, 343n2
Lewis, David K., 317n12, 317n14, 325n30
Lewis, Sinclair, 330n28
Liddel Hart, B. H., 309, 350n81
Lincoln, Abraham, 92, 99-100, 102-3, 106-8, 112, 123, 127
Litwack, Leon F., 332n41
Livy (Titus Livius), 16
Lloyd, Henry, 28-36, 42
Logue, William, 324n17
London, 86-87, 89, 205-6, 220, 244, 247, 268, 274-76, 287, 289
Longmate, Norman, *If Britain Had Fallen*, 222, 224-27, 229-32, 342n50
Lovejoy, Owen, 102
Lucretia, 18-19
Lynch, Deidre, 334n68

MacDonald, Ramsay, 340n7
Mackay, Robert, 249, 344n11
Mackie, Penelope, 317n12

Mackie, Philip, 286, 347n49
Macmillan, Harold, 281, 345n27
Mandler, Peter, 339n2, 340n11
Marcus Aurelius, 58–59, 61, 63–65, 95
Marshall, Thurgood, 136–39, 174
Marx, Karl, 67
Mass Observation, 249
McIntire, Dennis P., 333n62
McKenzie, John, 206
McLuhan, Marshall, 74
McSherry, Frank, Jr., 333n62
Mead, Margaret, 340n11
Meade, George Gordon, 102–6, 329nn13–14
Means, Howard, 333n62
Megill, Allan, 316n8, 317n11
Mellon, Stanley, 322n4
Mencken, H. L., "The Calamity of Appomattox," 115–17, 121, 126, 140, 145, 151
Meyer, John R., 127–29, 331n35
Michelet, Jules, 65–66
Mihailescu, Calin-Andrei, 325n29
military history, 3–5, 50, 52–53, 57, 70, 106, 118, 122, 139, 141, 143–44, 155, 194, 207–8, 214–15, 333n65; critical, 26–28, 36, 40, 44–45, 47, 87
Mill, John Stuart, 74
Miller, Andrew H., 318n16
Milliken v. Bradley, 133, 332n49
Mitchell, Edward Page, "The Clock That Went Backward," 160, 163, 165, 186
Montaigne, Michel de, 320n17
Montana, Ron, 175, 337n33
Moore, Michael S., 315n1
Moore, Ward: *Bring the Jubilee*, 143, 147–51, 153–55, 157–60, 188–89, 335n4, 335n6; *Greener Than You Think*, 334n1
morale, during wartime, 216, 246–50, 266
More, Kenneth, 347n49
Morris, William, 85
Morselli, Guido, 327n42
Morson, Gary Saul, 318n16
Morton, H. V., 345n24
Moscow, burning of, 39, 42, 52–54, 56, 194
Mosley, Oswald, 195, 228–30, 234
Mouy, Paul, 324n20
Moyn, Samuel, 349n70
multiverse, 15, 71, 318
Murat, Joachim, 55
Murphy, George, 316n7

Nahin, Paul J., 336n14, 337n29
Nannen, Henri, 348n61

Napoleon III (Louis-Napoleon), 51, 60–61
Napoleonic Empire, 49, 51, 53–54, 238, 320
Napoleonic Wars, 35, 39, 54, 173, 241, 320
Nathan, Robert, 345n24
nation: and American Union, 98, 100–102, 107–8, 112–13, 115–16, 141; as character, 14–15, 66, 145, 237–47, 266–74, 304, 308–11; as daily plebiscite, 240, 251; in Disunited States novels, 174–78; as ethnos, 176–78, 251–54, 347n50; as liberal democratic state, 240, 250–51, 254–56; national character, 14–15, 91, 192–93, 201–7, 218–21, 226–37, 257–60, 339n2; state vs. people, 193, 237–50, 256, 258–78, 281–93, 306–9
National Front, 219
Nationalism, ethnic, 176–78, 251–54, 347n50
Nazi Britain novel, 346n35
Nazism, 219–20, 222–23, 227, 239, 251, 260, 273–308, 310, 316n8, 348n53, 348n61, 349n65, 349n69; neo-, 186, 219, 222, 273, 275–76, 282–83, 288–89, 297, 348n53
Nehru, Jawaharlal, 265
Neiman, Susan, 349n65
Némirovsky, Irène, 343n4
neoliberalism, 270
Nesselroth, Peter, 325n29
Neumann, Klaus, 350n79
New Left, 287, 305, 350n74
nexus, 52–53, 63–64, 74–75, 139, 166, 171
Nicole, Eugene, 326n31
Niethammer, Friedrich, 327n40
Nietzsche, Friedrich, 67–68, 155, 324n22
Nixon, Richard, 134, 317
Nolte, Ernst, 297
nonevent, 193–94, 292
normalization, of Nazism, 230, 282–97, 347n45, 348n53, 348n58
North, Douglas, 128, 331n36
novel genre, 8, 10–11, 14, 49, 72–75, 80, 83
Novikov, Igor D., 318n17
Nuremberg Trials, 224, 304, 306, 349n70

occupation, Nazi: of Britain, 90, 192–93, 204–5, 217–32, 238–45, 253–55, 267, 273, 275, 277, 283–85, 344n18; of Channel Islands, 233–36, 242n47, 242n50; of France, 224–25, 232, 236, 343n4
Olick, Jeffrey K., 347n45, 348n53, 348n58
Operation Sea Lion, 208–17, 220–21, 341
Ophüls, Marcel, 225–26, 306, 342n40
Opiz, Giacomo, 34

Orwell, George, 242–43, 248, 286–87, 291–94, 300–301; *Animal Farm*, 263–64; *The Lion and the Unicorn*, 256–66, 271–72, 292; *1984*, 286–87, 290–92, 300
Osborne, John, 277–78
Osley, Anthony, 344n12
Our Timeline (OTL), 11, 52–53, 56, 69, 73, 75–77, 80, 83–84, 89–90, 95, 122, 158, 165–66, 184, 186, 304, 336n18

Page, Jake, 338n36
Paris Commune, 49, 67
Parker, Geoffrey, 315n1, 317n9
Parry, Ann, 349n63
Pascal, Blaise, 23–24, 63, 319
Paul, Kathleen, 347n50
Pavel, Thomas G., 325n30
Perla, Peter P., 321n29
Pétain, Philippe, 230, 262
petites causes, 24–25, 119
Philadelphia Plan, 135
Philippe, Louis (king), 51
Phillips, U. B., 125–27, 129
Pius IX (pope), 60
Plessy v. Ferguson, 91, 112, 136–37
Posner, Eric A., 338n40
Powell, Enoch, 219, 230, 288
Powell, Lewis, 137, 333n58, 333n60
Poyer, David, 337n33
Prendergast, Christopher, 322n5, 323n12
Priest, Christopher, 310
Priestley, Joseph, *Lectures on History*, 21–22, 25, 30, 82, 320n15
probability, 5, 7, 12–13, 17, 23, 27, 30, 34–39, 42–43, 69, 129–31, 192, 321n36, 323n10, 335n8
Prometheus, 323n11
propaganda, WWII, 209, 242–43, 248–51, 253, 256, 259, 267, 269, 287, 290, 303, 348
providence, 4, 7, 17–18, 21, 24–25, 45, 67, 107, 323
Ptolemy (king), 324n25
Puckett, Kent, 346n38

Quisling, Vidkum, 229–31

race, 11, 91, 93, 96, 108, 110, 112–15, 120–25, 131–37, 140–43, 148, 151, 153, 159, 165–68, 174–79, 181, 186–88, 191, 251–55, 273, 287–92, 304, 331n31, 332n48, 333n60, 348n50
Randall, J. G., 123–24, 327n1

Randle, Kevin, 179, 337n33, 338n35
randomness, 18, 34, 39, 71
Ranke, Leopold von, 62
Ransom, Roger, 143–46, 157, 327n1, 332n40, 334nn66–67, 334n69
Reagan, Ronald, 297
Reconstruction, 37, 91, 97, 108–9, 112, 114, 116, 120–27, 134, 137, 139, 158–59, 186, 188, 327n1, 329n15; Second, 125, 131–32, 171
Regents of the University of California v. Bakke, 136–38, 333n60
Reisswitz, Georg Leopold von, 34
Renan, Ernest, 240, 251, 298, 343n2
Renouvier, Charles, *Uchronia*, 26, 49–50, 58–66, 72, 75–77, 80, 83, 85, 95–96, 110, 322n1, 324n17, 334n66
Republican Party, 98, 100–101, 103, 106, 112, 159
Rescher, Nicholas, 325n27
resistance, wartime civilian, 218–22, 224–27, 229, 232, 234–35, 243, 251–52, 268–69, 276–78
reversal, ironic, 21–22, 25–26, 78–79, 109, 114, 116–18, 165, 233
revisionism, Civil War, 126–30, 147
Rexroth, Kenneth, 335n4
Reynolds, Mack, 337n33
Richard, Jules, 323n11
Richer, Adrian, 25–26, 319n14
Ricoeur, Paul, 334n68
Rigaut, Jacques, 162–65, 336n18
Roberson, David W., 332n49
Roberts, Andrew, 236, 340n18
Robinson, Derek, 341n22
Roman Empire, 16, 19, 63–65
Ronen, Ruth, 325n30
Rosenfeld, Gavriel D., 285, 316n8, 317n10, 319n7, 339n1, 346n35, 347n44, 347n46
Roth, Philip, 90
Rothberg, Robert, 339n46
Rottensteiner, Franz, 337n29
Rudman, Stella, 339n5
Russel, Robert R., 331n33
Rwelamira, M. R., 339n46
Ryan, Marie-Laure, 325n30, 326n33, 326n35
Rymer, Thomas, 323n10

Sachs, Joe, 338n34
Sackville-West, Vita, 345n24
Saki (Hector Hugo Munro), 343n1
Sansom, C. J., 350n85

Sargent, Pamela, 338n36
satire, 23, 78–80, 147, 150, 152–53, 162–63, 264, 274, 276, 282, 335n8
Scheel, Walter, 348n53
Schellenberg, Walter, 342n39
Schenk, Peter, 341n29, 341n34
Schivelbusch, Wolfgang, 330n25
science fiction, 67–72, 83, 148–50, 162, 165–66, 171–74, 334n1
secession, Southern, 100, 112–13, 115, 178, 182, 188–89
secularization, and counterfactualism, 17, 22, 24
Sedgwick, John, 328n11
Seelöwe (game), 214
segregation, racial, 91, 109, 112, 121, 123, 132, 135, 137, 140, 142, 159, 178
Sell, William, 172
Serpell, Christopher, *Loss of Eden*, 244–45, 247, 249–50, 253, 256–57, 261, 263, 274, 290, 310, 344n7
Seven Years' War, 29, 32, 35, 39
Sextus Tarquinius, 18–19, 45
Shaw, Harry E., 326n39
Sheers, Owen, 350n85
Shelley, Percy, 78–80
Sickles, Daniel, 104
Sikkink, Kathryn, 316n5, 349n70, 350n78
Simpson, Lewis P., 330n25
Singles, Kathleen, 317n10
Skidelsky, Robert, 272
Skimin, Leonard, 337n33
slavery, 57, 91–92, 98–99, 102, 107, 112–16, 122–31, 135, 140–43, 146, 151, 167–71, 178, 181–82, 184–85, 190, 227, 327n1, 329n19, 331n3, 337n25, 338n40
slavery, and secession debates, 329n19
Słonimski, Antoni, 173
Sloterdijk, Peter, 294
Sluga, Glenda, 344n15
Smith, Hazel Knowles, 342n47
Smith, Martin Cruz, 175, 177, 179, 337n33
Smith, Robert Worthington, 331n33
socialism, 57, 260–69, 344n18
Soll, Jacob, 320n22
Sorrow and the Pity, The, 342n40
Sprague de Camp, L., 172, 337n28
Stack, George J., 324n22
Stampp, Kenneth, 126, 128, 331n33, 331n35, 332n41
Stansky, Peter, 206, 340n15
Stanton, Edwin, 101

Stapp, Robert, 177, 337n33
Steinbeck, John, 211
Stern, Der, 297–99, 348n61
Stokes, John, 348n51
Storey, Wilbur, 100
Suez Crisis, 218, 272
Sutch, Richard, 327n1, 331n39, 332n40
Suvin, Darko, 317n10
Swinton, William, 107, 329n14

Taylor, Kenneth A., 325n29
Taylor, Telford, 341n30, 341n34
teleology, 17, 22–25, 161
temporality, 44, 47, 134, 156, 261, 302; atemporality, 266, 282; backwards, 47; omnitemporality, 30, 46–47, 81–82; sideways, 45–47, 61, 173
Tetlock, Philip E., 315n1, 317n9
theodicy, 6, 16–17, 21–23, 61, 114, 304; Leibniz *Theodicy* (see Leibniz, Gottfried)
Third Reich, 190, 219, 269, 280, 285, 297, 299, 304, 306, 308, 349
Thompson, Dennis, 339n46
Thomsen, Brian, 333n65
Thoreau, Henry David, 99
Thurlow, Richard, 347n50
time-travel, backward, 1, 139, 147–48, 150, 152, 155–68, 172–74, 177, 179, 182–88, 335n8, 336n14, 336n18
To Secure These Rights, 131
Tourgée, Albion, *A Fool's Errand*, 109–12, 114, 121, 140, 152
Travers, Tim, 320n25
Trevor Roper, Hugh, 297
Truth and Reconciliation Commission (TRC), South African, 187, 339nn45–46
Tsouras, Peter, 141–42, 333n62
Tucker, Irene, 343n3
Turner, Henry Ashby, Jr., 342n44
Turtledove, Harry: *Guns of the South*, 182–84, 186–89, 338n44; *How Few Remain*, 339n47
Twain, Mark, 94, 173, 336n18

University of California, Davis, 136, 332n54
utopia, 2, 10, 15, 22, 49, 53, 56–58, 65–66, 71, 75, 85, 91–95, 147–50, 154, 157–58, 178, 238

Varlet, Théo, 336n18
Venturini, Georg, 321n30
Vermeule, Adrian, 338n40

Verwoerd, Wilhelm, 339n46
Villa-Vicensio, Charles, 339n46
Voltaire, 17, 23, 25, 79, 319n14
Vonnegut, Kurt, 346n38

Wade, Benjamin, 102
Waldron, Webb, 330n24
Wall, John W., 346n35
Walton, Jo, 347n42, 350n85
war, total, 247, 266, 277, 284
warfare, 5, 8, 22, 27–29, 31, 33–35, 39–40, 44, 46–47, 99, 266–67, 320n20, 346n38
Weisinger, Mortimer, 336n19
Weissman, Gary, 349n68
welfare state, 135, 148, 264, 266, 271, 297
Wellington, Duke of, 53, 322n7
Wells, H. G., 336n18, 338n38
Went the Day Well?, 210, 267, 344n18
Werle, G., 339n46
Westley, Robert, 332n43
Wheatley, Ronald, 341nn33–34
Williams, Bernard, 12, 317n12
Williams, F. P., *Hallie Marshall*, 84, 91–95, 98, 109, 112, 142, 147–48, 327n44
Wilson, Woodrow, 123
Winter, Jay, 7, 315n4
Wintjes, Jorit, 321n29, 321n32
Woodward, C. Vann, 132
Worcester, Battle of, 20, 25, 329n20
Wordsworth, William, 327n41
worlds, alternate, 15, 66–67, 77, 83, 90–91, 94–95, 110, 122, 148, 151–54, 157, 165, 176–78, 221–22, 226, 229, 232–33, 282–83, 286, 290, 293–94, 296, 302–4, 318n17
worlds, possible, 4, 6–7, 12, 15, 18–24, 45, 66–68, 70–71, 73–74, 77, 80, 82, 85, 153, 157–58, 171, 174, 303, 317n12, 317n14, 319n5, 325n27, 326n30
World War I, 85, 115, 119, 179, 196, 309
World War II, 1, 4, 97, 131, 140, 153, 179–81, 190–94, 196, 198, 210, 215, 220, 233, 276, 284, 297, 303, 310, 327, 341n36
Wurgaft, Benjamin Aldes, 347n46

www.ingramcontent.com/pod-product-compliance
Lightning Source LLC
Chambersburg PA
CBHW021931290426
44108CB00012B/802